CONTENTS

PREFACE

The Amateur Entomological Society has already published Handbooks on Lepidoptera, Coleoptera and Hymenoptera and leaflets for a number of smaller insect groups. The most glaring gap in its series has been the need for a Handbook on the Diptera, since this major group has previously only been treated in the form of a leaflet, long out of print.

The Dipterist's Handbook has partly adopted the style of its predecessors in catering for the needs of the beginner by providing the basic information on collecting equipment and methods. However, a strong feature of this Handbook is its emphasis on describing the fauna of different habitat types and the associations of flies with other animals and plants. The reason for this structuring of the Handbook has been the principle that the beginner will be able to get the most out of his field work if he knows what to look for and how to approach what may be totally unfamiliar concepts in ecology. With this background the novice can readily make a real contribution to the advancement of the study of Diptera since many gaps in knowledge and lines of investigation are indicated. It is, however, more than a beginner's guide since the format provides an invaluable reverence for the experienced dipterist. A great deal of published and unpublished information has been drawn together and much of the material has never been available in this form before; much original work is included. A wide range of amateur naturalists and professional ecologists and biologists will now be able to gain easier access to information on this important group of insects. It is hoped that the format will foster the many lines of investigation still required in order to understand fully the role of Diptera in the field.

In order to keep the cost of the Handbook within the resources available to the Society it has been necessary to restrict the range of topics and take some tough editorial decisions, such as the reduction in the number of references. No attempt is made to describe and identify adult flies in this work since such information is available in *Flies of the British Isles* by C. N. Colyer and C. O. Hammond (Warne, London 1951, revised 1968) and *Bibliography of key works for the Identification of the British fauna and flora* (Systematics Association, London, revised edition 1978*). The scientific names in the Handbook are those used in current standard works, including the *Check Lists of British Insects* published by the Royal Entomological Society. As an economy in space the authority names have not been given.

The Society wishes to express its thanks to all those concerned in the preparation of the text. The authors are named with the individual contributions and they have assisted each other with comments on drafts. Other people assisted substantially by reading drafts and submitting items for incorporation. These include Dr. John

*Key works to the Fauna and Flora of the British Isles and Northern Europe.

Coulson, George Else, Peter Hammond, Keith Harris, Richard Lane, Ron Payne, Dr. Stephen Trifourkis and Michael Ackland. It is clear that some of the authors have put a great deal of work into the Handbook. Ken Smith, who apart from his major contributions, has assisted with proof reading together with his wife, Vera, and Dr. Tony Irwin who drew the cover illustration have both spent much time preparing text for the book. It is also a pleasure to thank Dr. B. M. Hobby and the Trustees of the British Museum for permission to reproduce illustrations of larvae from the Entomologist's Monthly Magazine and British Museum publications respectively. My son, Stephen Cribb, prepared some of the sketches suitable for the printer. Major thanks are due to Alan Stubbs and Peter Chandler, the joint editors, without whose enthusiasm and hard work the Handbook would still be only an idea.

The Society also acknowledges considerable financial contributions towards the cost of producing the Handbook which have been made by the Royal Society and the Nature Conservancy Council and records its thanks to the Society and its Fellows and the Council for their support in this important project.

Peter W. Cribb

Hanworth, July, 1978.

INTRODUCTION

The Diptera constitute one of the largest orders of British insects, comprising some 6000 species, with the list being steadily added to by the studies of dipterists. That number represents about one quarter of all insect species in Britain or, put another way, it is approaching, and may soon exceed, the entire British fauna of Lepidoptera (2,400) and Coleoptera (4,000) combined.

The Handbook is prepared as a companion volume to the book by C. N. Colyer and C. O. Hammond, *Flies of the British Isles*. This superb introduction to flies has sparked the imagination of most of those who are today dipterists. It describes and illustrates the various families of flies and gives a useful insight into their biology in conjunction with the taxonomic account. However, one book cannot cover everything. The handbook sets out to become a companion reference on field craft and other related information. It has been prepared by dipterists with a considerable range of experience between them, yet they knew from the outset the difficulty of meeting some of the simplest requirements. No one has attempted to summarise the dipterous fauna of the major habitat types in Britain before, nor drawn together such biological information as the associations of flies with other animals and plants. If the Handbook achieves success, this will be best measured by the extent to which the information becomes reassessed and improved by further studies. The authors, however, believe that this step forward is best encouraged and aided by building something to step from, however incomplete. The Handbook is written at a time when there is an upsurge of interest in our two-winged flies. The Handbook reflects, we hope, the challenge that the present period of development in this branch of entomology has reached, a challenge equally open to amateur and professional alike. We have reached a point where most of the major groups of Diptera are moderately well known and there is a fairly broad groundwork of information on the early stages and other aspects of biology. Yet, looking out from this base, there remain vast fields of ignorance which, more than anything else, this Handbook sets out to recognise.

In taxonomy, how many groups of insects could claim an increase in the checklist by 800 species in 33 years, yet this is what has happened with the Diptera in recent years. The field is wide open for anyone to add new species and indeed it is a frequent occurrence for even the newcomer to Diptera to find new species. Very often these additional species have already been described on the continent of Europe but it is by no means uncommon for species new to science to be found in Britain. Though the base-line taxonomy is sorted out in many families, there remain some groups requiring primary revision by the more serious minded entomologists – and if you are not working at a specialist level, there still remains a great deal that one may contribute through collecting the material required and by drawing attention to differences in habits which may provide a clue to the need to look for taxonomic differences where none have been sought.

One of the largest gaps in knowledge concerns the inadequate information on life histories. Adults are abundant but larvae often seem to be non-existent. Just how do 6000 species of flies make a living in their early stages when spontaneous creation of adults seems the only explanation for their origin in the field? Many species are phytophagous, that means they eat plants, so we can look for leaf mines, galls and other evidence of attack on plants but preparation of the relevant section of the Handbook exposed the degree of ignorance even here. It is much more difficult to give a lead to finding larvae with other habits. Even of the 'known' life histories, many are based on a single certain or suspect identification and no adequate description of the early stages or the circumstances of occurrence are recorded. This is a field wide open to anyone to add to our knowledge – it does not take a specialist to rear material, the specialist can assist with the identification. The habits and behaviour of adult flies offer a multiplicity of original lines of study. We know sufficient to say that there is an incredible range of fascinating different things that flies do, but we are still at the tip of the ice-berg stage where anyone with an enquiring mind has a whole unseen world ahead.

Ecology is still a relatively new subject and in consequence there is little background at present. We are here concerned with the way a species lives in and interacts with its environment. It is often taken to be synonymous with habitat, but we need to know of habitat at both major and micro levels as well as the summation of life history, habits, behaviour, predators, parasites, etc. You do not need to be a professional scientist to help find out where and how a species lives.

One of the major events of recent years has been the development of recording schemes. These are often equated with an effort to map the occurrence of insects and indeed this is one of the major purposes but, certainly in the case of Diptera, they are concerned with all aspects of recording information. One might, at first sight, query the possibility of mapping the distribution of flies, yet the results obtained so far confirm that this is very much a viable proposition and, moreover, some groups of flies are especially easy to sample. At the time of writing about 850 species of Diptera are covered by recording schemes, with others under consideration.

The opening statement spoke of the diversity of species. Before turning to the following chapters it is worth reflecting upon the sheer abundance of Diptera. In many situations they are the predominant insects. A naturalist or ecologist should not ignore them whilst still speaking of an understanding of the countryside or even town. Diptera in their seemingly infinite life styles are playing a major role in the web of life. Whether approaching natural history from the view-point of a botanist, ornithologist, mammalogist, herpetologist, freshwater or littoral-marine biologist, lepidopterist, arachnologist or just about any other related biological discipline, Diptera are involved and the Handbook has been designed so that such naturalists can find a statement relating to their interests. It is because Diptera are just too significant to be ignored that many entomologists are drawn towards finding out more bout them, and we invite all naturalists to share in our studies. There are few fields of study open to the enquiring mind which offer such scope and challenge to contribute to the frontiers of knowledge.

Structure and use of the Handbook

The Handbook is divided into themes which should be readily recognised from the contents pages, which serve as an index. Each item is an introductory account and does not pretend to be exhaustive but a guide to further reading should assist follow-up studies and in some cases an appendix gives a fairly complete review of current information on the subject.

Several editing decisions have had to be made in order to economise on page space and also to meet the production deadlines. Thus there is no formal index to species and subject, though arguably this is not essential in view of the contents structure. Detailed reference information such as further reading and appendices has gone into small type face and the scope of the references remains sparse in some subjects. The citing of species names in the accounts on habitat types has had to be severely limited, especially where large numbers of species are involved — the main objective has been to give a general "feel" for the habitat or subject concerned. Authority names have been omitted, since all insect names are in line with the revised Check Lists published by the Royal Entomological Society, including revisionary notes in *Antenna,* and in the case of Hymenoptera the pre-publication text has been consulted. With other groups, the authors concerned have used the names given in standard identification works. *Key Works to the Fauna and Flora of the British Isles and Northern Europe,* (published by the Systematics Association, revised edition 1978) gives a through list of identification works on adult and larval Diptera as well as other groups of plants and animals.

To make the most effective use of the Handbook it is suggested that reference be made to the relevant section before going into the field. Thus if you are expecting to go out for the day to woodland or for a holiday to the coast, a read through the habitat discussion and the other relevant themes will insure that you have some orientation to your field work.

No one can expect to absorb all the information in a book of this sort, especially all the detail in appendices. To gain constructive results from your field work it is most sensible to concentrate on a few themes, having decided which ones particularly interest you. It is then possible to get to grips with a subject, follow up the literature and make progress in improving on the pre-existing knowledge. There is probably not a single item in this Handbook which cannot be radically revised and improved.

There is no pretence that the Handbook will enable everyone to become self-sufficient. There is much to be gained from the stimulus of working with others. If you are taking an interest in Diptera then please make contact with the Diptera Recording Schemes and if you are making a serious follow-up of any of the themes in this book then the authors will be glad to know of your work.

Chapter 1

Collecting and Recording

EQUIPMENT
by Dr. Anthony G. Irwin

Choosing, obtaining and using equipment is best done by seeking the direct advice of a more experienced dipterist. He will have all sorts of prejudices to balance the views in this account. Eventually you will find just the right selection of equipment to suit yourself, and the type of flies you collect.

First, remember that the list of essential equipment is very small - a net, a few tubes and/or a pooter, a killing agent, a pair of forceps, a few pins, some labels and a box. All the other equipment discussed here is simply designed to make life easier, though at times it can make life chaotic. My first specimens were caught with a home-made net, killed with a stain remover, impaled on dressmaker's pins and stuck into a shirt-box lined with corrugated cardboard. I may not have made any·major contribution to British entomology, but I enjoyed myself.

Field Equipment

The most serious mistake concerning field equipment is to carry too much. To be prepared for every eventuality will result in being so overloaded that every opportunity will be missed. Most equipment can be bought from the dealers listed on page 6, but beware of catalogue descriptions, and try to see and use any item before buying it. The best pooters are home-made, and no commercial supplier markets a satisfactory netbag.

Nets

No complete net can be recommended from the dealers. The four-fold 14" frames are satisfactory, and the 12" spring-steel pocket nets are convenient, though rather small. These frames are provided with a useless black bag. It may be better to buy a fisherman's landing net frame of 14" to 18" diameter, with a 3 ft. alloy handle (available at most fishing shops). The diameter of the new frame is a matter for personal choice. With a large frame it is easier to get inside the net to extract specimens, and a larger frame will catch more flies. A small frame, however, is cheaper, can be used with greater speed and less effort, and is more manoeuverable in thick vegetation.The net bag should be made of fine-mesh, pale-coloured nylon net which is available from most fabric shops. The length of the material should be 2 ½ times the diameter of the frame, and the width should be an inch longer than the circumference of the frame. The bag should have a rounded end and the leading edge should be protected with a strip of canvas or webbing. Terylene or polyester thread should be used for all the seams. These nets are very strong and can be used to sweep any vegetation except brambles. If they get wet, the net can be dried quickly by rubbing it on a piece of dry material such as a jacket sleeve or shirt front. Several serious mistakes may be found in home-made nets. Failure to provide a protective binding always results in the net leaving the frame. Use of weak cotton thread will result in parting of seams or puckering when it shrinks. Single seams tangle insects unless the netbag is always turned the right way out. If the bag is not long enough, flies will escape easily. If it is too long, it will catch everything but the fly.

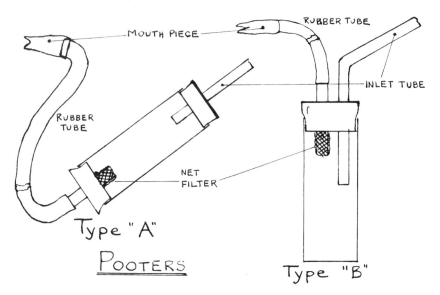

Pooters

There are two sorts of pooters - the straight-through variety (Type A) and the U-tube (Type B). With the former, the flies are killed in the pooter then transferred to a separate tube. With the latter the flies remain in the tube which is corked normally and a fresh tube is used on the pooter.

The following hints apply to both sorts of pooter, whether purchased or home-made. The pooter barrel or tube should be made of hard glass. Avoid plastic barrels, as these will react unfavourably with ethyl acetate. The inlet tube should be neither too large nor too small (3/16" to $\frac{1}{4}$" diameter), and in any case should be slightly smaller than the mouth tube. The tip of the inlet tube should be smoothed off in a flame, so that it does not strip the diagnostic bristles off the larger flies as they are sucked in. The inner end of the inlet tube should protrude well into the pooter, so that flies have difficulty finding an exit. The net or gauze filter on the mouth tube should be held firmly in place, close to the bung, using a slice of the tubing which forms the flexible mouthpiece. This mouth tube should be as long as your arm and is best made of clear polythene tubing. Make the tube a few inches longer than necessary to allow for nervous nibbling if you get very excited in the field. Note that rubber tubing tastes unpleasant unless a plastic or glass mouthpiece is used, but these will reduce overall efficiency. Use rubber bungs rather than corks for your pooter. Corks tend to slip and split.

When in use, a piece of soft crumpled paper or tissue should be placed inside the pooter. This provides a greater promenade area for the flies, as well as corners in which the smaller, more delicate species can hide. It will also absorb condensation. Some flies (usually the rare ones!) will crawl out of the inlet tube, so either a small cork or piece of tissue should be put in the end of the tube. Alternatively keep a finger over the end of the tube, but avoid carrying the pooter if there is a possibility of slipping. Very nasty accidents can occur if the pooter breaks!

Under some conditions, the use of a conventional pooter is not recommended. when collecting off dung, carrion or nest material, there is a real risk of contracting a serious disease by inhaling fungal spores, bacteria or viruses. To overcome this problem, one can use a large rubber bulb to create low pressure in the pooter, but this is never very satisfactory. Alternatively a blow pooter may be used. The blow pooter is impossible to buy, difficult to make (see Evans, 1975), and not very efficient. Fame, if not fortune, awaits the inventor of a suitable substitute.

Tubes

Some flies will not fit into the average pooter and for these it is best to use individual tubes. These should be made of hard glass and have well-fitting corks. Individual tubes are also useful for predatory insects and easily damaged flies such as culicids, bombyliids and therevids. Include a piece of paper in each tube to absorb condensation. Do not carry more than two or three sizes of tubes. Very small diameter ($\frac{1}{4}$") and small ($\frac{1}{2}$") are used for individual flies. Large (1") tubes are used for pooter contents. These can be kept in a cardboard box which insulates them from heat and shock. When a tube has been used a few times, it should be thoroughly washed and dried. Dirty tubes produce dirty flies.

Killing Agent

A few dipterists still use the ancient cyanide jar, and will be so eager to tell you of its advantages that I need not list them here. However the best killing agent is ethyl acetate, which is cheap, relatively safe, and easily carried in a small bottle for field use.

To introduce ethyl acetete into the pooter, wet a small twist of tissue with it and poke the twist into the inlet tube.Then blow sharply down the tube. Do not continue blowing into the pooter as this will cause condensation. Avoid sucking fumes or ethyl acetate-dampened tissue into the pooter. This can damage your health.

Ethyl acetate acts fairly quickly on most flies, but hymenopterans, beetles and spiders are more resistant, so include some extra ethyl acetate in the tube in which the catch is kept. This tube should be well-sealed and provided with tissue so that the flies neither dry out nor become damp.

Lens

For examination of specimens in the field it is worth buying a good quality folding pocket lens with a metal case. Tie it to a piece of string and tie the string to yourself. Next to rare flies the most frequently lost items in the field are lenses.

Collecting larvae

This tends to be a specialised business and is discussed further in Chapter 2. Several items of equipment will always be found useful, including a trowel for digging and a pair of secateurs for cutting. A stout knife can be used for both tasks. A fertiliser bag made of white or yellow heavy-gauge polythene can be used as a beating-tray, sorting dish, waterproof seat and emergency umbrella. It is also very cheap and easily carried. Assorted polythene bags can be used to carry home substrates when there is no time to examine them in the field. Use waterproof labels and a pencil so that data can be included in the bag.

To sort through flood debris, leaf litter, etc., use a garden sieve with $\frac{1}{4}$" - $\frac{1}{2}$" mesh. Alternatively use a Berlese or Tullgren extraction funnel (Southwood, 1966). For wet or freshwater material use a fine mesh kitchen sieve or a pond net. Pond nets need to be much stronger than insect nets and are correspondingly much more expensive. It is probably worthwhile spending time and effort to make your own frame. For convenience, a plastic kitchen sieve and wet arm are the ideal combination.

Other Field equipment

A notebook and supply of pencils are essential. The notebook should have a waterproof cover and stitched binding. Pencils are better than pens because they are waterproof and ethyl acetate-proof and do not need a top to stop the ink drying-out. Pencils should be attached to the field bag with a piece of string. A canvas shoulder bag with compartments inside is necessary to contain pooters, tubes, notebook,etc. One ought to be able to find any piece of equipment with one hand and without looking.

The final items of equipment are not entomological, but should be carried by anyone who is working in remote, inhospitable areas. If you fall thus breaking your pooter and cutting your finger, assorted surgical plasters can be used for temporary repairs to both pooter and finger. A map and compass, properly used, will not only get you off a mountain in mist, but will guide you to that small pond in the middle of a forestry plantation. A small torch is indispensable if out late in the day, and is also useful for examining the interior of hollow tree trunks and small caves.

Microscopes

Apart from cabinets, the most expensive item of indoor equipment is a stereoscopic microscope. This should have a range of magnification from 10X (or 20X) to 100X (or more), as well as a wide field of view and long working distance. The construction should be robust yet not too heavy.

Unfortunately second-hand microscopes are very scarce and suitable new microscopes cost over £150 (1978 prices). The following firms can provide models with a magnification range of at least 20X to 40X for under £200. (Trade name in brackets).

Gallenkamp & Co. Ltd., P.O. Box 290, Technico House, Christopher St., London, EC2P 2ER. (Olympus)

Newbold & Bulford Ltd., Carlton Park, Saxmundham, Suffolk, IP17 2NL (Grey 5-40)

Psyer-Britex Ltd., Fircroft Way, Edenbridge, Kent. (Swift)

Vickers Ltd., Breakfield, Coulsdon, Surrey, CR3 2UP (Vickers)

If you are considering the purchase of a new microscope, write to these firms for the latest details and prices. Most of them will agree to demonstrate their models to you, or even offer a free trial period.

Also write to the co-ordinator of the Diptera Recording Schemes who should be able to put you in touch with someone who can offer advice. When choosing a model, look for the potential of extending the magnification range through supplementary eyepieces and objectives. Although microscopes are expensive, they will last a lifetime and will not devalue as rapidly as a television set or motor cycle!

Petri Dishes

When sorting flies under the microscope, clear petri dishes will be found useful. Plastic dishes are cheaper than glass, but they react disturbingly with organic solvents and are also subject to static, so that small flies may stick to the dish, jump onto the lid and otherwise behave unpredictably. A cheap standby are paper bun cases, but these are very light and easily blown away.

Stackable plastic petri dishes are suitable for rearing batches of larvae, but be careful to buy those with close-fitting lids, to protect the larvae from drying-out.

Forceps

For sorting flies, fine forceps are needed. Swiss watchmakers' forceps are the best. The very fine ones (no. 5) can be used for dissection. To handle larvae, use light-touch storkbill forceps. These will not crush the larvae no matter how clumsy you are.

Entomological forceps are used for handling pins. Some of these forceps are poorly made and can cause a great deal of trouble. In general, the more you pay, the better the product, but there are exceptions, so ask for advice before spending money. If you find a good source, it may be worth buying several further pairs immediately. A good pair of forceps will securely hold the head of a pin at any angle. They will also hold the shaft of all sizes of pins securely at one of two angles. They should have little "shearing" movement and should close with a minimum of effort. Avoid any forceps which show strong magnetic properties.

Pins

The most useful continental pins (for direct pinning) are sizes 00, 0 and 3. If using micropins (for staging), the best range of sizes is .0056, .01 and .016 mm, with English no. 8 or no. 12 pins for the stage. Many other sizes of pins are available, so try out a selection before buying a large quantity. It is not necessary to stock every size of pin, but do order them in quantity since they are subject to production and delivery difficulties. In any case, buy stainless steel where possible. Brass pins should only be used for the stage, never for the fly.

Plastazote

Until recently, stages for micropins were made from polyporus, and cabinets and boxes were lined with cork. Expanded polystyrene is not a suitable substitute, since it does not "grip" pins. Now, however, an expanded cross-linked polyethylene material called Plastazote is available. It is white, comes in a variety of thicknesses and densities, is easily cut and is resistant to many organic solvents. Its finest quality is that pins can be inserted into it easily, yet remain held firmly, leaving no hole when they are removed. Unlike cork, it does not seem to deteriorate with age. Many dipterists are now using a system of micropinning flies into small (4" x 3" × ¾") clear plastic boxes lined with 5 mm thick Plastazote. the specimens are later staged on strips of Plastazote cut from 2mm sheets and then pinned into storeboxes or cabinets lined with 9mm Plastazote.

Cabinets and Storeboxes

For permanent storage of any insect collection, a cabinet is the best solution, but with prices now ranging from £15 to £35 a drawer, most amateurs will have to resort to storeboxes. Second-hand cabinets are a bit cheaper, but real bargains are seldom found. Home-made cabinets can be good, if the drawers are air tight but the present cost of wood and glass makes them expensive.

Storebox prices vary between suppliers, so shop around before buying many. Stick to one size of storebox for ease of storage. For temporary use, card boxes (e.g. shirt boxes) can be lined with Plastazote or cork, but they are open to attacks by pests and must be inspected regularly.

Suppliers

The following general and specialist suppliers will provide prices and details of specific items on request but may charge up to £1 for a catalogue.

Watkins and Doncaster, Four Throws, Hawkhurst, Kent. — General, but especially good for nets, pins and storeboxes

Griffin and George Ltd., 285 Ealing Road, Wembley, Middlesex, HAO 1HJ. — General, but best for plastic and glassware, chemicals and foreceps.

L. Christie, 129 Franciscan Road, Tooting, London SW178DZ. — Storeboxes and cabinets (as well as books). [Postal business only]

Wilford Manufacturing Co. Ltd., Grange Works, Great Northern Road, Dunstable, Bedfordshire, LU 4BU — Plastazote

Stephenson Blake & Co. Ltd., Sheaf Works, Maltravers Street, Sheffield S4 7Yl — New cabinets.

Further Reading

Evans, L.J., 1975. An improved aspirator (pooter) for catching small insects. *Proc.Brit.ent.nat.Hist.Soc.* **8**:8-11.

Southwood, T.R.E., 1966, *Ecological Methods*, Butler & Tanner, London

Other general reading on equipment can be found in the references to the following section.

CURATING
by Dr. Anthony G. Irwin.

Curating is one of those useful terms which covers everything which the collector does with his specimen after he has caught and killed it. Many books have been written on these aspects of entomology, so this account is biased to meet the needs of the dipterist. For more thorough treatment of basic curatorial techniques consult Oldroyd (1970), Cogan and Smith (1974) and the appendix in Colyer and Hammond (1968).

Curating a collection is always time well-spent. There are few sights more disheartening than half-eaten flies, dried-up larvae or illegible labels. Remember that a collection is not just a mass of dead flies. It also represents miles of travelling and years of labour in the field and at home. The amount of effort required to maintain the collection is comparatively small.

All specimens go through the same stages of processing - preparation, labelling, identification, storage and maintenance. In addition some may be sent to specialists and some may be dissected for the examination of genitalia or mouthparts. The discussion of these processes is followed with advice on the association of material and use of chemicals.

Preparation of Adult Material

The adult fly will remain the most important element in any collection. With the exception of a few chironomids and many cecidomyiids, all Diptera were described from adults, so accurate naming relies on the comparison of adults. Flies may be pinned, pointed, carded or packeted if dry, and can be stored in spirit or on slides if wet. It is possible to dry wet material and to wet dry material, so no matter how the specimen is collected, it can be treated to fit into the rest of your collection, but it is best to decide how to preserve your specimen before killing it.

Pinning

Two methods of pinning are available. Continental or direct pinning involves putting the fly and all its data labels on one long pin (Fig. 1). The fly should be near the top of the pin, leaving enough room to hold the pin with finger and thumb. In staging, the fly is impaled on a short micro-pin, leaving enough room to grip it with a pair of forceps. This is then stuck into a stage made of polyporus, Plastazote, celluloid or card and the stage is put on a large pin which also bears the data labels (Fig. 2). The disadvantage of the continental pinning method is that for very small flies the pin must be very thin and therefore is very weak. The disadvantage of the staging method is that it will take up more room than direct pinning. Without saying which method is right, it may be noted that very few British dipterists use continental pinning for anything but their largest flies.

The arrangement of the flies on the pin is very important. It is not necessary to spread the wings and legs of flies as though they were moths or dragonflies (Fig.3). In fact this is almost always wrong, because characters on the side of the thorax or upper part of the leg are obscured. The only exception may be in groups such as the Stratiomyidae or Syrphidae, where the adults do sit with wings spread, and

7

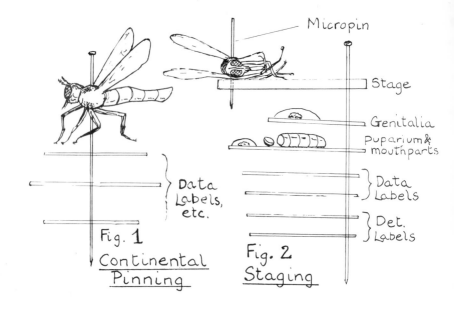

Micropin

Stage

Genitalia

Puparium &
mouthparts

Data
Labels,
etc.

Data
Labels

Det.
Labels

Fig. 1
Continental
Pinning

Fig. 2
Staging

preliminary field identification may be easier if part of the collection has been set that way. In general, it is best to set specimens with the legs, wings, mouthparts and genitalia all drawn away from the body (Fig.4). This can be done with specimens which are pinned from above, but it is easier to side-pin material. When doing this, make sure all the specimens face one way. It does not matter whether they face left or right, but all the specimens in your collection should be the same, so that comparative examination is easier. Push the pin from behind the level of the wing base to emerge at the other side in front of the wing base (Fig.5). In this way any part damaged on one side will be intact on the other. If you top pin specimens, place the pin slightly to one side of the mid-line, so the median bristles are not destroyed.

Micropinned specimens can be kept together in locality and date groups in small, shallow boxes, to be staged and labelled later. If you use plastic boxes, open the lids slightly for a few hours after pinning, so that the flies can dry properly. Large flies may take longer to dry fully. A sheet of thin paper over the pinning surface helps absorb moisture and enables lines to be drawn demarcating batches of flies with common data.

Pointing

If the specimen dries before it is pinned, do not try to relax it as though it were a butterfly. Naturally it is hazardous to try pinning brittle specimens, so the best alternative is to glue the specimen to a triangular card point (Fig. 6). Use good quality white card (of postcard thickness) and a heavy water-soluble gum (e.g. Seccotine). Avoid using too much gum, but equally beware of using too little, since the fly will spring off and be damaged if not attached firmly. It is best to standardise a few sizes of points to make the collection look neat.

Carding

An alternative method to pinning fresh material is to glue it to card or celluloid rectangles (Fig. 7): Such preparations give the specimen more protection but will also restrict examination from some angles. Never card a specimen as though it were a beetle. Flies should be carded on their sides and in a single step. Colyer and Hammond describe the technique well. Difficulty may be experienced with large cards rotating on their pins and damaging adjacent specimens.

Packeting

If voucher specimens need to be kept, conventional mounting methods may prove to be wasteful of space, time and money. In this case, or when the identity of common species is to be checked at a later date, specimens may be kept in envelopes loosely packed in a crush-proof box. For this purpose, the hard tissue envelopes sold for photographic negatives or stamps are best. Some flies, notably tipulids, travel well in envelopes. Others such as muscids may suffer damage, though seldom so much that they cannot be identified. A useful procedure during peak collecting periods is to select a few of the obviously interesting flies to pin and to put the rest in labelled envelopes. Later in the year, the packeted flies can be identified and if these are interesting, they can be mounted on card points. Note that several recording schemes prefer packeted material.

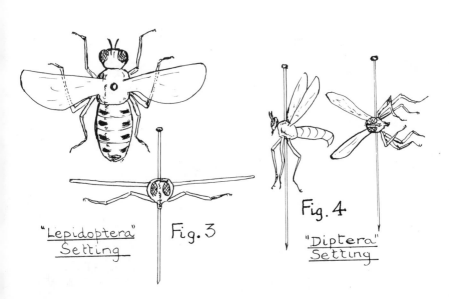

"Lepidoptera" Setting   Fig. 3   Fig. 4   "Diptera" Setting

Layering

This method involves placing the flies on layers of cellulose wadding or tissue within a stiff box or tin (Fig. 8). Each layer is provided with its own data label. Great care should be taken to ensure that flies do not jump from one layer to the next. The box should therefore be fully packed before it is moved. The contents of air-tight boxes must be allowed to dry before the lids are finally put on, unless the flies are very small. This method has no advantages over envelopes except that very large or bristly flies are more protected. It is important that each box should have a complete list of the data for its contents. Otherwise the boxes will have to be searched carefully and laboriously to find a particular batch of flies.

Wet preservation

For some families of flies, wet preservation is recommended, and some trapping techniques involve wet preservation for the whole catch. The techniques are the same as for larvae, except that they should not be killed in hot water.

Mounting adults on slides

For many very small flies, the use of a high-power compound microscope makes identification much easier. These flies should be treated as though they were genitalia, being macerated, cleared and then mounted in a suitable medium under a coverslip on a standard microscope slide. Some dissection will be necessary to display the characters properly.

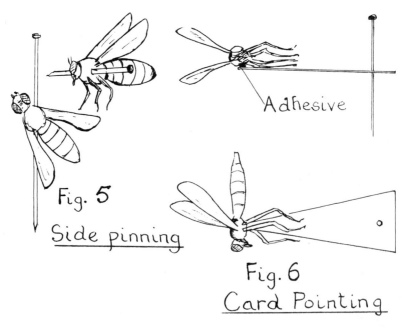

Adhesive

Fig. 5
Side pinning

Fig. 6
Card Pointing

10

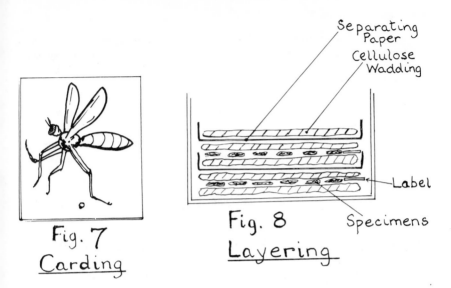

**Fig. 7
Carding**

**Fig. 8
Layering**

Separating Paper

Cellulose Wadding

Label

Specimens

Drying wet flies

If specimens have been collected in alcohol or water, they can be pinned and dried or dried and cardpointed. Also pinned specimens may become "wet", a condition in which grease from the fly's fat body comes through the cuticle and destroys the appearance of dusting. The technique for solving these problems is the same in all cases - simply immerse the specimen in a strong organic solvent for several hours, remove and dry. Xylene is an ideal solvent, but ethyl acetate will do. Labels must be taken off pins before immersion.

On removal, blow gently on the fly to aid drying. This is essential with hairy flies which will otherwise become matted. All the water and grease will have been removed from the specimen, so it will be very brittle. Because of this, it is essential to pin specimens *before* treatment. Although dusting patterns will be restored, they will not be absolutely "as new", so take care if using them as characters for identification.

Wetting dry flies

Normally there is little need to wet dry flies. If part or the whole of a fly is to be mounted on a slide, then it can be put straight into KOH (potassium hydroxide) for a while and treated as usual. Under some exceptional circumstances, dry specimens may be required for comparison with those which are wet-preserved. Some sucess may be obtained by soaing these specimens in a weak (0.25 - 0.5%) solution of trisodium orthophosphate (see Van Cleave and Ross, 1947). No recommendations are available for the length of time for immersion, so experiment with unwanted material. After immersion, the specimens should be washed then placed in preservative.

What method to use?

Considering the restrictions outlined in the previous two paragraphs, the choice of preservation technique may well be determined by how the flies are collected. Assuming, however, that the material is collected alive and freshly killed, the following recommendations should be followed.

Nematocera:
Culcidae, Chaoboridae, Bibionidae and Simuliidae should be micro-pinned. Dixidae, Chironomidae, Scatopsidae, Thaumaleidae, Psychodidae and Cecidomyiidae should be kept in alcohol, and may later be mounted on slides. All other Nematocera may either be pinned or packeted and subsequently card-pointed.

Brachycera:
All families should be pinned. The genitalia of female Tabanidae should be exserted.

Aschiza:
Phoridae should be micropinned dorsally (to leave the mesopleural bristles undamaged) or preserved in alcohol for later dissection and mounting on slides. Pipunculidae should be micropinned. Some dipterists advise controlled removal of the head, followed by gluing it to the end of the micropin. It may be that Pipunculidae are best preserved in alcohol - discussions continue! All other Aschiza, including Syrphidae, should be pinned. The identification of many species depends on the examination of the male genitalia, so these should be exserted.

Acalyptratae:
Braulidae should be kept in alcohol. All other families should be micropinned, but some genera, e.g. *Drosophila*, which have light bodies and dark bristles, may be more easily identified from material in alcohol. In some families, e.g.Anthomyzidae, very small species should be partly represented in alcohol, since pinned material is often distorted. Genitalia should be exserted in several families.

Calyptratae:
All should be pinned. Male genitalia should always be exserted.

Pupipara:
Preferably in alcohol, though Hippoboscidae can be pinned.

Labelling

Labels should be permanent, legible, accurate, complete and firmly fixed to or associated with the specimen. Use drawing ink on white card for all labels, unless you have them printed. Write in block letters and avoid abbreviations which may be ambiguous. Allow labels to dry before handling them or putting them in preservative.It saves time to buy some printed labels for localities which you visit regularly. Good quality labels are available from various suppliers. A stock of labels such as those in Fig.9 may be kept. On these write the locality, grid reference, habitat and date. These data, together with the county, country and collector already printed, are the essential items on a label. Some dipterists employ just locality and date, but these rogues can never have experienced the frustration of finding an interesting fly in and old collection, and not knowing whether it comes from Cornwall, Cork or California. Never assume your notebook will remain with your collection when you leave it to your local (or national?) museum. The data should be on a pin or in a tube with the specimen, and not in a book which can be so easily forgotten in the sorrow surrounding your departure.

Identification

When a species is given a name, that name is given to one particular individual, the type specimen. The most accurate way to name your specimen is to compare it with type specimens until you find one that is identical. This is seldom possible, so try comparing your specimen with examples which have been compared with type specimens. Such collections can be found in the British Museum or in the Hope Department at Oxford University. In some cases even these institutions do not have the necessary material. All is not lost however, for when the species is named, the author publishes a description of the type specimen. If your specimen agrees exactly with this description, it is probably (but not certainly) this species. When a taxonomist carries out a family or generic revision, he will try to see all the type material, and will often enlarge the original descriptions. He may also produce a key which is simply a graded grouping of species according to visible characters. Because, at most, a few characters are chosen for each grouping, some individuals will not fall into their correct groups. A good key will have an average of 95% success for each species, so do not worry if you have specimens which do not "key out". Most importantly, remember that a key is only a guide to identification. IT CANNOT BE USED TO NAME SPECIES WITH CERTAINTY. This is particularly so if you have one or two species in a large genus. It is not uncommon for experienced dipterists using a family key to "successfully key out" a fly in a completely different family!

The easiest way to name material is to have it examined by a specialist, so be tactful when you meet one. If the specialist retains some exceptionally rare specimen of yours, then that is his reward. Console yourself with the thought that accurately named common specimens are of more value than anonymous ranks of little flies which you cannot identify.

When the specimen is identified, a determination label should be attached. This should bear the name of the species, the author, the sex and the identifier's name, as well as the year of identification. This 'det.' label (Fig. 9) is placed below the data labels.

Storage

Good storage has two functions. One is to protect your specimens from damage. The other is to enable you to find any specimen quickly and easily.

Pinned specimens need to be protected from physical shock, damp (which causes mould), and pests. Careful handling and smooth-running drawers are the best guarantee against shock. Damp is not usually a problem, but if specimens do get mouldy, they can be brushed with a solution of phenol in xylene (1:3). The fungal hyphae can then be removed with fine forceps. The appearance of dusting may be altered by this treatment. To prevent the growth of mould, place thymol crystals in the drawer or box.

The pests which will eat dried insects include dermestid beetles, clothes moths,

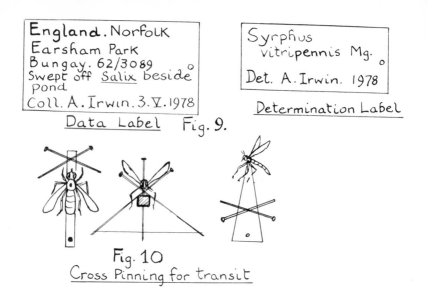

England. Norfolk
Earsham Park
Bungay. 62/3089
Swept off Salix beside
pond
Coll. A. Irwin. 3.V.1978

Data Label Fig. 9.

Syrphus
  vitripennis Mg.
Det. A. Irwin. 1978

Determination Label

Fig. 10
Cross Pinning for transit

booklice and mites. The best protection against these is tight-fitting lids. In addition, place flaked naphthalene or phenol crystals in the drawer or box. Dichlorvos ("Vapona" etc.) or paradichlorbenzene can be used but these are not recommended in domestic situations. With the exception of the latter these chemicals should be regarded only as deterrents. If an infestation occurs, the specimens and cabinet or boxes should be fumigated. This is not an easy task, but some success may be obtained by soaking small wads of cotton wool in ethyl acetate, and placing them in the box. This treatment should take place in a ventilated room. Indeed any use of chemicals in the collection should be restricted to a room which is not occupied for long periods. Specimens in spirit and on slides do not usually suffer from pests, but be careful to avoid drying-out or breakage of glass.

The layout of your collection will make it either easy or difficult to use. The normal convention for pinned material is to use one drawer for complete units, be they families, genera or species. Where possible, avoid dividing a genus or species into two drawers. The generic name should be at the head of the specimens and the species at their foot. Beyond this, the layout of the collection is determined by the size of the flies and the amount of material you have or intend to add. Try to leave a blank species space within each large genus where unidentified specimens can be placed. Within a genus, arrange the specimens alphabetically, as in the check-list. The outside of drawers or boxes should be labelled with the family and genus they contain. This avoids unnecessary movement of specimens.

Mailing

Sooner or later the need will arise to send specimens through the post. This should be avoided if hand carriage is available, but if necessary, then take the following precautions.

Pinned specimens should be securely pinned and cross-pinned (Fig. 10) in a stout box with a soft cork or Plastazote base. Around the edge pin some cotton wool. This will trap any loose specimens or pins and stop them damaging other specimens. This box is then put into another larger box which contains wood-wool or sponge rubber to act as a shock absorber. Do not use expanded polystyrene as a packing material, since this will transmit shocks through to the specimens. This outer box is then sealed, wrapped in stiff paper and tied with string. It should be clearly addressed and your address should also be given. Use a label to state what is in the box. This is obligatory if the specimens are being sent out of the country. "Dried insects for scientific study. Of no commercial value." is the standard description.

Wet-preserved material should be sent in full hard-glass tubes which are packed separately in cotton wool within a stout box or tin. This is placed in an outer box as described above. It is best to be over-cautious when packing specimens for the post. To ease your mind about the safe arrival of your specimens, enclose a stamped, addressed, ready-written postcard.

Genitalia

Colyer and Hammond (1968) give a detailed account of how to make a genitalia preparation by macerating the specimen in KOH and mounting in Canada balsam. Euparal is an alternative mountant which has the advantage of also being a clearing agent. Thus specimens can be transfered direct to it from 95% alcohol, without the need for complete dehydration. In some cases the genitalia are best examined whole rather than in just two dimensions. In this case the preparation is best kept in a drop of glycerine in a microvial (3/8" x 1/8") which is pinned by its cork with the specimen. These microvials are very difficult to obtain, but the enterprising glassworker should be able to make his own. With large calypterates such as *Sarcophaga*, the male genitalia can be dissected dry by removing the enclosing tergites. In this case, they can be mounted laterally on a card slip which is pinned below the specimen. This is only useful for those genitalia which can be seen without the need for maceration.

Associated Material

There are many occasions when two specimens should be associated. Mating pairs, predators and prey, parasites and host, adult and larva, leaf-mine or gall are all cases where two specimens should be connected either physically or by writing. The safest solution is to pin the prey on the same stage as the predator, or to enclose the parasites in the same tube as the pupa, etc. If this is not possible, e.g. larval skin on a slide and pinned adult, then give each specimen full data and refer to the other material being preserved. If necessary use a code number to avoid confusion.

15

Preserving Plant Material

Leaf mines may be pressed and dried between sheets of absorbent paper as befits a botanical specimen. Small leaves may be kept in completely transparent stamp collector's envelopes or mounted on sheets of paper. Empty galls and stem mines can be pinned into a storebox when dry.

Chemicals

The following notes on chemicals cover those mentioned in both this and the previous sections. It should be possible to find a local supplier in the telephone directory. If there is a problem, contact Griffin and George (see "Suppliers" above).

Acetic Acid (Glacial): Used to neutralise KOH, and to soften tissues. Unpleasant, pungent fumes

Alcohol: Used as a liquid preservative (70 - 80% in water). Buy ethanol or industrial spirit. Do not use "meths" as sold in chemist's shops. A special purchasing permit is required from customs and excise. Vapour is inflammable. Poisonous.

Amyl Acetate: Used as a solvent for celluloid. Inflammable, toxic vapour. Poisonous.

Canada Balsam: Dissolved in xylene and used as a mountant for microscopic preparations.

Cellulose Wadding: Obtainable from chemists as "nappy padding".

Cyanide: Potassium cyanide lumps are embedded in plaster for use as a killing agent. Fumes toxic. Solids extremely poisonous if taken internally. Not recommended for Diptera.

Dichlorvos: Used as a killing agent or pesticide. Normally bought in impregnated plastic strips ("Vapona" etc). Fumes toxic, probably carcinogenic (causing cancer). Dangerous to handle.

Ethyl Acetate: Used as a killing agent and solvent. Inflammable, toxic vapour. Poisonous.

Euparal: A mountant for genitalia, etc. Soluble in "Euparal Essence". May be used direct from 95% alcohol.

Formalin: Used as a fixative, but unsuitable as a preservative. Pungent vapour. Unpleasant on contact, but not dangerous unless taken internally.

Glycerine: Used with preservatives to avoid complete desiccation. Also used as a preservative for very small specimens.

Naphthalene: (moth balls) Used in its flaked form as a pest deterrent, but not very effective with some pests. Poisonous.

Pampel's Fluid: Used as a fixative. It is made up from 35% formalin, 95% ethanol, glacial acetic acid and water in the ratio 6 : 15 : 2 : 30. Poisonous.

Phenol: Used as a fungicide when dissolved 1 : 3 in xylene.

Potassium Hydroxide: (KOH) Used as 10% solution in water to macerate specimens prior to microscopic examination. Corrosive and poisonous. Dangerous on contact when hot.

Propylene Phenoxetol: (2-phenoxyethanol) Used as a preservative, but material *must* be fixed first. It is difficult to dissolve in water. To overcome this make up a solution of propylene glycol, propylene phenoxetol and water in the ratio 5:2 : 93 and shake well. Poisonous, but otherwise not unpleasant.

Thymol: Used as a fungal preservative in crystal form. Will affect plastics. Poisonous.

Trisodium orthophosphate: Used as a 0.25 - 0.5% solution in water to reconstitute dried material. Poisonous and dangerous to handle.

Xylene: General purpose organic solvent. Inflammable, toxic vapour. Poisonous.

DO NOT TAKE RISKS WITH CHEMICALS. KEEP THEM IN SECURE, WELL LABELLED BOTTLES AWAY FROM CHILDREN AND FIRES. VERY LARGE QUANTITIES OF INFLAMMABLE CHEMICALS SHOULD BE KEPT AWAY FROM THE HOUSE.

Further Reading

Colyer, C.N. & Hammond, C.O.., 1978. *Flies of the British Isles* 2nd ed., Warne, London.
Cogan, B.H. & Smith, K.G.V., 1974. *Instructions for Collectors* No.4a. Insects. 5th ed., British Museum (Natural History), London.
Oldroyd, H., 1970. *Collecting, Preserving and Studying Insects.* 2nd ed. London.
Van Cleave, H.J. & Ross, J.A., 1947. A method for reclaiming dried zoological specimens. *Science* 105 (2725):318.

TRAPPING DIPTERA
by Ian McLean.

The techniques described in this section will enable the collector to obtain more material of some families than can be found by active collecting in the field. Almost certainly additional species will be found even in well worked localities, and the species composition and relative abundance will be different from, for example, sweep samples. Working a locality regularly through a season with traps can give valuable information on seasonal changes in abundance and species composition, especially when records are linked with additional data such as weather and position of traps in relation to habitats. Traps will continue to collect flies when the collector is elsewhere, so if collecting time is limited, traps can increase efficiency, providing time is available for sorting the catch.

Traps are passive and rely for their success upon the activity and mobility of flies. They are particularly useful for studies which involve counting the numbers of individuals and applying some degree of statistical analysis in comparing traps or separate trapping sessions. The amateur as much as the professional can gain useful information by keeping note of quantitative results, but it is necessary to take account of the limitations of traps in providing unbiassed samples.

As several of the traps require preservation of the material in alcohol, some families may be difficult to identify if the key characters are obscured. Dusting is not visible in alcohol, wing venation may be less easy to see and the colours may be altered. Sometimes colours return on drying out and specimens can even be point mounted but this is not the way to treat critical material. In alcohol however, structural features such as genitalia and chaetotaxy can still be used, and the specimens are pliable and easily manipulated. Some specialists will welcome alcohol material of their group, but please find out in advance if they have time to look at your samples, and always send sorted specimens only. Other orders collected may be of interest - see if you can find a colleague who will find your "rejects" useful.

Finally, always obtain permission from the landowner before setting up traps, and try to ensure that trapping will not adversely affect rare or vulnerable species. For example, large numbers of water traps can catch many queen bumblebees in spring. Place conspicuous traps well away from roads or pathways where they may be vandalised in your absence and do not erect traps in fields where there are grazing farm animals or across deer paths in woods.

Water Traps

These are cheap, easy to make and catch most families of flying Diptera. They are excellent for Phoridae, including small species which may be otherwise overlooked, and flower visitors such as Syrphidae and Anthomyiidae are well represented. Construction is shown in Fig. 11. The pie tin should be nailed to the top of the stake after the latter has been firmly driven into the ground. Yellow is the best colour for the bowls, a little detergent added to the water increases the catch by lowering the surface tension and formalin (1-2 ml) helps to preserve the insects caught. The traps should be emptied at least once per week and the water level kept high to prevent the bowls being blown off. The insects caught can be filtered out by pouring the trap contents through fine terylene curtain net stretched over a small plastic bucket, with the water being re-used. The insects are removed with forceps and placed in 80% alcohol. The stake can be dispensed with provided the trap is sited where it is clearly visible to flying insects, above the ground vegetation and in an insect flyway.

Light Traps

Although nocturnal Lepidoptera predominate in light trap catches, many other groups of insects are taken including Diptera, particularly Tipulidae and Chironomidae. A.E.S. Leaflet No. 33 "Insect Light Traps" should be consulted for details of construction and operation. Tipulidae obtained in light traps will usually have a different species composition from those found by sweeping in the same locality during the day or even from suction traps run concurrently with light traps. In buildings certain light fittings catch large numbers of flies. Of particular value are the white glass globes around bulbs and the box-shaped diffusers under fluorescent strip lights. The specimens are faded but structural characters are still usable. A technique for attracting flies to light is described in the section on Sand Dunes and this presumably also has application in other habitats.

Bait Traps

Traps of the designs shown in Fig. 12 may be baited with a variety of substances depending on the groups required for study. For example, pulped fermenting fruit (apple is best) is attractive to Drosophilidae (Shorrocks, 1972), dung is a bait for Scathophagidae and Sphaeroceridae, carrion for Piophilidae and Heleomyzidae etc. and carbon dioxide (as "dry-ice" wrapped in polythene for slow release) for blood-sucking species. Other baits which can be tried include fish, fungi, crushed snails, rotting eggs and amyl acetate. There are many designs for bait traps, two of which are illustrated in Fig. 13. Small plastic funnels make entrance cones, while tins, zinc gauze and plastic sheeting can be used to construct the main body of the traps. Where possible traps should be sited away from direct sunlight.

Manitoba Trap

The Manitoba trap for Tabanidae (Fig. 14) has been used successfully by several workers in North America for faunal studies. The general construction is shown in the diagram but note that the trap should be firmly staked to prevent over-turning

Fig. 11.
Water Trap.

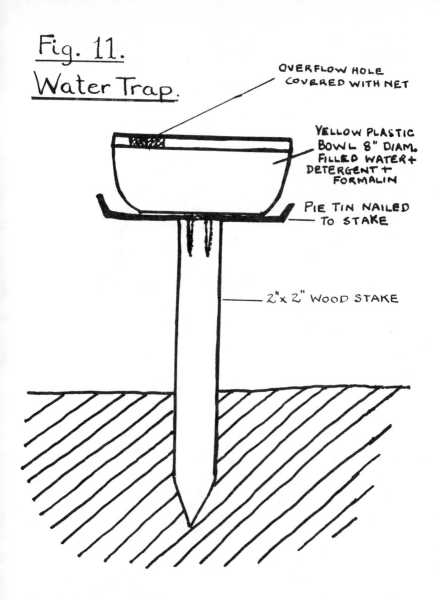

OVERFLOW HOLE
COVERED WITH NET

YELLOW PLASTIC
BOWL 8" DIAM.
FILLED WATER +
DETERGENT +
FORMALIN

PIE TIN NAILED
TO STAKE

2"x 2" WOOD STAKE

by strong winds. The cone is made from 215° sector of a circle of three foot radius using a flexible clear plastic. A ring of plastic tubing or wire should be used to maintain a circular configuration for the base of the cone, while at the apex a hole should be cut to allow the flies to move into the collecting chamber. This should contain a killing agent such as dichlorvos ("Vapona") – see the section chemicals (p.16) Manitoba traps are reported to work best in forest clearings beside ponds or slow-moving streams, and less well in open areas or in dense forest. Shelter from wind will increase catches.

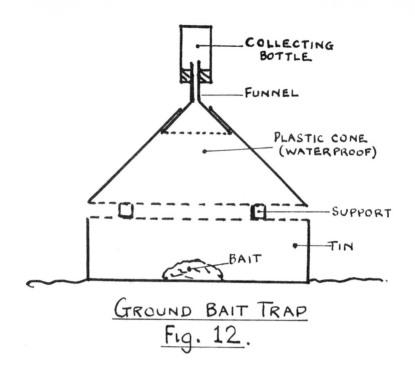

GROUND BAIT TRAP
Fig. 12.

Malaise Trap

The principle is as follows— a vertical screen of fine black netting is set up in a likely flight path, the ends block lateral escape and the insects, rising up the screen from either side are guided by the canopy into a collecting unit. Many designs have been proposed for this trap, the references given should be consulted for details. It is excellent for collecting flying Diptera, though it has the disadvantages of cost (about £20 for materials at 1977 prices) and time needed for construction (about 10 hours). Before making a Malaise trap it is advisable to see a made up example, e.g. at the BM (NH). The basic tent-like design is shown in Fig. 15, the guy ropes, attached to the supporting poles and corners of the trap are omitted from the figure. Terylene netting is a suitable material for construction, 36 feet of 44 inch wide material will be required. The edges of the netting panels are strengthened with half inch cotton tape (98 feet pre-shrunk is needed) before they are sewn together (the ridge seams are pinned together and then sewn after all the other panels are joined) and aluminium or wood poles are used to support the complete trap. The collecting unit is illustrated in Fig. 16; it is constructed from two screw-top plastic bottles with the lids cut open and glued together, the insects caught can be collected into alcohol or killed with dichlorvos ("Vapona") in the collecting jar. A wire screen across the entrance can be used to exclude large insects such as bumblebees and butterflies which can damage the smaller and more fragile Diptera.

Correct siting of the trap is very important for achieving the best results. Sheltered areas are best and placing the trap across insect flyways such as paths, wood margins, beside streams or across gulleys should give good catches. The end of the trap with the collecting unit should be placed towards the light, facing open ground or less dense vegetation.

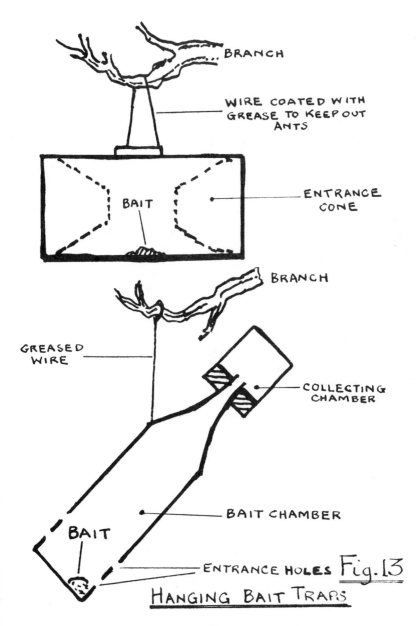

BRANCH

WIRE COATED WITH GREASE TO KEEP OUT ANTS

BAIT

ENTRANCE CONE

BRANCH

GREASED WIRE

COLLECTING CHAMBER

BAIT CHAMBER

BAIT

ENTRANCE HOLES

Fig. 13

HANGING BAIT TRAPS

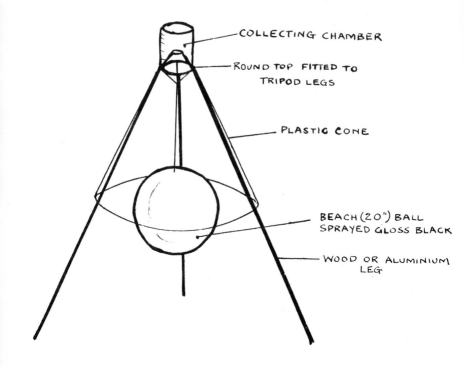

COLLECTING CHAMBER

ROUND TOP FITTED TO TRIPOD LEGS

PLASTIC CONE

BEACH (20") BALL SPRAYED GLOSS BLACK

WOOD OR ALUMINIUM LEG

Fig. 14. Manitoba Trap.

PLAN FOR PLASTIC CONE

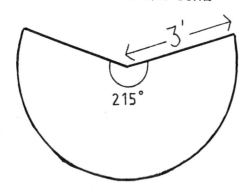

3'

215°

Herting Trap

The construction of this trap is shown in Fig.17. It will collect a variety of Diptera, but needs to be operated for long periods to obtain the best results. The trap, as illustrated, must be regularly inspected throughout the day, the insects required are removed from the plastic window with a pooter. The addition of a pitched roof with a Malaise collecting unit (see Fig. 16) at the roof apex on the window side of the trap could reduce the attention needed for the trap. It should be sited in a sheltered situation with the window facing the light and wind, while there should be cover and shade behind the trap, for example a woodland area, bushes or a tree.

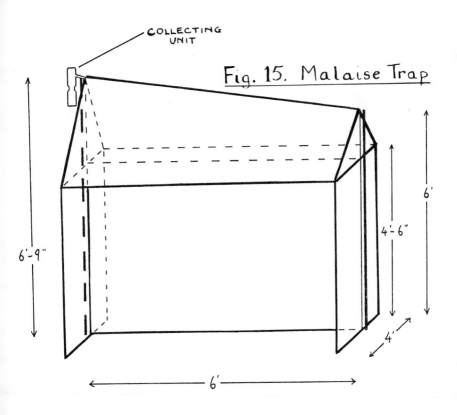

Fig. 15. Malaise Trap

Fig. 16. Malaise Trap
Collecting Unit

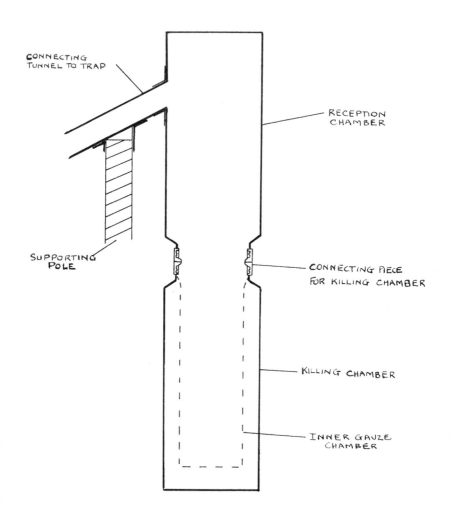

CONNECTING TUNNEL TO TRAP

RECEPTION CHAMBER

SUPPORTING POLE

CONNECTING PIECE FOR KILLING CHAMBER

KILLING CHAMBER

INNER GAUZE CHAMBER

Emergence Traps

An alternative to bringing home leaf litter, tussocks, dead wood or fungi for breeding Diptera is to place an emergence trap over the micro-habitat in the field. Although the precise biology of the species reared may not be known exactly, valuable information on position of breeding site is gained for the flies which emerge. The essential features of any emergence trap are that it should consist of an insect-proof cage flush with the ground or the surface of the breeding substrate, and a collecting bottle at the top where the emerging adults will congregate. Examples of emergence traps are given in Fig. 18. For collecting species which have aquatic larvae and emerge from the water as adults, a modification as in Fig. 18a) may be used, with the base frame attached to floats.

Pitfall Traps

Few Diptera are usually found in pitfall traps but species from grass tussocks and small mammal runs may be taken. Ground beetles will make up the bulk of the catch, so collect into water plus formalin to prevent the more fragile Diptera being damaged.

Autocatcher

A large net with a rectangular mouth (and anchored tail) mounted on a car roof rack has been termed an 'autocatcher' by the coleopterists who use it. The idea is

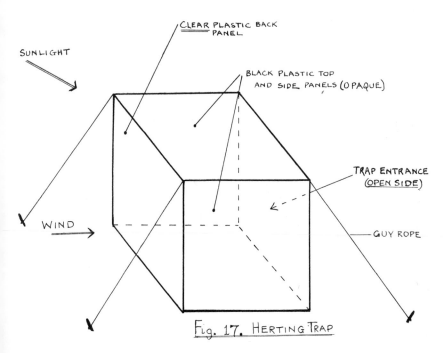

Fig. 17. Herting Trap

25

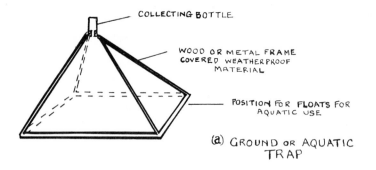

COLLECTING BOTTLE

WOOD OR METAL FRAME COVERED WEATHERPROOF MATERIAL

POSITION FOR FLOATS FOR AQUATIC USE

(a) GROUND OR AQUATIC TRAP

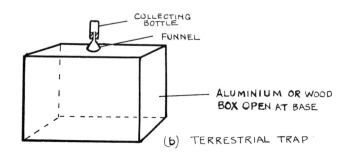

COLLECTING BOTTLE

FUNNEL

ALUMINIUM OR WOOD BOX OPEN AT BASE

(b) TERRESTRIAL TRAP

Fig. 18. EMERGENCE TRAPS

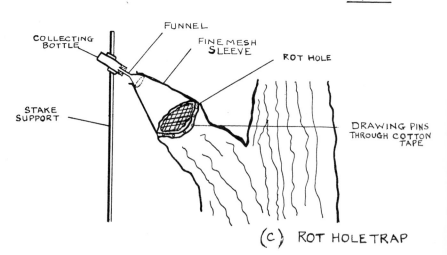

FUNNEL

COLLECTING BOTTLE

FINE MESH SLEEVE

ROT HOLE

STAKE SUPPORT

DRAWING PINS THROUGH COTTON TAPE

(c) ROT HOLE TRAP

to drive along country lanes when warm weather encourages plenty of insects to fly, and thus take a large aerial sweep sample. Though the records gained are of no ecological consequence, coleopterists have gained important district records of species rarely found by normal field methods. Numbers of Diptera may be obtained with an 'autocatcher' but no one has made a study of the material obtained in this way. If the 'autocatcher' is to be used, it is preferable that material from different habitat districts is kept separate.

Other Traps

Sticky traps have been successfully used in some studies but in general should not be used as the Diptera are often indeterminable. Suction traps (see Southwood, 1966) are expensive and not portable so are of limited use to collectors. "D-vac" portable suction samplers tender to damage the Diptera caught and are expensive to buy.

Sorting of Bulk Samples from Traps

The use of a logical sequence of steps when sorting large numbers of insects preserved in alcohol will save time and prevent damage to specimens. Two pairs of fine forceps will be needed.
1. Place sample in a flat dish (a petri dish is suitable)
2. Remove large Lepidoptera, Coleoptera, Hemiptera and Hymenoptera before placing the sample under the microscope. Any large Diptera such as syrphids or tabanids can also be removed to storage bottles at this stage.
3. Under low microscope magnification remove the medium-sized Diptera (such as muscids, tipulids, etc.) to separate storage bottles.
4. If any other groups such as staphylinid beetles or parasitic hymenoptera are being kept they can be separated at this stage, together with groups of Diptera such as the small acalypterates, empids and dolichopodids. If there are few categories here and the sample is not too large, sorting is much quicker if the insects are first separated into small piles in the dish rather than placing them directly into the storage bottles (this section is then combined with 5).
5. The small Diptera such as Cecidomyiidae and Phoridae are best left until last. They are seperated into small piles in the dish and then carefully placed in storage bottles. Plastic capped bottles are very useful for keeping insects in alcohol and don't forget to keep the collecting data associated with all the sorted material.

Further Reading

Cogan, B.H. and Smith, K.G.V., 1974, *Instructions for Collectors* no. 4a, *Insects*, BM (NH), London, 169pp.
Heath, J., 1970 *Insect light traps*, AES leaflet no. 33.
Herting, B., 1969. Tent window traps used for collecting tachinids (Dipt.) at Delmont, Switzerland. *Commonwealth Institute of Biological Control Technical Bulletin* **12**: 1-19. (gives details of the Herting trap, together with a list of tachinids caught 1966-68).
Malaise, R., 1937. A new insect trap *Ent.Tidskr.* **58**: 148-160 (The original Malaise trap design).
Oldroyd, H., 1970 *Collecting, preserving and studying insects* (2nd ed.), Hutchinson, 336 pp.
Shorrocks, B., 1972. *Drosophila* (Invertebrate Types Series), Ginn & Co., 144 pp (Gives details of *Drosophila* trapping programmes).

Southwood, T.R.E., 1966. *Ecological methods with particular reference to the study of insect populations*, Chapman and Hall, 391pp. (The authoritative work with many references).

Thompson, P.H., 1969. Collecting methods of Tabanidae (Diptera), *Ann. ent. Soc. Am.* **62**: 50-57. (Gives details of building and operating Manitoba traps).

Townes, H., 1972. A lightweight Malaise trap. *Ent. News* **83**: 239-247. (A recent detailed paper on the construction of a portable Malaise trap).

COLLECTING TECHNIQUES
by Alan E. Stubbs.

Consideration is here given to active as opposed to passive ways of collecting. These entail only the use of the basic equipment that every dipterist should have.

Sweeping

This is a procedure whereby the net is swept through vegetation with alternating backhand and forehand strokes. This can be employed in step with walking through vegetation or whilst standing still. Everyone has their own timing and vigour of approach and it must be through experience that individual style is adapted to conditions and the groups of flies required. For tipulids a firm sweep deep into herbage is often preferable, but on occasions when they are very active a quicker lighter sweep over the tips of vegetation is more likely to be successful. It is important to realise that a very different fauna may reside in tree and bush foliage compared with the ground layer. Even sweeping over dead leaves or bare mud can be productive.

Commercially available sweep nets have canvas bags and are designed for beetles and caterpillars. One cannot see the flies inside without opening the net sufficiently for all the flies to shoot out. A bag of netting material must be used for diptera, even though special care to avoid thorns is necessary. On completing a series of sweeps, the tip of the bag is pointed towards the brightest part of the sky so that at least in theory all diptera go to that end whilst the collector's head and pooter have accesss via the mouth of the net.

Sweeping does not catch all flies, especially those which are deep within or low down in vegetation, and including those which take evasive action by dropping to the ground or flying off as the source of disturbance grows nearer. Though in many respects inefficient, sweeping is one of the most productive general purpose collecting methods.

Stalking

Many flies are best stalked individually. They may be too fast for capture by general sweeping or it is preferable to watch the habits of a fly in the field and then capture it to check identification. Each collector must develop his own skills and techniques to suit himself but some general guide lines are offered.

Flies on a horizontal flat surface, such as fast ones sun bathing on bare sand, are best approached slowly. Move the net as close as possible before completing a quick swatting downward stroke. On a vertical surface, especially a curved tree trunk, it is difficult to know what to do - often an upward stroke will catch the fly by surprise. The speed of approach needs to be such that the fly has just lifted off the surface but has not had time to evade the net - success or failure is measured in hundredths of a second. Sometimes the fly just sits there regardless of the net; it may have a different plan next time or simply popping a glass tube over the top is all that was required in the first place. The latter technique with a 3 x 1 inch tube has considerable application, especially in spots where a net cannot be wielded. A pooter is useful for collecting small inconspicuous flies on tree trunks, such as empids and psychodids.

Some dipterists are keen on small diameter nets of about 6 inches across. These are useful for picking off flies where a large net would cause too much disturbance - as in selectively collecting off flower heads or in tight corners on bramble bushes. Having scanned flowers for interesting flies, a random sweep with a large net afterwards will often yield small species which were overlooked.

It is essential in any sort of stalking not to allow your shadow to pass over the fly and frighten it away. All movement should be smooth, avoiding sudden action until the final stroke of the net. In windy weather, the collector has the advantage in bringing the net in from the downwind side.

Sifting and Rummaging

This is often a hands and knees operation applying to a variety of situations where the most sedentary flies have to be searched for. The pooter should always be at the ready. The tussock fauna is discussed under Lowland Grassland. The collecting kit can easily accommodate about a square metre of thin light coloured plastic sheeting on which tussocks can be shaken out. The net with material taut across the mouth will act as a standby but the inevitable folds and small area are disadvantages. On a winter expedition for this operation a sieve is worth the effort of carrying it, or material may be brought home in a large plastic bag for sieving. The early warmth of spring is a particularly good time since flies are encouraged to the warm outer layer of the dead leaves of *Carex paniculata* tussocks or towards the sunny surface of sedge litter on the ground - large handfuls thrown on a sheet are often productive. Leaf litter and moss are also worth a try. On other occassions there is always an excuse for sitting on the ground and rumaging slowly through vegetation to locate the many small flies that run and skip through the denser layers on or near the ground.

On the banks of lakes, rivers and streams small flies may be walking around and are easily pooted. It is worth looking underneath stones and drift material. Sea shore or freshwater strand line debris often has large numbers of small flies running under or within.

Some of these activities are likely to reveal larvae (see Chapter 2).

A Sheet

A pale coloured sheet of plastic (this is best because it does not matter if it gets wet or dirty), especially white or yellow, may attract flies because of the colour or to sunbathe. The section on Sand Dunes discusses the use of an illuminated sheet at night. A sheet may also act as a swarm marker or if placed under a swarm of chironomids, predatory ceratopogonids may fall onto the sheet with their prey (patience is recommended!).

HOW TO SET ABOUT FIELD WORK
by Alan E. Stubbs.

A field entomologist must be an opportunist, recognising the potential of the time and place in which he finds himself. However, there is a great deal that can be done to reduce the element of chance and to plan ahead in reaching the places where opportunities are greatest. Much of the Handbook is concerned with background knowledge which will assist the reader to develop techniques and field craft which help obtain the best results for the time spent in the field, though there is nothing that will replace direct experience. There is, however, more to field work than just obtaining a few flies, since the value of that time and effort ultimately depends on records made, or not made!

Background Preparation

The winter is a valuable period. This is the time to check and repair equipment, and ensure that it is assembled where you can find it. The first sunny day of spring can be a sad affair if you have forgotten where half your equipment lies and the net is still full of holes from the previous season. This is the time also to read up on points where it is possible opportunities were lost on earlier occasions because of inadequate information.

One of the most valuable aids in deciding where to go is a map, whether of your home district or a proposed holiday area. The 1:50,000 Ordnance Survey maps are ideal. These may not tell you everything but they give a good lead in locating potentially useful spots. A wood with a small stream running through or along a southerly aspect is a much better bet than a wood with no stream and a northerly aspect. Woods in topographically sheltered spots and with rides are more likely to be useful than ones on exposed hill tops and with no rides. If there are marshes indicated, those with some shelter in a valley or along a wood edge, perhaps with ditches and ponds, may be promising. Similarly river banks are all the better if woods or marshes lie adjacent. In upland situations streams in gulleys and boggy ground should be apparent. On the coast the saltmarshes of estuaries are indicated, sand dunes are recognisable and one may assess the prospects of finding sea cliffs and shores of various characteristics. A stream running to the coast, no matter what the coastal type, will usually offer greater opportunities than a coast without streams.

It is possible to show some additional cunning with the aid of a geological map, since this gives a lead on soil types. One should be able to recognise the distribution of limestone, clay, sand, gravel, etc. and thus increase the chances of sampling from different habitat conditions within a given area. A broad interpretation may be made from solid geology maps at 10 miles to the inch Covering the whole of Britain in two sheets) or for greater accuracy Drift maps at one inch or 1:50,000 are preferable. The main stumbling block is that rock type may vary even within a single colour code on a map; there are various books that can be consulted, such as the series published by the Institute of Geological Sciences entitled *British Regional Geology.*The books and maps published by HMSO can be ordered through most bookshops or obtained at the Geological

Museum in London.

In your home district, it is often worth using the winter to explore for suitable spots so that on those precious sunny days of summer it is possible to head straight for areas with good potential.

Conservation

The chances of locally exterminating a species of fly by collecting is small but there is still no need to collect long series of species which you know may be locally rare. The greatest impact is likely to be by destruction of habitat. In a few species it might be possible to remove all the larvae, as by collecting all infected seed heads or leaf mines from a locally rare plant. Rotten wood is one of the most vulnerable habitats and this should only be inspected with restraint. By far the greatest impact from the collector of Diptera is likely to be by thoughtless trampling or sweeping in fragile vegetation (which action can totally alter a habitat to the detriment of the species living there). It is illegal to dig up plants without the landowner's permission.

Collecting Strategy

Having arrived on site, the first thing is to assess the weather and time of day. Are flies coming in reasonable numbers to flowers? If not then that is one technique which may not warrant prime attention if other strategies may provide a better return for effort. If flies are at flowers in the morning of what could turn out to be a hot day, or sun may be of short duration then it is best to concentrate on flowers while the going is good. Alternatively, it may be noted that the sun will not reach certain flowers until later in the day.

Under windy conditions, the main consideration is to find sheltered spots where collecting is still productive. Sometimes strong wind conditions can be used to advantage since large numbers of flies will have been blown into the lee of obstructions. Thick tree foliage on the lee side of a wood may be teeming with flies as revealed by sweeping. A hedge, embankment, ditch, stream gully, river bank, clump of rushes or other thick vegetation, hollows in dunes, etc. are all spots where on occasion large numbers of Diptera may congregate.

Rain is more of a problem since a wet sweep net reduces flies to a soggy blob. If rain has been light or only recently started, the vegetation may be dry enough to sweep within a wood. Once the vegetation is saturated one can best hope to find flies sheltering on the underside of leaves but if the temperature goes right down even this is rather unproductive. However if it does remain warm, then a surprising number of flies remain active and conspicuous - these are best tubed direct off vegetation. Once the rain stops, the first consideration is to find where vegetation will dry out fastest - sunny spots and areas where the wind will help. Tree foliage will often dry fastest, especially in a breeze.

Even in Britain there are occasions when it can get too hot for flies. Sultry, very high humidity weather suits flies, but a hot dry day can often send flies into cover. On such days the mornings and evenings offer the best collecting, or if out in the full afternoon heat then the cooler conditions of woodland offer the best prospect. Further aspects of collecting strategy will be deduced from the chapters on habitat.

Survey Techniques

The minimum data when recording a species is date and locality. The value of a record can be substantially increased if details of the circumstances of capture and ecological setting are described. Whilst the effort of individual treatment may be justified with a rare species, few entomologists will have the time or inclination to make detailed notes about each specimen. Thus a balance has to be struck between recording detail and time available.

A simple procedure may be adopted in survey work. The unique date and locality label still applies, but during that day's field work the catch is collected in a series of sub-samples, each with its own code letter. Thus 'a' may be a batch of flies on spear thistle flowers at the edge of a meadow adjoining an oak wood, 'b' may be a sample swept from tree foliage at the edge of the wood and 'c' some flies at a seepage on an oak trunk within the wood and 'd' a single fly waving its wings whilst walking over a bramble leaf in a shaft of sunlight in the wood. The code letter should be written in pencil on a label in the tube and in a field note book. On returning home the coding is listed in a permanent notebook and the code letter placed after the date on the locality label on the specimen. Ideally the habitat data should be written out on a second label on the specimen in case the note book is lost. In this fashion it is possible to apply fairly precise habitat information to even large catches of flies and usually more than enough material for sorting has been gained well before 'z'. In working in this way, it is useful to have 2 or 3 pooters so that it is possible to carry on working without stopping for emptying every time.

To gain the most out of one's studies, it is most rewarding to carry out a survey of at least one of the localities that can be visited regularly, or a nice looking spot on holiday. As the locality becomes familiar and the species list grows, it becomes easier to appreciate the habitat features which govern the distribution of individual species and search for the 'missing' species brings its own reward in success or interesting questions of reasons for absence. The interpretation of distribution patterns becomes all the more meaningful if there are some well worked localities as a base line. If carrying out such a survey it is best to form your own system of annotations for sub-divisions of an area and to select representative spots as main sampling points. Such a procedure will give better balanced and more meaningful end results than wandering haphazardly taking a few flies here and there. If at all possible, use a variety of passive trapping techniques as well as active collecting methods so as to sample as wide a range of the fauna as possible; sweep samples only provide a biassed view of the overall species composition. Quantitative information is always of value if this can be obtained.

Studies on Biology of Flies

As is explained elsewhere, there is still a great deal to be learnt about the life history, behaviour and other aspects of the biology of flies. For anyone wishing to take on a small study, it is worthwhile considering the biology of a single species or the sequence of flower visitors to a single species of plant during the day. There are all manner of opportunities, many of which are most likely to arise by chancing upon an interesting feature worth following up, but it is as well to try to look into at least one field of study thoroughly to get worthwhile results. A few examples may help give some ideas. Many adult flies are predatory on other flies and insects yet little is recorded on the subject. When, how and by what pattern of behaviour do individuals find each other to mate, and do the males have distinctive behaviour in fending off other males? Observations on egg laying may help give a clue to where larvae live. The scope for locating and rearing larvae from virtually all potential media is endless. Anyone with botanical leanings could help find out more about the phytophagous species and the microhabitat distribution of infected plants. Even for Tephritidae there is plenty to be done in checking plant host associations (some even lack known associations) and to assess how it is that several species can co-exist on the same host. Rearing parasites of tephritids is often easy and much remains to be discovered overall about parasites of Diptera and the parasitisation by Diptera of other invertebrates. These thoughts should be sufficient for plenty of other ideas to be recognised further on through the Handbook.The main needs are a field notebook and the careful noting of observations in the field that may be put on more permanent record on reaching home. A seemingly unimportant observation may eventually come to be recognised as crucial to making sense of a study but a balance has to be met in practice between distinguishing the trivial from the potentially important.

Keeping Records

There are various alternative methods of keeping records, with varying advantages singly or in combination. A permanent notebook may be used to keep a log of records and observations for each day's field work, and this should be indexed. Alternatively, a loose-leaf file enables re-sorting into localities or subject areas of biological information - but take care not to lose pages. Some dipterists have favoured card indexes arranged by species and with another index for locality cards or biological subjects. The index arrangement has some advantages in relation to the recording schemes cited below but has the disadvantage of restrictions on space. The writer prefers to keep loose-leaf files where space is unrestricted and to extract records onto standard cards where these are sought by the organisers of recording schemes.

Photography provides a further means of recording, including habitats, leaf mines, galls and the insects (for techniques see Lindsley, P., 1977 *Insect photography for the amateur*, Amateur Entomologists' Society).

RECORDING SCHEMES
by Alan E. Stubbs

In recent years there has been a growing recognition of the need to encourage and co-ordinate the recording of information about insects. The momentum has mainly been concerned with producing distribution maps but in many cases, as with Diptera, recording is taken to encompass virtually all aspects of the natural history of flies. A distribution map is only satisfactory if it can be interpreted and this requires a wider understanding of the biology and ecology of the fly concerned. The body which oversees all the recording schemes in Britain is the Biological Records Centre (BRC) at Monks Wood, near Huntingdon (within the Institute of

Terrestrial Ecology). These schemes cover the vascular plants, lichens, mosses, terrestrial vertebrates and a range of terrestrial, freshwater and marine invertebrate groups. In all cases the aims include the assembly of records into data banks and the production of distribution atlases, the BRC operations in Britain largely being carried out under contract to the Nature Conservancy Council. The British activities in turn form a component of the European Invertebrate Survey (EIS) which co-ordinates the national programmes of all the countries in Europe. A programme of distribution maps for the Western Palaeartic is already under way but does not yet include Diptera. In turn EIS is to form part of a world mapping project funded under the umbrella of UNESCO. The British system was the model and catalyst for this development.

British mapping of invertebrates is on a 10Km square grid, but it cannot be emphasised too strongly that all records should have a six figure grid reference, or as second best the 1 Km square reference, since distribution can only be interpreted in terms of exact localities - a 10 Km square map only gives the broad impression. European mapping uses 50 Km squares on a UTM grid.

There is considerable advantage in all naturalists following the same pattern of map display and a similar organisation of data banks. There are already British maps for flowering plants, so one may readily check whether the distribution of a fly matches the distribution of a supposed food plant. Also there are maps of molluscs, so it is a simple matter to compare the distribution of sciomyzids with their known hosts. there are bumble-bee maps to compare with forthcoming conopid maps. Many invertebrate schemes, as with those for Diptera, are still in the early phases of operation but as momentum gathers it will be possible to consider quite complex multiple distribution patterns and, of course, physical factors such as geology, soil and climate. As will be apparent later in this Handbook, Diptera inter-relate with a vast range of plants and other animals so the common efforts of dipterists and specialists in other organisms is all to mutual benefit. The map is not the ultimate tool, it is an index to a data bank which ought to include sufficient detailed facts to enable meaningful interpretation. The organisers of most invertebrate schemes are usually able to provide help and advice in identifying non-dipterous insects which may be found associated with flies.

British Diptera Recording Schemes

There are (at the time of writing) seven schemes covering certain groups of Diptera. Each scheme has one or more organisers and additionally there are regional representatives who act as ambassadors for all schemes. These dipterists form the Central Panel (of Diptera Recording Scheme Organisers) to co-ordinate the schemes and to act as a panel in the sense of being prepared to advise on Diptera. It is as an element of this advisory role that the Central Panel has acted as the focus for the production of the Handbook, drawing in other specialists to assist with the project.

The recording schemes are as follows

Craneflies (Tipulidae, Trichoceridae, Anisopodidae, Ptychopteridae) 330 species
Dixidae   14

Larger Brachycera (Tabanoidea, Asiloidea)	152
Hoverflies	250
Conopidae	24
Sciomyzidae	65
Sepsidae	26
	total 861 species

Each scheme organiser is the focal point for gathering information for his own group. Experienced dipterists provide data in the required format and the less experienced are able to send in their collections for identification. Even if someone does not study some of the groups, he is encouraged to send in field samples placed in envelopes for all schemes. The envelopes are easy to post or store in a crush-resistant box or tin. The scheme organisers and regional representatives act as relay points for any type of relevant material.

A newsletter, called a Bulletin, is circulated as a means of keeping recorders informed of progress. This announces various meetings, such as an annual meeting in London each autumn and a number of field recording meetings. The latter may be for a day or weekend to cater for regional participation or national week long meetings in any part of Britain. Various working keys and advistory notes are also produced. In addition to the formal schemes, there are a number of smaller scale projects operating, usually involving at least an identification service. These currently include Mycetophilidae, Bibionidae, Culicidae, Phoridae, Platypezidae, Calliphoridae, Rhinophoridae, *Pollenia*, Sarcophagidae and *Pupipara*. Enveloped or pinned material is satisfactory for all except Phoridae which must be in 70 % alcohol. One of these projects is concerned with getting people to send in bait samples of Calliphoridae from anywhere and any time of year, with a special co-ordinated effort once a year for gardens under the banner 'National Fish Skin Week.' It is expected that some of these projects will lead to recording schemes if the interest and support is sustained.

The Interpretation of Distribution

Given detailed records, it is possible to make use of more vague data (and unfortunately most pre-existing data is vague since the nearest town on a data label may be several miles from the actual locality). The rhagionid *Symphoromyia immaculata* was regarded as a rarity, but it was found that there was a pattern to recent records since they all came from chalk grassland or roughly comparable habitat, a fact which had never been reported. Chasing up all available records from the literature and collections in private and museum hands produced a total of 45 localities. These mostly vague records were plotted as accurately as possible and it was found that nearly all of them related to chalk or limestone outcrops reasonably closely. Thus chalk and limestone grassland seemed the limiting factor, but why was the fly unrecorded for certain areas? By superimposing climatic maps, a close fit was obtained which, at least in theory, explained the distribution in terms of availability of a certain type of grassland with a certain type of climate. The test is then to see whether the negative information on the distribution map is true or false - and so far all additional records have been in predicted positive areas and search in predicted negative areas has been unsuccessful. The life history is unknown, but if that were investigated it may be possible to appreciate how and why the habitat and climate are limiting factors. Is the hypothesis true or a completely false red herring? Only time and the results of further field study will lead towards an answer, but that is how an understanding of natural science progresses.

The first cranefly maps to be published involved an analysis of data on *Ptychoptera* species. This revealed interesting distribution patterns and the first considered statement of the habitat differences between species. All sorts of problems remain - has *P. contaminata* really become extinct in Scotland by retraction of its range, why does *P. minuta* show a clumped distribution, how do species pairs in similar habitat avoid competition and what is the meaning of *P. scutellaris* seemingly having different habitat requirements in northern England compared with southern England? The cranefly recording scheme, if not directly answering these questions, at least continues to increase the strength of the data on which explanations can be posed and tested.

The distribution pattern of the asilid *Leptarthrus brevirostis* is decidedly odd. It is restricted to chalk grassland in some parts of England but occurs in a wider variety of terrain in the west and north, yet is decidedly clumped in distribution with mysterious and apparently genuine gaps in distribution. The evidence on a world basis that asilid larvae are often parasites or predators of scarabaeid beetle larvae raises the prospect that the fly is using different hosts in different parts of its range. The Larger Brachycera Scheme is new and one hopes that the day may come when the coleopterists map their scarabaeids, thus enabling a multidisciplinary approach to the problem.

The Hoverfly Recording Scheme is bound to reveal many interesting distribution patterns. One of the recent discoveries is that *Xylota florum* of the British list is in fact two species, with *X. coeruleiventris* in the north and west and genuine *X. florum* in the south and east. The amazing aspect of the maps at present is that the two species have almost touching yet mutually exclusive ranges. This is not implausible since some other insects are known to have species pairs of this sort and, moreover, the boundary may move as climate changes. Real or imaginary? Explicable or beyond explanation?

It is hoped these few examples will show that recording is a worthwhile exercise. All aspects of the taxonomy, biology and ecology of flies are inter-related. As should become clear from the themes in the chapters below, Diptera cannot be intelligently studied without placing them in the context of how they live and interact with their physical environment and with other species, whether plant or animal.

Further Reading

Stubbs, A. E., 1967-1968. Geology as an ecological factor in the distribution of an insect. The fly *Symphoromyia immaculata* F. (Dipt., Rhagionidae). *Entomologists's Rec. J. Var.* **79**: 292-3, 313-6; **80**: 22-35, 56-59, 80-83.

Stubbs, A.E., 1972. A review of information on the distribution of the British species of *Ptychoptera* (Dipt.: Ptychopteridae). *Entomologist* **105**. 23-38, 308-312.

DISPOSAL OF COLLECTIONS

It is preferable that instructions to next of kin invite the British Museum (Natural History) to advise on the disposal of a collection and leave it to their complete discretion whether a named or unnamed museum, society or individual should receive all or part of the collection. If all collections and associated note books were handed on in this way, there would be considerable confidence that the efforts of dipterists today can indeed be viewed as a scientifically valuable inheritance for future generations of entomologists.

Chapter 2

The Immature Stages of Flies
by Allan Brindle and Kenneth G.V.Smith

Introduction

Diptera undergo a complete metamorphosis, i.e. with the four stages egg, larva, pupa and adult. The Hippoboscidae, Nycteribiidae and Streblidae, collectively known as the 'Pupipara', do not lay eggs but retain the egg and resulting larva within the body until pupation is imminent and then give birth to the mature larva. In some Calliphoridae and Sarcophagidae the eggs are hatched internally and living larvae produced. In *Ocydromia glabricula* (Empididae) living larvae are dropped (as opposed to placed) onto dung, in which they breed, by the female as she hovers slowly above, the only such case known in the viviparous Diptera (Hobby & Smith, 1962). In the Cecidomyiid genus *Miastor* paedogenesis occurs i.e. young daughter larvae are produced from eggs, within the parent larva's body, which they destroy before reaching the pupal stage; thus the adult stage may be dispensed with for several generations. Another form of development known as pupal paedogenesis occurs in some Cecidomyiidae and also in some Chironomidae. Here sometimes larvae emerge from the adult fly while it is still inside the pupal skin, though a normal life cycle also occurs (Wyatt, 1961)

Eggs of flies have been little studied and as one might expect we know most about species of economic or medical importance. The eggs of some mosquitoes are laid in floating 'rafts' and others have various flotation devices. Aquatic Chironomidae lay their eggs in gelatinous strings. Many eggs laid in semi-liquid media have flotation devices and other adaptations which aid respiration or help in avoiding desiccation or drowning when it rains (Hinton 1961). Some of these adaptations are illustrated (figs. 78 - 84). Eggs are fairly easily collected from pregnant females and useful work could be done in describing and illustrating eggs thus obtained, since the identity can be established with certainty from the adult. Many eggs have complex microsculpture which may be diagnostic at species level (e.g. Syrphidae, Chandler, 1968; see Aphids). If the fly belongs to a group where some knowledge of the natural pabulum exists one can attempt rearing through to adult, but this is not easy unless the precise food requirements are known.

Larvae and adults of flies often live entirely different lives in different pabula and take different food. Dipterous larvae are without true legs (apodous) but sometimes (e.g.*Ephydra, Limnophora*, figs. 51, 62) have secondary organs of locomotion (pseudopods or prolegs). In the Nematocera and most Brachycera a distinct head capsule is present but in the Cyclorrhapha the head armature consists mostly of the mouthparts (cephalo-pharyngeal skeleton) and the larva is usually pointed at the head end and called a maggot. Blunter ended larvae are popularly called grubs. The form of the mouthparts is useful in identification. Respiration is usually via spiracles which vary in number from ten pairs in *Bibio* to the more usual one anterior and one posterior pairs, which again are often useful in identification. Respiration in truly aquatic insects is often via respiratory siphons and the larva must seek the surface to breathe (e.g. mosquitoes). In other aquatic larvae external gills have developed to cope with the problems of respiration (e.g. Chironomidae). Parasitic larvae often have large and complex posterior spiracles to solve their respiratory problems. Keilin ;(1944) describes many respiratory adaptations of larvae.

Pupae of Diptera are less well-known than the larvae but can be identified to family and sometimes further with experience. The Nematocera and Brachycera have pupae in which the adult anatomy is largely visible externally (figs. 69-70) and from which the adult emerges through a slit in the back. In the Cyclorrhapha the true pupae remains inside the cast larval skin, which forms a protective puparium (figs. 71-77) from which the fly emerges by forcing off a cap (usually in two parts) by inflating a sac on its head called a ptilinum. When rearing flies the pupal 'trappings' should always be preserved, especially the bits of the puparial cap of Cyclorrhapha as the mouthparts of the third larval instar are attached and can be vital to identification. It is also advisable to segregate mixed pupae or puparia into individual containers for rearing to avoid confusion of the various bits and pieces. Respiratory horns and other adaptational modifications are often useful in identifying pupae or puparia (figs. 71-72).

Good general works on the immature stages are provided by Hennig (1948-52), and Brauns (1954), which are in German, but well illustrated and Hennig includes a full bibliography. Peters (1957) provides useful illustrations; illustrated keys to larvae of medical importance are provided by Oldroyd and Smith (1973) and to those invading the body of man and animals (myiasis) by Zumpt (1965). Séguy (1950) and Oldroyd (1964) give much useful biological information and Keilin (1944) discussses respiratory systems. A bibliography of rearing techniques is given by Wong (1972). Other works on specific families or of special interest are given in the *Bibliography of Key Works* published by the Systematics Association.

Collecting Techniques

Larvae of various kinds of Diptera are often accidentally encountered when searching for other kinds of insects, and it is well worth attempting to rear these larvae. They are usually the larger ones, often well grown, and if some of the material in which they are found is included with them, there is often little difficulty in obtaining the adults. It is assumed that whatever they are actually eating exists in the material and not infrequently the species turns out to be one which is not often seen in the adult stage.

Apart from accidental encounters, however, the systematic collecting of larvae does present problems. The extent of possible habitats is so large that some kind of sampling is really necessary. As one would expect, none of the habitats are sharply defined and typical soil-inhabiting larvae may be found in wood debris, amongst leaf litter or in dung and a succession of different larvae inhabiting increasingly wetter soils leads imperceptibly into semi-aquatic and aquatic habitats. Some larvae normally associated with running water can be found in still water and some terrestrial larvae may occur in aquatic moss. There are some larvae, however, which only occur in very strictly defined habitats. The larval habitat may change with the age of the larvae and some semi-aquatic larvae migrate to dryer habitats before changing to the pupal stage.

Amongst terrestrial habitats, soil is perhaps the most extensive and as a general rule the wetter the soil the more productive it becomes. Black friable woodland soil is generally good, especially that formed below mosses on stones or soil, whilst heavy clay soil is poor. Peaty soil is generally poor, although low-lying peaty soil, when drained, may be productive and it is often useful to sample various soils to investigate their potential. Early spring is the most productive period, although collecting should be carried on through the summer to obtain those species which are adult in late summer or autumn. Hand searching of soil is useful but this is only practicable in fairly dry friable soil which crumbles easily in the hand. In bare soil a strip about 3 ft by 6 inches is dug out to a depth of about 3 inches, using a trowel. A second strip is then searched by crumbling the soil by hand and the rejected soil pushed into the dug-out portion. Successive strips are then dealt with, working away from the original strip. The back of a large knife can be used in preference to the hand to 'comb' the soil back into the dug-out portion. If the soil is grass-covered, the grass is uprooted and shredded above the loosened ·soil. To some people there is no advantage in using a white or pale coloured plastic sheet over which the grass can be shredded since too much debris results and the larvae are often more easily seen against a dark background. *Tipula* larvae are readily found in this way even through they are grey or brown and the numbers found depend on the type of the soil and the operator. Other collectors prefer to use a coarse sieve to remove the larger debris and to shake onto a sheet a small quantity of soil or litter at a time; if left for a minute the *Limonia* larvae in soil covered silken tubes show up easily when they begin to move (a coloured sheet e.g. yellow helps show up white larvae). There is sometimes a considerable difference between apparently identical soils, even at the same time of year, and some larvae are localised, a large number being found close together, whilst otherwise the site may be somewhat barren. As the soil becomes more moist, the strip method becomes less useful since the particles cling together and a rapid method of dealing with such soils is to use a sieve. Sieves sold by general dealers for flour are useful, and consist of a circular piece of mesh, about 16 holes to the inch and 10-12 inches in diameter, enclosed in a deep but thin wooden rim of about 4-6 inches in depth. The mesh usually used now is nylon or similar material, which has replaced the former wire mesh, and the nylon is less apt to injure any larvae. Soil is placed in the sieve and the latter washed in any nearby water, when the soil particles pass through the mesh and leave any larvae behind. The speed of this method is its advantage; the necessity of a water supply is one limitation. Sandy soils are ideal since the material rapidly passes through the mesh leaving little debris behind. Woodland soils tend to leave a good deal of debris but some of this can be washed whilst the sieve is immersed and thrown away. Peat soils leave too much debris, but even so the larvae are washed clean and often being pale coloured tend to become conspicuous.

Many larvae curl up during the sieving, but some active larvae often crawl through the mesh. It is better, therefore, to wash the soil for only a short time before a first inspection so that any larvae seen may be removed before subsequent washings. A glance on the underside of the mesh takes care of any larvae which have passed

40

through. Picking up a larva using wetted fingers works well but care is needed with a wire mesh not to injure the larva against the mesh.

Another method of sampling soils is by the use of orthodichlorobenzene, using about half an ounce of the liquid to one gallon of water. This method seems to rely on the vapour interfering with the respiration of the larvae, so that they come to the surface. A square yard of ground is first cleared by cutting any vegetation short to enable any surfacing larva to be seen and two gallons of the mixture are then poured over the area; any larvae should surface before half an hour or so. The orthodiclorobenzene is immiscible with water so a little liquid detergent is recommended; this produces a milky fluid which penetrates the soil well, providing this is fairly well drained. In marshy soils, of course, the liquid does not penetrate as well as in more porous soils. The first indication that the liquid is working is given by the emergence of worms which surface quickly; Diptera larvae emerge later and much more inconspicuously. The proportion of the chemical can be varied and the best proportions found for various soils. It is better to err on the side of a weaker solution, since a strong solution can kill the larvae. Earthworms are much more affected than the larvae of Diptera and a very rapid exodus of earthworms indicates that the liquid is too strong. It has been suggested that the same effect of driving the larvae to the surface of soil could also be done by using water alone to flood the area or by leaving a plastic sheet over the wet soil for some time. In fact Tipulidae and *Lucilia* larvae sometimes appear on the soil surface in large numbers after periods of heavy rain.

An excellent method of sampling soils, which also brings the smaller larvae to view, is by flotation, using commercial epsom salts, (magnesium sulphate) at the rate of about one pound to one gallon of water. This is really only practicable for indoor work. The principle behind this method relies on the specific gravity of the larvae, which is only slightly greater than that of water. Alternatively the addition of some common salt to water will cause any contained larvae to float, provided that they are free-living and not enclosed in other material. The material to be sampled is placed in a large plastic bowl and the solution poured into the bowl, the mixture being well stirred by hand. Any contained larvae then float to the surface and can be picked off and placed in clean water. This is probably advisable since magnesium sulphate is used as an anaesthetic for aquatic animals in zoological techniques, though provided the larvae are removed fairly quickly there do not appear to be any ill effects. A number of soil samples can be used before the water becomes so turgid that the larvae cannot be easily seen. If the soil is sieved first most of the colouring matter is removed and prevents the flotation water becoming too darkened. Some larvae, and most pupae, tend to collect around the edges of the water which should be closely inspected.

It has been found, however, that none of the previous methods are entirely satisfactory for some larvae. Those of the genus *Limonia* (Tipulidae) for example, often construct a silken tube in which they live, and this tube is covered with soil or other debris. Unless they come out of the tube they may not be seen since the tube does not float. In this case the simplest method, but a slow one, is to place washed soil in clean water in a white dish and watch for movement. Other case-making larvae such as *Thaumastoptera calceata* (Tipulidae) are most easily found in this way.

The methods outlined are all useful and can be effectively combined. For example, it is difficult to see small larvae in the sieve and yet the flotation method requires the bringing back of samples. This latter can be concentrated and much of the colouring matter can be got rid of by using the sieve; this concentrated material can be very productive since a large area can be dealt with and the concentrate brought back in a plastic bag.

Many larvae are susceptible to a dry atmosphere and quickly die if kept for a short time in such conditions. The use of a Berlese or Tullgren funnel is perhaps unsuitable for small delicate larvae but it does produce the more resistent larvae such as those of *Fannia* (Fannidae) and *Sargus* (Stratiomyidae). These larvae, however, are best searched for by hand, using a white sheet or plastic sheet and shredding the compost heap or other material over it, since they are more easily seen against a pale coloured background.

Terrestrial mosses, growing on walls or stones usually contain larvae of *Tipula* (Tipulidae) and sometimes those of *Ptiolina* (Rhagionidae) and various muscid larvae also occur. Shredding the moss is probably the most effective method. Old trees are worth attention, especially when the bark has detritus or mould beneath , when larvae of Lonchaeidae, Stratiomyidae, Clusiidae and Muscidae occur with others. In all these, hand searching, using a knife or trowel when necessary, appears to be most useful. In harder wood the use of a knife for paring off thin slices may reveal tunnels of delicate larvae, such as those of *Epiphragma, Austrolimnophila* and *Lipsothrix* (Tipulidae), and more robust methods, using a hammer and chisel are often needed to get at the larger *Tanyptera* (Tipulidae) and other larvae. Decayed wood may contain Mycetophilidae, Stratiomyiidae, Tipulidae, and others; inspection of holes with silken webs may produce such larvae as *Keroplatus* (Mycetophilidae) and others.

Dung is always worth an enquiring prod with a trowel; apart from Bibionidae, Anisopodidae and Trichoceridae, such Syrphidae as *Syritta* and *Rhingia* occur. This material is generally unsuitable for the methods previously mentioned, though well decayed dung can be investigated by flotation.

Fungi frequently have larvae of various groups. Mycetophilidae are often white with dark heads; the latter can easily be seen when moving even though the bodies remain invisible. Well decayed fungi support saprophagous larvae. Slime fungus can harbour such larvae as *Phronia* (Mycetophilidae), some of which bear superficial coverings.

Aquatic larvae can be obtained using the normal water net in both still and running water, or by lifting stones out of the water to find such larvae as *Antocha* (Tipulidae) or Simuliidae, although both will turn up in water nets used in the usual way in streams and rivers. *Limnophora* (Anthomyiidae) are often frequent in mosses in running water with Hemerodromiinae, although these cling tenaciously to the moss and the latter, being very small, are best located with the moss in water in a white dish, since they are quite active.

Other sections of the Handbook give further details on such topics as dead wood, dung, fungi and water.

Preservation

A good method of killing larvae consists of immersing them in hot (60-70°C.).

water, which expands the larvae fully and kills them immediately. Alcohol or other similar killing fluids are not instantaneous and tend to contract the larvae; the usual method of collecting samples from Berlese or Tullgren funnels in alcohol produces retracted larvae which may be difficult to examine. Retractile structures, such as anal papillae, are usually well expanded with hot water, although other methods can also be used. The larvae should be allowed to move freely before dropping them into the water.

After killing, the larvae are first preserved in Pampel's fluid which seems to give consistently better results than alcohol. The larvae are eventually transferred to 70% alcohol for permanent storage, with a small proportion of glycerine added, but no definite time limit is used before this transference. Pampel's fluid is unpleasant to work with and storage in alcohol is preferred; the same applies to other formalin based preservatives for permanent storage. The formula for Pampel's fluid is as follows:-

Glacial acetic acid	4 volumes
Formaldehyde (40%)	6 volumes
Alcohol (95%)	15 volumes
Distilled water	30 volumes

The preserved larvae are stored in 50 mm x 12 mm glass tubes which have polythene stoppers; these latter have transverse ridges which grip the tube and leakage of alcohol is nil or almost so. If many larvae are involved, larger glass vials, 6 or 4 are used; these have polythene press-on caps and are similarly practically free from evaporation problems. A label with the data written with waterproof Indian ink on a small piece of white card is placed lengthwise in the tube with a piece of cellulose wadding pushed down, before inserting the larvae, to hold the label against the side. These tubes can be stored in small trays, each holding a genus or species, arranged in those banks of filing cabinets having shallow small drawers (about 14 inches x 9 inches x 2 ½ inches). Over a period of some twenty years no serious faults have been found with these tubes or vials, although occasional tubes may be faulty. Alternatively tubes or vials can be placed in any other form of system, in plastic boxes etc. The former method of inverting tubes, sealed by a plug of cotton wool, in a larger jar, has been abandoned for two reasons – (1) evaporation of alcohol was very difficult to eliminate completely, and (2) the examination of any particular tube was a somewhat messy procedure and the selection of a tube more difficult.

Dead, dry or alcohol contracted larvae can be softened in warm caustic potash (10% KOH) and, when expanded, transferred to alcohol or Pampel's fluid for storage.

Key to Families of Diptera Larvae

Key to suborders of larvae

1. Mandibles opposed and moving in a more or less horizontal plane, or abdomen with at least nine distinct segments. Head capsule typically complete, free, and usually non-retractile

   (In a very few, e.g. *Forcipomyia*, Ceratopogonidae, the mandibles move

43

vertically, but the head capsule of these is complete and free. In the Cecidomyiidae the head capsule is often reduced and the mandibles may be almost aborted or not opposed, but there are at least nine abdominal segments, and the respiratory system is usually peripneustic. In the Tipulidae the head capsule is retractile and may be reduced, but the mandibles move horizontally) ....Nematocera

– Mandibles not opposed, and moving in a more or less vertical plane, with their apices parallel and directed ventrally. Head capsule typically incomplete and retractile. Abdomen with not more than eight segments

(In the Xylophagidae and Stratiomyidae the head capsule is strongly sclerotized and non-retractile, but the mandibles move vertically. In the Therevidae and Scenopinidae the abdomen appears to consist of more than eight segments due to secondary segmentation, and the head may be almost completely sclerotized) 2

2. Head capsule always with a distinct, even if incomplete dorsal sclerotization; mandibles usually sickle-shaped; antennae well developed and situated on a sclerotized plate; maxillae and maxillary palpi distinct and usually well developed; sclerotized rods projecting posteriorly from the head into the body not united ....Brachycera

— Head capsule not sclerotized dorsally; mandibles usually shorter and broader; antennae absent or reduced, and if present situated on a membranous area; maxillary palpi almost always absent or indistinct, maxillae fused with mandibles; sclerotized rods extending posteriorly from the head into the body united in a cephalopharyngeal "skeleton". In the Lonchopteridae, the maxillary palpi are distinct but small ....Cyclorrhapha

Key to families: Nematocera. For convenience the figures illustrating this key are placed in the order in which they appear in the British Check List.

1. Head reduced, often greatly reduced; venter of thorax with a sclerotized "sternal spatula" (fig. 19); often pink or bright red, orange or yellow in colour, sometimes white; size small; in soil, humus, under tree bark where they may occur in masses, or in galls; very inactive. (Some Sciaridae are pink in colour and may also occur in masses, but the heads are more prominent) ....Cecidomyiidae

— Head usually prominent and complete to form a head capsule, reduced in some Tipulidae but there the reduced head is retractile and the larvae are active and larger; no sternal spatula 2

2. Head capsule complete, or incomplete and reduced to a number of sclerotized bars, but always retractile; typically elongated, mainly whitish or yellow, but may be darker brown or grey; body with only one pair of spiracles, and these at the end of the last segment (metapneustic), except the aquatic *Antocha* which lacks spiracles (apneustic); prolegs occur in some pediciines; in marshy soils, or in drier soils, sometimes aquatic, or in mosses or decayed wood;

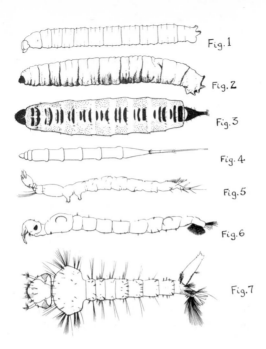

Fig. 1

Fig. 2

Fig. 3

Fig. 4

Fig. 5

Fig. 6

Fig. 7

movement active in carnivorous larvae, herbivorous larvae slower moving (fig.2)..Tipulidae
— Head capsule complete and non-retractile 3

3. Abdomen long and slender, with posterior margins swollen and with a retractile respiratory tube on the anal segment which can be very long and slender when extended; in marshy soils or mud (fig.4) ......Ptychopteridae
— Abdomen not so long and slender, any respiratory tube much thicker, shorter, and non-retractile...4

4. Prolegs present on at least one body segment.....,...................................5
— Prolegs absent...9

5. Prolegs on first two abdominal segments only; usually curved in a U-shape in life; dorsum of abdomen may have setae arranged in rings on some segments; anal segment tapering posteriorly, with a pair of flattened leaf-like processes, one at each side, wider surface facing dorsoventrally; on water surfaces of slower moving water, on wet rocks or mosses, etc.; very active (fig.5) Dixidae
— Prolegs on thoracic segments or on posterior abdominal segment............6

6. Sessile, fixed by anal segment to stones, weed, etc., in flowing water; head conspicuous and with mouth brushes; abdomen prominently widened distally (fig.12)..Simuliidae
— Not sessile; abdomen not prominently wider distally.................................7

7. Prolegs on first thoracic segment and on the end of the abdomen, with or without additional anal gills; both sets of prolegs paired; aquatic in flowing or still water, or terrestrial in wet habitats such as mosses; movement very active or slower; aquatic larvae often swim with a looping movement (fig11).....
....Chironomidae
— Prolegs on thoracic segments only, and not paired, although they may be bifurcated; anal segment may appear to have short processes but in this case the head is peculiarly shaped (Thaumaleidae) or the body has conspicuous setae (Ceratopogonidae) 8

8. Body smooth, almost parallel-sided, without prominent setae but with sclerotized darker dorsal areas; head shape distinctive; on wet rocks, mosses, etc., where a film of water flows (hygropetricous); movement sinuous and active (fig.8)..Thaumaleidae
— Body not smooth, less parallel-sided, and with conspicuous setae, which may be spatulate, or long and filiform; in moist habitats, under bark, in soil; water drops often adhere to the setae; movement slow (fig.10)...........................
....Ceratopogonidae (part)

9. Body very slender, almost thread-like, and rather like a small nematode; semi-aquatic or aquatic, in sphagnum or similar wet mosses, or in sand of river banks; sometimes freely aquatic; movement sinuous and active (fig.9)........
....Ceratopogonidae (part)
— Body not so slender 10

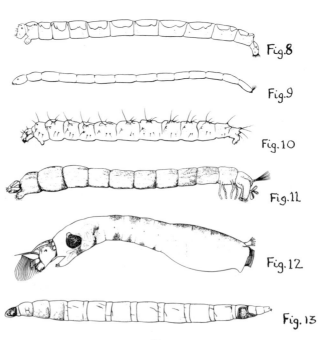

Fig.8

Fig.9

Fig.10

Fig.11

Fig.12

Fig.13

10. Thoracic segments fused together, forming a more or less enlarged section of the body which is usually distinctly wider than the abdomen................11
—   Thoracic segments not fused nor distinctly wider than the abdomen.....12

11. Antennae prehensile, with long, strong, apical spines, and without definite mouthbrushes; thorax and antepenultimate abdominal segment with paired hydrostatic organs which appear dark; thorax broader and anal segment with a siphon*(Mochlonyx)*, or thorax more slender and siphon absent *(Chaoborus)*; in still or slow moving water; active, and hold a horizontal position in the water (fig.6)...Chaoboridae
—   Antennae not prehensile, without such strong apical spines, and with mouthbrushes; no hydrostatic organs; hold an oblique position in the water usually; siphon present but short in *Anopheles* and these surface in a horizontal position; in still or slowly moving water (fig.7)...........Culicidae

12. Body with short processes, glabrous; anal segment with longer processes; body characteristically curved in life; ten pairs of spiracles; in decaying organic material, in rich soil, dung, etc., usually communal; very inactive (fig 14) ....Bibionidae
—   Body otherwise; less than ten pairs of spiracles.......................................13

13. The two posterior spiracles each on the tip of a cylindrical process; dark coloured larvae or at least yellow or brown; rather hairy; in dung, soil, or in drier habitats where decaying, material exists, e.g. bird's nests; very inactive (fig.18)...Scatopsidae
—   The two posterior spiracles not on such processes...................................14

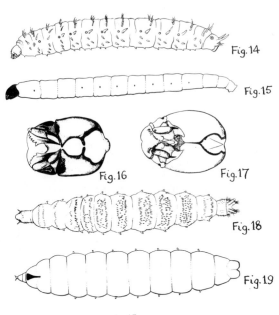

Fig.14

Fig.15

Fig.16

Fig.17

Fig.18

Fig.19

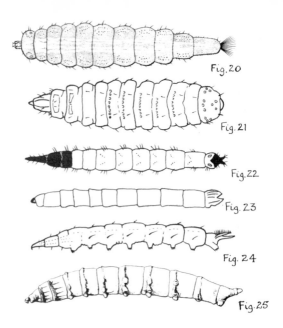

Fig.20

Fig. 21

Fig.22

Fig. 23

Fig. 24

Fig.25

14. Last abdominal segment with a short non-retractile respiratory tube, or tergites of bodies with numerous distinct transverse sclerotized plates; sometimes body segments with numerous processes; in decaying organic material, often in wet habitats; inactive (fig. 3)..........................Psychodidae
— Last abdominal segments without such a tube; abdomen without numerous distinct transverse sclerotized plates...15

15. Abdominal segments divided superficially into three more or less equal parts; anal segment with four lobes around the posterior spiracles; whitish to grey, in drier dung, in soil, or in more moist habitats where decaying organic material occurs; slow moving (fig.1)..Trichoceridae
— Abdominal segments not divided superficially into three more or less equal parts...16

16. Abdominal segments 2-6 divided superficially into two unequal parts; five reduced lobes around posterior spiracles; body slender; in moist habitats where decaying organic material occurs, in deliquescent fungi, or in drier habitats such as dung, soil, old plant stems, etc.; active (fig.13)...............
....Anisopodidae
— Abdominal segments not so divided; sometimes superficially ringed but in this case the rings are narrow, darker and equal; anal segment without any lobes; sometimes with a superficial covering of debris or other material; most common larvae are white with a distinct dark head; in fungi, under bark, in silken webs in holes in old trunks, in soil or in decaying plants or roots, etc. often active, some slower moving (fig.15-17).......Mycetophilidae, Sciaridae

48

Key to families: Brachycera

1. Posterior spiracles close together and more or less concealed within a terminal fissure on the anal segment 2
— Posterior spiracles widely separated on the anal, penultimate, or antepenultimate abdominal segment, and not concealed 4

2. Terminal fissure vertical; head capsule not strongly sclerotized, and retractile; body cylindrical and cuticle smooth; mainly in moist or wet soils, sphagnum, etc.; inactive (fig.25) .... Tabanidae
— Terminal fissure transverse; head capsule strongly sclerotized, and non-retractile; body depressed, and cuticle roughened 3

3. Anal slit on the central part of the anal segment, bordered with teeth-like projections, and a row of similar projections arranged transversely anterior to the anal slit; thoracic tergites with a more or less well defined smooth area on the medium part of each tergite; amphipneustic; inactive under bark of decaying trees (fig.21) .... Xylomiidae
— Anal slit without such teeth-like projection, nor with anterior transverse row of similar projections; thoracic tergites uniformly roughened; holo-or peripneustic; inactive; in woodland debris, dung, compost heaps, or other decaying organic material of vegetable origin; or more or less aquatic, in ponds, ditches, etc. (fig.20) .... Stratiomyidae

4. Posterior spiracles on the last apparent body segment 5
— Posterior spiracles anterior to the last body segment 9

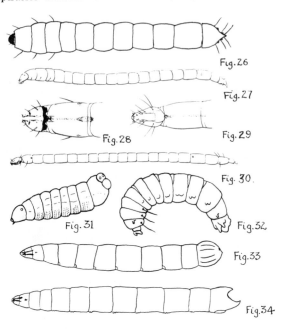

Fig.26

Fig.27

Fig.28

Fig.29

Fig.30

Fig.31

Fig.32

Fig.33

Fig.34

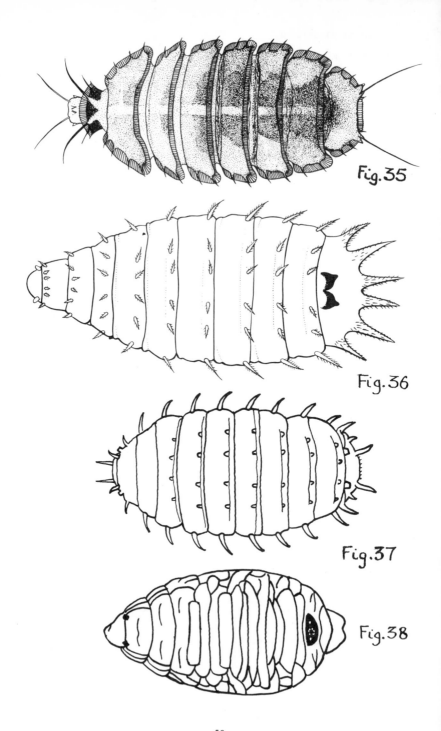

Fig. 35

Fig. 36

Fig. 37

Fig. 38

5. Head capsule very short and minute; body broad and soft; last abdominal segment without processes but with two distinct spiracles, anterior spiracles on prothorax small; in the early triungulin free-living stage the larvae are elongated with long setae, very small 0.5 mm, active endo-parasitic on spiders; inactive (fig.31) ....Acroceridae
— Head capsule prominent; last abdominal segment usually with processes; free-living 6

6. Head strongly sclerotized, elongated; posterior spiracles on a bifurcated sclerotized plate on the dorsum of the anal segment; under bark of decayed trees, sometimes within old burrows; inactive (fig.22)............Xylophagidae
— Head not strongly sclerotized; posterior spiracles not on a bifurcated plate.7

7. Anal segment ending in two or four fleshy lobes, subequal in size, in soil, sometimes marshy soils, slow-moving (fig.23); or with two long fringed processes (fig.24); in flowing water, body retractile, active; or with two small hook-like processes, green in colour, inactive, in moss on stones and walls *(Ptiolina)*...Rhagionidae (incl. Athericidae)
— Anal segment otherwise...8

8. Anal segment with a single median projection below the posterior spiracles, or almost entirely rounded; mainly in soil; inactive (fig.33); or, aquatic larvae which occur in still or flowing water, anal segment with several finger-like lobes and body with pseudopods or welts (Hemerodromiinae, Clinocerinae) ....Empididae
— Anal segment usually with four lobes, the ventral pair being the longer; sometimes with two ventral lobes; in marshy soils, in aquatic mosses, in saline marshes, in wet sand, etc. (fig.34) or amongst seaweed on beaches; sometimes the anal segment is evenly rounded in plantmining species; at most one pair of prolegs on abdomen ....Dolichopodidae

9. Posterior spiracles on the apparent penultimate segment; abdominal segments not subdivided, the body consisting of 11 or 12 apparent segments, exclusive of head..10
— Posterior spiracles on the apparent ante-penultimate segment; abdominal segments 1-6 subdivided, the body apparently consisting of up to 20 segments exclusive of head...11

10. Thoracic segments each with two long setae, one on each side on ventro-lateral margin; anal segment with six or more long setae; free-living, in soil or decayed wood; inactive (fig.26)...Asilidae
— Thoracic segments without setae or with weak ones; anal segment without setae; predatory or parasitic or inquilines in nests of bees and wasps or in egg cases of grasshoppers, etc. Rather like a bee or wasp grub; inactive (fig.32). (In the early, free-living stage, as a triungulin, the larvae are slender, active, each thoracic segment with one long seta on each side, and the anal segment with two very long setae; active)..Bombyliidae

11. Dorsal extension of head capsule extending into the thorax from the head posteriorly, with a spatulate apex; head capsule with two ventral projections; in soil, often sandy soils; active, snake-like in movement or moving by jumps. (figs. 27, 28) ....Therevidae
— Dorsal extension of head capsule extending into the thorax from the head posteriorly not spatulate at apex; head capsule without ventral projections; in fungi or in domestic habitats, in debris, etc., active, movement as for Therevidae (figs. 29, 30)...Scenopinidae

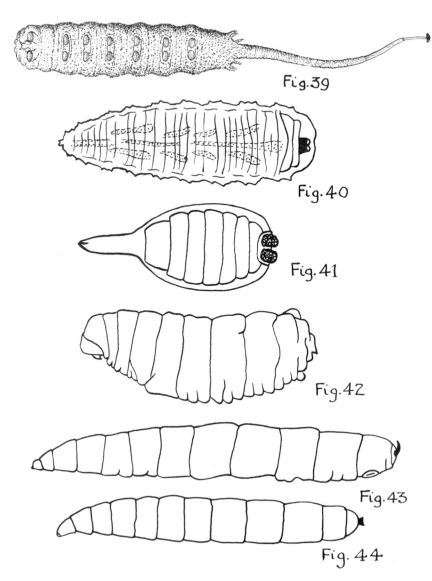

Fig. 39

Fig. 40

Fig. 41

Fig. 42

Fig. 43

Fig. 44

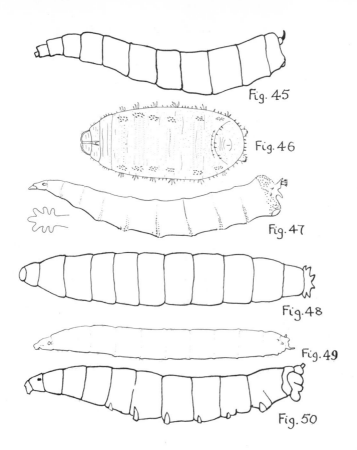

Fig. 45

Fig. 46

Fig. 47

Fig. 48

Fig. 49

Fig. 50

Key to families: Cyclorrhapha

1. Strongly depressed and sclerotized larvae, uniformly yellowish-brown to darker brown in colour; segmentation prominent and often with processes; posterior spiracles on short processes which are well separated 2
— Less strongly depressed and sclerotized larvae 3

2. Tergal plates distinct, but without obvious processes; seven apparent body segments; apparent head narrower and with two pairs of long filiform appendages; posterior spiracles near to the posterior margin of the last apparent tergite and widely separated; inactive; in decaying organic material, often in wet or moist habitats (fig.35) ....Lonchopteridae
— Tergal plates usually with obvious processes laterally and dorsally; apparent head gradually narrowed and without long filiform appendages; posterior spiracles on dorsum of last apparent tergite; sometimes active; in decaying organic material, usually in drier habitat (fig.60) (some Phoridae may run here but the tergal processes are unbranched and the posterior spiracles are usually closer together - fig.36)..Fanniidae

3. Posterior spiracles on a prominent large sclerotized plate; endoparasitic in Homoptera; inactive (fig.38)..Pipunculidae
— Posterior spiracles not on a prominent large sclerotized plate...................4

4. Anterior spiracles close together on the dorsal surface of the prothoracic segment; mainly in leaf mines; inactive (fig.54)......................Agromyzidae
— Anterior spiracles well separated, more or less lateral in position, or absent 5

5. Each posterior spiracle with numerous small pore-like openings; endoparasitic in insects or cattle 6
— Each posterior spiracle with three elliptical or slit-like openings; occasionally with up to six similar openings 8

6. The small openings of each posterior spiracle extending completely round the spiracular plate, the spiracular scar in the centre; a small spine occurs near the dorsal edge of each plate; endoparasitic in bees and wasps; inactive (fig.41) ....Conopidae
— The small openings of each posterior spiracle not extending completely round the spiracular plate, the spiracular scar lateral in position, towards the inner margin; no spine near the dorsal edge of the spiracular plate; not endoparasitic in bees and wasps 7

7. Openings of spiracle arranged in three radiating lines; endoparasitic in insects (known hosts are Heteroptera) (fig.59)................Tachinidae (part-*Alophora*)
— Openings of spiracle arranged circularly, but not extending completely round the spiracular plate, the inner side of plate more or less devoid of openings; endoparasitic in cattle, deer, and sheep (figs. 55, 67, 68).............Oestridae

8. Posterior spiracles on the end of short or longer processes, these sometimes very elongated; the processes are united throughout their length, so that an end view shows the two spiracles distinct although closely adherent. Variable in form as the following groups:-
(a) segmentation obscure, rounded; in ants nests; inactive (*Microdon*).
(b) rather depressed and more or less parallel-sided, narrowing anteriorly; pale in colour, sometimes with reddish or yellowish median bands, sometimes darker with more prominent lateral and dorsal processes active, feeding on aphids etc. (*Syrphus*, etc., fig.40) inactive, in stems, roots, fungi, (*Cheilosia*, etc.) or in decaying organic material in wet habitats (*Platycheirus*).
(c) depressed but with a longer apical siphon; in dung (*Rhingia, Syritta*); in decaying wood or sap from tree wounds (*Brachypalpus* etc.); semi-aquatic or aquatic with siphon pointed (*Lejogaster*, etc.), inactive.
(d) Cuticle with numerous sharply pointed processes; active; in wasp's nests (*Volucella*).
(e) Apical siphon very long, retractile; in mud where water is contaminated with organic material, active (*Eristalis*, etc. fig. 39)....................Syrphidae
— Posterior spiracles not in the end of united process...............................9

9. Neck region of the anterior part of the larvae with a sclerotized prominent collar or ring, the ring incomplete...10
— Neck region of anterior part of the larvae without such a collar..........11

10. Larvae more slender, last segment long and tapering, and anterior segments tapering towards head; numerous papillae ventrally and laterally on body; free-living, feeding on aphids, etc.; active (fig.46)................Chamaemyiidae
— Larvae short, broad. last segment broad and rounded, anterior segments not tapering towards head; papillae confined to anterior segments and much smaller; in wax cells of hive bee, feeding on pollen paste; inactive. Braulidae

11. Anterior spiracle simple, unbranched; larvae with an oval outline, with 48 lateral branched appendages (*Callomyia*) or more or less parallel-sided, somewhat depressed, with or without short lateral and dorsal processes *Agathomyia*, (Platypezinae); inactive; in fungi (fig.37). (Some Phoridae may run here but the posterior spiracles are usually closer together - fig.36)
....Platypezidae
— Anterior spiracle branched or absent..12

12. Borders of each posterior spiracular plate with a complete ring of branched setae; in decaying seaweed, etc., on beaches; active...................Coelopidae
— Borders of each posterior spiracular plate without setae or setae present as isolated groups..13

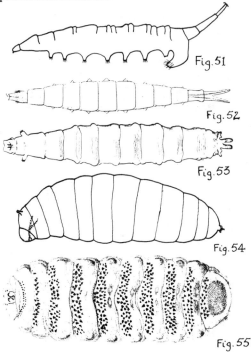

Fig.51

Fig.52

Fig.53

Fig.54

Fig.55

13. Posterior spiracles on short processes ending in a sharp apex 14
— Posterior spiracles on processes not ending sharply.................................15

14. Anterior spiracles absent; aquatic, in plant stems, or as leaf miners; or terrestrial and carnivorous; inactive or slightly active ....
....Ephydridae (Notiphilinae)
— Anterior spiracles present; terrestrial, in leaf mines; inactive....................
....Drosophilidae (*Scaptomyza*)

15. Posterior spiracles on elongated processes forming a pair of diverging branches from a cylindrical elongated base, or at least the branches are united at the base (in Canacidae (couplet 21) the spiracular branches are not forked or
– Posterior spiracles not on the inner side of the spiracular processes.....16

16. Posterior spiracles on elongated processes forming a pair of diverging branches from a cylindrical elongated base, or at least the branches are united at the base (in Canacidae (couplet 21) the spiracular branches are not forked or diverging but are on elongated processes). Mouth-hooks with accessory sclerites...17
— Posterior spiracles on the surface of the last segment of the abdomen or on short processes which are not united at the base. Mouth-hooks with accessory sclerites (small sclerites by mouth-hooks). *Limnophora* (Muscidae) is an exception in having the spiracles on diverging processes united basally but the mouth-hooks have accessory sclerites - these are aquatic larvae in moss in running water (fig.62)..24

17. Spiracular field with short lobes; mouth-hooks united by a sclerotized bridge; thoracic segments longer and narrower than the abdominal segments; dark coloured active larvae, usually in ditches, ponds, etc. terrestrial, acquatic or semi-aquatic, feeding on snails, etc. The body is retractile (fig.48)............
....Sciomyzidae
— Spiracular field without lobes; mouth-hooks not united by a sclerotized bridge; thoracic segments not longer and narrower than the abdominal segments; not dark coloured active retractile larvae...18

18. Spines or setae on at least the posterior body segments, apart from any on segmental borders..19
— Cuticle smooth, without spines or setae on the surface of the body segments, although tubercles may occur 22

19. Posterior part of body obviously swollen, bulbous in shape; anterior spiracles with a more or less elongated central axis from which arise lateral processes; in decaying organic material, such as dung, carrion, etc., active (fig.47)...
....Sepsidae
— Posterior part of body not obviously swollen; anterior spiracles usually fan-shaped, sometimes elongated 20

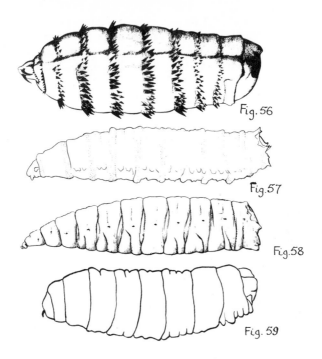

Fig. 56

Fig. 57

Fig. 58

Fig. 59

20. Each posterior spiracle at the end of an elongated cylindrical process which projects from a tubular siphon derived from the last abdominal segment; ventral pseudopods are often present; aquatic on plants, often anchored by the posterior pseudopods, or in semi-aquatic habitats which are contaminated with organic material..21
— Each posterior spiracle much shorter, without a basal tubular siphon derived from the last segment; in decaying organic material, such as fallen leaves in which they may mine, or in bird's nests...................................Lauxaniidae

21. Posterior spiracular process not forked, spiracles united..............Canacidae
— Posterior spiracular process forked, spiracles not united (figs.51, 52).........
....Ephydridae

22. Anterior spiracles with a basal cylindrical part from the distal end of which arise several finer filaments; or anterior spiracles absent; saprophagous, in decaying fruit or other vegetable material, dung, fungi, etc., active (fig.53)
....Drosophilidae (part)
—. Anterior spiracles present but not so formed..23

23. Anterior spiracles with a very long slender central axis from which arise short lateral processes; posterior spiracles on an elongated siphon or process; body narrow, with ventral pseudopods; in sap from tree wounds, etc; inactive .
....Aulacigastridae

57

— Anterior spiracle with a long but broader central process, the distal end broadened and bearing the spiracular openings; no lateral processes; body broader, without ventral pseudopods; in larval tunnels of beetles (e.g. Scolytidae, etc.), inactive (fig.50)..Odiniidae

24. Cephalopharyngeal skeleton with accessory sclerites by mouth-hooks; posterior spiracular openings straight or sharply bent about midpoint; under bark, under moss, in soil, etc.; inactive.....................Muscidae (Phaoninae)
— Cephalopharyngeal skeleton without accessory sclerites by mouth-hooks; in case of any doubt then posterior spiracles with strongly sinuous openings.
....25

25. Posterior spiracles with three strongly sinuous openings whose axes lie approximately parallel to the spiracular borders (fig.66); left mouth-hook rudimentary or rudimentary accessory sclerites by mouth-hooks; in decaying organic material, dung, etc. fairly active or inactive...Muscidae (Muscinae)
— Posterior spiracles with straight openings (fig.65), or (*Eriothrix* - Tachinidae) if openings are sinuous their axes lie tangential to outer spiracular border. 26

26. Each posterior spiracle with obvious spines or lobes on its border (fig.43)
(a) In decaying organic material; inactive (fig.43)..........Micropezidae (part)
(b) In decaying wood of fallen trees; inactive. ....Clusiidae
(c) In plant stems, roots, etc. sometimes in galls; inactive (fig.44) Psilidae
(d) In stems of grasses, umbelliferae, in flower heads of Compositae etc, or under bark ....Pallopteridae (part)
(e) Under bark, in dung or decaying fruits, etc. ....Lonchaeidae (part)
(f) Under bark? possibly in decaying organic material?.............Diastatidae
— Each posterior spiracle without such spines or lobes.............................27

27. Posterior spiracles united, the three spiracular openings of each weakly or strongly bent; endoparasitic in horses; inactive (fig.56)........Gasterophilidae
— Posterior spiracles separate·...28

28. Posterior spiracles in a distinct deep depression; in decaying organic material of animal origin, carrion, etc. active (fig.57)..........................Sarcophagidae
— Posterior spiracles not in a depression...29

29. Apex of each posterior spiracular process separated into three, on each of which is an opening; associated with ants, or attached to predatory flies and feeding on their prey (Milichiidae) or in refuse in bird's nests (Carnidae). Milichiidae, Carnidae or plant feeders, or aphid feeders (e.g. *Thaumatomyia notata*)..Chloropidae (part)
— Apex of each posterior spiracular process normal...................................30

30. Anterior spiracle with a more or less elongated central axis, from which arise short or longer processes laterally; spiracular openings short, elliptical; in

carrion, dung, bird's nests, etc, usually associated with decaying organic material..Sphaeroceridae
— Not as above..31

31. Posterior spiracular openings rather sinuous, all openings more or less parallel to each other and to the outer border of the spiracle; mouth-hooks strongly curved near base, rest of cephalopharyngeal skeleton united; under bark; inactive...Megamerinidae
— Not as above..32

32. Posterior spiracles with three very short elliptical radially arranged openings 33
— Posterior spiracles with elongated, slit-like openings; anterior spiracles, when present fan-like..34

33 Anterior spiracle fan-like..Chloropidae (part)
In plant stems, etc., phytophagous..............................Anthomyzidae (part)
— Anterior spiracle with central axis elongated, in plant stems, etc., phytophagous..Opomyzidae, Anthomyzidae (part)

34. Posterior spiracles on the surface of the last segment, without processes. 35
— Posterior spiracles on the end of more or less obvious processes, always short 36

35. End of last segment of abdomen with obvious tubercles arranged in a more or less circular sequence around the posterior surface; spiracular scar usually in the rather narrow but strongly sclerotized spiracular border; in decaying organic material of animal origin, in wounds of animals, or in dung, etc.; active (figs.58, 65)..Calliphoridae
— End of last segment with less obvious tubercles; spiracular border without the spiracular scar, the scar always situated inside the border (figs.42, 64)
(a) in plant stems or roots
(b) in flower heads sometimes causing galls
(c) in leaf mines
(d) in fruits...Tephritidae

36. Endoparasitic larvae in insects, Isopoda, etc..37
— Free living larvae...38

37. Endoparasitic in insects mainly..Tachinidae (part)
— Endoparasitic in Isopoda..Rhinophoridae

38. Body, including last segment, without obvious papillae or tubercles.
(a) Platystomatidae in decaying organic material of vegatable origin
(b) Otitidae.

59

(c) Ulididae.

(d) Micropezidae (part)

(e) Lonchaeidae (part) under bark, in dung or decaying fruit

(f) Helcomyzidae (part) in decaying seaweed on beaches

(*Heterocheila buccata*)

(g) Heleomyzidae in fungi, carrion, dung, decomposing material.

— Body, including last segment, with a ring of papillae or tubercles around the spiracular field and with others on other segments; cuticle may have spines or hairs

(a) Dryomyzidae in fungi, dung, etc.

(b) Helcomyzidae in decaying seaweed (*Helcomyza ustulata*) (fig.45)

(c) Neottiophilidae in bird's nests, feeding on blood of nestlings

(d) Heleomyzidae (part) in fungi, carrion, dung, decomposing material or rotten wood

(e) Drosophilidae (part) in decaying or fermenting vegetable material or from animal material

(f) Scathophagidae in dung, in plant stems or leaf miners (docks, reed, water-lilies, orchids, etc.)

(g) Anthomyiidae leaf miners, in stems or roots, fungi, rotten wood (fig.63).

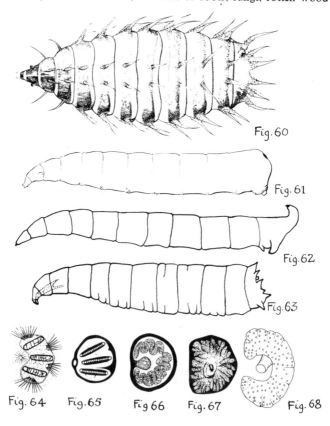

Fig. 60

Fig. 61

Fig. 62

Fig. 63

Fig. 64   Fig. 65   Fig 66   Fig. 67   Fig. 68

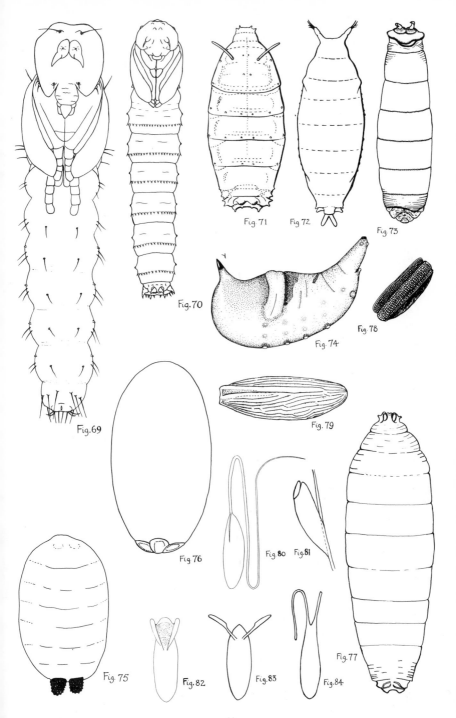

Fig. 69

Fig.70

Fig. 71

Fig. 72

Fig. 73

Fig. 74

Fig. 78

Fig. 79

Fig. 76

Fig.80 Fig.81

Fig. 75

Fig. 77

Fig.82

Fig.83

Fig.84

Families Not Included in Key

Hippoboscidae, Nycteribiidae : larvae distinct by spiracular field, spiracular openings connected by branching tubular structures; larvae pupate soon after they are "laid" by the female. (Pupa of Hippoboscidae shown in fig.76)
N.B. Phoridae are included twice under couplets 2, (Fanniidae) and 11, (Platypezidae).
Larvae not known, or only known from tropical species or others widely separated from Europe -Tanypezidae, Chyromyiidae, Acartophthalmidae, Periscelidae, Asteidae, Camillidae, Tethinidae

Legend to Figures (not to any uniform scale)

Larvae of Diptera Nematocera (Plates 1, 2 & 3).
Fig. 1. *Trichocera* (Trichoceridae) lateral
Fig. 2. *Tipula* (Tipulidae) lateral
Fig. 3. *Psychoda* (Psychodidae) dorsal
Fig. 4. *Ptychoptera* (Ptychopteridae) dorsal
Fig. 5. *Dixa* (Dixidae) lateral
Fig. 6. *Chaoborus* (Chaoboridae) lateral
Fig. 7. *Aedes* (Culicidae) dorsal
Fig. 8. Thaumaleidae lateral
Fig. 9. *Culicoides* (Ceratopogonidae) lateral
Fig. 10. *Forcipomyia* (Ceratopogonidae) lateral
Fig. 11. *Chironomus* (Chironomidae) lateral
Fig. 12. *Simulium* (Simuliidae) lateral
Fig. 13. *Sylvicola* (Anisopodidae) lateral
Fig. 14. *Bibio* (Bibionidae) lateral
Fig. 15. *Bradysia* (Sciaridae) lateral
Fig. 16. *Bradysia* (Sciaridae) head, ventral (epicranial plates meet at two points)
Fig. 17. *Leia* (Mycetophilidae) head, ventral (epicranial plates meet at one point)
Fig. 18. *Scatopse* (Scatopsidae) dorsal
Fig. 19. Cecidomyiidae, dorsal

Larvae of Diptera Brachycera (Plates 4 & 5)
Fig. 20. *Odontomyia* (Stratiomyidae) dorsal
Fig. 21. *Solva* (Xylomyiidae) dorsal
Fig. 22. *Xylophagus* (Xylophagidae) dorsal
Fig. 23. *Rhagio* (Rhadae) lateral
Fig. 24. *Atherix* (Rhagionidae) lateral
Fig. 25. *Tabanus* (Tabanidae) lateral
Fig. 26. *Dioctria* (Asilidae) dorsal
Fig. 27. *Thereva* (Therevidae) lateral
Fig. 28. *Thereva* (Therevidae) head, dorsal
Fig. 29. *Scenopinus* (Scenopinidae) head, dorsal
Fig. 30. *Scenopinus* (Scenopinidae) lateral
Fig. 31. *Acrocera* (Acroceridae) lateral
Fig. 32. *Bombylius* (Bombyliidae) lateral
Fig. 33. *Rhamphomyia* (Empididae) lateral
Fig. 34. Dolichopodidae lateral

Larvae of Diptera Cyclorrhapha (Plates 6, 7, 8, 9, 10 & 11)

Fig. 35. *Lonchoptera* (Lonchopteridae) dorsal
Fig. 36. *Megaselia* (Phoridae) dorsal
Fig. 37. *Platypeza* (Platypezidae) dorsal
Fig. 38. *Cephalops* (Pipunculidae) dorsal
Fig. 39. *Eristalis* (Syrphidae) ventral
Fig. 40. *Syrphus* (Syrphidae) dorsal
Fig. 41. *Physocephala* (Conopidae) ventral
Fig. 42. *Xyphosia* (Tephritidae) lateral
Fig. 43. *Micropeza* (Micropezidae) lateral
Fig. 44. Psilidae (Chloropidae, Sphaeroceridae similar) lateral
Fig. 45. *Helcomyza* (Helcomyzidae) lateral (Clusiidae similar)
Fig. 46. *Leucopis* (Chamaemyiidae) ventral
Fig. 47. *Sepsis* (Sepsidae) lateral with detail of anterior spiracle
Fig. 48. *Pherbellia* (Sciomyzidae) dorsal
Fig. 49. *Piophila* (Piophilidae) lateral
Fig. 50. *Odinia* (Odiniidae) lateral
Fig. 51. *Ephydra* (Ephydridae) lateral
Fig. 52. *Teichomyza* (Ephydridae) dorsal
Fig. 53. *Drosophila* (Drosophilidae) ventral
Fig. 54. *Melanagromyza* (Agromyzidae) lateral
Fig. 55. *Oestrus* (Oestridae) ventral
Fig. 56. *Gasterophilus* (Gasterophilidae) lateral
Fig. 57. *Sarcophaga* (Sarcophagidae) lateral
Fig. 58. *Calliphora* (Calliphoridae) lateral
Fig. 59. *Compsilura* (Tachinidae) lateral
Fig. 60. *Fannia* (Fanniidae) dorsal
Fig. 61. *Musca* (Muscidae) lateral
Fig. 62. *Limnophora* (Muscidae) lateral
Fig. 62. *Limnophora* (Muscidae) lateral
Fig. 63. *Hylemya* (Anthomyiidae) lateral
Figs. 64-68. Posterior spiracles of : 64 *Ceratitis* (Tephritidae); 65. *Lucilia* (Calliphoridae), 66. *Musca* (Muscidae); 67. *Oestrus* (Oestridae); 68. *Hypoderma* (Oestridae)
Fig. 69. Pupa of *Rhamphomyia* (Empididae) ventral
Fig. 70. Pupa of *Chrysopilus* (Rhagionidae) ventral
Fig. 71. Puparium of *Megaselia* (Phoridae) ventral
Fig. 72. Puparium of *Drosophila* (Drosophilidae) ventral
Fig. 73. Puparium of *Clusia* (Clusiidae) ventral (adult emerged, 'cap' off)
Fig. 74. Floating puparium of *Elgiva* (Sciomyzidae) lateral
Fig. 75. Puparium of *Physocephala* (Conopidae)
Fig. 76. Puparium of *Ornithomyia* (Hippoboscidae) ventral
Fig. 77. Puparium of *Lonchaea* (Lonchaeidae) dorsal or ventral
Fig. 78. Egg of Muscidae showing surface sculpture
Fig. 79. Egg of *Delia* (Anthomyiidae)
Fig. 80. Egg of *Sepsis* (Sepsidae)
Fig. 81. Egg of *Gasterophilus* (Gasterophilidae)
Fig. 82. Egg of *Scathophaga* (Scathophagidae)
Fig. 83. Egg of *Drosophila* (Drosophilidae)
Fig. 84. Egg of *Orygma* (Sepsidae)

Further Reading: General

Brauns, A., 1954 *Terricoler Dipterenlarven. Puppen terricoler Dipterenlarven.* 2 vols. Musterschmidt, Gottingen, Frankfurt, Berlin.

Brindle, A.,1961-9. Taxonomic notes on the larvae of British Diptera. *Entomologist.* **94-102.**

Hennig, W., 1948-52. *Die Larvenformen der Dipteren.* 3 vols. Akademie-Verlag, Berlin (reprinted 1968) (covers world literature).

Hinton, H. E., 1961. How some insects, especially the egg stages, avoid drowning when it rains. *Proc. Trans. S. London Ent. & Nat. Hist. Soc.* **1960:** 138-154

Keilin, D., 1944. Respiratory systems and respiratory adaptions in larvae and pupae of Diptera. *Parasitology* **36:** 1-66

Oldroyd, H., 1964. *The Natural History of Flies* Wiedenfeld & Nicholson, London

Oldroyd, H. & Smith, K. G. V., 1973. Eggs and larvae of flies (pp.289-323). *IN* Smith, K. G. V. *Insects and other Arthropods of Medical Importance* British Museum (Nat. Hist.), London.

Peters, A., 1957. *Larvae of Insects* II, Edwards, Ohio. 416pp

Seguy, E., 1950. La Biologie des Dipteres, *Encycl. Ent.* **26:** 1-609 Paris

Wong, H. R., 1972. *Literature guide to methods for rearing insects and mites.* Information Report NOR-X-38. Northern Forest Research Centre, Edmonton, Alberta (Canada)

Zumpt, F., 1965. *Myiasis in man and animals in the Old World.* Butterworths, London

Chapter 3

Some Micro-Habitats

The heading of this Chapter is not ideal. The chosen subjects are those which are relevant to a number of the Major Habitats or there are special considerations including rearing techniques, as in water and dead wood. Dung and carrion could justifiably be called minor habitats whilst many water bodies are far from minor. This chapter is therefore concerned with smoothing the way for the discussion on Major Habitats and the items are complementary.

DEAD WOOD AND SAP RUNS
by Ivan Perry and Alan E. Stubbs

This topic should be read in conjunction with the item on Woodland in the next Chapter; there is a small amount of overlap but the subject is considered in detail here.

Over 200 species of Diptera breed in dead wood situations where they may utilize dead rotting timber or the sap flows and rot holes of living trees. Few species are restricted to a particular species of tree, although most seem confined to either deciduous or coniferous trees and many Diptera show preferences within these major tree types. Elm, oak, ash, beech and poplar are particularly favoured, but the most important thing appears to be the state of decay of the wood, the size of the timber, whether sap is present or not and degree of dampness. The larvae may be saprophagous, or on fungal hyphae and other vegetable matter, or carnivores preying on other larvae, whilst a few are commensals or predators in the galleries of wood boring beetles.

As a general guide line the districts with plenty of old mature trees are the most productive, but such trees are not easy to find. Woodland, or at least a copse, is better than isolated or parkland trees. It is not essential to look for dead trees since plenty of dead wood situations can occur on a live tree, such as rot holes, including hollow trunks (even at root level) and places where a branch has fallen off. Fallen branches and logs are at their best when only a few years old and the more massive the timber the better, the most productive usually being that which had developed heart rot or other rotten portions before it fell to the ground. Some studies have shown that aerial logs (dead branches which have not yet fallen) contain a different fauna from fallen timber, but that has yet to be proven with Diptera; likewise there ought to be differences of fauna depending upon height above ground of the rotten or fallen timber. One of the most important criteria is that the dead wood should not be so exposed that the sun bakes it dry (heat sterilisation) - thus shaded situations are best or those where wood is only in the sun for part of the day. As yet little is known of the sequence of Diptera that invade dead wood as it decays and this is where observation over a period of years can be invaluable. In Windsor Forest beech trees are numbered for recording purposes, but anyone can devise their own notebook numbering system without marking the trees in their own district.

The classic areas for dead wood Diptera are the New Forest, Windsor Forest and Epping Forest but one needs to know where to go. As is so often the case, it is possible to find many of the specialist species in other districts if one takes the trouble to look and given some luck in finding suitable trees. Of all types of Diptera collecting, this is the most unpredictable and fortuitous, whether in classic areas or not. Adults may be found between May and September depending on species, but May and June are the peak months for Syrphidae and Tipulidae. Larvae and pupae are often most easily found in February, March and April when the wood is very moist; also one does not have to wait long for the adults to develop. However, there is something to be found throughout the year.

Collecting Adults

Finding the adults of wood breeding Diptera is not always easy. Some appear to be particularly secretive, indeed certain species such as *Chrysopilus laetus* (Rhagionidae) have never been seen as an adult in Britain yet their larvae are fairly frequent in Windsor Forest. There are several basic strategies in collecting.

Standing Timber

Adult Diptera may be found on the surface of a tree trunk so approach to a suitable looking tree should be gentle. Small diptera may be seen running over the surface in short jerky sprints; these will often include *Tachypeza* (Empididae) and *Medetera* (Dolichopodidae). All sorts of other flies may be resting there, not always breeding in the tree itself, including craneflies, muscids and many other Diptera. If there is a patch of dead wood on a living trunk, you may be lucky enough to find *Paraclusia tigrina* (Clusiidae), a strongly marked fly which may not be as rare as is often supposed.

Hollows in trees are particularly favourable. Even where no mature dead wood seems to be available, it is often possible to locate trees with small hollows at the base of the trunk between a fork in the roots. Such spots on a sunny day in May or June attract insects which look like bumble bees - but do not be fooled - if you net them there is a good chance they will prove to be mimics among the hoverflies, such as *Criorhina*. Any supposed bumble bee near a tree trunk at this time of year is worth checking and those that are interested in hollows higher above ground may be *Pocota*. If there is a shaft of sunlight on a trunk with hollows, various wasp and bee mimicking hoverflies, muscids and other species may be attracted for sunbathing. One special type of tree trunk is that which has broken off to expose a hollow. If the trunk still rises 2 metres or more it may attract mimic hoverflies which look like hive bees, *Brachypalpus laphriformis*. A low hollow stump may act as a nice sun trap for sunbathing hoverflies such as *Xylota*, or in suitable localities, *Caliprobola*. *Brachyopa* (a syrphid resembling a *Phaonia* with grey thorax and orange abdomen) likes stumps.

Having searched the trunk, it is worth sweeping a net over the surface in case you have overlooked something and it is especially worth sweeping inside or over the entrance of hollows. Also, one may see patrolling males of wood breeding muscids in the air close to the tree or its branches. Trunks in sunny positions, where they contain beetle burrows may attract the wasps which nest in such holes as well as the grey and black anthomyiid *Eustalomyia*, a cuckoo parasite of the wasps, which is often seen about the entrances to their tunnels.

Fallen Timber

Once felled, a piece of wood undergoes a cycle of decay, often with fungi playing a major role. We need to know far more about the associated sequence of Diptera species. Some are known to be associated with the beetles invading dead wood, such as *Medetera* breeding in bark beetle burrows at the very early stages of decay. Others are primary invaders in their own right but many are probably associated with the middle stages of decay.

The adult Diptera may be found on the surface of fallen wood, including sun bathers such as *Xylota*, or again one may keep watch for bumble bee mimics which usually show an interest in hollows or the underside of large logs. The large brightly coloured tipulids of the genus *Ctenophora* may be flying around massive logs mimicking ichneumon wasps of the most terrifying appearance. One feature of mimics is that they often overdo the act and are distinctive in being too good to be genuine, at least to our eyes.

Shaded ends of large fallen trunks often harbour numerous Diptera, especially Nematocera. Naturally shattered ends of trunks are the favourite spot for *Ctenophora* and one may find such interesting species as the empid *Oedalea apicalis* hovering. It is best to creep up on such spots and then quickly sweep the net back and forth. The shaded underside of a log may also provide dark crannies worth sweeping. Where there is herbage growing on or around a log, it is often possible to get a good haul by sweeping, the catch often including flies which breed in the log. In general the thicker the wood the better. However, some species apparently breed in quite small fallen branches and this seems to account for the abundance of the tipulid *Austrolimnophila*. A useful ploy where there seems to be no dead wood is to look for coppice stools (the stumps which have frequently had the regrowth cut, as in hazel coppice) since there is often a good quantity of dead wood in these.

Perhaps the greatest opportunities exist in timber yards, especially those on large estates with plenty of woodland. At times there may be numbers of commercially useless trunk bases with rot holes so adult Diptera can be attracted in reasonable numbers. You will usually need to ask permission to enter these woodyards but this gives an opportunity to ask whether the trees, and hence emerging flies, are all gathered locally or not. In wood yards, or in the forest, recently cut logs from live timber attract a distinctive fauna, presumably because of the sappy content of the cut ends. For instance this is the best way of finding the drosophilid genus *Chymomyza* which sit on the cut ends.

Flowers and other spots

Though flowers are considered in detail elsewhere it is worth emphasising a few points in this section. Many of the dead wood hoverflies are most easily found on flowers, especially those of shrubs. Hawthorn flowers in late May or early June in a sunny spot inside or at the edge of woodland are one of the finest lures. Even rhododendron flowers can on occasion be productive. In the autumn, ivy in East Anglia can attract the syrphid *Callicera spinolae*. It is also worth watching for hoverflies sunbathing on foliage and net anything along woodland rides or edges which could even remotely be a bee or wasp mimic, especially in May and June.

Collecting Larvae

The best way to obtain species breeding in dead wood is to collect the larvae and rear them through. This is almost the only way to obtain some species and in a number of cases it is much easier to find the larvae than it is the adults. By rearing, one has a chance to find out much more about the biology of the species and its special requirements during the early stages. The only equipment you will need to collect larvae is a trowel, stout knife, some tubes and polythene bags.

To find the species breeding under bark look for recently fallen trees and branches, where the bark is still quite tight on the heartwood and where there is sap underneath. Prize off the bark with your knife and examine the larvae present, but do not destroy too much of the habitat. The smooth whitish larvae of Lonchaeidae are often common in this situation together with the larger muscid larvae which will be preying on them. The hard, reddish brown larvae of *Solva marginata* and the smaller flattened greyish larvae of *Pachygaster orbitalis* are sometimes common under poplar bark together with the elongate, yellowish larvae of the tipulid *Gnophomyia viridipennis*. The yellowish maggot-like larvae of *Medetera nitida* can be found quite commonly in the galleries of the elm bark beetle *Scolytus scolytus* and if some of this bark is taken home you may be able to rear *Odinia meijerei* whose larvae are commensals in the borings of this beetle.

After a year or so the sap will dry up and the bark will come away from the wood. It will then be invaded by woodlice and at this stage will not be attractive to Diptera, though the rhinophorid *Paykullia maculata* may parasitise some of the woodlice and the larvae of *Tipula irrorata* are sometimes present. However several years later, depending on the type of tree, the heartwood will begin to decay and other species of Diptera will utilise it. Look for damp, well rotted logs in shady places which may have moss growing on them. Gently remove some of the moss and look for grey leatherjacket larvae of *Tipula irrorata*. Other species may be in the rotted heartwood such as *Ctenophora*. Take a sample of the rotting wood home and place it in a jar so that you can rear out any of the smaller species, such as clusiids, which may have been missed. Do not destroy too much of the habitat and replace any bark and moss before leaving

Rot holes often support larvae of interesting and seldom seen Diptera. The best situations are those in living trees which are saturated with sap. These are often a considerable height from the ground and escape detection until the tree is felled. When you have located a suitable rot hole remove some detritus with your trowel, place it in a polythene bag, and take it home for sorting. The long, almost transparent larvae of the uncommon tipulid *Rhipidia ctenophora* are occasionally numerous in elm. Larvae of *Pachygaster tarsalis* and *Systenus* species sometimes occur in elm and beech rot holes and the handsome *Solva maculata* has been reared from beech and oak. Several species of Syrphidae breed in rot holes, the rat-railed maggots of *Myathropa florea* are sometimes common, but other rarer species may also be present. Several species of Muscidae can be found in rot holes and also the spiny larvae of *Fannia aequilineata*.

Comment is made on the possibilities in submerged wood under Flowing Waters.

Rearing Techniques

Rearing species found in dead wood situations is not always easy, as they require a considerable amount of time and attention. Glass tubes and jars covered with muslin are suitable containers for rearing, old sweet jars being particularly good for large samples. It is also practical to place samples still in their polythene bags, with their mouths open, in an aquarium or perspex seed propagator (with muslin over the air vents) so that emerging adults do not die and rot in a moist container (this is only practical with large samples, each in a separate container). One or two larvae can be reared simply in a glass tube with a little of their media but leaving enough air space for emergences. Do not use metal containers because they corrode.

Where possible, separate larvae into different species; any predatory muscid larvae are best placed in a tube on their own as they may devour each other. Do not overcrowd the larvae and give them a generous amount of the substrate. Pupae should be separated as they may quickly lead to emergence and easy host/pupal skin association. Pay particular attention to the degree of moisture and try to maintain it at the same level by adding small, but regular amounts of clean rain water. Place the cultures in a cool, unheated place, but protect them from frost. Some species can be reared quite easily with very little attention, whereas others will require some form of additional food. Tipulid larvae found in rotten logs are normally quite easy to rear, especially if a layer of living moss is placed on top of the dead wood to provide some extra food. Muscidae are often carnivorous and will need to be fed on other larvae. Collect all the larvae you find with them and use some of these as food (even bark beetle larvae will do). Lonchaeid larvae, which are often common under bark, provide excellent food for Muscidae. Most other species appear to benefit by being provided with some form of extra food. If short of such food, it is possible to buy some uncoloured maggots from a fishing tackle shop and store them in a fridge. When you want to use them take them out and plunge them into hot water to kill them, cut them open to expose the body contents and place them in the rearing jars. Most larvae will find them quickly and soon dispose of them, but any that are left over after a day or so should be removed to prevent mould forming. By using this method a number of species have been reared where previously success was unattainable.

It should be remembered that some species of syrphid which breed in rot holes develop very slowly and may spend several years in the larval stage. When they are ready to pupate they seek a drier situation, so pile up some dry moss and bark in one corner of the jar for them.

When the flies emerge, transfer them to a dry tube for 24 hours so that they have a chance to mature and harden before being killed. Try to keep the empty pupal skins and mount them with the appropriate specimens.

By rearing from dead wood, one is able to obtain species which are considered to be rare because of the difficulty of obtaining the adults during the normal course of collecting. It well repays the time and effort and helps to further our knowledge of the species involved.

Sap Runs

These are part of the general story of an unsound tree and with a fauna which shares much in common with the dead wood fauna. There is however a very distinctive species composition. Sap runs were easiest to find on elm but that tree is now decreasing. Virtually any species of deciduous tree with a sap run may attract interesting species, even horse chestnut in a park. Seepages in most cases flow best in the spring and early summer and may be dry at other times of year. Both adults and larvae are best sought during this period. The regular sap flows from trees attacked by the Goat Moth *(Cossus)* occur also in the autumn when a concentration of some drosophilids and *Fannia* may result; *Amiota variegata* may be abundant in this situation and the scarce muscids *Phaonia pratensis* and *P. trigonalis* may occur.

The hoverfly *Brachyopa insensilis* can be found on or hovering close to sap runs on elm. Another hoverfly, *Ferdinandea cuprea*, also requires this habitat but just sits on the tree trunk and often sunbathes. Blackish fungus gnat like flies usually prove to be the anisopodid *Mycetobia pallipes* (but other species could yet be found in Britain) and in the same family the brownish mottled winged *Sylvicola cinctus* is often common. The dolichopodid *Systenus* spp. occur locally and many small dark acalypterates attracted to sap runs include drosophilids (especially *Drosophila tristis*, *D. subobscura* and *D. subsilvestris* but occasionally other spp.), periscelids (*Periscelis annulata* is the most frequent) and *Aulacigaster leucopeza*.

Larvae may be seen on the surface or discovered within the wet sludge contained in the seepage. Very elongate larvae usually belong to anisopodids, squat rather immobile larvae with a 'tail' consisting of fused posterior spiracles are syrphids whilst a variety of cyclorrhaphous maggots include the combination of saprophagous acalypterates and carnivorous calypterates. Larvae and pupae may be reared by placing a small amount of sludge in a tube and keeping a regular watch for emerging adults. When the wings are expanded these adults should be placed in a dry tube for 24 hours to harden off.

Further Reading

Chandler, P.J., 1973. Some Diptera and other Insects associated with decaying elms (*Ulmus procera* Salisbury) at Bromley, Kent, with some additional observations on these and related species. *Entomologists' Gaz.* **24** : 324-346.

Shillito, J.F., 1948. Notes on insects visiting diseased elms. *Entomologists's mon. Mag.* **83** : 290-292

Teskey, H.J., 1976. The Diptera larvae associated with trees in North America. *Can. Ent. Mem.* **100** : 1-53

Uffen, R.W.J., 1962. Some flies (Diptera) breeding in wounds of elm trees in Hyde Park. *Lond. Nat.* **42** : 25

APPENDIX: Diptera Breeding In Dead Wood and Runs

All records without comment apply to rotting or decaying wood. There is often inadequate information on trees utilised, but typical examples are given where this may be helpful. A few abbreviations are used:– ub = under bark; wd = wood detritus; rh = rot holes; s = physically soft wood; h = physically hard wood; occ = occasional, not usual habitat. *Cossus*, the Goat Moth, forms large burrows with sappy detritus. Note that most species are in deciduous trees and that conifers usually support a separate fauna. The physical condition of decay is often more important than the tree species, but certain trees decay more readily (e.g. poplar, elm). English names are used for trees:– aspen *(Populus tremula)*; beech *(Fagus)*; birch *(Betula)*; conifers *(Pinus, Picea, Larix* etc); elm *(Ulmus)*; hazel *(Corylus)*; hornbeam *(Carpinus)*; horse chestnut *(Aesculus)*; oak *(Quercus)*; pine *(Pinus)*; poplar *(Populus)*; sycamore *(Acer pseudoplatanus)*; willow *(Salix)* and yew *(Taxus)*.

Trichoceridae: *Diazosma hirtipennis* (probable); **Tipulidae:** *Ctenophora*. all 6 spp.; subgenus *Ctenophora* in large timber, esp. beech; *.Tipula marmorata* ub, occ; *T. irrorata* wd, ub; *T.flavolineata* h, beech, birch; *T.scripta* ub, occ; *T.cava* wd; *T.peliostigma* occ (also bird nests); *T.selene* reared from a small ash branch on fen peat; *Limonia dumetorum*; *L.ctenophora* sappy rh, elm, sycamore; *L.uniseriata* sappy rh, elm, beech; *Epiphragma ocellaris* h; *Austrolimnophila ochracea*; *Gnophomyia viridipennis* gregarious ub, poplar; *Idiognophomyia* sp. wet detritus in hollow beech. **Psychodidae:** *Trichomyia urbica* h; possibly other spp. in wet detritus. **Ceratopogonidae;** (The larval morphology is more diverse than the adults, the taxonomy related to rearing records is confused). *Forcipomyia bipunctata* ub; *F.kaltenbachii* ub; oak, pine, poplar sap. *F.nigra* oak logs; *F.picea* ub; *F.pulchrithorax* wd, elm, sap; *Dasyhelea versicolor* elm sap, rh oak (also *Arctium* roots), *D.*spp. some probables; *Culicoides chiopterus* very doubtful record, elm sap; *Atrichopogon* sp. on green algal growth on exposed bare wood surface. **Chironomidae:** Some terrestrial spp. (f.lignicolous fungi) but needs clarification. **Anisopodidae;** *Mycetobia pallipes* sap, wd; *Sylvicola cincta* sap. **Mycetophilidae.** *Diadocidia ferruginosa* ub, silk tubes; *Symmerus annulatus*; *Macrocera stigma* web; *Macrorrhyncha flava* web; *Keroplatus testaceus* web; *Platyura marginata* web; *Orfelia nemoralis* web; *O.nigricornis* web; *Neoempheria pictipennis*; *N.lineola*; *Phthinia humilis* hornbeam; *Acnemia nitidicollis* cocoon; *Boletina flaviventris*; *B. trivittata*. **Sciaridae:** *Sciara thomae* wd; *Trichosia caudata*; *T.coarctata*; *T.pilosa*; *Plastosciara pernitida*; also "*Sciara*" *egertoni* and *keilini (Plastosciara* in Edwards); probably most other *Trichosia* and *Plastosciara*; *Xylosciara lignicola* oak, birch; *Epidapus gracilis*, beech. **Scatopsidae;** *Holoplagia richardsi*, beech; *Ectaetia lignicola*, *E.platyscelis*, wd. beech. **Cecidomyiidae: Lestremiinae** (probably entire sub-family): *Lestremia* and *Aprionus* adults about old beech logs, *Lestremia leucophaea; Aprionus acutus; A.bidentatus; A.flavidus; A.flaviventris; A.miki; A.spiniger; Cordylomyia bifida* newly felled birch stump; *C.xylophila* over burnt larch stump; *Monardia magna* cherry; *M.ulmaria* rotten elm stump; *Pezomyia vanderwulpi* over hazel stump; *Trichopteromyia modesta* old beech and oak log. **Porricondylinae** (includes a number of rotten wood feeders, especially tribe Heteropezini which has paedogenetic larvae): (Wyatt, 1967) *Heteropezula tenuis* chestnut logs; *Leptosyna nervosa* ub, chestnut; *Miastor castaneae* chestnut bark; *M.metraloas* ub, birch. **Cecidomyiinae:** *Brachineura quercina* over oak log.

Stratiomyidae: *Pachygaster atra* beetle burrows in elm (also decaying veg); *P.leachii* wd, elm, oak (also decaying veg); *P.minutissima* ub, pine; *P.orbitalis* holly, horse chestnut, poplar; *P.tarsalis* beech, elm, poplar, pine. **Xylomyiidae:** *Solva maculata* rh, beech; *S. marginata* ub, elm, poplar; **Xylophagidae:** *Xylophagus ater* preys on beetle larvae, deciduous trees and pine; *X.cinctus* pine, Scotland; *X.junki* pine, Scotland. **Rhagionidae:** *Chrysopilus laetus* wd, beech; *Rhagio scolopaceus* wd, beech, occ. **Asilidae:** *Laphria flava* large pine, Scotland; *L.gilva* pine; *L.marginata* oak etc. **Therevidae:** *Psilocephala melaleuca* beech. **Empididae:** *Drapetis arcuata* hollow horse chestnut; *D.assimilis* (probable); *D.simulans* owl's nest in hollow willow; *Tachypeza fuscipennis* wd, willow, horse chestnut, etc; *T.*spp. (probable); *Tachydromia umbrarum* (possible); *Leptopeza flavipes* elm; *Oropezella sphenoptera* (possible); *Oedalea apicalis* beech, *Cossus* infected oaks; *O.flavipes* oak; *O.holmgreni* (probable); *O.stigmatella; O.tibialis; Euthyneura halidayi; E.myrtilli* beech; *Dryodromia-testacea* (possible); *Rhamphomyia albidiventris*   pine bark; *R. dentipes* stump; *R.marginata* fir stump; *Hilara lurida.* **Dolichopodidae:** *Sciapus platypterus* ub; *Medetera,* several spp. in burrows of bark beetles e.g. *diadema, truncorum, dendrobaena* (general), *impigra* (beech), *nitida* (elm), *ambigua, obscura* (elm), *pinicola* (pine); *Systenus bipartitus* elm sap; *S.leucurus* elm, beech; *S.pallipes* elm sap; *S.scholtzii* beech, elm; *S.tener* beech; *Achalcus melanotrichus* wd, lime, elm, horse chestnut (the other 2 *Achalcus* are probably on decaying veg.); *Neurigona quadrifasciata* possibly ub (possibly all other *Neurigona*).

Phoridae: (There is a lack of information). *Anevrina* spp. (*thoracica, urbana*) presumably ub; possibly several *Megaselia*. **Syrphidae:** *Ferdinandea cuprea* sap; *F.ruficornis* sap in *Cossus* trees; *Myolepta luteola* rh. beech, hollow poplar; *M.potens* (probable); *Brachyopa insensilis* sap; *B.bicolor* sap; *B.scutellaris; B.pilosa* beech; *Hammerschmidtia ferruginea* adult on aspen logs, Scotland; *Callicera aenea; C.spinolae; C.rufa* rh, pine, Scotland; *Volucella inflata* oak with *Cossus; Xylota abiens* oak; *X.coeruleiventris; X.florum* (probable beech); *X.segnis* stumps rh. yew, wet sawdust, silage; *X.sylvarum* oak, beech, wet sawdust; *X.tarda; X.xanthocnema* rh. yew; *Xylotomima lenta* beech; *X.nemorum* beech; *Brachypalpus bimaculatus* tall hollow stumps, beech, ?ash; *B.eunotus* (probably damp wood,? alder)` *Caliprobola speciosa* wet detritus in hollow beech stumps, oak; *Pocota personata* rh, high up in living trees, beech, etc; *Criorhina asilica; C.berberina* rh; *C.floccosa* rh at ground level, elm, birch, beech, ?ash; *C.ranunculi; Blera fallax* sap runs, Scotland; *Mallota cimbiciformis* rh, wd, horse chestnut, elm; *Myathropa florea* wet wd, wet rh, ub damp.

Otitidae: *Homalocephala albitarsis* (probable); *H.bipunctata* pine; *Myennis octopunctata* poplar. **Micropezidae:** *Rainieria calceata* probably beech. **Megamerinidae:** *Megamerina dolium* oak etc. **Tanypezidae:** *Tanypeza longimana* probable. **Chyromyidae:** *Gymnochiromyia flavella* (= *minima*) wd, elm. **Pallopteridae:** (bark beetle burrows) *Palloptera muliebris; P.umbellatarum; P.usta; P.ustulata.* (*chorea*, elm, also other decaying veg. **Lonchaeidae:** *Lonchaea* most species under bark or wood detritus. **Lonchaeidae:** *Lonchaea* most species under bark or wood detritus, predatory larvae often associated with bark beetles, most in deciduous trees, e.g. *corusca, patens, britteni, flavidipennis, fugax, palposa, sylvatica, peregrina; L. chorea* elm, also other decaying veg.; *L. laticornis* elm, conifers; *L. laxa, L. collini* in conifers; *Dasiops trichosternalis* aspen. **Clusiidae:** (all in dead wood) *Clusia flava* beech, birch; *Paraclusia tigrina* beech, elm; *Clusiodes* 7 spp; *Heteromeringia nigrimana.* **Odiniidae:** *Odinia hendeli* with *Ischnomera* (Coleoptera), elm; *O.maculata* visits oak; *O.meijeri* with *Scolytus* (Coleoptera), elm; *O.pomona* apple branches; *O.xanthocera* with *Saperda* (Coleoptera), aspen. **Acartophthalmidae:** *Acartophthalmus* possible (but at least *nigrinus* on fungus). **Periscelidae:** *Periscelis annulata* sap; *P.winnertzi* sap; *P.annulipes,*? sap. **Aulacigastridae:** *Aulacigaster leucopeza* sap, elm. **Asteiidae:** *Asteia amoena* sappy wd. **Drosophilidae:** *Amiota variegata* sap; *A.alboguttata* sap, dead beech; *Chymomyza costata* sap; *C.distincta* cut ends of fresh logs; *C.fuscimana* cut ends of fresh logs; *Drosophila immigrans* sap; *D.subsilvestris* sap; *D.obscura* sap; *D.tristis* sap. **Milichiidae:** *Madiza britannica,* wd, beech.

Tachinidae: (parasites) *Loewia phaeoptera* on centipedes; *Triarthria spinipennis* on earwigs; *Trichopareia maculisquama* on tipulid larvae; *T.seria* on tipulid larvae; *Xylotachina* *ligniperda* on *Cossus* (Lepidoptera). **Rhinophoridae:** (woodlice parasites) *Paykullia maculata; Melanophora roralis.* **Sarcophagidae:** (parasites in crabronid wasp nests) *Amobia signata; Ptychoneura cylindrica; P.rufitarsis.* **Anthomyiidae:** *Hylemya nigrimana* ub; *Eustalomyia* 4 spp. cleptoparasites in crabronid wasp nests. **Fanniidae:** *Fannia aequilineata* wd, elm, sap; *F.canicularis* wd, sap; *F.difficilis* sap; *F.gotlandica* wd, beech, elm; *F.polychaeta* stump; *F.postica* stump; *F.umbrosa* wd, oak. **Muscidae;** *Dendrophaonia querceti* rh elm (+ other habitats); *D.setifemur* rh beech; *Phaonia* (various species can occur under bark, though not exclusive to dead wood habitat:- *pallida, palpata, populi, subfuscinervis, variegata);* more specific dead wood species are *canescens* ub; *cincta* sap, elm, horse chestnut; *gobertii Cossus* borings; *mirabilis* rh elm, sycamore; *mystica* ub, under moss; *pratensis* sap, birch; *trigonalis* rh birch, sap; *Helina pertusa* ub, rh; *H.rothi.*

DUNG
by Peter Skidmore

The association of flies with dung is so implanted on the public mind that it is widely assumed that all flies breed in excrement of some sort or other, from whence these pests make sorties onto the Sunday joint. Neither is this an altogether modern view although it has been greatly substantiated by several generations of students of the housefly, *Musca domestica.*

The earliest description of a fly larva from human faeces was probably the figure, apparently of *Fannia scalaris,* by Swammerdam, in his Book of Nature, reprinted in 1758. Réaumur, studied the life cycles of several stercoricolous insects including *Scathophaga stercoraria, Mesembrina meridiana, Musca domestica* and *Rhingia campestris,* some 20 years before they were given their Linnaean names. His study of *S.stercoraria* was so complete that relatively little has been added to it since, whilst he found that *Musca domestica* only breeds in situations where the temperature is increased by fermentation, regarded by many workers as the basic requirement in its economy. Réaumur discovered the remarkably low fecundity of *Mesembrina meridiana,* and postulated that buoyancy of eggs laid in fluid substrates is greatly assisted by the elongate processes which adorn many fly eggs. He compared the faunas of different types of dung and found that each had its characteristic associates, whilst his discovery that cow dung was the normal pabulum for *Rhingia* larvae was not confirmed until 1926, some 200 years later. Following Réaumur, little work ensued (apart from the first monograph on *Musca domestica* by von Gleichen in 1790 and Bouché's researches in the 1830s) until after 1880 with Portschinsky's studies in Russia. He found that many muscids have predaceous larvae, which are important controllers of fly populations, e.g. *M. domestica* and *Stomoxys calcitrans* were sometimes eradicated locally by such species as *Hydrotaea dentipes* and *Muscina stabulans.* Portschinsky's work led to the researches into predaceous muscids by Keilin & Tate (1930), Thomson (1937) and others. Whilst Thomson was studying the morphology of the muscid inhabitants of cow dung in W. Scotland, Hammer (1941) was investigating the ecology of the cow dung community in Denmark, dealing primarily with Muscidae. A very useful supplementary paper is Laurence (1955) on the Sphaeroceridae of the cow dung community.

The science of copromyiology has developed mainly along two paths, the one concerned with human faeces, especially relevant from a medical or public health view point, the other centred upon domestic animals and hence more relevant to veterinary science. The disproportionate attention given to human faeces and cow dung is apparent from the appendix where 172 are recorded from cow dung and 161 from human faeces. It is also apparent that while the majority of records from the latter are of adults (cf.Howard, 1900; Gregor & Povolny, 1964 and earlier works), a much greater proportion of the cow dung species are known to breed. This probably indicates reticence of collectors rather than a statement of fact! Hopefully this list will reveal the massive gaps in knowledge of this subject. Enormous scope exists for valuable pioneer work, especially in the dung of other animals and birds. Disney (1972) reared a few flies from samples of dog dung and speculated on its medical importance in cities, which calls for detailed study; having seen large gatherings of *Sarcophaga*, *Calliphora* and *Lucilia* feeding on dog dung and on fish lying on adjacent fishmonger's slabs, I am sure there is some significance. The flies breeding in accumulating guano in the massive urban pigeon and starling roosts or in duck and goose droppings in ornamental parks have also not been studied. Whatever their provenance, accumulations of dung are likely to be colonised by flies, some of which may prove to be quite specific to the chosen medium.

Only when all species of mammals and birds have been adequately studied in the present context can a meaningful comparison be made between different dung types though it is clear that different types have characteristic faunas. Many researchers have commented on this with respect to cow and horse dung in the field. It is known that the predatory larvae of *Polietes albolineata* may even prevent the survival of many of their co-inhabitants of horse dung, including other Muscidae, but they are also highly cannibalistic.

There is typically a great faunal difference between small amounts of dung, such as individual cowpats, and masses, such as manure heaps. Hammer (1941) and Elton (1966, The Pattern of Animal Communities, Methuen & Co.) discuss the physical factors involved in some detail. Basically different thermal regimes operate, due to heat from fermentation and fungal metabolism being maintained as long as dung is being added. This does not happen in individual cowpats and by such means organisms are able to survive outside their natural geographical range, and here the high thermal requirements of *Musca domestica* are relevant since this is an alien, albeit a long established one. In Britain and much of the Holarctic *S.calcitrans* and *M.domestica* are much more strongly eusynanthropic in cooler latitudes such as Britain than in tropical regions. Thus *Stomoxys* is only doubtfully recorded breeding in cow dung in pastures in N.W.Europe, whilst in warmer regions this is quite commonplace.

Various techniques have been used by workers in this field, but valuable work has been accomplished with a minimum of equipment. Hammer, Gregor & Povolny and others have relied heavily on direct observation of flies in the field visiting the appropriate attractants. If capture for subsequent examination entails pootering then obviously a blow pooter is essential. A watch should always be kept for ovipositing females and any eggs laid may be collected along with some of the pabulum, and secured in a container which will allow gaseous exchange but will not exacerbate desiccation. If possible the dung *in situ* can be covered with fine gauze cones (Hammer, 1941) but this is impractical in most situations. I have always found the simplest methods adequate for rearing adults from larvae or puparia collected from dung, or from the soil immediately below; namely to enclose in a tube, pill box or other receptacle. Plastic bags are less satisfactory unless extensively perforated with a pin beforehand. More elaborate methods are available in standard textbooks on laboratory culture methods, but whatever system is adopted the importance of note-keeping cannot be over-stressed, since seemingly irrelevant facts later prove to be highly significant. It is valuable to note or retain any other insects present, which may be interrelated with the Diptera. Thus coprophilous fly larvae are parasitised by various chalcidoids (i.e. *Spalangia*), cynipoids (i.e. *Eucoila, Figites* etc.), braconids (many *Alysiinae*) and cryptine Ichneumonidae as well as staphylinids of the genus *Aleochara*. How many of these parasites are specific?

Finally, but most importantly, *always* retain pupal exuviae or puparia, with the emergent flies in your collection. I prefer to mount these on the same pin as the adult since they are then immediately correlated. If retained separately one or other may be lost. Since very important features are present on the ventral face of puparia (i.e. abdominal ambulatory welts and anal plate), these should not be obscured by adhesive. The value of identified puparia is enormous since sometimes empty puparia are found which one would dearly wish to identify. Many flies have a very short flight period and location of the species may be most easily accomplished by recognising the puparium. Also of course puparia are very durable and commonly occur in archaeological sites, but as yet most cannot be identified except in some of the better worked groups (i.e. Muscidae). *Always* keep your puparia, even if they fail to hatch.

Whilst the appendix will inevitably be greatly extended, it includes the vast majority of published records. In view of this it is interesting to note that only about 5% of the British Diptera fauna has been recorded as coprophilous and a mere 2% exclusively so in the larval stage.

Further Reading

Disney, R. H., 1972. Some flies associated with dog dung in an English city. *Entomologist's mon. Mag.* **108**: 93-94.

Gregor, F. & Povolny, D., 1964. Eine Ausbeute von Synanthropen Fliegen aus Tirol. *Zool. Listy., Folia Zool* **13** 3: 229-248.

Hammer, O., 1941. Biological and ecological investigation on Flies associated with pasturing cattle and their excrement. *Bianco Lunas Bogtrykk.* A/S. 1-258.

Howard, H. O., 1900. A contribution to the study of the insect fauna of human excrement (with special reference to the spread of typhoid fever), *Proc. Wash. Acad. Science* **2**: 541-604,

Keilin, D. & Tate, P., 1930. On certain semi-carnivorous Anthomyid larvae. *Parasitology* **22**:19-68.

Laurence, B. R., 1955. The ecology of some British Sphaeroceridae (Borboridae, Diptera). *J. Anim. Ecol.* **24** (1): 187-189.

Skidmore, P., (in prep.) On the taxonomy of the immature stages of the Muscidae of the Palaearctic Region, with notes on their biology and phylogeny.

Thomson, R. C. Muirhead, 1937. Observations on the biology and larvae of Anthomyiidae. *Parasitology* **29**: 273-358.

West. L. S.. 1951. The Housefly. its Natural History. medical importance and control. Comstock. New York.

APPENDIX:

Review of records from dung: based on British and foreign literature together with results from personal studies

15 excrementous substances are tabulated thus - bird, small rodent (i.e. mouse, rat, vole), rabbit, hedgehog, dog, pig, human, sheep, deer, horse, cow, chicken manure, cow/horse manure, privies (incl. cess pits, urinals etc.) and sewage (incl. sewage beds). Within each of these pabula a species may occur as adults only .(a), breeders (b), casual invaders or adventives from adjacent biotopes (c), or in the egg stage only (o). Capitals indicate greater frequency. Where a species has only been recorded breeding in a particular biotope the letter "e" is added thus - cow (b,e).

Trichoceridae: *Trichocera hiemalis*, rodents (a); *T.regelationis*, cow (b); *T.saltator*, cow (b). **Tipulidae:** Following species have been reared as casuals from cow dung - *Nephrotoma flavipalpis*, *N.quadrifaria*, *Tipula cava*, *T.vernalis*, *T.paludosa*, *Limonia tripunctata*, *Cheilotrichia cinerascens*. **Psychodidae:** *Pericoma trivialis* "dung"; *Psychoda albiipennis*, horse (B), cow (B), sewage (B); *P.alternata*, privies (B), sewage (B); *P.brevicornis*, cow (B); *P.cinerea*, sewage (b); *P.grisescens*, cow (B); *P.minuta*, cow (b,e); *P.parthenogenetica*, horse (B), cow (B), chicken manure (B), sewage (B); *P.phalaenoides*, cow (B); *P.pusilla*, cow (b,e); *P.setigera*, cow (B); *P.surcoufi*, cow (b); *P.trinodulosa*, cow (B,e). **Ceratopogonidae:** *Forcipomyia bipunctata*, cow/horse manure (B); *F.brevipennis*, horse (b), cow (B); *Culicoides chiopterus*, cow (B); *C.dewulfi*, cow (b); *C.nubeculosus*, cow/horse manure (B). **Chironomidae:** *Camptocladius stercorarius*, cow (B); *Mesosmittia flexuella*, cow (b); *Metriocnemus hygropetricus*, sewage (B); *M.hirticollis*, sewage (B); *Limnophyes minimus*, sewage (B); *Smittia aterrima*, small rodent (a), cow (b); *S.contingens*, cow (b). **Anisopodidae:** *Sylvicola fenestralis*, cow/horse manure (b), sewage (B); *S.punctatus*. cow (B,e). **Bibionidae:** *Dilophus febrilis*, cow (b). **Mycetophilidae:** *Pseudexechia trivittata*, horse (a) (see Fungi). **Sciaridae:** *Lycoriella auripila*, sewage (b); *Bradysia brunnipes*, "dung"; *Scatopsciara vivida*, small rodent (b); *"Sciara" semialata*, cow (b); *Pnyxia scabiei*, cow/horse manure (b). Laurence (1953) stated that at least 4 additional species of *"Sciara"* develop in cow dung. **Scatopsidae:** *Holoplagia albitarsis*, small rodent (b), cow (b); *Coboldia fuscipes*, cow/horse manure (b); *Scatopse notata*, cow (B); *Reichertella pulicaria*, privies (B); *Anapausis soluta*, cow (b). **Cecidomyiidae:** ? sp. cow (b,e).

Stratiomyidae: *Chloromyia formosa*, cow (c), cow/horse manure (b); *Microchrysa polita*, cow (b), cow/horse manure (B), privies (b); *M.flavicornis*, cow (B,e); *M.cyaneiventris*, cow (b,e); *Sargus bipunctatus*, cow (o); *S.splendens*, cow (b), cow/horse manure (B); *S.cuprarius*, cow/horse manure (B,e).**Asilidae:** *Asilus crabroniformis*, cow (o). **Empididae:** *Drapetis humilis*, horse (a), cow (B), cow/horse manure (a); *D.nigritella*, cow (B), cow/horse manure (a); *Ocydromia glabricula*, cow (B,e); *Empis trigramma*, cow (c). **Dolichopodidae:** *Dolichopus griseipennis*, cow (c); *D.ungulatus*, cow (a). **Phoridae:** *Megaselia fusca*, small rodent (b,e); *M.giraudii*, small rodent (b,e); *M.rufipes*, small rodent (a); *Borophaga femorata*, privies (a); *Conicera floricola*, small rodent (a); *Dohrniphora cornuta*, human (b). **Syrphidae:** *Rhingia campestris*, cow (B,e); *Syritta pipiens*, cow (b), cow/horse manure (B), privies (b); *Eristalis tenax*, human (a), cow/horse manure (B), privies (b), sewage (b).

Otitidae: *Physiphora demandata*, dog (a), pig (a), human (a), cow/horse manure (b); *Ulidia erythrophthalma*, human dung and privies (?); *Seioptera vibrans*, bird (a); *Ceroxys urticae*, cow/horse manure (b); *Herina lacustris*, human (a). **Dryomyzidae:** *Dryomyza anilis*, human (a); *D.flaveola*, human (a), cow (c). **Lauxaniidae:** *Tricholauxania praeusta*, cow (c). **Heleomyzidae:** *Heteromyza rotundicornis*, bird (b,e); *Tephrochlamys flavipes*, small rodent (b); *T.rufiventris*, human (a), privies (b); *Neoleria inscripta*, human (a); *Oecothea fenestralis*, small rodent (b); *Eccoptomera ornata*, small rodent (a); *Scoliocentra villosa*, rabbit (A); *Heleomyza modesta czernyi*, privies (b); *H.serrata*, human (a), chicken manure (B), privies (B). **Chyromyidae:** *Chyromya flava*, bird (a). **Sepsidae:** *Saltella sphondylii*, cow (B,e); *Themira putris*, human (a), cow (a), privies (a); *Meroplius stercorarius*, human (a), cow (a); *Nemopoda nitidula*, human (A), cow (a), privies (A); *N.pectinulata*, human (a); *Sepsis biflexuosa*, cow (c); *S.cynipsea*, cow (B,e); *S.flavimana*, cow (b); *S.fulgens*, human (a), cow (B,e); *S.neocynipsea*, human (a); *S.nigripes*, cow (b,e); *S.orthocnemis*, human (?), cow (B,e); *S.punctum*, pig (b), human (A); *S.thoracica*, human (a), cow (c); *S.violacea*, human (a), cow (b), cow/horse manure (B), privies (B); *S.duplicata*, cow (b,e).**Sphaeroceridae:** *Sphaerocera curvipes*, human (a), sheep (a), horse (B), cow (c), cow/horse manure (B), privies (b); *S.monilis*, cow/horse manure (b); *S.denticulata*, horse (a), cow (b), cow/horse manure (B); *S.pusilla*, human (a), horse (b), cow (a), cow/horse manure (a), privies (B); *S.pallidiventris*, horse (b), cow (c); *Copromyza atra*, dog (b), human (b), sheep (b), horse (b), cow (B), privies (A); *C.flavipennis*. horse (a), cow (a); *C.glacialis*, small rodent (a); *C.nigra*, human (a), horse (b), cow (b), cow/horse manure (B); *C.nitida*, human (a), horse (a), cow (B,e); *C.roserii*, small rodent (a), horse (a), cow (a); *C.costalis*, horse (a), cow (a); *C.nitidifrons*, horse (a), cow (b,e); *C.sordida*, horse (a), cow (b,e); *C.uncinata*, horse (a); *C.vitripennis*, horse (a), cow (b,e); *C.equina*, dog (a), human (a), horse (B), cow (b), cow/horse (B), privies (A); *C.similis*, human (b), horse (b), cow (B), cow/horse manure (b); *C.stercoraria*, small rodent (B), human (b), horse (?), cow/horse manure (B); *Leptocera curvinervis*, pig (b), sheep (b), horse (b), cow (b); *L.fontinalis*, cow (a), privies (B), sewage (B); *L.fuscipennis*, pig (b), sheep (b), horse (b), cow (b); *L.fenestralis*, horse (a), small rodent (a); *L.scutellaris*, bird (?), rabbit (a), human (a), deer (a), horse (a), cow (B,e); *L.appendiculata*, cow (a); *L.bifrons*, sheep (b), horse (b), cow (b), cow/horse manure (b); *L.claviventris*, small rodent (b); *L.collini*, cow (B,e); *L.clunipes*, human (a), horse (b), cow (B), privies (A); *L.denticulata*, cow (B,e); *L.flaviceps*, cow (a); *L.flavipes*, horse (a); *L.grenstedi*, cow (a); *L.longiseta*, horse (a); *L.mirabilis*, cow (a), cow/horse manure (?); *L.moesta*, cow (b); *L.palmata*, cow (a), *L.pseudoleucoptera*, cow (B,e); *L.pullula*, small rodent (b,e), horse (a); *L.ochripes*, "dung"; *L.rufilabris*, cow (a); *L.silvatica*, cow (B), cow /horse manure (b); *L.talparum*, small rodent (b), mole nests; *L.vitripennis*, sheep (a), cow (a); *L.humida*, cow (a); *L.atomus*, cow (a); *L.leucoptera*, "dung"; *L.coprina*, cow (b,e); *L.melania*, horse (a); *L.minuscula*, cow (a); *L.spinipennis*, horse (B), cow (b); *L.aterrima*, cow (b), cow/horse manure (?); *L.pilosa*, cow/horse manure (a); *L.quadrispina*, cow (B,e); *L.acutangula*, dog (a), sheep (a), horse (B), cow (b), privies (B); *L.ferruginata*, pig (b), sheep (b), horse (B), cow (a), cow/horse manure (B); *L.hirticula*, cow (a); *L.hirtula*, small rodent (b), rabbit (b), horse (a); *L.lugubris*, rabbit (a), dog (a), sheep (a), horse (b), cow (B); *L.pseudolugubris*, horse (a), cow (a); *L.vagans*, sheep (b), horse (b), cow (?), cow/horse manure (b), privies (b). **Lonchaeidae:** *Lonchaea chorea*, cow (b) (identity unconfirmed); *L.sylvatica*, cow (?), (identity unconfirmed). **Piophilidae:** *Piophila casei*, human (b), privies (a); *P.varipes*, human (a); *P.vulgaris*, human (b); *P.latipes*, human (a). **Ephydridae:** *Scatella stagnalis*, privies (b); *Teichomyza fusca*, privies (B), sewage (B). **Drosophilidae:** *Drosophila funebris*, privies (a); *D.repleta*, human (a), privies (B); *D.busckii*, human (b), cow (c), privies (a); *D.melanogaster*, human (a). **Milichiidae:** *Leptometopa latipes*, privies (B,e).**Carnidae:** *Meoneura* sp., human (a).

Oestridae: *Hypoderma* spp., deer (c), horse (c), cow (c), (puparia only). **Gasterophilidae:** *Gasterophilus* spp., horse (c) (puparia only). **Sarcophagidae:** *Sarcophila latifrons*, human (a), horse (a); *Ravinia pernix*, human (a), cow (b); *Sarcophaga albiceps*, human (a), horse (a); *S.aratrix*, human (a); *S.carnaria*, dog (a), human (a); *S.haemorrhoidalis*, human (a); *S.incisilobata*, human (b), horse (a); *S.laciniata*, human (a); *S.melanura*, human (a); *S.scoparia*, human (a); *S.sinuata*, human (a); *S.teretirostris*, human (a). **Calliphoridae:** *Calliphora alpina*, human (a); *C.loewi*, human (a); *C.subalpina*, human (a); *C.uralensis*, human (a), privies (b); *C.vicina*, human (A), privies (A); *C.vomitoria*, human (A), privies (A); *Bellardia agilis*, cow/horse manure (b); *Melinda gentilis*, human (a); *Cynomya* *mortuorum*, small rodent (a); *Lucilia ampullacea*, human (a); *L.caesar*, human (b), horse (a), privies (A); *L.illustris*, human (a); *L.sericata*, human (a), cow/horse manure (b); *L.silvarum*, small rodent (a), human (a); *Pollenia rudis*, human (a), horse (a), cow (a), cow/horse manure (c); *P.varia*, human (a); *P.vespillo*, human (a); *Phormia regina*, human (a); *P.terraenovae*, human (a), privies (A). **Scathophagidae:** *Spaziphora hydromyzina*, sewage (B); *Scathophaga furcata*, dog (a), human (a), sheep (b), privies (B); *S.inquinata*, "dung (A)"; *S.lutaria*, human (a); *S.scybalaria*, "dung (a)"; *S.stercoraria*, dog (a), human (a), sheep (a), horse (a), cow (B,e), cow/horse manure (A). **Anthomyiidae:** *Fucellia fucorum*, cow/horse manure (a); *Pegohylemyia fugax*, small rodent (b); *Lasiomma meadei*, human (b), cow (a); *Hydrophoria conica*, human (a); *Anthomyia pluvialis*, human (A); *A.procellaris*, human (a); *Hylemya nigrimana*, cow (b,e); *H.partita*, human (a); *H.strenua*, human (A), horse (a), cow (B), cow/horse manure (b); *H.variata*, human (a), cow (b); *Paregle cinerella*, human (A), cow (B), cow/horse manure (B); *P.radicum*, hedgehog (B), dog (b), human (A), horse (a), cow/horse manure (b); *Calythea nigricans*, pig (b), human (a); *Nupedia aestiva*, cow (B,e); *Emmesomyia socia*, human (A), horse (a).

Fanniidae: *Fannia aequilineata*, "dung"; *F.armata*, human (a), privies (B); *F.canicularis*, small rodent (B), rabbit (b), dog (b), pig (b), human (b), horse (b), chicken manure (B), cow/horse manure (B), privies (B), (also in ferret dung); *F.difficilis*, human (a); *F.fuscula*, human (a); *F.genualis*, human (a); *F.incisurata*, human (B), privies (B); *F.manicata*, rabbit (b), human (a), chicken manure (B); *F.monilis*, dog (b), human (a); *.F.mutica*, human (a), horse (a); *F.scalaris*, pig (b), human (a), chicken manure (B), cow/horse manure (B), privies (B); *F.vespertilionis*, bat droppings. **Muscidae:** *Polietes albolineata*, dog (a), human (a), horse (B,e), cow (a); *P.hirticrura*, human (a), cow (b,e); *P.lardaria*, dog (a), human (A), deer (a), horse (A), cow (B,e); *Mesembrina meridiana*, human (a), horse (a), cow (B,e); *Pyrellia ignita*, human (a); *Dasyphora cyanella*, human (a), horse (a), cow (B); *D.cyanicolor*, human (a), sheep (b); *Orthellia cornicina*, human (a), cow (B,e); *O.viridis*, human (a), horse (a), cow (B,e), cow/horse manure (a), privies (A); *Morellia aenescens*, horse (B), cow (b); *M.hortorum*, human (A), horse (a), cow (B,e), cow/horse manure (a); *M.simplex*, human (A), cow (B,e); *Musca domestica*, rabbit (b), dog (a), pig (B), human (B), sheep (b), horse (B), cow (b), chicken manure (B), cow/horse manure (B), privies (B); *M.vitripennis*, human (a), horse (a), cow (B,e); *M.autumnalis*, dog (a), human (a), horse (a), cow (B); *Azelia cilipes*, human (a), horse (b), cow (B); *A.macquarti*, pig (b), human (a), horse (b), cow (B), cow/horse manure (B); *A.triquetra*, human (a), horse (a); *A.zetterstedti*, cow (b); *Thricops longipes*, cow/horse (a); *Alloeostylus diaphanus*, human (a), cow (c); *A.simplex*, human (A); *A.sudeticus*, human (a); *Trichopticoides decolor*, cow (B), cow/horse (B); *Drymeia hamata*, cow (c); *Dendrophaonia querceti*, birds (b), rabbit (b), dog (b), human (b), privies (B); *Ophyra capensis*, human (B), chicken manure (B), privies (B); *O.leucostoma*, human (b), chicken manure (B), cow/horse manure (B), privies (B); *Hydrotaea albipuncta*, cow (B,e); *H.armipes*, pig (b), human (b), horse (B), cow (?), cow/horse manure (B), privies (b); *H.dentipes*, rabbit (b), dog (a), pig (b), human (B), horse (b), cow (c), chicken manure (b), cow/horse manure (B), privies (B), sewage (b); *H.irritans*, human (A), horse (a), cow (c), cow/horse manure (c); *H.meridionalis*, cow (b,e); *H.meteorica*, human (a), cow/horse manure (b?); *H.militaris*, human (a), cow (B,e); *H.occulta*, human (a), chicken manure (b), cow/horse manure (b); *H.palaestrica*, human (a); *H.pandellei*, human (a); *H.pellucens*, human (a), cow (b,e); *H.similis*, human (a); *H.tuberculata*, cow (B,e); *H.velutina*, cow (B), cow/horse manure (b); *Muscina assimilis*, small rodent (b), human (a), horse (a), cow/horse manure (?), privies (a); *M.pabulorum*, human (a); *M.stabulans*, rabbit (a), dog (a), pig (a), human (a), horse (a), cow (a), chicken manure (B), cow/horse manure (B), privies (B); *Phaonia apicalis*, human (a); *P.errans*, human (a); *P.erronea*, human (a); *P.incana*, human (a); *P.pallida*, human (a), horse (a); *P.rufipalpis*, human (a); *P.siebecki*, human (a); *P.signata*, human (a); *P.variegata*, human

78

(a), deer (c); *Helina duplicata*, human (a), cow (b); *H.depuncta*, human (a), cow (b); *H.flagripes*, human (a); *H.impuncta*, human (a), cow (b); *H.obscurata*, cow (b); *H.quadrum*, cow (b); *H.quadrimaculella*, human (a), cow (b); *Gymnodia humilis*, horse (B), cow (?); *Hebecnema affinis*, cow (b); *H.fumosa*, human (a), cow (b); *H.nigricolor*, human (a), cow (b); *H.umbratica*, human (A), horse (a), cow (B); *H.vespertina*, cow (?); *Mydaea ancilla*, dog (b), human (a), privies (B); *M.anicula*, human (a); *M.deserta*, human (a); *M.scutellaris*, human (a), cow (B,e); *M.urbana*, human (A), horse (a), cow (B); *Myospila hennigi*, human (A), horse (a); *M.meditabunda*, dog (b), pig (b), human (b), horse (a), cow (B), privies (B); *Graphomya maculata*, human (a), cow/horse manure (?); *Coenosia tigrina*, cow (a); *Lispe tentaculata*, "dung"; *Stomoxys calcitrans*, rabbit (b), pig (b), human (b), sheep (b), horse (b), cow (b), cow/horse manure (B), privies (B); *Haematobia irritans*, cow (B,e); *Haematobosca stimulans*, cow (B,e).

CARRION
by James P.Dear

The study of the dipterous fauna of carrion can be a useful, interesting and rewarding exercise, but not always particularly pleasant. Overstimulation of the olfactory organs for instance can occasionally prove excessive! Very careful observation is required if the results obtained from carrion studies are to be of scientific value. The balance and faunal composition within this micro-habitat is controlled by many external factors, so comprehensive notes should be made at all times. Nature and size of the carrion, state of decay (see below), position in relation to sunlight, type of habitat, weather, time of day, season, latitude and altitude are all important factors and should be noted. The most useful and interesting results are obtained when both the breeding and visiting species are collected. This can only be done really successfully by using carrion bait within a trap.

Most Diptera that visit carrion are extremely fast fliers and usually aware of the approaching dipterist. Great agility with the net is therefore required to capture the the larger species. Although two or three sweeps will sometimes capture some of the smaller species these tend to move off in short flights to the surrounding vegetation when disturbed. They can generally be pooted up as they re-appear. Some species remain on the carrion and can be easily taken using the blow-pooter. Blow-pooters are not always very successful as they can become damp with condensed breath; to avoid this short, sharp breaths with the lips pursed (as in producing a bugle-note) should be used. The ordinary sucking pooter should not be used for specimens on carrion as it is dangerous to health, apart from being very unpleasant. The females of the larger species, especially *Sarcophaga*, can also present dangers to health if pooted inside the net as eggs or larvae may enter the eyes or mouth and result in naso-pharyngeal myiasis. Some Diptera prefer to scavenge between the carrion and they should be collected by gently lifting the bait. Larval samples should also be taken, especially if they are migrating for pupation.

The relative attractiveness of various carrion baits can be a useful study, especially using various whole animal corpses such as birds, mammals, fish and reptiles. It is however necessary to use traps for this type of work if complete data on faunal succession is to be made. It does however mean that both the breeding and visiting species can be recorded. Although some traps will slightly alter the overall ecological picture of the carrion by eliminating some species in other orders

(Coleoptera) the alteration in the dipterous fauna will be minimal. Work of this sort is best carried out in as natural a habitat as possible. When studying small corpses a simple trap can be used (Fig. 1), however for larger corpses it is not feasible to use traps. When using the simple trap 80% ammonia solution can be used as a 'knock down' agent. This is done using an inverted wash bottle so that only vapour enters the trap and placing a hand over the gauze at the top. Other reagents tend to taint the bait and should not be used. For larger carrion continuous observation is the only method for obtaining accurate results, and a strict routine must be followed with careful notes made at all times. Obviously the more frequent the visits the more complete the data.

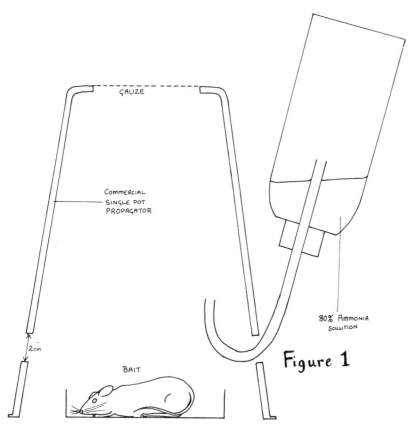

GAUZE

COMMERCIAL
SINGLE POT
PROPAGATOR

2cm

BAIT

80% AMMONIA
SOLUTION

Figure 1

The faunal seccession on crrion in the open can be divided into approximately eight distinct phases which can be closely correlated to the state of decomposition. However, the species composition will be very different when diverse habitats and conditions are considered. The general succession on corpses is as follows:—
1st wave. Fresh carrion usually has only a slight smell. Blood, musty fur, fishy, for instance. These are extremely attractive to the keen senses of blowflies, especially

Calliphora and *Lucilia* spp. These two genera can arrive at carrion within minutes of it being exposed and are even able to locate it from 100' above ground level. In spring and autumn *Calliphora* dominates the initial invasion but in summer *Lucilia* almost certainly attract *Calliphora subalpina, C.loewi* and *C.uralensis, C.alpina,* an extremely rare species in Britain appears to occur only at the tree line and could possibly be trapped there. Females of both *Calliphora* and *Lucilia* will begin to oviposit at this stage in and around the natural openings. Muscidae attracted at this stage are not usually breeding species, generally *Musca* and *Muscina.*

2nd wave. A faint odour develops and in corpses the abdomen begins to distend. *Lucilia* an *Calliphora* are still the most common visitors at this stage but in northern habitats *Cynomya* may dominate but this needs some investigation. Muscidae, Fanniidae, Piophilidae and Sphaeroceridae are also prominent, including *Graphomya* and *Hydrotaea. P.latipes* and *P.varipes* are the most common piophilids. Some species of Anthomyiidae can also be found feeding on juices around the natural orifices.

3rd wave. A strong odour has now developed and any fats present turn rancid. *Calliphora* and *Lucilia* larvae are mostly fully developed and begin to migrate for pupation. Larvae or ovipositing females of *Fannia, Microchrysa* (Stratiomyidae), *Piophila,* and *Neoleria* (Heleomyzidae) may now be present. Sphaeroceridae and Platystomatidae adults will also be present at this stage.

4th wave. Butyric fermentation with a cheesy smell attracts many acalypterates including Drosophilidae, Sepsidae, *Piophila casei,* Milichiidae, Ephydridae and Sphaeroceridae. In larger corpses in the more liquid parts *Eristalis* (Syrphidae) can also develop.

5th wave. Ammoniacal fermentation takes place and eventually the sanious fluids evaporate. .*Ophyra* spp. are especially attracted at this stage of decay and Phoridae also invade as the carrion dries. A rare acalypterate family, Thyreophoridae (included in Piophilidae in the check list) which has not been collected since the beginning of this century, and is presumed extinct (although adults may appear very early in the year and so be overlooked), is supposedly attracted at this stage. The other waves are generally concerned with Coleoptera species but Sphaeroceridae and Phoridae will remain on carrion even when it is completely dry.

The following is a list of the families of European Diptera, with the important genera, that have been recorded as visiting carrion. In brackets is given the season when they occur on carrion and the number of species within the genus or family that have been recorded. (Sp = spring, S = summer, A = autumn):−

Calliphoridae: *Calliphora* (Sp,A,5), *Lucilia* (S,7), *Phormia* (S,1), *Pollenia* (early S,5), *Melinda* (S,1), *Cynomya* (S,1); **Sarcophagidae** (S,18); **Rhinophoridae** and **Tachinidae** (S,12); **Fanniidae:** *Fannia* (Sp,S,A, 18); **Muscidae:** *Azelia* (S,1); *Ophyra* (Sp,A,2), *Hydrotaea* (Sp,A,19), *Muscina* (S,2), *Pyrellia* (S,1), *Musca* (S,2); **Anthomyiidae;** *Phorbia* (S,4), *Paregle* (S,2), *Anthomyia* (S,1), *Fucellia* (S,*maritima* complex); **Scathophagidae** (A,2); **Sepsidae** (late Sp,S,6); **Sphaeroceridae** (late S, A,12); **Platystomatidae** (S,4); **Dryomyzidae** (S,A,1); **Heleomyzidae** (S,A,4); **Piophilidae** (Sp,S,A,6); **Milichiidae** (late Sp,S, *Meoneura* spps); **Agromyzidae** (S,A,2); **Chloropidae** (S,2); **Clusiidae** (Sp,1); **Ephydridae** (S,3); **Sciomyzidae** (A,1); **Coelopidae** (Sp,S,A,1);

Empididae (S, 2 preying on other flies?); **Syrphidae** (S,6); **Stratiomyidae** (late S,A,1); **Simuliidae** (S,1).

Obviously many in the above list are visiting carrion for feeding purposes rather than breeding and much more work is required to differentiate these two categories.

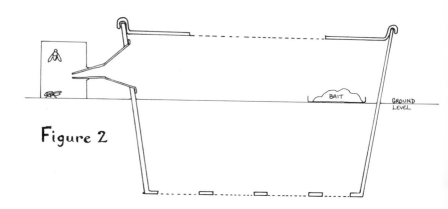

Figure 2

Rearing of carrion-flies is best done in natural habitats using the apparatus shown (Fig.2). The bait should be exposed for 1-3 days and then the lid replaced. The development time, larval stages, effect of temperature, humidity and sunlight can then be studied. Work of this sort supplies invaluable information on these most important flies for use in veterinary, public health, forensic and medico-legal fields. Some species are very important as vectors in disease transmission. Samples of larvae should always be collected from carrion so that all stages of the breeding species can be identified. Larvae should be sorted into as many different types as can be recognised. A sample of each type should then be preserved in alcohol. The rest can be left to pupate in dry peat or sand in a shallow tray. The puparia should then be retrieved and be placed in glass corked tubes; when flies emerge it is important not to lose the 'caps' (usually in two pieces) which are forced off, as these often contain the mouthparts that are so vital in identification. If more than one species emerges from each sorted group then the mouthparts from the puparia can be compared with the larval mouthparts from the alcohol-preserved specimens. In this way a correct larva-adult association can be made.

Further Reading

Lane, R. P., 1957. An investigation into blowfly (Diptera: Calliphoridae) succession on corpses. *J.nat. Hist.* **9**:581-588.

Nuorteva, P. numerous papers after 1965 (see Zoological Record).

Smith, K. G. V., 1975. The faunal succession of insects and other invertebrates on a dead fox. *Entomologist's Gaz.* **26**: 277-287.

MUD

by Dr. Anthony G. Irwin

"Mud, mud, glorious mud!"
These words must sum up dipteran feelings about this medium. Most fly larvae are very susceptible to desiccation and require wet conditions in order to survive. True, many species, particularly in the Nematocera, live in open water, but there they succumb to constant predation by fish. Moreover, open water is not an easy medium in which to move, especially if the larva lacks limbs. The wriggling of a maggot is more effective in a thicker liquid. And the most abundant thick liquid in the world? ————— mud!

Sub-aquatic Mud

A lot of mud is found at the bottom of ponds, lakes and rivers. Living in this mud which is permanently covered by water poses a number of problems. Mud, by its very nature, contains much organic matter. It is also seldom disturbed. Under these conditions, a great deal of bacterial action takes place and oxygen levels are often low. The major problem is how to breathe. Chironomid larvae, which form most of the sub-aquatic mud fauna, have overcome this by both physiological and behavioural adaptation. (They have respiratory pigments and make tubes through which they pass comparatively pure water.)
Other families resort to more cunning means to obtain air. Most remarkable are those larvae which 'plug-in' to the air supplies of aquatic plants. *Notiphila riparia* (Ephydridae) and *Chrysogaster hirtella* (Syrphidae) are two species which have specially adapted posterior spiracles which they use to pierce the stems or roots of emergent vegetation. Similarly the pupa of *Erioptera squalida* (Tipulidae) has specialized thoracic spiracles which can tap the air spaces in such plants. Obviously it is much simpler to live in mud which is exposed to the air. The rest of this section investigates such mud.

Where to find Good Mud

The margins of ponds, lakes, rivers and streams have mud which is both wet and exposed to the air. Here there are no fish from which to hide, and no problems getting enough oxygen. The main problem arises if the water level drops and the mud dries out. Some larvae will burrow deeper into the mud. Yet others (notably among the Stratiomyidae) possess peculiar cuticles which resist desiccation, until the mud is damp again.
Other suitable areas of mud can be found around springs and seepages where it is never too wet or too dry and consequently there are interesting assemblages of flies. In upland areas of north-west Britain, rainfall is so frequent and drainage so poor, that semi-permanent areas of mud can be found in the open. Peat is simply a mud with very low mineral content.
Because of the low rate of ground-water evaporation in woodland, this habitat often has patches of mud especially along rutted rides and even dry woodland often has local spots prone to become muddy. In its extreme condition the woodland/mud combination takes the form of alder or sallow carr.

In Britain, the most extensive areas of mud are found by the sea. This mud is permanently damp, for it is soaked twice a day by the tide.

How to Find Fly Larvae in Mud

Having found mud the next stage is to find larvae (or adult flies). This is not difficult, but can be messy. Although one might expect larvae to be distributed evenly throughout the mud, in fact they tend to concentrate around more stable objects. This is probably to ensure that the pupa does not become buried too deeply if the mud is disturbed, and of course mud under an object is less likely to become dry. Several examples will illustrate this point.

Beside eutrophic lake margins, the pupae and predatory larvae of the scathophagid, *Spaziphora hydromyzina*, can be found under stones lying on mud, but are absent from the surroundings. On saltmarshes, larvae of the stratiomyid genus *Nemotelus* are found under stones and driftwood, where they are protected from probing shorebirds. The stable object need not be a discrete item such as a stone, but could be an algal mat, like those covering some mudflats. In North America, the larvae of *Canace macateei* (Canacidae) are found in large numbers in such mats of filamentous algae. A similar habitat is probably the home of our British *Xanthocanace ranula*. The mixture of filamentous algae and mud is ideal for dipterous larvae. Many species are known to feed on the algae, and of course these are attended by their predators. The seepages found on coastal cliffs are interesting in that they are the only vertical mud habitat available. It is the filamentous algae which retain the mud and stop it being washed away. Tipulids, stratiomyids (*Oxycera*), dolichopodids and ephydrids form the main component of the seepage fauna. These larvae may be subject to heavy parasitism. Certainly parasitic hymenoptera can often be seen searching over the algae. As many of the seepage species of Diptera are little-known, investigation of their parasites could be well-repaid.

How to Collect and Rear Fly Larvae from Mud

Finding larvae in mud is only the beginning. Rearing adult flies from them is more difficult. Because of this, it is a good idea to collect large numbers of larvae. Thus although some may die despite lavish care, sufficient will survive to enable some to be preserved and some to be bred out.

The easiest way to collect large numbers of larvae is to sieve them in still water so that the mud washes away, but it is then necessary to collect enough substrate to accommodate them. Tough polythene bags are useful for this. As soon as possible, the larvae should be sorted into species and size classes. This is important, for in the confines of a rearing jar or dish, cannibalism and predation may be rife. If the species sorting is done carefully, it may not be necessary to separate individuals, but if more than one species emerges from one batch of larvae, then adult/exuvia associations may be difficult to establish. Algal and detritus feeders will find enough food in the substrate, but predatory larvae should be given a few surplus small larvae.

No doubt you are now wondering how to tell whether a larva is predatory or not. Unfortunately it is not possible to give an easy answer, but of the families of flies found in mud, there seem to be some dietary trends. Empididae, Dolichopodidae, Scathophagidae and Muscidae have predatory larvae. All the other families (Nematocera, larger Brachycera and acalypterates) have larvae which are primarily algae and detritus feeders, but there are many exceptions.

Although food is important for survival, greater mortality of collected larvae probably results from conditions which are too wet or too dry. There is no substitute for constant checking of humidity. When the larvae are nearing pupation, slightly drier substrate should be provided for those species collected from marginal mud, where the larvae might normally crawl to drier areas. If the larvae were collected from under stones, place small stones on the mud in the rearing container. Remember that mud is seldom warm in the field, so do not place rearing containers in a warm room.

Collecting Adult Flies

Although rearing larvae provides useful information about the species which breed in mud, flies are more easily found by collecting adults. These can be classed in two groups - those which breed in the mud and those which only visit it as adults. Of the visitors, most come to mud to drink. One does not usually remember that adult flies require water as much as any other animal. Some get all their requisites from their prey, from nectar or from dew, but many visit mud and suck water from it. Notable among the latter are hoverflies and horseflies. Naturally such a source of water is in greater demand in drier years and in drier areas of the country.

Some large hoverflies such as *Eristalis* and *Helophilus* sit on mud and may oviposit in it. The mature larvae however are normally found in sub-aquatic mud. Catching these larger flies may prove to be hazardous. Swiping at them often results in a netful of nothing ———— or mud! A better technique is to bring the net down from above, holding the tail of the net aloft, so that the insect flies up into it. Alternatively search or sweep the surrounding vegetation. This not only secures the visitors, but will also result in the capture of many species which breed in the mud. Of the latter, several species, including all the Nematocera, will leave the mud as soon as they emerge and will only return to oviposit.

Other mud-breeders spend their whole adult lives on the surface of the mud. Many species of Dolichopodidae and Ephydridae seldom fly, but rather run or hop across the mud and great skill is needed to skim the net at just the right height.

Some flies are reluctant to fly, and for these species, direct use of the pooter, including muddy knees and elbows, seems to be the best method. This is probably one of the most frustrating of all the dipterist's activities. Just as the fly comes within pooting distance, it hops or runs away. No doubt some unsporting funnel trap could be devised to secure these flies. Certainly emergence traps can be used with great effect on patches of mud.

Summer is not necessarily the best time to collect mud flies. If the mud has dried out, then it is unlikely that adults will oviposit. Thus, at least among the Nematocera and acalypterates, larger numbers of species will be found later or earlier in the year. Certain Ephydridae can be found more frequently during the winter than in summer. It may be that these species are adapted for cooler climates, so that the heat of the midsummer must be avoided, and thus the pupa aestivates.

It is often possible to catch large numbers of flies from mud. This can be advantageous, for several species of similar appearance may be present in different ratios. Thus collecting several hundred *Scatella* (a small ephydrid bearing dark wings with white spots) may produce only two or three of the rarely recorded *S.crassicosta*, while the rest will be the common *S.stagnalis*. Unfortunately these cannot be separated in the field, so one must collect at least a hundred from any saltmarsh before declaring *S.crassicosta* absent.

A Word of Warning

Although collecting flies in and on mud is rewarding, exciting and just good, clean (?) fun, it can be dangerous, particularly beside lakes and the sea. A long net handle should be used to test the depth of mud before venturing onto it. However, if you seem to be sinking rather deeply, it is best to swallow pride and dignity, by lying on the mud and rolling to firmer ground. It is certainly better than swallowing mud, or looking dignified just from the neck up!

WATER
by Peter Cranston

The freshwater aquatic environment, although unexploited by adult Diptera, provides numerous diverse habitats for larval development. The larvae of the Culicidae, Dixidae, Chaoboridae, Simuliidae and Thaumaleidae are all aquatic, while the majority of Chironomidae and Ceratopogonidae develop in water. Representatives of nearly all of Nematocera families may be found in water, while several families of Brachycera and a few families of Cyclorrhapha have aquatic immatures.

Collecting Adults

Many of the imagines of the aquatic Diptera are weak fliers straying only short distances from the emergence site so collecting the adults of these insects is relatively easy. Sweeping the vegetation beside a body of water or pooting directly from the underside of bridges, marginal leaves or overhanging banks will always ensure numbers of flies, particularly Nematocera. Midges can also be collected by sweeping the characteristic mating swarms which often form at dusk or dawn. These swarms are monospecific and where two species use the same marker there is usually a height difference between the swarms. Predaceous Ceratopogonidae including *Ceratopogon* and the larger Palpomyiini can be collected on the ground under chironomid swarms: the predators attack individual Chironomids and drop to the ground with the prey.

Many aquatic Diptera, Chironomidae, Ceratopogonidae and Culicidae, particularly can be collected at light near a body of water, while a Malaise trap across a stream will collect many of the Diptera which move up and down streams.

Historically many freshwater ecosystems have been studied with the aid of emergence traps which collect the adult flies emerging at the water surface. Although there has been criticism of the use of these traps for quantitative studies (in standing waters the ascending pupae may avoid the trap and in running waters the trap may act as a drift net catching pupae floating down from upstream) the traps are still very useful in giving a sample of the insects emerging from a known area. Some traps have been designed to collect both the cast pupal skin and the adult insect.

Collecting Immatures

The phenomenon of drift in running waters is well exemplified by the numbers of simuliid larvae which become attached to submerged parts of any emergence trap. Drift can be used to collect all aquatic larvae and pupae. A drift net is strung across a stream in such a manner that all organisms and detritus which meet the net are deflected by the net into a central submerged tube similar to that of the Surber sampler (described below). The contents of a drift net will include floating adults which have failed to emerge, as well as the immatures. It is possible with luck to find adults with the pupal skin attached, and pupae with the larval skin and head capsule attached, and thus identify all stages of a species without rearing. Naturally care must be taken with the association of the stages.

Collection of larvae and pupae and rearing through to the adult is probably slightly more difficult for the aquatic groups than for terrestrial Diptera, but the results are equally rewarding. In most of the aquatic families there are new life histories to be discovered while in some families the majority of immatures are undescribed. Only in the Simuliidae, Dixidae, Chaoboridae and Culicidae can the immatures be described as reasonably well known but there are still gaps in our knowledge. In some water habitats immatures may be collected by visual examination of the medium - in most cases more or less specialised equipment is necessary for collecting them. In standing waters up to half a metre deep a standard fine mesh pond net is effective for larvae living above the benthos (bottom) such as Culicidae and Chaoboridae and also for surface dwelling larvae including the meniscus midges or Dixidae. A sturdy pond net can be used for taking samples of the bottom material (benthos) but here a grab sampler can give better results. A grab sampler is essential for sampling the deeper lakes where it is lowered from a boat or jetty. The grab, with jaws open, is sent on a line to the bottom where the weight of the grab embeds the jaws into the benthos. A metal weight, the messenger, is sent down the line where it operates a spring loaded jaw release. Provided the bottom is not too stony (which may prevent the jaws from closing) the closed grab is brought to the surface for sorting.

For collecting immatures in running waters a pond net can be used to good effect in some slower streams and ditches, but the Surber sampler used by freshwater ecologists is an extremely useful piece of equipment. The sampler consists of two square frames at right angles to each other, one of which encloses the substrate to be sampled while the other is the frame of a tapering net. This net terminates in a plastic jar secured to a strengthened net tail by a jubilee clip. This jar can be unscrewed from the net. The sampler can be used quantitatively since the frame enclosing the substrate is of a known area, but for the purpose of collecting larvae for rearing it can be used qualitatively. The sampler is placed in the stream with the substrate frame on the bed and the net opening facing upstream. The user is free to use both hands to clean the stony substrate from upstream into the net, or the bed can be stirred with the feet in front of the net. Organisms and substrates are concentrated in the jar and the debris adhering to the sides of the net can be washed down into the jar.

Sorting Samples

Sorting aquatic samples is easiest in a white tray using a pipette (dropper) to extract the larvae. Aquatic mosses and macrophytes (larger plants) provide ideal conditions for dipterous larvae and although the numbers may be high, separation is not easy. Careful sorting of plant material is necessary teasing the strands apart to reveal the smaller Chironomidae especially *Cricotopus* and *Orthocladius*. Mud and fine sediments are also rich in larvae and similarly difficult to sort but the use of a series of sieves gives the best results, taking any single sieve to remove some of the sediments. The sample is placed in the sieve and agitated while the sieve is held partly immersed in water. The finer sediments are lost and hopefully the majority of the larvae retained, and these are now more readily visible in the sorting tray. The judicious use of a combination of different mesh sized sieves will permit extraction of all sizes of larvae.

When the larvae are collected live for rearing, care must be taken to prevent death from thermal stress for most aquatic larvae have a low lethal temperature, particularly marked in those from running water. The larvae should be collected into a thermos flask containing water at the same temperature as the source of the larvae. Care should be taken not to include any predatory species such as many of the Pediciini and Hexatomini (Tipulidae), Chaoboridae, Tanypodinae (Chironomidae), *Atherix* (Rhagionidae) or the larvae or adults of dytiscid beetles, since any of these can decimate a thermos flask of larvae in a short time.

Rearing Larvae

When rearing larvae with the intention of associating larvae and pupae with adults it is essential to rear each larva separately, one in each container, to prevent misassociation. Multiple rearing of larvae which look alike has led in the past to misassociations which still cause problems today in chironomid larval work. Many dipterous larvae are killed by low oxygen levels in the incubating medium. This may be caused by collecting too much vegetation in the thermos, which uses up the dissolved oxygen by respiring in the dark, or more commonly by the larva itself using the oxygen which is not replaced by diffusion from the atmosphere. This may be avoided by using 50 mm diameter, 12 mm deep petri dishes with a 5 mm depth of water in the bottom. This allows a relatively large surface area of water for gaseous exchange. However many larvae will develop with a good chance of success in a 50 by 12 mm diameter tube.

Simuliid larvae present a rearing problem because they are filter feeders which require a continuous current of water bringing particles through their fan-like mandibles. This can most easily be attained by the use of an air current from a pump, compressed air cylinder or, with ingenuity, from a running tap. This air current is directed through a nozzle placed just below the water surface close to the edge of the dish, causing a circular current of water in the dish.

With many of the smaller larvae including the orthocladiine Chironomidae, the Ceratopogonidae and the Psychodidae, the water from the site of collection is adequate for a rearing medium since it usually contains enough algae and detritus for the larval development. With the larger Chironomidae and Culicidae it may be necessary to add some substrate to the water they were collected in and a small amount of fish food can be added. Care must be taken not to add food to excess since this will develop a fungal film rapidly and can kill the larvae. The use of fungicides is not recommended although occasional use of chlorinated tap water has been observed to reduce the rate of fungal development, without any ill effects on the larvae. Where petri dishes are re-used it is important that they are sterilised before re-use.

Predaceous larvae present different problems. Most prey heavily upon chironomid larvae and these can be used as food, as can copepods and oligochaete worms. Outdoor domestic water bodies such as fish ponds, water butts and bird baths contain plenty of potential food for predaceous Diptera larvae.

Rearing Pupae

Most families of Nematocera with aquatic larvae have aquatic pupae and these should be left in the rearing vessel. If there is only one larva per vessel the larval skin can safely be left in the vessel until all three stages are removed. Cast larval skins are rapidly eaten by other larvae and many other aquatic creatures and the same applies to the pupal skin. Fungal or bacterial activity is much slower and the skins can be left for several days.

Simuliid pupae which darken with age should be removed when dark and placed on a piece of damp blotting paper in a tube to await the emergence of the adult. Among the Tipulidae, Tabanidae and at least *Odontomyia* in the Stratiomyidae the final instar larvae leave the aquatic habitat to pupate in drier conditions. If the larvae have been recognised as belonging to one of these groups they can be removed from a partitioned drier part of the rearing vessel (a mound of sand for example) to a separate tube to pupate.

Pupal development is essentially a much faster process than larval development, taking at most a week in the larger species and less than a day in some orthoclad Chironomidae. The emerged adult should be allowed a day if possible for the cuticle to harden. At the moment only Chironomidae, Chaoboridae, Dixidae Ceratopogonidae and Psychodidae should be collected in 80% alcohol or Berlese fluid; other adult Diptera should be pinned or pointed dry. If the adults are preserved in fluid all stages should be kept in the same tube, and if the adult is kept separately from the immature skins they should be unambiguously referable to each other.

Seasonal Collecting

The largest numbers and greatest diversity of aquatic insects emerge from late spring to autumn. Larval collections at this time of year will frequently contain large numbers of final instar larvae which are easy to rear and quick to emerge. Final instar larvae can be recognised by the developing pupal thoracic structures visible within the anterior larval cuticle giving rise to a swollen thoracic area. For obvious reasons most collecting is done in these warmer months and in all families our summer emerging species are better known. British collectors have tended to neglect the winter and early spring emerging species, a criticism not restricted to those working on freshwater Diptera. Winter collecting, even in lowland sites, has added numerous species to the British list of Chironomidae, particularly those species with either a boreo-alpine or arctic distribution in Europe. There is certainly scope for more 'unseasonal' collecting of both adults and immatures in Britain.

APPENDIX: Diptera with Aquatic Larvae

Since many Diptera breed in wet soils it is often difficult to draw a line between truly aquatic and aquatic transitional. Undoubtedly many undescribed dipterous larvae remain to be recorded during investigations of flowing and standing water. This list is based upon confirmed observations of larvae or on a reasonable interpretation of adult occurrence. There are substantial differences from the list of P.Maitland (1977, A Coded Check-list) which included a number of entirely terrestrial genera and, on this reassessment, made some omissions. Even now, a finite list is not possible.

Tipulidae: Many species live in wet soil and marshy seepages. Ground close to flowing and standing water tends to be rich in species but the larval habitat is often too vaguely known to specify whether certain species are normally, occasionally, or never occurring as aquatic larvae. Aquatic and sub-aquatic moss provides further options. The list includes species with known aquatic larvae and those with larvae found in aquatic marginal situations. The annotations are f = flowing water, s = standing water and m = aquatic or sub-aquatic moss.

Tipula (A.) maxima; T. (A.) fulvipennis; T. (A.) vittata, fs; *T. (S.) cheethami*, m; *T. (S.) rufina; T. (Y.) coerulescens*, f; *T. (Y.) couckei*, f; *T. (Y.) lateralis*, fs; *T. (Y.) marginata*, f; *T. (Y.) pruinosa*, s; *T. (Y.) solstitialis*, s; *Nephrotoma aculeata*, f; *Prionocera*, s; *Phalacrocera replicata*, m; *Triogma trisulcata*, m; *Antocha vitripennis*, f; *Elliptera omissa*, f; *Limonia (D.) didyma*, fm; *L. (D.) mitis* typical, f; *L. (D.) omissinervis*, f; *L. (D.) ventralis*, s; *Helius*, fs; *Pedicia (C.) littoralis*, f; *P. (C.) straminea*, f; *P. (L.) claripennis*, f; *P. (L.) lucidipennis*, f; *Pedicia* other sub-genera, fs; *Dicranota*, f; *Hexatoma*, f; *Limnophila (L.) punctata*, f; *L. (L.) pictipennis*, s; *L. (Phylidorea)*, s; *L. (Euphylidorea)*, s; *L. (B.) nemoralis*, fs; *L. (Eloeophila)*, f; *Dactylolabis transversa*, f; *Pilaria (P.) discicollis*, fs; *P. (P.) fuscipennis*, fs; *P. (N.) batava*, f; *P. (N.) filata*, f; *Gonomyia (Idiocera)*, f; *G. (Gonomyia)*, fs; *G. (P.) abbreviata*, f?; *Rhabdomastix*, f; *Lipsothrix*, fs; *Erioptera (T.) pilipes*, s; *E. (Erioptera)*, fs; *E. (I.) areolata*, f; *E. (I.) vicina*, f; *E. (M.) bivittata*, s; *Ormosia lineata*, f; *Molophilus pusillus*, f.

Psychodidae: Many of the species are abundant by streams and ditches. The larvae are most prevalent in wet leaf litter but some species may be classed as aquatic. **Ptychopteridae:** all species are aquatic, the larvae occurring in mud at the edge of water or very shallowly submerged. *Ptychoptera lacustris*, *P.longicauda* and *P.paludosa* are only found by flowing water, especially small streams. The others may be found at the edge of standing water or very sluggish flowing water. **Dixidae:** both *Dixa* and *Dixella* have aquatic larvae on the water meniscus. *Dixa* is associated with flowing water and most *Dixella* with standing water or sluggish streams. **Chaoboridae** and **Culicidae:** standing water is the habitat for all species. **Thaumaleidae:** flowing water is the sole habitat, including rock face seepages. **Ceratopogonidae:** many species are unknown in the early stages and even within the same genus there can be aquatic and non-aquatic species. In the Ceratopogoninae most are aquatic except the biting midges (Culicoidini) which mainly develop in sub-aquatic mud. Some Dasyheleinae are aquatic but others occur in rot holes or sap runs. Most Forcipomyiinae are terrestrial but there are some aquatic examples in *Atrichopogon*. Aquatic larvae are active and thread-like. **Chironomidae:** all are freshwater with the following exceptions, the marine genera *Thalassomya, Psamathiomya, Halocladius, Clunio* and *Thalassosmittia* and terrestrial groups, *Bryophaenocladius, Camptocladius* (dung), *Gymnometriocnemus, Mesosmittia, Pseudosmittia* (? except *recta*), *Smittia* (? except *contingens*).

Paraphaenocladius and *Pseudorthocladius* include some possibly semi-terrestrial species. **Simuliidae:** all species are confined to running water.

Stratiomyidae: Only the Clitellariinae (*Nemotelus, Oxycera, Vanoyia*) and Stratiomyiinae (*Odontomyia, Stratiomys*) are aquatic. **Rhagionidae:** *Atherix* and *Atrichops* larvae live in rivers and streams. **Tabanidae:** most larvae occur at the margins of still or sluggishly flowing water, in saturated soil but migrate to drier soil in the third instar. *Chrysops* and some *Hybomitra* are truly aquatic, the former in running water, the latter in standing water. **Empididae:** very few empid larvae are known. In the Hemerodromiinae there are strong associations with water in *Heleodromia, Chelifera* (especially flowing water) and *Hemerodromia*; in the Clinocerinae, *Clinocera* and *Wiedemannia* are aquatic. **Dolichopodidae:** though adults are often common by water, very few larvae have been described. There is no obvious grouping of genera or species which might be aquatic as larvae. Most of the genera of Dolichopodinae and Hydrophorinae are likely to contain some species which are truly aquatic; Aphrosylinae are marine littoral. Other genera which may be good candidates solely or in part are *Rhaphium, Syntormon, Argyra, Campsicnemus* and *Sympycnus*.

Syrphidae: aquatic species are largely limited to the Eristalini with rat-tailed maggot larvae structurally modified for aquatic life. *Myathropa* and *Mallota* are rot hole species considered under dead wood. Only *Chrysogaster* does not belong to this group; at least *C.hirtella* has the posterior spiracles adapted for piercing the air cavities of aquatic or sub-aquatic plants. The generic list is thus *Eristalis, Eristalinus, Helophilus, Anasimyia, Lejops, Parhelophilus* and *Chrysogaster*.

Ephydridae: this is one of the few families of acalypterates with aquatic larvae but though adults are often in high numbers at the margins of water, relatively few have truly aquatic larvae. Many species breed in wet mud; the separation between species living in wet mud as opposed to aquatic mud is not always simple. Some species are terrestrial. *Notiophila* is truly aquatic, plus ? *Dichaeta*. The Ephydrinae are wet mud and semi-aquatic species, this also being largely true of the Parydrinae. Certain *Hydrellia* are associated with aquatic plants, though not always below the water surface. The Gymnopini and Atissini breed in mud. The Discocerini are river bank species, probably breeding in terrestrial situations subject to flooding. *Clanoneurum* (a leaf miner of saltmarsh plants) and *Parydroptera* occur in sea shore habitats subject to flooding with salt water. *Psilopa* and *Discomyza* are terrestrial, as also may be *Trimerina* and the Philygriini. **Sciomyzidae:** many are aquatic, or live on emergent vegetation or in the transitional zone to marsh. Those with completely aquatic larvae are *Knutsonia, Sepedon, Elgiva, Dictya, Renocera striata*, some *Tetanocera* (see Chapter 5, Mollusca). **Scathophagidae:** the best known aquatic species are *Spaziphora hydromyzina* which can be abundant on sewage filter beds (also along lake shores) and *Hydromyza livens* which mines water lilies. **Muscidae:** most Limnophorinae (e.g. *Limnophora riparia, Lispe* spp.) are aquatic; many Coenosiinae probably develop in mud and some may be truly aquatic. *Phaonia mirabilis*, larvae in tree rot hole pools.

Chapter 4

Major Habitats

The approach in this Chapter is directed towards giving a general ecological introduction to major habitats rather than attempt to give an exhaustive review of the Diptera. Most of the major habitat types are here taken as very broad headings, each type subject to a great deal of variation both in character and geographical setting. Even were selected localities described, there would not be enough space to do justice since a typical fauna may run into many hundreds of species, and very few sites in Britain have received thorough survey. Only in the case of the seashore, where the fauna is small and fairly well defined, is it possible to attempt a reasonably comprehensive review but even here there must be many more species which have not come to attention. The main aim has been to give a general 'feel' for the approach to field studies. Thus the text has drawn in some of the ecological factors which are relevant to the dipterist, many of the more general points not being easily available for reference by the amateur entomologist.

Chapters 3, 5 and 6 consider a variety of minor habitats and the niches available through associations with other animals and plants. Considerable information relevant to the major habitats is within these chapters.

It is of interest to note that the two best studied localities in Britain have over 1100 recorded species though survey has by no means been fully exhaustive. These localities are Bookham Common, Surrey (clay woodland, grassland and ponds) and Leckford, N. Hants (fens, chalk grassland and poor woods). Other extensive surveys include Spurn Head, E. Yorks (coastal spit with dunes and saltmarsh); Ainsdale, Lancs (dunes); Holden Clough, Lancs (small valley); Malham, Yorks, (upland, with fens and lake); Rhum, Inner Hebrides (island with uplands); Moorhouse, N. Pennines (upland). The surveys for Leckford and Ainsdale are unpublished and the references below often do not include all currently recorded species. There are, of course, a larger number of partial surveys in various parts of Britain, but it cannot be emphasised too strongly that there is a need for a wider range of localities and habitat types to receive comprehensive survey as a base line of knowledge from which to view the information on lesser known sites.

Further Reading

Brindle, A., Bryce, D. and Henson H. In The Insects of the Malham Tarn Area *Leeds Phil. Lit. Soc.* (Scientific Section) **9** (2). 91pp.

Coulson, J.C., 1959. Observations on the Tipulidae (Diptera) of the Moor House nature reserve, Westmorland. *Trans. R. ent.Soc. Lond.* **III**: 157-174.

Hincks, W.D., 1953. The Entomology of Spurn Head, XII Diptera. *Naturalist* (reprint): 159-169.

Kidd, L.N., 1971. In *Holden Clough*, Oldham Public Libaries, 199 pp.

Nelson, J.M., 1971. The invertebrates of an area of Pennine moorland within the Moor-house nature reserve in northern England. *Trans Soc. Brit.Ent.* **19**: 173-235.

Parmenter, L., 1950, 1960, 1966. The Diptera of Bookham Common. *Lond. Nat.* **29**: 98-133, **39**: 66-76, **45**: 56-59.

Steel, W.O. & Woodroffe, G.E. (eds.) 1969. The Entomology of the Isle of Rhum National Nature Reserve. *Trans. Soc. Brit. Ent.* **18** (6): 91-167.

UPLANDS AND MOORLANDS
by Dr. Henry Disney and Alan E.Stubbs

The definition of uplands is not too precise. A useful concept was that they are areas of land rising above 1000 ft (305 m) but a recent conference adopted 800 ft as the critical limit in order to accord with the EEC definition of 'less favoured areas'. These definitions have in common the notion that there is ecological significance to an altitude at which growing conditions for plants become rather hostile, above which forests do not flourish and agriculture is restricted to hill pasture grazing.

The western and northern parts of Britain, including the Pennines, contain extensive areas of uplands whilst the high ground of the Cotswolds and the Downs of the south-east Britain keeps (with minor exceptions) conveniently below the arbitrary 1000 ft. However, it is important to appreciate that even in upland areas there are extensive lowland situations such as along valleys. Also the tree line, which is often very ill defined, is much lower in areas such as north Scotland than in the south because climate rather that altitude is the main limiting factor.

The term moorland is readily understood but is difficult to define. Usually it is an upland habitat, ideally with areas of heather and bog. The lowland equivalent is defined as heathland but it becomes very difficult to sustain a clear distinction in western and northern districts where moorland may come right down to the coast in the absence of any heathland belt. Essentially moorland is an area of heath with higher rainfall and a bleaker climate. Moorland is simply a type of upland vegetation, indicative of acid and usually peaty soils. Other upland vegetation types include upland grassland, bracken and species rich limestone communities.

Uplands are very demanding areas for the existence of insects. The climate is often severe and unpredictable. Rainfall is often high, but this factor is aggravated by the hours of mists, drizzle and light rain. Thus the proportion of rainfall hours is high relative to the quantity of rain compared with a lowland area. However, there can be long periods when the wind has a strong drying effect. The temperature is low, periods of snow and frost are long and the hours of sunshine often reduced. However, it is important to appreciate that very marked differences in climate can occur even within a single area of uplands. For instance the north and south sides of a mountain may have different climate and warmer conditions are likely to rise higher up a mountain on the south side. Also the rainfall may vary with aspect to the prevailing wind. Sheltered areas may reach very high temperatures on a good sunny day out of the wind, contrasting markedly with exposed situations.

The soil type and geology can have a very marked effect on vegetation and on the degree of waterlogging. Limestone areas are likely to contain a very different flora from acid terrain or peaty moorland.

Wide areas of the uplands can be poor in Diptera so it is essential to learn to recognise the spots with greatest potential. Thus the worst areas are uniform areas of grassland on well drained and relatively dry ground. The ideal sheep grazing hill land is often poor. Extensive stands of bracken are also a poor omen. Bleak featureless hills with no shelter hold few moorland and upland Diptera. The main problem is that an apparently uninteresting piece of hillside as seen from a distance may prove to have extremely good habitat once one is on the ground. The best ground for Diptera is likely to be that with a mosaic of vegetation types including boggy areas and streams, sheltered hollows being an additional advantage. Using a map it is easy to see where the streams run and there may be symbols indicating boggy ground. The contours on a map give a lead in recognising relatively sheltered terrain. A scan with binoculars may reveal a mosaic of vegetation and it may be possible to spot small ravines with bushes. The best general ploy in the uplands is to follow a stream or head for vegetation types which indicate boggy ground. If you are on the windy side of a hill, every advantage should be taken of even the smallest physical features which may provide shelter. If there is a strong wind it may still be possible to find plenty of Diptera by searching among vegetation and along the edges of peat hags and stream banks with a pooter and specimen tubes (such edges can be swept even when conditions are wet). However, under favourable conditions sweeping is the best all purpose collecting method.

Habitat Features

It should first be mentioned that the richest collecting in the uplands tends to be in the lowland valleys. The available habitat of course varies with the district but it is important to realise that many of the flies in Britain with a northern and western 'upland' distribution are in fact confined to the valleys where the climate and flora have characteristics not normally found in the more extensive lowland belts. The climate in some of the valleys can be surprisingly warm and the sunshine hours may be high in contrast to the surrounding hills. There are strong anomalies such as the species which occur on the lowland heaths of southern England and in the Spey Valley of the Scottish Highlands. The syrphid *Microdon eggeri* is an example with such disjunct distribution. Where the low ground abounds in flowers, there is often a rich syrphid fauna, including such species as *Eristalis rupium*.

The true upland habitat has a great variety of special features. Seepages are especially worthy of attention, either with associated acid bog vegetation or in particular as flushes where base rich conditions favour a diverse flora. Both acid and basic seepages support a rich fauna including many tipulids and among the special members of the base rich flushes are the sciomyzids *Dictya umbrarum* and *Renocera striata*, the otitid *Herina frondescentie* and the stratiomyid *Oxycera pygmaea*. Moorland bog may have plenty of small pools which support a good fauna and, if *Carex* is plentiful, this may yield various *Cordilura* species and *Pogonota barbata* (Scathophagidae) especially in Scotland. With both seepage areas and moorland, patches of *Juncus effusus* usually indicate areas worth sweeping. Streamsides are particularly productive.

Drier habitat types have features of interest but these tend to be of a specialised nature. The limestone pavement of the Malham and Ingleborough area may well include an interesting fauna breeding in fissures but this has yet to be studied.

However, the larvae of the ceratopogonid *Dasyhelea lithotelmatica* are often abundant in water filled solution hollows on the bare limestone surfaces. Screes with some vegetation may provide especially dry well drained soils and this would seem to explain the local occurrences of the cranefly *Tipula cava* (which is most at home on lowland heath). High level crags have yet to be recorded in detail but there ought to be some interesting species, especially where limestone provides a rich flora with plenty of flowers. The more exposed high ground has some specialities, such as *Tipula montana* on stony grassland in July and mountain and hill tops frequently act as an assembly point for various Diptera which come from other habitats, either blown by the wind or possibly using the hill top as a swarm marker. There are some strange habitat associations, such as the lowland wood edge *Tipula varipennis* occurring above 600 m on limestone grassland in the north Pennines.

Faunal Features

The fauna of upland areas above 305 m is particularly rich in Nematocera, as one might expect in high rainfall areas. Many of the families in other sub-orders are scarce or absent, in particular those with a predominant requirement for woodland (e.g. Clusiidae) or lowland marsh (most Micropezidae). Also Syrphidae have few species, for predictable reasons such as reduced amounts of sunshine, few aphids and lack of woodland. Other warmth requiring groups such as Asilidae are not found at a high level. One possible surprise is the scarcity of Tachinidae yet Lepidoptera larvae are common by comparison even if the species diversity is low. One of the most dominant groups, however, are the Anthomyiidae both at low and high levels in the uplands.

The seasonal pattern in the uplands holds the key to success in field work. Even at 750 m in the northern Pennines, the first peak of activity begins in mid May, exemplified by the large numbers of Tipulidae and other Nematocera. The exact time obviously depends on the degree of advance in the season for the district concerned, but the point is that a great deal will be missed if one is not onto the hills as soon as the weather allows in May. *Tipula subnodicornis* and *Molophilus ater* for instance are rarely recorded later than early June. There is still plenty to find right through the summer, though tipulids are sparse, but another peak comes surprisingly late for uplands, in October. Again Tipulidae and other Nematocera are important components of the fauna.

Uplands and moorlands are particularly rich, in fact infamous, for their biting Ceratopogonidae. When the conditions are right *Culicoides* can spoil an otherwise perfect evening. *C.impunctatus* is probably the most frequent species caught biting man, but many species can be collected. The Ceratopogonidae are well represented in upland areas by other genera. The striking predatory *Serromyia* is readily swept from moorland vegetation. Chironomidae and many other Nematocera abound in upland areas, where the prevalence of small pools and streams are a reflection of the damp climate. Emergence traps and water traps are useful means of collecting. Bibionidae occur in large populations in grasslands. Sciaridae are an important but neglected family in moorland habitats. Spring trickles are characterised by Thaumaleidae. Mycetophilidae are few in species, but *Boletina gripha* may be very numerous and some species are apparently peculiar to this habitat (e.g. *Mycomya clavigera, M.lambi*); at higher altitudes several *Exechia* spp. and some *Macrocera* (e.g. *aterrima* and a 'variety' of *pava*) predominate, while the large *Gnoriste longirostris* has only been collected once on a high crag in Scotland. Among Brachycera some northern species of Empididae and Dolichopodidae are frequent in upland areas. The two common *Haematopota* and locally *Hybomitra montana* add to the variety of the biting flies. The grey rhagionid *Symphoromyia crassicornis* is often numerous amongst low vegetation in flushes while *Rhagio* spp. such as *notatus* may be seen basking on stones when the sun breaks through. The Aschiza are poor in species. The Platypezidae and Pipunculidae are virtually absent (except in the valleys). The Syrphidae may include a number of strays, especially the most ubiquitous species of Syrphinae. *Sericomyia* spp. are characteristic of moorland where the larvae breed in boggy pools. *Cheilosia sahlbergi* would seem to be generally found above 600 m on mountain flowers. *Melanostoma* include *M.dubium* (details in press, Speight). *Parapenium flavitarsis* males have been found swarming over bare soil at 400 m. For hoverflies the main strategy is to seek out spots with flowers in a moderately sheltered postion. Yellow tormentil, *Potentilla erecta*, is widespread on acid ground and attracts the small species and *Succisa pratensis* is suitable for *Sericomyia* and *Arctophila*. Little is recorded on flower visiting on the more specialist mountain flora where Anthomyiidae are probably among the most important pollinators, being indifferent to all but the worst weather.

Plenty of Cyclorrhapha are to be found in upland and moorland habitats. Phoridae abound, *Phora* spp. being the most likely to be noticed as the males may use people as a swarm marker. Sphaeroceridae occur in considerable variety and often in vast populations. The abundant Ephydridae are mostly *Hydrellia*, particularly *H.modesta*; some other genera are frequently swept in October. Chloropidae are well represented by *Oscinella* spp., which are frequent at flowers of yellow Compositae. Blowflies and Scathophagidae are well represented; in grazed areas dung flies are very numerous and the determined collector is likely to turn up some of the boreal species of *Scathophaga* and *Calliphora*; some other northern Scathophogidae (e.g. *Microprosopa, Ernoneura*) occur locally in Scotland. Muscidae,

With the afforestation now occurring in our uplands we are likely to witness an increase in the variety of Diptera. Mycetophilidae certainly benefit as well as numerous acalypterates such as the Lauxaniidae. With close packed conifers the shading out of the ground vegetation reduces elements of the Diptera fauna but the edge of plantations are often particularly worth searching. Recently there has been a greater readiness to plant broad-leafed trees around conifers and up gills running through conifer plantations. These mixed-woodland banks of gills are particularly rich hunting grounds for the dipterist. In young plantations the ungrazed tussock-grass vegetation is well worth searching with a pooter, working into the litter layer.

Pitfall traps and water traps are highly successful in upland and moorland habitats, where they are not going to be disturbed by livestock. For Nematocera, Phoridae, Drosophilidae and other families where wet specimens are acceptable these two techniques are particularly commended.

Acknowledgement

Dr. J.C.Coulson has commented on a draft.

LOWLAND HEATHLAND
by Alan E.Stubbs

In the south-eastern half of England there used to be extensive tracts of dry heath on well drained sandy soils and wet heath and bogs on related waterlogged soils. Much or all of the heathland had been maintained through thousands of years of improverishment by man's grazing and burning which encouraged a special fauna adapted to poor soils and hot sunny open conditions. Much of this country has been lost or reduced in value through destruction for agriculture and building, planting with pine forests, natural invasion by trees or by devastating uncontrolled fires; the bogs become drained. It is now an increasingly scarce habitat and much of the finest area has been lost, e.g. beneath the Bournemouth and Poole conurbation. In general the richest areas are those in the south – the Dorset heaths, New Forest, the Weald and north-east Surrey, whilst further blocks of heath remain in the Breck and other parts of East Anglia.

Lowland Heath merges into moorland in upland areas, as for instance around the edges of Dartmoor. There are also coastal heaths of rather different character again. Through the Midlands and the coastal belt of Wales there is a variety of lowland heath situations. The further north one goes the more difficult it is to maintain a clear distinction between upland and lowland heath.

This section describes the hot sunny heaths of the south-east of Britain, thus complementing the section on moorland. For intermediate situations, one will need to refer to both accounts.

Dry Heath

This habitat is confined to acidic sandy soils, either derived from the sandy rock beneath or, as is often the case in East Anglia, from superficial deposits lying on top of the solid rock. Dry heath is often characterised by stands of pure *Calluna* (a type of heather) with little humic soil beneath. Sometimes another heather, *Erica cinerea*, is also present and gorse (*Ulex*) may occur. Though such simple vegetation communities contain a very rich invertebrate fauna, Diptera are relatively scarce since few are adapted to breeding in dry soils with sparse dry litter. Many of the Diptera come in from other habitats where they breed or they are parasites or make use of secondary habitats such as dung.

It is necessary to recognise two very important components of the habitat which contribute enormously to the richness of a heath. Firstly, bare sandy ground along paths, in sand pits and on sparsely vegetated ground is essential for the occurrence of a variety of Diptera which enjoy sitting on the sand despite its intense heat in the sun. Secondly, it is often difficult to distinguish species which really require fringes of trees and clumps of bushes for their occurrence.

The most interesting component of the dry heath fauna is that of bare sand. This is the ground for a bombyliid with boldly marked wings, *Thyridanthrax*, as well as asilids including *Lasiopogon, Epitriptus, Eutolmus* and, in a few localities, *Asilus*. Where solitary bees and wasps are in evidence, parasitic calypterates are usually sitting camouflaged near burrows - e.g. *Metopia, Miltogramma, Leucophora*. This is also conopid country. Our largest species, *Conops vesicularis*, is confined to dry heath and is best found in May or June. Some *Myopa* such as *M.testacea* are also heathland insects, the latter being found flying along paths. Other parasites include many tachinids, of which the very common reddish mottled *Linnaemya vulpina* sits well camouflaged on heather shoots and our largest species *Tachina grossa* flies around like a large black bumble bee. The hoverfly *Microdon* has larvae which live in ant's nests and though all three species have been recorded on heathland, it is *M.eggeri* which is characteristic of Surrey heaths. This requires dry open heath with old birch or pine stumps and logs infested with the common black ant *Lasius niger*; puparia may be found under loose bark in ant galleries in the spring.

A few Diptera have soil dwelling larvae on heaths. Though a moisture-loving group, surprisingly craneflies live in even the driest situations. *Nephrotoma scurra* and *Tipula cava* occur as adults in the full heat of July and it is probable that the Sussex rarity *N.sullingtonensis* requires the same habitat. Though the first two species can occur on open heath, they are easiest to find by sweeping bush foliage. On a few occasions *Limonia dilutior* has been found associated with gorse, including *Ulex minor*.

When the heather is in flower, large numbers of hoverflies come to feed. Many of these probably do not breed on the dry heath but have been attracted from nearby habitats. Some species may yet be shown to specialise in heath, such as *Sphaerophoria philanthus* and *S.rueppellii*. Others, such as *Paragus*, are found along sandy tracks where yellow tormentil flowers are available. Sweeping heather usually yields a wide variety of Diptera, even in winter. *Sepsis cynipsea* is often abundant, possibly having bred in dung, and *Scathophaga stercoraria* likewise. *Tephritis* species are often to be found throughout the winter on mild days, having bred in composite flowers on the margin of the heath.

Dry heath may include grass heath which is considered under Lowland Grassland. Here one may note that dry *Molinia* and *Agrostis setacea* heath are very poor for Diptera.

Wet Heath and Bog

A peaty soil contrasts markedly with dry heath situations. Wet heath lives up to its name during the winter, though in dry summers it is less recognisable since *Calluna* may continue to be conspicuous. Wet heath is perhaps most easily characterised by the cross-leaved heather, *Erica tetralix* (and on the Dorset heaths by *E.ciliata*). A much greater variety of plants may be present including *Juncus squarrosus*. Bare peat surfaces or a thin carpet of *Sphagnum* moss may be visible between these plants.

Wet heath may grade into bog, in the south-east usually valley bog. Here water-logged conditions are associated with a build up of thick peat which is squashy or even quaking underfoot. If you are not used to bogs, or do not know the locality well, considerable care is necessary so as not to get stuck or worse. *Sphagnum* moss is often a dominant component of bogs but other plants are generally also present and small pools may occur within the main body of a bog. Many valley bogs include areas which have advanced in succession to be covered by bushes, especially of sallow, but also birch. Such wet woodland, which is often swampy, is termed carr.

Wet heath is a good place for craneflies early and late in the year. *Tipula subnodicornis* and *Molophilus ater* occur locally in April whilst in September and October *T.melanoceros* and *T.luteipennis* may be found. This is good ground for many small flies, including *Hydrophorus nebulosus* which may be swept from wet bare peat, especially where there is a slight mat of reddish algae.

Bog is so variable that it is difficult to generalise. Craneflies include *Limnophila meigeni* and *Erioptera nielseni*. The ephydrid *Ochthera mantis* with its mantis-like front legs is especially distinctive. Small pools may have a variety of adults, including the dolichopodid Hydrophorus bimaculatus, on the surface. Surprisingly even sciomyzids can occur where acidity is not too great, *Hydromya dorsalis* and *Knutsonia lineata* being among the more frequent one. Hoverflies include *Sericomyia* and the tabanid *Atylotus fulvus* may occur locally.

Carr is extremely rich in Diptera and is an essential collecting area for virtually any group of flies. Certainly it is especially rich in Tipulidae, Mycetophilidae and many groups of acalypterates. Wet grass heath, as dominated by *Molinia*, is poor in Diptera but is better where covered by carr. Rushes, especially *Juncus effusus* and *J. acutiflorus* are usually indicators of good spots for sweeping.

Heath Woodland

Many heaths merge into woodland, especially around the margins. Birch and pine woodland are considered under Woodland. Here it is only necessary to note that these woods can be rich in Diptera especially where there is a good herbaceous layer, even bracken. One must particularly emphasise the rich mycetophilid fauna associated with the profusion of fungi which can occur in heath woodland. Isolated bushes, especially the dense regrowth after fire, often yield a rich fauna, particularly of empids, by sweeping foliage.

Heath Verge

This term is adopted here to describe the habitats frequently found round the edge of a heath, or in a sand pit, which do not represent true heath or heath woodland. In some respects one might speak of grass heath, but often there is a wide mixture of plants, with flowers attractive to insects, which in origin include roadside and wasteland casuals as far as heathland flora is concerned. Generally the soil is much richer than on the heath proper. Wood edge situations are usually present. This is a rich area for Diptera, in part because of the transition of habitat types but also because of flowers which at some seasons provide the only nectar source for hoverflies and other flower visitors.

The grassland is worth sweeping for asilids such as *Dioctria atricapilla* and *Dysmachus trigonus*. Because this is usually attractive ground for bees and wasps, in association with the flowers, conopids are often also present and bare sandy paths with aculeate burrows will have their attendant flies. Acalypterates usually abound, including tephritids associated with composite seed heads and distinctive species such as *Lauxania cylindricornis* are best found by sweeping. Tachinids are often plentiful because of the range of Lepidoptera larvae available.

General

Many heathland localities contain a complex of very varied habitat and in consequence provide very rich collecting including streams, ponds and lakes which have not been considered in this section. In March and April one would search sallow blossom in the carr and along the verge areas as well as sweeping dry heath for the overwintering fauna. In April the wet heath sees the emergence of an interesting fauna. By mid-May all habitats except dry heath are very productive, continuing into June. July is still generally productive, especially for the dry heath fauna of bare sand. August may still be good for bee and wasp parasites, hoverflies are often abundant on heather flowers and *Nephrotoma scurra* will still be found. However, apart from the fact that *Asilus* is late and continues into September, late summer and early autumn is overall a difficult period. October sees another flourish of activity in wet and wooded localities, especially for Nematocera and acalypterates but dry heath is poor apart from the possibility of *Limonia dilutior* about gorse. Right through from November to March mild periods are still collectable, especially late autumn for fungus gnats in wooded heath.

LOWLAND GRASSLAND
by John Ismay

At the present time much of Britain is covered in grassland. This situation is mainly due to human activities, since the natural climax vegetation of lowland Britain is forest. Besides clearing forests, man has planted large areas for pasture and his grazing animals have turned forest to grassland by preventing regeneration of trees.

The character of grassland is greatly influenced by the underlying geology. Chalk and limestone grassland is usually well drained and has its own characteristic and often diverse flora and fauna. Acid grassland, as on sand and gravel, may be well drained but usually has a poorer flora. Grasslands on clay vary between drained or poorly drained, and depending on the amount and seasonality of rainfall, they may be seasonally dry or marshy; the flora varies in diversity, but is especially rich on calcareous clays. Thus grassland is a very varied habitat, and quite small areas may have an interesting fauna.

The richest grassland is so called semi-natural grassland or unimproved pasture. This means that apart from grazing, the land has not been disturbed for perhaps hundreds or even thousands of years. The flora, and fauna associated with it, has consequently had a long time to colonise and develop. Such areas can be particularly rich for Diptera but are becoming scarce as modern agriculture demands a higher productivity of the land. Even steep slopes can be ploughed, new seed mixtures oust the native plants and the application of herbicides and fertilisers eliminate much of the diversity of the flora. A meadow of monotonous grass is of little value to the entomologist compared with the former meadows rich in flowers, although some of the agriculturally important species of Chloropidae may be abundant eg. *Chlorops pumilionis.*

However, even where the semi-natural grassland has not been interfered with, the habitat can be lost or impoverished. Commons and downs which once were grazed by sheep often remained in good condition since, when sheep husbandry became less frequent, rabbits were able to continue the grazing. However, when myxomatosis virtually wiped out rabbits in the 1950's and 1960's, the artificial habitat started to revert to scrub and then woodland. Even where the scrub and trees did not invade, the coarse grasses tended to smother the weaker plants. Thus in recent years many of our grasslands have seen a fundamental change in character but the precise effect on the Diptera fauna was not recorded and there is little background documentation which will allow assessment of the degree of recovery of the fly fauna, relative to the recovery of the flora, once grazing is reintroduced.

It will be seen that despite the apparent structural simplicity, grassland is a fairly dynamic habitat and it offers plenty of scope for study. The richest areas would seem to be those with long grass and other herbage, which offers maximum structural diversity. The areas poorest for Diptera are very short closely grazed turf which provides little shelter, though a few species thrive under such conditions. A mosaic of short and long turf is ideal but not always easy to find or maintain, though trampled areas often provide short grassland. Open grassland can be very poor in Diptera on a windy day. Usually the richest areas will be found in the lee of bushes and hedges. On steep hillsides it is often the bottom of the slope which is richest, especially if there is a hedge providing shelter, and such areas generally have a moister and richer soil.

Dry grassland (calcareous and neutral)

There is a strong difference between calcareous and neutral grassland but space does not allow detailed discussion of this subject. The early part of the season is best, especially May and June.

Tipulids are few but characteristic, especially *Nephrotoma appendiculata* and *Tipula vernalis* in May and early June, *N.flavescens* in July and *Tipula paludosa* (avoiding driest grassland) in late August and September. The smaller species are largely confined to hedges and scrub margins, such as *Limonia sericata* and *Limonia mitis* form *lutea*, both of calcareous areas in May. Other Nematocera include a succession of Bibionidae through the season, the large *Bibio marci* being out in May; the non-biting Ceratopogonidae include several species, Cecidomyiidae are often plentiful and there are generally Sciaridae and Scatopsidae to be found. The Brachycera are well represented by Empididae, especially around bushes in May and June; various Dolichopodidae such as *Chrysotus; Tabanus glaucopis* (locally on chalk), *Rhagio scolopaceus* and *R.lineolus* near trees; *Epitriptus cingulatus, Machimus atricapillus, Leptarthrus brevirostris* (calcareous), *Leptogaster, Dioctria atricapilla* (Asilidae); *Thereva* around hedgerows, bramble patches, etc. (Therevidae); Acroceridae; *Bombylius major* (Bombyliidae). Of the Aschiza, *Lonchoptera*, Phoridae and Pipunculidae are typically present and, of course, this is good ground for Syrphidae especially if flowers are plentiful. Among the latter group are *Melanostoma*, some *Platycheirus*, *Cheilosia* and *Microdon devius* (on chalk) but many others are attracted to the flowers from other habitats.

The Conopidae include the small black species *Thecophora atra* and *Zodion cinereum*, which are best found by sweeping, as well as *Conops*, *Physocephala rufipes* and *Sicus ferrugineus*. Acalypterates are numerous. Good tephritid plants such as composites often abound, and the rich flora supports many Opomyzidae, Agromyzidae and Chloropidae. Some other characteristic species are *Herina germinationis*, *Dorycera graminum*, (Otitidae), *Micropeza corrigiolata* (Micropezidae), many Chamaemyiidae; *Minettia rivosa*, *Calliopum aeneum* (Lauxaniidae), *Sepsis* (Sepsidae); *Pherbellia cinerella*, *Coremacera tristis*, *Dichetophora obliterata*, *Limnia unguicornis*, *Trypetoptera punctulata* (Sciomyzidae), *Discomyza incurva*, *Psilopa nitidula* (Ephydridae) and many Calypterates.

Acid Grassland

This has a very different fauna although some of the species considered above do occur. The early part of the season is again best, which is not surprising since in a hot summer the vegetation can become rapidly parched. The more resistant grasses, such as *Molinia* and *Agrostis setacea* provide poor collecting compared with the taller *Agrostis* species and areas of mixed vegetation. Among the characteristic species are the asilid *Dysmachus trigonus* and the lauxaniid *Lauxania cylindricornis*. This habitat often occurs on lowland heathland.

Wet Grassland

This grades into marsh. However, it is sufficient to note that wet meadows with lush grasses and other herbage provide very rich collecting for Diptera. Also the families considered above are represented, but the Brachycera are usually more diverse especially in Stratiomyidae, Rhagionidae and Tabanidae whilst Asilidae and Therevidae are virtually absent. Damp, lush grassland dominated by such grasses as *Deschampsia* or *Dactylis* and with a high floral diversity is often rich in the more moisture dependent groups such as Sciomyzidae and Brachycera. Flowers are visited by a range of syrphids - *Cheilosia* and *Helophilus*, and the aphidivorous species including *Platycheirus*, *Melanostoma* and *Pyrophaena*.

Grass Tussocks

There are many species of Diptera associated with grasses, sedges and rushes which are not readily taken by sweeping. Searching with a pooter may be the only way to locate these, and one of the best microhabitats is large tussocks such as occur in old, especially damp, pasture, or fen or dune slacks may be productive. After selecting a suitable tussock, divide it down the middle to the level of the roots. Press down both sides lightly so that the grass is compressed slightly but not compacted. The slight pressure seems to encourage insects to leave, but if there is too much compaction they may be unable to escape. Take care that spiders do not get into your pooter; they kill and damage most the Diptera and cover the rest with silk making them useless as specimens. Large tussocks may be dissected and the pieces shaken over a sheet. This method works well for flightless species. Always put the tussock back together when you have finished, to conserve the habitat. You may know a specialist on bugs or beetles who uses similar techniques, and it would be worthwhile exchanging specimens.

The Diptera found in tussocks comprise some species that live and breed there and many more which only overwinter or shelter. Tussocks will yield Diptera at any time of the year - many are as abundant in winter as in summer; it is much warmer inside a tussock than outside.

General

Most species of grassland Diptera can be caught by sweeping. Although Diptera can be found in grassland throughout the year, the most productive time is early summer (May - e.July) when most flowers and grasses are in bloom. There is a second peak of emergence of some species in the autumn. In prolonged drought the numbers of Diptera drop, but even naturally arid areas are well worth sweeping since some otherwise uncommon species e.g. *Trixoscelis* sp. (Heleomyzidae) may turn up.

In late summer sweeping is made difficult by the large quantity of grass seeds that are netted, but if you spread these out over the bottom of the net most of the Diptera will crawl out, and they can be pooted as they walk up the sides of the net. Where field voles have constructed runs through the grass, Sphaeroceridae may be found, including the short-winged *Leptocera fenestralis* v.*nivalis*; the small piles of droppings and cut grass left by the voles are particularly attractive to Diptera.

MARSHES AND FENS
by Peter Chandler and John Ismay

Marshes and fens occur where a high water table creates waterlogged ground for at least part of the year. There may be marsh at the transition between open water and higher ground, on areas kept wet by ground water seepage, in an area where a river floods or in a hollow. The level of the water table of marshes and fens varies considerably. Where fed by a spring or seepages the water table may be constant and such sites remain productive even in droughts. Those marshes associated with rivers and lakes usually dry out to some extent during periods when the main water body decreases but they rarely dry up completely and if you find a small wet patch in a dry marsh many Diptera may be congregated there. During floods, conditions can be productive, if some vegetation is left exposed on which Diptera assemble. Flood refuse is often rich in Diptera, including larvae, but remember that many species have been washed out of their natural microhabitat. In wet periods fens can be treacherous, especially those by tidal rivers.

Marshes and fens are very variable in nature but are often characterised by strong lush growth of vegetation in contrast to the demanding conditions in a bog. A bog is in effect an acid marsh and at the other extreme there is a fen which is a base rich marsh. Both bog and fen are on peat since the conditions enable plant debris to build up faster than it can decay. The term marsh may be used for areas where mineral soils are present, with or without some intermixture of peat, and the pH is generally more neutral. Wetland is a non-committal term also embracing any open water that may be present.

Fens are of restricted distribution, some of the best being in East Anglia (the Norfolk Broads, Wicken, Woodwalton) the Test and Itchen valleys in Hampshire and in Anglesey and the Lleyn Peninsula of North Wales, but small examples are present in many parts of the country. Marshes are more widespread. Both fens and marshes are under intense threat from agricultural reclamation and today we see only a fraction of what formerly existed. On many reclaimed marshes and fens the fauna and flora is largely restricted to drainage channels which have been dug across them. These can provide productive collecting where a good growth of emergent and marginal vegetation supports a diverse flora with plenty of flowers ('improved', deep, vegetation free ditches are rarely worthwhile). Areas with open muddy edges, as where cattle trample, can add further to the opportunities for finding a wide range of flies.

As in other habitats, marshland and fenland is dynamic. Open water becomes invaded by rafts of floating vegetation which together with the build up of litter and silt deposition, leads to the creation of new fen. Fen may be invaded by sallow or alder scrub leading to wet woodland (carr), or if the water table is lowered, scrub is able to invade as a precursor to woodland.

Like other wetlands, marshes and fens are particularly susceptible to pollution. High levels of organic pollution reduce the diversity of Diptera, but some species thrive in this situation like *Themira putris* (Sepsidae) and some sphaerocerids and ephydrids.

General aspects of the Fauna

The dipterous fauna of wetlands is dominated by species with larvae living in still or slow moving water or muck and the phytophagous types developing in marsh plants. Nematocera are often dominant since so many species breed in water or at the aquatic transition but they become more obvious in the evening when they are less "shy" in these open habitats. Chironomidae and Tipulidae, especially *Limnophila* and Eriopterinae, may be abundant. Biting species, both *Culicoides* and mosquitoes (including *Aedes* species and sometimes *Anopheles maculipennis*) may be prolific. Bibionids, e.g. *Dilophus febrilis* and some common *Bibio* species, may be abundant in the spring; *B.clavipes* (and its variety *lepidus*) appears in autumn. *Ptychoptera* species occur on the vegetation bordering ditches in which the larvae develop.

Stratiomyidae provide an attractive element to the marsh fauna, both some with terrestrial larvae (*Microchrysa, Chloromyia*) and those which develop in shallow water. *Nemotelus* (*pantherinus, nigrinus*) and *Odontomyia* (especially *viridula*) may be seen on flowers of Compositae at ditch margins. Several *Oxycera* species, *Vanoyia* and *Stratiomys potamida* may occur less frequently. The rhagionid *Chrysopilus cristatus* is often abundant and *Rhagio scolopaceus* occurs although it prefers trees to settle on in the vicinity. Sometimes large numbers of freshly emerged *Haematopota* and *Chrysops* (*relictus*, less often *viduatus*) including males are observed; larger Tabanidae are seen less often although *Hybomitra bimaculata* and *Tabanus autumnalis* occur locally in marshy areas.

Aphidivorous Syrphidae are not well represented except by several *Platychirus* (e.g. *fulviventris, scambus*). Species of *Anasimyia, Parhelophilus* and *Eristalinus sepulchralis*, which have aquatic larvae, are best sought in marshes. *Eristalis intricarius* is also usually seen on waterside flowers. Marshes are often good for Pipunculidae, which may be located hovering amongst rank vegetation.

Some cursorial Empididae (e.g. *Platypalpus cursitans* and *Tachydromia*) may be found running over marsh vegetation. Swarms of *Hilara* occur wherever shallow water is present. *Lonchoptera lutea* is generally abundant while *L.scutellata* occurs locally. Many Dolichopodidae (e.g. *Dolichopus picipes, Argyra vestita* and several *Rhaphium*) and small acalypterates are obtained by sweeping. Chloropidae, Ephydridae (e.g. *Notiphila, Hydrellia*), Anthomyzidae and Chamaemyiidae may be abundant. *Asteia concinna* (Asteiidae) is found mainly on coastal marshes. *Melieria crassipennis, Ceroxys urticae, Herina frondesceniae* and locally *H.lugubris* may be conspicuously wing waving on marsh vegetation. Several Sciomyzidae, such as *Pherbina* and *Knutsonia albiseta* are common and in fens *Psacadina* species sometimes occur. The stilt-legged *Micropeza corrigiolota* and some *Calobata* species (commonly *cibaria*, more locally *ephippium* or *sellata*) (Micropezidae) may be seen on broad leaves.

Calypterates are not usually very obvious in open marsh but this habitat can be rich in the small predatory Coenosiinae (e.g. *Spanochaeta dorsalis, Coenosia pumila, C.sexnotata*). *Melanomya nana* is common, running on coarse herbage and larger species include *Nyctia halterata, Pollenia vespillo* and the anthomyiids *Hydrophoria divisa* and *H.ambigua*.

Reedbeds and other vegetation types

The main expanses of marsh and fen vegetation offer the richest collecting if either there is a diversity of different communities including many plants which support phytophagous Diptera or if there is a good representation of a high quality community. The best areas are those with the lushest vegetation and greatest floral diversity including a variety of flowers attractive to flies. Lush vegetation normally coincides with moist or wet ground and provides ideal conditions for flies which require moist soil in their early stages. As in all open habitats shelter is an important factor for Diptera; a hedge, tall vegetation along a path or carr edge may have a richer fauna than the open marsh or fen - at least larger flies are more prevalent there. Sweeping and collecting off flowers are the most productive collecting methods but it is important to appreciate that many species, especially small acalypterates, have secretive habits so that tussocking and rummaging deep within vegetation is necessary to gain a representative species list.

A large stand of the common reed (*Phragmites*) is both difficult to collect in and unproductive except at the margins, but this plant supports a small but characteristic dipterous fauna including the chloropid genus *Lipara*. The common *L.lucens* forms galls also inhabited by the early stages of *Calamoncosis minima* and *Cryptonevra flavitarsis* (Chloropidae), *Anthomyza collini*, several Cecidomyiidae and the predatory scathophagid *Cleigastra apicalis*. Several

Agromyzidae and the large chloropid *Platycephala planifrons* also frequent *Phragmites*.

Stands of rushes *(Juncus)* and sedges *(Carex)* are often productive. *Loxocera* species are associated with the former while the latter (e.g. *acutiformis, riparia*) support *Cordilura* especially *impudica* and *ciliata*; the life histories of this genus, which probably all develop in leaf sheaths of *Carex*, require elucidation. Tussocks of *Carex paniculata* may conceal many small Diptera especially Chloropidae and Sphaeroceridae (including the short winged *Elachiptera brevipennis* and *Copromyza pedestris*); the empid *Stilpon graminum*, the dolichopodid *Achalcus cinereus* and the Lauxaniid *Trigonometopus* are often present (see Lowland Grassland regarding tussock collecting).

The grass *Glyceria aquatica* adds further chloropids and anthomyzids. The reedmace *(Typha)* should be searched for the local *Anthomyza bifasciata*. Where the flowering rush *(Butomus)* occurs, the associated agromyzid *Metopomyza ornata*, known from a single British locality, may be sought. The stems of meadowsweet *(Filipendula ulmaria)* often contain early stages of the anthomyiid *Pegomya rubivora*, while *Cheilosia grossa* and *C.albipila* (Syrphidae) develop in stems of marsh thistles. Where comfrey *(Symphytum)* is present, blotch mines of *Agromyza ferruginosa* may be conspicuous on its leaves.

Flowers

Sallow *(Salix)* catkins are important early in the year for *Egle* species (anthomyiids which breed in the catkins) and for early hoverflies such as *Cheilosia grossa* which is on the wing in March and early April. Late in April and early May osiers *(Salix)*, sloe *(Prunus spinosus)* and marsh marigold *(Caltha palustris)* are important, the latter being attractive to hoverflies such as *Lejogaster, Neoascia, Cheilosia* and *Tropidia scita*, the last also frequenting the yellow flag *(Iris pseudacorus)*. In June and July hogweed *(Heracleum)* and later into August *Angelica* is important; these umbels attract a wide variety of Diptera especially hoverflies and calypterates but some Nematocera such a *Anapausis soluta* and *Sciara thomae* may sometimes be abundant. Meadowsweet, marsh thistle *(Cirsium palustre)*, valerian *(Valeriana officinalis)* and buttercups *(Ranunculus)* are also well attended by Diptera in marsh areas.

Carr

Wet or swamp scrub woodland growing on peat may be referred to as carr. On the mineral soils of marshes the term marsh scrub or marsh woodland may be more appropriate. These areas can be extremely rich in Diptera so it is well worth sweeping the underlying vegetation and also the bush foliage. The fauna is very different from open habitats and will often contain a greater diversity of species. Tipulidae are much richer in species under scrub. Empididae and Dolichopodidae are usually abundant and *Xylophagus ater* may be breeding in the dead wood of sallow. Some Syrphidae occur where a reasonable amount of sunshine can get through. Acalypterates are numerous, including Lauxaniidae (which are relatively sparse in open vegetation) and Sciomyzidae are often diverse in species, including *Renocera pallida*. In some carrs the tephritid *Myoleja caesio* is abundant though its host plant is still not certain. Calypterates are diverse and the Scathophagidae include species such as *Leptopa filiformis* and *Megaphthalma pallida* whose biology remains unknown.

Scrub edge can be particularly worth searching, since it provides shelter for species living in open habitats as well as sun and flowers for hoverflies and various other Diptera which breed within. Sweeping of bush foliage is often very productive in Empididae and acalypterates

FLOWING WATERS
by Peter Cranston and Alan E. Stubbs

Entomologists often think of collecting sites in terms of major habitat types such as heathland or woodland without paying enough attention to rivers and streams as important habitats in their own right. Clearly there is a wide range of character in flowing water from springs and seepages through streams to the largest rivers. Amongst the factors which affect the aquatic fauna is the flow rate which ranges from sluggish lowland meanders, resembling more the characteristics of lakes, to the torrential mountain streams. Within the length of a river the flow rate does not necessarily change gradually with increasing distance from the source but within short stretches the flow may vary considerably. It is a characteristic of many streams that short stretches of rapid shallow water or riffles are followed by deeper pools with a corresponding change in physical parameters and fauna. The flow rate and bed of the water course are related and both affect the fauna. In fast flow stretches any suspended matter will not be deposited on a bed which is either boulders or bed rock. In slower current speeds deposition of particles takes place and the bed consists of gravel, sand, and in the slowest stretches mud. Among the other physical factors which affect the fauna are the frequency of flood and the seasonal variation in volume of water in the water course. The specialised fauna of winterbournes (chalk streams which are dry in the summer months) includes the simuliid *Metacnephia amphora*. Aquatic insects are not solely affected by factors originating within the water body: the broader environment of the river must also be considered. The organically poor acid moorland streams can be contrasted with the shaded woodland water courses which have a high input of leaves and other organic matter.

It can be seen that the habitat discussed here is extremely complex consisting of many minor habitats. Inclusion of the riparian (river side) habitats will increase the variety still further. The richness of riverside faunas stems from the mingling of three very different faunas. Firstly, the truly aquatic fauna, the larvae living submerged in the water or wet marginal sediment. Secondly, the large number of terrestrial and semi-terrestrial species living in the river bank, including many species which specialise in this habitat. Thirdly, there are large numbers of species which may come to a river bank from adjacent terrestrial habitats. The variety of riparian and riverine habitats makes accurate recording of habitat data necessary.

Collecting

The larvae of aquatic groups, techniques for their collection and extraction and their rearing have been considered in previous chapters. Adult Diptera may be collected by searching and sweeping marginal vegetation but one should not assume that all Diptera collected this way are aquatic. The Dolichopodidae, Tabanidae, Empididae and Ephydridae collected from marginal mud usually have larvae which develop in this mud, while Sphaeroceridae, Mycetophilidae and many Muscidae which are so frequently found beside running waters will have bred some way from water. Naturally, since the aquatic environment is so hospitable for many Diptera and other orders of insects, predatory flies abound. The ceratopogonid genus *Forcipomyia* is recorded attached to the wing veins of Odonata and Ephemeroptera, but further observations on the distribution of these parasites and the degree of host specificity are necessary. The early stages of some water mites attach themselves to Diptera for dispersal.

Streams and rivers and their banks, where free of vegetation, are used by many insects as flight paths and a well-sited Malaise trap will catch many aquatic and terrestrial Diptera. Many of the aquatic Diptera form more or less discrete swarms; although the swarms of midges are most familiar, the empid genus *Hilara* forms swarms just above the water surface which are surprisingly difficult to sweep without getting a wet net.

Sheltered spots on river banks have a different fauna to the open, possibly sunny, sites. Where the soil around tree roots has been eroded by flood waters leaving damp hollows many Tipulidae including *Limonia nubeculosa* and *Dolichopeza albipes*, Mycetophilidae, Sciaridae, Psychodidae and Anisopodidae will be found hiding. These sites together with undercut shores provide the sort of damp, sheltered environment preferred by many Nematocera, most of which do not breed in the water. The numbers of flies in these places can be very large but there seem to be few specific associations with the sites. The underside of stones on the bank is a likely site for the tipulids *Rhabdomastix* and *Hexatoma* as well as dolichopodids.

Waterlogged rotting logs at the edge of the water provide the breeding site for the rare crane-fly *Elliptera omissa* and the hoverfly *Brachypalpus eunotus* may be found resting on such a log. These logs provide extremely interesting species in Northern Europe and Canada, and a further close investigation of partially submerged rotten logs in Britain would provide interesting records.

Many adult flies appear to sunbathe in open situations, resting on leaves or tree trunks. These species may rest on leaves higher in trees than the collector and here a long handled net to sweep the foliage is necessary. In deeply wooded habitats the margins of rivers and streams may provide the only places where sunlight reaches the lower foliage of the trees. Where sunlit foliage overhangs a river one may find adult *Atherix* (Rhagionidae) basking, and where flood debris is left suspended in the branches of marginal trees there may be clusters of female *Atherix* around their eggs on the underside of the ball of debris. *Atrichops* (Rhagionidae) rests beneath leaves and is only readily found by wading.

Adult Diptera may be collected from sites within the river bed where there are emergent stones or vegetation. The cranefly genus *Dicranota* may be found on platforms of emergent vegetation, while many adults of the running water chironomids may be collected, after emergence, on aquatic emergent vegetation. In sites with sluggish flow and a great deal of emergent vegetation where there are many snails, Sciomyzidae are frequent, presumably searching for the snails which are host for the larvae. The uncommon sciomyzids, *Colobaea distincta* and *Antichaeta brevipennis*, may occur in *Juncus* or grass tussocks at the water's edge. Long herbage at margins of streams and rivers may conceal several *Themira* spp. (Sepsidae) which are uncommon elsewhere.

Springs

Streams may start from an underground source, particularly in limestone or sandstone regions. Springs are usually unaffected by pollution since they arise from underground aquifers and the fauna of these areas is of unusual interest due to the stable temperature. The temperature of springs are almost constant at 8°C winter or summer, and in many invertebrate groups the fauna can be described as glacial relict. When the last ice age retreated·cold adapted forms either retreated behind the ice sheets or were isolated in regions of thermostable cold water, the springs. For this reason it is suggested that the isolated occurrence of some northern cranefly species in S.E.England, up to a hundred miles from the nearest locality, may be due to survival in cold springs, insulated from possibly lethal higher air temperatures. There is scope for more study of lowland spring faunas by dipterists. The presence of natural woodland around a spring is a good sign that the fauna of the spring may be natural. In some cases cold water species occur in rivers where springs arise in the river bed.

Mountain and Moorland streams

The productivity of these streams is usually low since suspended organic matter, which is the food for most aquatic larvae, is low. Many of the species present in these streams emerge early and late in the year. Dominant among the early emerging species are the Diamesinae and *Orthocladius* (Chironomidae). The specialised running water genera such as *Rheocricotopus* and *Eukiefferiella* have several generations each year, and in some years emergence may continue until the winter months.

Collection of adult flies is facilitated by finding sheltered sites in the lee of a bank, a bridge, or a stand of *Juncus*. The fauna of moorland may often be concentrated in such sheltered sites which saves the collector many hours of frustrating collecting over a wide barren area of moorland. The craneflies present one of the major groups of upland Diptera associated with running water, particularly the Pediciini, notably *Dicranota*. *Dolichopeza albipes* mentioned earlier as a species of wooded streams may also be found in shady areas where the stream has undercut the peaty banks. *Tipula coeruleiventris* is a species apparently confined to upland streams in limestone districts; it has a spring and summer emergence in some districts, suggesting two generations a year.

Streams and Upper Reaches of Rivers

The richest regions are those where the stream is shaded providing additional shelter, and well provided with organic matter from the surrounding land; a summer drought is less apparent where the humidity remains high. The summer lull in adult insect numbers is less obvious and stream temperatures are less affected by high air temperatures allowing the emergence of cool adapted species throughout the summer.

In upland areas stretches of shaded streams are worth searching for, similarly stretches of water running through shaded ravines. In the absence of woodland, a line of alders along the water will give similar conditions of shelter for the adults and shade for the larvae.

Small lowland streams are particularly productive, especially those in chalk districts. As the moss and macrophyte levels increase through the season, the larval populations increase correspondingly. A submerged plant provides an anchorage against the current for larvae such as *Simulium* and the epiphytic Chironomidae, and also provides a larger surface area for development of the algae on which many of the chironomids feed.

Mosses provide a trap for organic matter descending the stream and again provide an anchorage or site of resistance to current for many tipulid, psychodid and chironomid larvae. The heavy plant growth in chalk streams provides an exceptionally rich substrate for aquatic larvae throughout the summer months with a correspondingly rich adult fauna.

In the damp marginal habitats and seepages which form tributaries to the major water body a special fauna has developed which is intermediate between the fully aquatic fauna of the stream and the semi-terrestrial fauna of the waterlogged banks, usually termed the hydropetricous fauna. Dominant in this fauna in upland areas are larvae of Thaumaleidae, of which adults have been overlooked by dipterists and a study of their distribution and early stages would be a useful contribution.

The collector should not miss the seepages of water in the banks of streams for these are the breeding sites of many species not found in the principal water bodies, such as many Limoniine craneflies, Psychodidae, Ceratopogonidae and Ephydridae. The adults may be swept from the vegetation and substrate surrounding the seepage. Where a seepage runs through mosses a specialised fauna may be found which includes larvae of the stratiomyid *Oxycera* and the empids *Chelifera, Hydrodromia* and *Wiedemannia*. The latter are found particularly where the seepage is rich in lime and depositing tufa. Similarly certain tanytarsine Chironomidae are found in these tufa depositing seepages, often making their tubes in the tufa.

Lower Reaches

The lowland reaches of rivers, where they flow through the alluvial plains, show many characteristics of standing waters. The current is slower and the finer sediments which remain suspended in the faster stretches are deposited on the bed. The substrate, particularly near the edges, is of gravel, sand and in the slowest parts fine organic detritus. Where there is emergent vegetation, a characteristic of the lowland rivers, deposition of sediments is higher. Thus the substrate of these stretches is similar to that of a lake, and many species can live in either habitat. Larval sampling deeper than the marginal sediments is not easy, but most of the larvae found in the deeper parts of rivers are Chironomidae, and Ceratopogonidae to a lesser extent. In the marginal sediments the larvae of Tabanidae, Ephydridae, Dolichopodidae and Tipulidae will be found. Unfortunately the lowland stretches of our rivers may be polluted by substances which reduce the dissolved oxygen levels in the water. This dramatically affects the fauna of the rivers such that in heavily polluted waters only the blood worms, the larvae of *Chironomus*, can survive in the deeper sediment and in marginal habitats the rat tailed maggots, the larvae of the syrphid *Eristalis*, live in the water shallow enough to extend their tails to the air.

In rivers with emergent reeds and rushes adult Diptera can be found resting on the vegetation, similarly on riverine trees and bushes. In these lowland areas the Chironominae dominate with numbers of larvae as high as 100,000 per square metre of river bed in summer. The correspondingly high number of adults emerging, as well as causing problems to humans, attract many predatory flies to the river banks including Empididae, Dolichopodidae and Ceratopogonidae.

Where the river bank is sandy, craneflies of the genus *Nephrotoma* can be found in the shade whilst sunny stretches may yield the parasites of wasps and bees nesting in the sand. The banks of rivers are frequently sites for many flowers while the emergent vegetation may carpet the water surface with flowers. These will be visited by many Diptera particularly Syrphidae. In some districts the river banks may be the only area of flowering plants for some distance and a rich fauna can be found.

Canals

Many of our canals may perhaps be better included in standing waters since disuse has overtaken such a large number but most canals have gently flowing water. In the less used canals macrophytes may flourish and a large and diverse larval fauna develops in association with emergent vegetation at the edge. Hedgerows and flowers along a towpath may provide good collecting. However, canals are particularly variable in quality and one soon realizes whether collecting is to be worthwhile or not.

Snails are often abundant in the canals as are their predators. Sciomyzid and chironomid larvae are found in the shells of *Physa* and *Limnaea*. Dragonflies can be numerous and it is worth catching some to examine the wing membrane for attached ceratopogonids feeding from the veins.

STANDING WATERS
by Peter Cranston and Dr. Henry Disney

Bodies of standing waters in the British Isles range in size from temporary pools and pot holes with surface areas of a few square centimetres, through ponds and pools to the 400 sq. kms of Lough Neagh. The enormous range of habitats found in standing waters is not necessarily governed by the size of the body: similar faunas may be found in the sheltered margins of both lakes and small ponds, while some of the greatest differences may be between an acid moorland pond and a similar sized dewpond on the Chalk. The factors affecting the fauna include the chemistry of the water, the temperature regime, depth and oxygen availability, nutrients, the nature of the substrate and the vegetation.

In the British Isles natural lakes and ponds are largely the by-product of the Ice Age and are thus relatively young. In the geological time scale lakes are transient features which are liable to silt up and become covered in vegetation to form a marsh. Ponds, especially in lowland areas, can vanish fairly rapidly. Many upland lakes have a low increment of sediment and are poor in plant nutrients so these are longer lasting, though a marsh is usually present where any stream is depositing a delta as it enters the standing water. Lowland lakes and ponds in such areas as the Cheshire Plain have considerable natural antiquity. However, in many districts man has dammed streams and rivers for water supply, fishing or industry and virtually all ponds and lakes in southern England are artificial. Some are many centuries old such as the hammer ponds of the Weald and a rich well established community of plants and animals may be present, whilst recently constructed reservoirs provide plenty of opportunity for studies of the colonisation and ecological adjustment of aquatic organisms. Such man-made water bodies should not be ignored by the collector, since some of the early colonists may include rare species, as has sometimes been the case with Chironomidae.

As with the running water species, there are many life histories to be described amongst the Diptera of standing waters. Attention should be drawn to the Tabanidae and Ceratopogonidae in particular.

Rot holes and Plant-held Water

Among the smallest bodies of standing water but one with the most specialised Diptera fauna are the holes in trees referred to as rot holes. Three species of mosquito *Anopheles plumbeus*, *Aedes geniculatus* and *Orthopodomyia pulchripalpis* and the chironomid *Metriocnemus martinii* are virtually restricted to these rot holes, while the ceratopogonid *Dasyhelea dufouri* often found in rot holes may breed elsewhere. Larvae of the syrphid *Myathropa florea* are found in rot holes and rarely elsewhere, while other Syrphidae including *Eristalis* species may be found.

In the tropics, plants may hold water in their axils or in pitchers; in fact plant-held water may be the major habitat for aquatic larvae. In temperate regions this habitat is less important but similar habitats include the leaf bracts of the wood clubrush (*Scirpus sylvaticus*), and hogweed (*Heracleum sphondylium*) and teasel (*Dipsacus*). The larvae of several families of Diptera including Culicidae, Ceratopogonidae and Chironomidae have been found here, none of them belonging to common species. Investigation of other plants which trap water would repay the dipterist.

The Surface Film

This is a surprisingly interesting situation for the dipterist. Many flies with aquatic larvae (e.g. Chironomidae, Culicidae, Chaoboridae, Ceratopogonidae and others) are found and these along with a constant rain of small terrestrial insects trapped there, attract many predatory arthropods, including Diptera as well as gerrid bugs and lycosid spiders.

Some of the predatory flies are characteristic of the surface film, e.g. the dolichopodid genera *Hydrophorus* and *Campsicnemus*, *Lispe* spp. (Muscidae) and among the ephydrids, *Ephydra* and *Hydrellia* spp. may be present. Hunting Empididae are sometimes seen but more often fly to and fro rapidly above the water. *Hilara* may be observed to drop suddenly to the surface film and rapidly rise again; if secured the fly will frequently be found to have picked up a small insect. Even *Scathophaga stercoraria* regularly hunts on the surface of ponds.

Some other flies are attracted to the refuse of dead insects floating at the surface; the empid *Wiedemannia bistigma* has been recorded using this food source and other *Wiedemannia* and possibly *Hydrodromia* may have similar habits. The film itself is also nutritious (being made of lipoprotein and containing micro-organisms such as bacteria and protozoa). Sciarids and sphaerocerids (especially *Leptocera humida*) have been observed sucking at the film and/or dead insects there. *Hydrellia* spp. have these habits in addition to their predatory behaviour, which involves securing prey by tumbling it over until it becomes trapped in the film. The Diptera to be found on the surface film of ponds and lakes merit much further study. Some of the more interesting species occur more frequently early and late in the year, possibly because other predatory animals (like *Gerris*) are too numerous in the summer months.

Benthic and Planktonic Fauna

As previously mentioned size is not the major factor governing the numbers and composition of the standing water fauna. Perhaps the main factor is the level of nutrient present, which is linked with the availability of oxygen in the depths. Where nutrient levels are high the demand for oxygen from the decomposers, especially in summer, leads to an oxygen deficiency. Few aquatic organisms can cope with this and the fauna is often poor in diversity, although high in numbers. Ecologists term the nutrient rich lakes eutrophic. The nutrient levels encourage a high weed and zooplankton growth, and large numbers of epiphytic larvae are found on the macrophytes. Culicidae and Chaoboridae feed just under the water surface and *Chaoborus* larvae (known as phantom midges on account of their transparency) are able, like *Chironomus* and relatives, to withstand the inclement conditions at the bottom of a eutrophic body of water. In ponds and lakes with very low oxygen levels, often due to over enrichment by pollution, the rat-tailed maggot larvae of the syrphid genera *Eristalis* and *Helophilus* can be found with their tails extended to the surface of shallow water. These larvae can be found in places as noxious as the run-off from cattle sheds and manure heaps.

The term dystrophic is used to describe water bodies which have high levels of suspended vegetative matter, usually peat, in a form which is broken down too slowly to affect the oxygen level of the water body. Just as the bacterial breakdown of peat is slow, the potential as a food source for Diptera larvae is low. These dystrophic bodies of water are found on moorland and even lowland peaty areas. *Chaoborus obscuripes* and Culicidae can be found in these ponds, while the larvae of many tanytarsine chironomids construct their tubes from the particles of peat.

The third category, oligotrophic water (poor in nutrients) is largely restricted to upland areas. Lakes of this type are on rocks which do not easily give up their chemicals, such as granites and slates, so, in the often cold water, plant growth is minimal. The fauna tends to be restricted to Chironomidae, Tipulidae and Ceratopogonidae. Numbers are never high, but the diversity is greater than in many other bodies of water. The small number of such ponds and lakes is diminishing as even hill farmers apply fertilisers to their soils, artificially enriching the waters and affecting the delicately balanced communities.

Margins of Lakes and Ponds

The marginal waters of ponds and lakes have a greater number of families of larval Diptera present than in the depths and open waters. In larger bodies the waves ensure that the water is fully oxygenated and the increased light permits a richer growth of mosses and submerged plants. Some species otherwise known only from fast flowing waters can be found on exposed shores of lakes, while the fauna also shows many similarities to that of slowly flowing lowland rivers. The fauna associated with submerged plants is of particular interest. The larva of the tipulid *Phalacrocera*, green in colour, can be found in *Sphagnum* moss in acid pools. The larvae and pupae of *Mansonia richardii* are unique amongst British Culicidae in spending all of their existence below water obtaining oxygen from the submerged roots and stems of *Glyceria, Typha* and certain *Ranunculus.* The larvae use a modified siphon and the pupa the respiratory trumpets to pierce the tissues of the plants and extract the gas from the vascular system. Similar adaptations are also known in *Erioptera squalida* (Tipulidae) and *Chrysogaster hirtella* (Syrphidae). Ptychopteridae and the syrphid genera *Eristalis* and *Helophilus* have telescopic breathing tubes (siphons) as an adaptation to living in shallowly submerged marginal mud. Many chironomid larvae live epiphytically on aquatic plants and several mine the leaves and stems. These include the *Potamogeton* mining *Cricotopus brevipalpis* and the genera *Glyptotendipes, Endochironomus* and some *Polypedilum.* A number of ephydrid larvae, notably *Hydrellia*, are leaf and stem miners on both submerged and emergent aquatic plants.

The marginal mud and stones cannot really be separated from the saturated mosses and soil adjoining water bodies. Man-made reservoirs are particularly subject to seasonal draw-down of the water and the margins are ill defined. Larval Ephydridae, Dolichopodidae, Tipulidae and Ceratopogogonidae are found in such marginal muds.

The Marginal Transition Area

Whilst there may be a sharp margin to the water's edge around some bodies of standing water, in many cases there is a transitional shoreline grading into marsh or swamp woodland (carr). Where this transitional area is wide there may be a distinct zonation of plants, not only of aquatic plants growing in different depths of water but also a zonation as the ground rises on the landward side. The landward zonation is generally related to different degrees of waterlogging and, if relevant, to any seasonal fluctuations in extent and height of the water level. The Diptera thus have a range of soil wetness and plant structure to choose from and many species probably have quite narrowly defined preferences which have still to be described. The fauna includes the true water edge and aquatic species plus those which breed in the more terrestrial marsh habitat. Groups such as the Sciomyzidae include both life styles and tabanid larvae are reported to belong to different species along a gradient of soil moisture. Often the adults of individual species will concentrate in the areas where they breed but there may also be extensive straying and mixing of faunas. To the rich resident fauna may often be added species from further afield, especially if there is an abundance of flowers.

WOODLAND
by Peter Chandler

The natural climax vegetation of most parts of the British Isles is forest of various types and it is not therefore surprising that a large percentage of the British Diptera fauna is primarily adapted to life in a wooded environment. Now the original forest cover is much reduced and what remains has been highly modified for the purposes of forestry. Commercial plantations, particularly monocultures, are poor in Diptera although some ubiquitous species may be abundant there. Those woods which retain something of a semi-natural condition are likely to be most productive, particularly where there is a diversity of trees and a good ground flora. The trees should preferably be of differing ages and including a proportion of partly decayed trees and dead wood; the presence of rides or clearings will also greatly increase the variety of niches. Sometimes small neglected corners of otherwise uniform woods may hold a great diversity of species concentrated in one spot.

The dominant tree species in native woodlands varies considerably according to soil, climatic conditions and management history. The principal factors affecting the composition of the dipterous fauna are whether the wood is broad-leaved or coniferous and the level of the water table. Those woods with streams or seepages are generally richer although the dry beechwoods on the Chalk have their own characteristic species. Woods on acid soils, mainly birch or pine are usually more open and allow more open ground insects to exist than are found in the closed canopy oak or alder woods on more neutral soils. Native coniferous forest exists only in the central Scottish Highlands and a range of boreal species are associated with it.

Basic collecting in woodland may be accomplished by sweeping over the leaf litter or through the ground flora if present or the accessible foliage of trees and shrubs. For collecting from dead wood or fungi, gentle sweeping may be employed although visual examination will be more instructive. Individual collecting is also the preferred technique for flies settled on tree trunks or feeding at flowers. In wet weather it is often possible to continue collecting longer in woods when shielded from the full force of a shower. Pooting flies sheltering under the foliage of trees may be the most productive method when the vegetation is too wet for sweeping. The most obvious limitation to collecting in mature woodland is that it is far more of a three dimensional habitat than other types of vegetation; the collector usually is only able to sample within his reach and any flies which habitually live in the canopy are missed. The application of techniques for sampling the upper levels of a woodland are a possible line for future investigation. Woodland is a suitable medium for use of certain trapping methods such as Malaise traps (in rides or glades) and suction traps.

Broad-leaved Deciduous Woods

Woodland Diptera may be considered as either shade or sun-loving and in general the Nematocera, some Empididae, Phoridae and acalypterates belong to the first category while the bulk of the Brachycera and Cyclorrhapha, which are usually more robust and hairy or bristly, fall into the second. The precise situation in which flies occur in a wood will, however, depend on a combination of their larval and adult habits.

Shade-loving Diptera

Most Nematocera, Empididae (especially *Hilara*), Dolichopodidae and some acalypterates such as *Leptocera humida* and Diastatidae gravitate towards damp situations and large concentrations of flies may be found in the vicinity of a woodland stream or around seepages. Alderwoods, which have a high water table are especially rich in these delicate bodied flies which avoid desiccation; they are usually the most productive habitat for the smaller crane-flies, many of which develop in mud as larvae.

Overhangs along the banks of woodland streams and other similar dark hollows are a good place to seek adult fungus gnats (Mycetophilidae), of which a large variety of species may often congregate in such spots, where a moist micro-climate is provided in an otherwise dry habitat.

Shaded woodland ponds have their own fauna. A larger variety of Psychodidae may be found running about on foliage around such a pond than would perhaps occur in a comparable open situation, especially if it is relatively stagnant. Some mosquitoes, e.g. *Anopheles claviger* and some *Aedes* and *Theobaldia* spp. favour such ponds. A few mosquitoes which habitually occur in woodland develop in water filled tree holes (see Standing Waters). The syrphid *Myathropa florea* develops in such holes or in very wet rotten wood but the adult fly is found at flowers or sunning itself.

Where no surface water is present the ground flora may provide a moist habitat where many flies shelter and general sweeping is the best method of sampling. Leaf litter also provides harbourage for many small Diptera such as Phoridae, Sphaeroceridae and *Lonchoptera*; sweeping over leaf litter in a beechwood, where the ground flora is usually sparse, will produce numbers of *Lonchoptera tristis* and several Heleomyzidae, e.g. *Scoliocentra caesia*, *S. amplicornis* and *Morpholeria ruficornis*. The mouths of animal burrows in such woods will also be worth searching for some of the latter family, e.g. *Scoliocentra villosa* and *Oecothea fenestralis*.

Ground flora

The ground flora of woods varies according to the type of soil. On acid soils where birch is the dominant tree, woods are often relatively open and a heathland vegetaion may co-exist. In many drier woods bracken *(Pteridium aquilinum)* covers large areas of ground and is used for shelter by many flies, especially Nematocera including fungus gnats and in the winter months Trichoceridae. Several *Chirosia* spp. (Anthomyiidae) are very common amongst bracken, in which the larvae develop; most are small greyish flies but the larger blackish yellow-winged *C.flavipennis* is often conspicuous. The large light brown tachinid *Dexiosoma caninum* is regularly seen sitting on bracken, although it is especially evident in rides; it is recorded as a parasite of the cockchafer *(Melolontha)* larva but in view of its abundance must also attack other beetle larvae.

In the dense canopy woodland a vernal (spring) flora dominated by Ranunculaceae, *Primula* spp. or locally *Allium* is developed and on heavier soils brambles *(Rubus* spp.) are much in evidence; many other plants will also occur, dependent on the amount of light that is admitted later in the season. The composition of the ground flora will dictate which phytophagous Diptera are present. Where a good herb layer is available, many Agromyzidae may be found either by sweeping or searching for the mines, several species on Ranunculaceae and *Phytomyza primulae* being common. A rather large species, *Phytomyza nigripennis*, is commonly swept from *Anemone* in the spring but has not been reared and may develop in the roots.

Many dipterous leaf miners whose food plants more normally grow in exposed situations will often prefer to attack a plant growing in shade where it may be etiolated and more delicate than typically and often failing to flower. This especially applies to Anthomyiidae and Tephritidae which make blotch mines, .e.g. *Pegomya dulcamarae* on *Solanum dulcamara*, *P.steini* on *Cirsium vulgare*, *Trypeta immaculata* on *Taraxacum* and *T.cornuta* on *Eupatorium cannabinum*. One picture-winged tephritid which is commonly swept from the herb or shrub layer in shady woods is *Myoleja caesio*; it has been reported as mining red campion, *Silene dioica*, but this requires confirmation (an anthomyiid *Pegomya albimargo* also mines *Silene*) as a supposed continental relative *M.lucida* develops in the fruit of *Lonicera*. The coltsfoot leaf miner *Euleia cognata* is usually found as an adult sheltering amongst the herb layer or under foliage of shrubs in woods. Some of the plant feeding Scathophagidae occcur in woods although they are usually restricted by the occurrence of their food-plants. Some of the *Cordilura* species occur in marshy woods where *Carex* spp. are present. *Norellia spinipes* is found about its food-plant *Narcissus* in the spring but has been swept from bracken in the autumn. *Delina nigrita* and *Parallelomma vittatum* mine the leaves of orchids especially in shady places. *P.paridis* is localised by its host *Paris quadrifolia*.

The flowers of woodland herbs are attractive to many Diptera not commonly found as flower visitors in more open situations and more observations are required on this, both with respect to the flies involved and their preferences. Some flies such as *Tipula* species, *Pelidnoptera* (Sciomyzidae) and some Empididae have been noted as visiting woodland flowers, particularly of Umbelliferae, only in dull damp weather. Other species are very specific in their choice of flowers, such as *Portevinia maculata* which is only found on large

117

stands of wild garlic, *Allium ursinum*, in bulbs of which its larvae probably develop. *Sphegina* species, which are overlooked by most syrphid collectors, normally visit flowers of woodland plants such as *Conopodium, Lycopus* or *Angelica* in diffuse sunlight or may be obtained in numbers by sweeping herbage in damp woods.

The largest British pipunculid, *Nephrocerus flavicornis*, has usually been collected by sweeping low vegetation in shady woods; there has been much speculation about its possible host, once thought to be the cicada, *Cicadetta*, but as it came to be collected in many localities outside the New Forest the large oak feeding homopteron *Ledra aurita* was suggested. A recent find of *N.flavicornis* in an alderwood where *Aphrophora alni* was abundant suggested that this might serve as a host and any further observation on the fly would be of interest.

Decaying Wood and Associated Habitats

Where a reasonable quantity of decaying wood, preferably including some entire fallen trunks and rot-holes in partly living trees, has been allowed to remain in a wood this will greatly enhance the quality of the dipterous fauna. Dead wood is most attractive to flies when it is in a shaded situation; once exposed to the sun it quickly becomes desiccated. Flies are usually only able to make use of decaying trees in parkland or other open situations when the tree is still partly living and kept moist by the presence of some surviving sapwood.

Sweeping about decaying logs and stumps in shade will usually produce some wood feeding flies such as clusiids (especially *Clusiodes* species and *Clusia flava*) or empids including *Oedalea* spp. (several are common but the scarce *O.apicalis* is confined to a few old forests), *Leptopeza flavipes* and *Oropezella sphenoptera*, a local species which has not been reared but probably develops in rotten wood. Dead wood in shade provides a moist micro-climate and many Mycetophilidae, Sciaridae and Cecidomyiidae may also be swept around large bodies of it. The many flies found about decaying wood in less heavily shaded places are dealt with fully under Dead Wood and Sap Runs.

Decaying wood provides a pabulum for the development of fungi and enriches the fungus flora of a wood, together with the many associated Diptera. Although some fungus feeding flies are polyphagous and may occur on fungi in other habitats, most are more restricted in their choice and many are confined to fungi growing on wood or forming mycorrhizal associations with trees, so are normally found most readily in the woodland environment. Sweeping about fungi will produce Mycetophilidae, Platypezidae, Muscidae, e.g. *Phaonia* or *Mydaea*, some *Fannia* and *Pegomya*, many *Suillia* spp., some Heleomyzidae such as *Neoleria ruficeps* and *Tephrochlamys* species, several Sphaeroceridae and when they have begun to decay, many Drosophilidae.

A growth of mosses on the surface of wood will also create a moist habitat for the development of dipterous larvae, such as *Tipula* species and some Muscidae. The rhagionid fly *Ptiolina obscura* is known to develop amongst mosses but the fly itself may sometimes be swept in comparatively dry places in woods as well as in damp mossy places. The smaller black rhagionid *Spania nigra*, which is rather local in damp shady spots, is a leaf-miner of liverworts.

Woodland snails are also more prolific where logs, loose bark, etc. are available to provide shelter; these are the hosts of sciomyzid flies. *Tetanura pallidiventris, Pherbellia scutellaris* and *Pelidnoptera fuscipennis* are examples which are found most readily about rotten wood. *Tetanocera phyllophora* parasitises woodland snails, so occupies today a more restricted habitat than the closely related slug parasite *T. elata*.

Tree Trunks

Close inspection of tree trunks will usually reveal many small cursorial flies adapted to this habitat such as *Tachypeza nubila* (occasionally *T.fuscipennis* in old woods), *Drapetis assimilis* and several *Medetera* spp.; these are predatory flies feeding on small insects, e.g. Psocoptera. The somewhat larger dolichopodids *Sciapus platypterus* and *Neurigona quadrifasciata* also run about on tree trunks where their green dusted bodies harmonise with algal or lichen growth. Sweeping tree trunks may disclose some flies not immediately obvious; many phorids and some mycetophilids of the genera *Cordyla* and *Docosia* are best found in this way. *Docosia* occur mainly in spring on lichen covered trunks.

Several arboricolous flies have brown wing markings, which may be a means of camouflage against predators like the grey-green dusting of *Medetera* and the tessellated bodies of muscids, etc. (see Rides). The large phorid *Anevrina thoracica* with brown tipped wings is habitually found on tree trunks but so is the clear winged *A.urbana*. The lauxaniid *Peplomyza litura* rests in crevices in trunks with its brown marked wings held in a tent formation. The large acalypterate, *Neottiophilum praeustum*, with brown spotted wings, may be beaten from tree branches or from ivy on tree trunks but it is more easily obtained by rearing from the bird's nests in which it develops. Where a growth of ivy is present on a tree trunk, *Palloptera* species and many lauxaniids may be beaten from it and several of these, e.g. *P.muliebris*, *Homoneura* spp. and *Lyciella decempunctata* also have spotted wings. Phorids of the genus *Phalacrotophora* are sometimes found aggregating on the tree trunks; these distinctive orange and black banded flies are parasites of ladybirds (Coccinellidae).

Where there is a discharge of sap from a living tree a distinctive fauna may be found, which is dealt with under Dead Wood and Sap Runs.

Other Temporary Habitats (Dung and Carrion) in Woodland

Dung deposited in woodland has a distinctive fauna of flies associated with it. *Scathophaga lutaria* replaces *stercoraria* as the common dung fly. *Dryomyza anilis* and *D.flaveola* are much in evidence. *Polietes lardarius* is usually numerous and large concentrations of the muscid *Alloeostylus simplex*, which is not often found by general collecting, may occur.

Carrion in woods possibly has a distinctive fauna; the commonest flies are *Piophila* (especially *P.nigriceps*) and the heleomyzid *Neoleria inscripta* while Calliphoridae are less in evidence. The occasional large gatherings of *Sepsis* species found on low vegetation in woods are probably due to mass emergence but it is not clear whether this has usually been from carrion or dung.

Sweat Flies and Biting Flies

When walking through woods in the summer months the collector will often be surrounded by hordes of sweat sucking flies. These are mostly the dull grey muscid *Hydrotaea irritans*, although in some old forest areas they are accompanied by *H.borussica* which has yellow patches on the male abdomen and small shining black spots in the female. *Musca autumnalis* is a common sweat fly in the south but becomes scarce in the north and west and information on its northern limit would be of interest. Other sweat flies are *Morellia* species and *Pogonomyia decolor*, the latter is widespread but easily overlooked because of its resemblance to *H.irritans*.

Biting flies are less in evidence in woods than they are in open or marshy places where large mammals or suitable breeding sites are more available. The several woodland mosquitoes, which are most prevalent in deep shade, have been mentioned above. The commonest woodland tabanid is *Chrysops caecutiens*, which usually approaches stealthily from behind; occasionally *Hybomitra distinguenda* or *H.bimaculata* (especially form *bisignata*) will occur. *Hybomitra micans* is a very local species in old woods; its males have been recorded at damp patches on woodland tracks and at *Heracleum* flowers. The large *Tabanus sudeticus* is found in some large forests in the south but is now frequent only in the north and west. Where deer are present, the curious deer ked *Lipoptena cervi* may sometimes alight on the collector although it is more often found by sweeping.

Foliage of trees and shrubs

Many flies may be found settled on or under the foliage of trees in the shadier parts of woods, particularly where the ground vegetation is sparse. Flies commonly found on tree foliage are the lauxaniid *Tricholauxania praeusta*, small tachinids such as *Lypha dubia* and *Cyzenis albicans*, which parasitise arboreal Lepidoptera larvae, and various empids. *Trichinomyia flavipes* is very common on tree foliage in the autumn and the uncommon *Euthyneura gyllenhali* is sometimes found settled under leaves. The small predatory muscid *Allognota agromyzina*, is commonly seen running about on leaves of shrubs and bushes.

Many species of Phoridae and Platypezidae may be found most readily when they are running about in an erratic way on the foliage of broad leaved trees and shrubs such as *Acer, Castanea, Aesculus* and *Rhododendron* as well as some herbaceous plants. Both sexes occur equally and it is possible that they are feeding on small particles or exudations. In the Platypezidae *Callomyia* and some *Agathomyia* species are found mainly in shade or diffuse sunlight while the Platypezinae and some *Agathomyia*, including the very local *A.falleni*, prefer foliage in more open places.

In late summer and autumn "honey dew" deposits on the foliage of various trees, especially sycamore, are very attractive to many Diptera, including lauxaniids and muscids like *Azelia* species.

Few phytophagous Diptera attack woody plants, only a few cecidomyiid galls and several species of Agromyzidae which are leaf or stem miners. Common leaf miners are of *Agromyza* on birch and alder and *Phytomyza ilicis* on holly (*Ilex*);

120

the latter is usually obvious wherever holly occurs.

Dolichopodids of the genus *Chrysotus* and many cursorial empids habitually run over the foliage of trees and shrubs where they capture their prey. They are most in evidence in open woodland or at edges of woods; the bulk of them belong to the large genus *Platypalpus*, of which the many dusted species occur in sunnier places, than the shining black or yellow species which usually prefer low herbage in the shade. *Phyllodromia melanocephala* and *Drapetis ephippiata* also commonly inhabit sunlit foliage. *Hemerodromia* and *Chelifera* species are also found on foliage of woody plants but usually near streams or in marshy places. The mainly yellow fungus gnats of the genus *Leia* are found more often on the foliage of trees than elsewhere. The many larger flies which bask on sunlit tree foliage are discussed below.

Rides, clearings and woodland edge

A wood is much richer in insect fauna when there are clearings or rides, letting in sunlight and encouraging the growth of many herbaceous plants not found in shady situations; flowering shrubs are also better developed at the edges of woodland. In a natural forest such clearings are provided by the death of mature trees but are usually artificially created in modern woods.

Sun-loving flies bask on the foliage of trees, shrubs and herbaceous plants in these open areas. These are mainly Syrphidae, Muscidae, Calliphoridae, Tachinidae and some larger Brachycera. Examples of moderately large flies found sunning themseves on the foliage of woody plants are *Xylota* spp, *Didea fasciata*, *Cheilosia* spp. (often *C.variabiis*), *Sargus* spp, *Phyllomya volvulus*, *Nemorilla floralis*, *Thelaira nigripes* and *Ernestia* spp.

Sunlit tree trunks are a resting site of many flies; tessellated muscids of the genera *Phaonia* and *Helina* are camouflaged against light coloured bark. Some flies are more conspicuous like the black *Mesembrina meridiana* with its orange wing bases and the metallic green tachinid *Gymnocheta viridis* which occurs on sunlit tree trunks in the spring before trees are fully in leaf. The so-called downlooker flies, *Rhagio scolopaceus*, settle facing downwards on tree trunks usually in open situations at the edge of marshy woods; their maculated wings make them inconspicuous in this position. The scarcer *R.strigosus* is found occupying a similar position in dry woods on the chalk.

Some Syrphidae tend to fly amongst low vegetation at the edge of woodland rides, e.g. *Pipizella* and *Neocnemodon* spp., *Chrysotoxum bicinctum*, *Xanthogramma* spp. and the scarce *Doros conopseus* has usually been found in this situation in relatively dry woods. Tachinidae of the genus *Gonia* (*divisa, picea*), now much less frequent than formerly, fly in early spring amongst long grass in woodland clearings. The rather slender ichneumonid-like fly *Megamerina dolium* may be seen in some older mixed woods running about on the foliage of low shrubs or flying along rides. Where a stand of woodrush (*Luzula sylvatica*) is present, whether at the edge of rides or in more diffuse sunlight, sweeping will usually produce the fly *Loxocera sylvatica*, which may develop in this plant although proof is not yet forthcoming.

As berry-bearing shrubs flower best at woodland edges, the tephritids which developing in their fruit are best found here e.g. *Phagocarpus permundus* on hawthorn (*Crataegus*), *Rhagoletis alternata* on rose hips (*Rosa* spp.); the fruit of white bryony (*Bryonia dioica*) scrambling over shrubs provides food for *Goniglossum wiedemanni* of which the adult flies are difficult to find. These flies and many other woodland edge species are able to colonise hedges in open country and now have more scope than those species which require the wooded environment. The large empid *Empis tessellata* has rather curious mainly dark legs in open country forms, now much commoner than a largely yellow legged form which is confined to woods in the south.

Several species of the large predatory asilid flies may be found in open parts of woods and are frequently seen settled or in flight along woodland tracks. *Neoitamus cyanurus* is common in mixed woods, usually settling on the ground; the scarce *N.cothurnatus* is known from a few southern woods. *Machimus atricapillus* will be seen settled on tree trunks or palings, often lying along a crevice in the bark from which it will rapidly dart out to catch its prey in the air. *Laphria marginata* flies over bracken or other low vegetation in old oakwoods; the fine *L.gilva* occurred in several mixed woods on acid soil in the south during the fifties but may now be extinct. Several *Dioctria* spp. are common amongst coarse herbage; *D.linearis* prefers the shadier parts of oakwoods, *rufipes* likes sunnier places in mixed woods, *baumhaueri* is most common in birchwoods, often amongst heather while *atricapilla* occurs in lusher vegetation in damper woods. The more local *D.oelandica* is usually seen on the foliage of trees about 5-6 feet from the ground and has been found in various woodland types; it is perhaps commoner in the north.

The collector should progress warily along woodland tracks as some sun-loving flies prefer to bask on the ground. The large tachinids *Trixa coerulescens* and *Servillia ursina* are inconspicuous when settled. The *Bombylius* species which are associated with the nests of burrowing Hymenoptera also occur close to the ground in woodland rides especially where there are banks or bare patches suitable for the nesting of their hosts. *B.major* and the more local *B.discolor* are best sought where there are plenty of primroses in flower in the spring as their long probosces are specially adapted to probe these flowers.

Flower visiting

There is a larger variety of flowering plants in open parts of woods and this is a good place to study the range of flies visiting selected flowers. In the spring, flowering trees such as *Crataegus* and *Prunus* species can be most productive of flies especially syrphids, muscids and empids. In old woods some local Syrphidae e.g. *Criorhina* spp., *Brachyopa* spp., *Psilota anthracina*, *Epistrophella euchroma* and *Parasyrphus* spp. (e.g. *annulatus*, *punctulatus*) are best sought in this situation. The scarce yellow empid *Dryodromia testacea* has been found at *Crataegus* and *Sorbus aucuparia* blossom in dry woodland rides.

The broad heads of Umbelliferae are usually the most productive herbaceous plants, especially *Heracleum* and *Angelica* in drier and wetter woods respectively during the summer months; the great quantities of *Anthriscus* produced earlier in the year are usually patronised by fewer Diptera. In woodland, such syrphids as

Melangyna spp., *Cheilosia illustrata, Leucozona lucorum* and *Eristalis* spp. many Tachinidae, *Empis* and *Rhamphomyia* spp. and a few flower visiting Mycetophilidae (*Macrorrhyncha flava* and *Antlemon servulum*) may be found commonly on umbels. Some of the scarce tachinids parasitic on Hemiptera may occasionally be found in this situation; *Gymnosoma rotundatum* is very local in the south, while *Alophora hemiptera* is more widespread but commoner in the north and west.

Devil's-bit Scabious (*Succisa pratensis*) is also very attractive and may attract *Conops* spp., *Nowickia ferox* or *Arctophila fulva*. The very local *Rhingia rostrata* is mainly found at purple flowers like *Succisa, Knautia* and *Mentha* along woodland rides, while the more widespread *R.campestris* is common outside woods. In marshy woods watermint (*Mentha aquatica*) flowers are visited by many flies; *Tachina fera* is usually in evidence. Bramble flowers (*Rubus* spp.) are frequented by many Syrphidae (especially *Volucella*), Tachinidae, Calliphoridae and other flies. The fruit of brambles when beginning to decompose is very attractive to flies especially *Bellardia* (Calliphoridae).

In the autumn, ivy (*Hedera helix*), which normally only flowers well in sunlit situations such as the edges of woods, is extremely attractive to flies as there are fewer alternatives available; muscids, anthomyiids, lauxaniids, *Apiloscatopse picea* and *A.flavicollis* are abundant. Occasionally, Conopidae of the genus *Leopoldius* which parasitise *Vespula*, may be found. The syrphid *Callicera spinolae* has been noted in recent years as a magnificent visitor to ivy flowers.

In woods on acid soils, heather (*Calluna* and *Erica*) flowers are very attractive to many flies especially Syrphidae including the common *Syrphus, Helophilus* and *Platycheirus* species but *Scaeva selenitica, Sericomyia* spp. or *Microdon eggeri* might also occur. The tachinid *Linnaemya vulpina* is often abundant at heather flowers and the large *Tachina grossa* may occasionally be found. Some conopids e.g. *Sicus ferrugineus* are also common at heather flowers.

Hovering and swarming flies

Along woodland tracks, certain hover flies may commonly be seen suspended high in the air, usually within reach of a long-handled net; the commonest species with this habit are *Volucella pellucens, Eristalis, Syrphus* and *Epistrophe* spp. but occasionally something more unusual may be found. In early spring, *Criorhina ranunculi* might occur in this way but is is much less frequent than formerly.

Many empids are "woodland edge" insects and this is largely because their males form swarms in the air which use part of an adjacent tree or shrub as a marker. They are most prolific in spring and early summer; *Microphorus, Trichina,* some *Hilara*, many *Rhamphomyia* and *Empis* have this habit. *Rhamphomyia sulcata* is a common spring species, which preys on *Dilophus febrilis* (Bibionidae), also abundant in spring along edges of woods. In the autumn fewer species occur but *Rhamphomyia erythrophthalma* (with its hairy-legged male form *hirsutipes*) is abundant then; the larger *R.spinipes* appears very local but may be overlooked because of a short autumnal flight period.

Other swarming Diptera, such as Chironomidae, Bibionidae, *Dicranomyia, Trichocera,* the stratiomyid genera *Beris* and *Chorisops*, Lonchaeidae, *Calythea nigricans* (Anthomyiidae) and many *Fannia* species occur in similar situations, under or close to a tree but usually near a clearing or the edge of a wood. Platypezidae are recorded as forming swarms in a "funnel" between trees or shrubs where a shaft of light penetrates but more observations on this are required. In all these cases the males form single species swarms to which the females are attracted.

The small black *Microsania* spp. (Platypezidae) swarm in the smoke of smouldering fires usually in wooded areas, preferably where the fire is sheltered to some extent. There are four British species all with this habit and they are rarely seen elsewhere, although on one occasion *M.pectinipennis* was caught about the topmost branches of a sycamore. The scarce empid *Hormopeza obliterata* has only been twice recorded in Britain about smouldering pine wood; they fly in low and settle on the ash or partly burned wood, their whitish wings making them inconspicuous. *Hormopeza* has been recorded as swarming in smoke and also preying on *Microsania*. Recently a small yellow and black asteiid *Astiosoma rufifrons* has turned up, attracted to smouldering wood and more particularly to wood ash in the vicinity of old woodland, and investigation of fires and bonfire sites in wooded areas will certainly repay further investigation.

The Scottish Pinewoods

These are usually open woodland with trees of various ages and frequently with a complete ground cover of grasses, heather, bracken or other plants. Sometimes there is a mixture of birch woodland or in wetter places, along streams and rivers, alder and willows. Many of the boreal insects which find a foothold in Britain in the central Scottish Highlands are restricted to waterside situations in the river valleys, others are more widespread in the pine forest while some (especially empids and muscids) occur on higher ground above the forested level.

Some boreal empids such as *Rhamphomyia* and *Hilara* spp. e.g. *H.abdominalis* occur by wooded riverbanks; *H.canescens*, although more widespread, is commonest in this habitat. *Wiedemannia phantasma* occurs on rocks by the rivers. *Chelifera* and *Hemerodromia* species are commoner on waterside trees than in the south. The aggregations of fungus gnats, which occur near river and stream banks include some species peculiar to this environment, e.g. *Dynatosoma nigromaculatum* and *Mycetophila caudata*. The large *Gnoriste bilineata*, which is probably associated with mosses, was thought to be confined to these woods but has recently been found to be more widespread in Scotland and mainly in deciduous woods.

Sweeping low vegetation will produce many Muscidae, Anthomyiidae and small acalypterates. *Calobata stylifera* and *Piophila signata* are only known from this area and Psilidae are more common than in the south. The Scottish species *Psila humeralis*, which is associated with *Heracleum* and *Myrrhis*, may be common and *P.pallida* is also frequent. Where flowers are present a local concentration of Syrphidae may be found including such species as *Metasyrphus lapponicus*, *Megasyrphus annulipes*, *Didea intermedia* or *Chrysotoxum arcuatum*. Heather flowers are attractive to *Linnaemya rossica*, (Tachinidae) which is as abundant here as *L.vulpina* is in the south.

Dead wood has its own special dipterous fauna in these forests, such as *Xylophagus cinctus, X.junki*, the otitid genus *Homalocephala* and the large golden haired asilid *Laphria flava*, of which the larvae may be predaceous on beetle larvae in large bodies of decaying pine wood. *L.flava* is local but widespread and may be observed settling on dead trees in fairly open pinewoods. Apart from widespread species, some local Clusiidae (*Clusiodes caledonica* and *C.geomyzina*) may be obtained and two of our four *Tachypeza* species (*heeri* and *truncorum*) have only been found on pine in Scotland.

The beautiful syrphid *Callicera rufa* is very local in association with decaying pinewood. Two other large striking syrphids, which are also confined to the central Highlands, i.e. *Blera fallax* and *Hammerschmidtia ferruginea*, are associated with deciduous trees, the former with sap runs and the latter has been found on decaying aspen stumps.

The tachinid *Anthomyiopsis nigrisquama* (= *Ptilopsina nitens*) was only known in association with aspen (*Populus tremula*) in the same locality as *Hammerschmidtia*, but it has subsequently been found on aspen in Wiltshire; it is a parasite of chrysomelid beetles and may occur more widely on this tree.

In addition to *Laphria flava*, one other less conspicuous dark coloured asilid *Rhadiurgus variabilis* is confined to the Scottish pinewoods, where it is locally common. The small syrphids of the genus *Chamaesyrphus* (especially *scaevoides*) are best found by sweeping under pine in patches of denser woodland where the ground flora is sparse.

Some of the mammalian parasites, particularly those associated with deer are commoner in the Scottish Highlands. *Cephenemyia auribarbis* is the widespread deer bot fly and *Hypoderma diana* is a warble fly which attacks deer. These are large hairy bee-like flies which are fast flying and not often collected. The reindeer bot fly *Cephenemyia trompe* has been introduced with its host, but it is not clear whether it has become established, while another parasite of the red deer, *Pharyngomyia picta*, was formerly recorded but is now thought to be extinct. Pine has been widely planted in much of Britain since the 1800's but a good dipterous fauna in dead wood only occurs in the Scottish Highlands where pine is native.

SAND DUNES
by Brian Cogan

This harsh environment is surprisingly rich in Diptera. Ardø (1957) listed nearly 750 species recorded during his investigations on the dunes of southern Sweden, but this figure included the fly fauna of the littoral zone, dealt with under Sea Shore below. However, only a relatively small proportion, less than 50 of the total 750 species were considered by Ardø to be truly confined to dunes (i.e. stenotopic dune species).

In Britain most dune systems are coastal in position. The main prerequisite for the development of a dune is an exposed coastline with an extensive wind fetch over a sandy shore. Dunes occur widely around the British coast but are highly localised in extent. They may occupy bays or occur on spits, bars and other accretionary coastal landforms whilst a few examples even 'climb' sloping cliffs. The machair of the Hebrides is a type of dune. Inland dunes are very rare; the best examples are situated in the Breck of East Anglia and in Worcestershire. An idealised mature dune system may be considered, for the purpose of delimiting its fauna, as a series of zones conforming to the stages in its development.

Fore Dune

The first zone on the seaward side is the fore dune, this being best developed on growing dunes but it may be absent on eroding or semi static-dune fronts. It occupies the top of the beach, an area characterised by strong abrasion from wind blown sand and often by the pioneer grass colonists *Agropyron junceiforme* or, sometimes, *Elymus*. The sand is usually fairly mobile and only precariously trapped by the plants to form a low dune. The outer fringe locally may support various other plants, notably those characterising the highest drift line such as *Cakile maritima*, the strand line being relatively rich in plant nutrients due to the rotting organic matter.

The fore dune can be relatively rich in Diptera sheltering in the low herbage or sitting on the sand. Some may be truly resident such as the chloropid *Meromyza*. However, most of the flies taken here are ubiquitous species, often casual visitors to the shore line or flies extending their range from the littoral, such as *Fucellia*, *Coelopa* and *Tethina*. The latter are usually confined to flowering vegetation and some flowers, such as *Cakile*, can attract hoverflies from more landward areas During calm conditions, the fore dune is also the hunting ground of the dune asilids, particularly *Philonicus albiceps*, a common species found throughout the dune system, and the empid *Chersodromia incana*, confined to the open sand. The scatopsid *Aspistes berolinensis* may be found in the foredune area, where it frequents open sand into which its eggs are laid; both adults and pupae are capable of digging into the sand when conditions become too dry (Ardø, 1957).

Dune Ridge and Yellow Dunes

As the fore dune becomes increasingly colonised, principally by marram, *Ammophila arenaria*, it accumulates blown sand and its elevation increases to form a dune ridge. There is frequently extensive hummock development with patches of bare sand, the latter giving rise to the term yellow dune. The hummocky ground provides sheltered areas where flies may congregate on a windy day. This bare sand is the favourite resting place of the dune therevids, *Thereva annulata* and *Dialineura anilis*, which are often found in large numbers in early summer; the males of these species are silver coloured, as are many other species (often both sexes) on bare sand, e.g. the muscid, *Helina protuberans*. Other species are mottled brown, e.g. the small heleomyzid *Trixoscelis*.

Marram tussocks provide shelter for a number of dune species; sweeping over dense stands will net, among others, species of *Dexiopsis* (Muscidae), the empid *Platypalpus strigifrons* and the acalypterates *Tetanops myopinus* and *Pherbellia cinerella*. The cranefly *Nephrotoma submarmorata* is often abundant in May and early June. Closer observation of the bases of the tussocks reveals many of the more delicate species, particularly the acalypterates *Asteia concinna*, *Stiphrosoma sabulosum* and *Gymnochiromyia minima*, the larvae of which are to be found in the rotting plant matter that has accumulated at the bases of the marram stems.

Also associated with the tussock grasses are a number of *Chamaemyia*, the larvae of which are predators on coccids living around the base of the grass and on their roots or on aphids in the flower heads

Fixed dunes

Landwards of the dune ridge the dunes become progressively more stable due to plant cover, often with a preponderance of lichens on the stable sand (grey dunes) or other vegetation may form a complete cover. Gradual replacement of marram inland by less xerophytic species of grasses, herbs and shrubs leads eventually to the production of dune grassland or heath. The latter, characterised by heather (*Calluna*), develops on older dune ridges where leaching of the sand by rain has produced a very acid and impoverished soil. The fly fauna changes correspondingly, with a greater proportion of dryland and ubiquitous species rather than stenotopic dune species. Flies characteristic of the zone are species of Anthomyiidae, *Delia* (esp. *alula* and *candens*) and Sarcophagidae, e.g. *Senotainia conica* and *Metopia argyrocephala*, which may be found searching for the burrows of sand-wasps and other aculeate Hymenoptera. *Phthiria pulicaria*, a small bombyliid, may be swept from flowers (where its larvae lie in wait for their hosts, flower-attending aculeates). A large bombyliid, *Villa*, is also frequent, especially in late July and August. Although not confined to dunes, the asilid *Dysmachus trigonus* is often a dominant species, preying on any insect it can subdue, regardless of size. The female of this species lays its eggs into the inflorescences of grasses, for which its ovipositor is well adapted; the other common dune asilid, *P.albiceps*, oviposits in sand.

Dune slacks

An additional zone, sometimes present in a dune system is the aquatic or marsh habitat termed dune slack. A slack is an area where the water table is close to the surface, often fluctuating in level and even sometimes flooding the surface during the winter. Such areas tend to occur between dune ridges and in major hollows; in some cases even large permanent lakes are produced. Such areas are often very rich in Diptera, the fauna contrasting markedly with the dry dunes.

The composition of the fly fauna will vary appreciably depending on the degree of salinity. Three families of Diptera predominate in and around the more saline slacks - Chironomidae, Culicidae and Ephydridae. Among chironomids, species of *Halocladius* and *Chironomus*, including *C.salinarius* and *C.halophilus* are found. The larvae of the halophilic culicids *Aedes caspius* and *A.detritus* are also found in the slacks, around which the adults are noticeable due to their persistent man-biting habit. Ephydrids are represented in this area by species of *Ephydra*, *Setacera* and *Scatella*, the larvae of which are aquatic, feeding on algae, while the adults are confined to the surface film, or the mud banks around the water's edge. The latter habitat is the larval home of a common and persistent biting-midge *Culicoides halophilus*. Less saline aquatic slack has a diverse fauna more typical of freshwater ponds and pond edges; sciomyzids are often plentiful and several tipulids such as *Tipula solstitialis* and *Erioptera stictica* may be common. Marshy areas often have a rich fauna; and in May creeping willow, *Salix repens*, has catkins which are very attractive to hoverflies and a variety of other Diptera. Slacks may develop areas of sallow or alder scrub and it is well worth collecting both in and around this habitat.

General

Dunes in Britain and probably elsewhere in north western Europe, harbour species that are at the limit of their range. Since most dunes are coastal, this means that they occur in areas which often have relatively high amounts of sunshine and the bare dry sand can reach high temperatures. It is perhaps not surprising, therefore, that some very interesting distribution patterns are discernible. The tipulid *Nephrotoma quadristriata* is confined to a few dune systems in Devon and Wales where it frequents the fixed secondary dunes and the areas around dune slacks (adults in August). *Tipula juncea* is confined to dunes in the Moray Firth area (plus sandy banks of the River Spey) yet it is not so strongly associated with dunes (or river banks) on the continent. The validity of the British records of the asilid *Dasypogon diadema* are disputed and this species may await rediscovery on the dunes of Wales and western England. *Pamponerus germanicus* is confined to some of the dunes on the east side of the Irish Sea, plus the Isle of Man and N.Devon. *Epitriptus cowini* is confined to coastal dunes from Dublin to Kerry in Ireland and to dry ground in the Isle of Man. The apparently rare agromyzid, *Cerodontha superciliosa*, is a leaf miner on marram grass, but has been recorded in this country only from Culbin Sands in Scotland; the factors that control its distribution here have yet to be elucidated. The muscid *Lispocephala rubricornis* has a particularly disjunct distribution in Britain, having been recorded from Studland (Dorset), Porthcawl (S.Wales) and Culbin Sands (Scotland).

One characteristic that most stenotopic dune species have in common is their pale colouration, pale buff-brown to grey. This colouration they share with many of the littoral species particularly those occurring above the drift line; their pale vestiture is probably for camouflage although it may also be protective in view of the intense solar radiation to which sand-dwelling species are subjected.

Collecting

Collecting techniques and equipment are not particular to dunes. Sweeping over the vegetation or direct pooting from the base of tussocks are the standard and most productive methods. Passing dry or slightly damp sand through fine sieves is an efficient method of extracting larvae and pupae from under and around tussock and cushion vegetation. Collecting around a light at night is often productive and many species that are difficult to catch in the heat of the day may be easily taken at light. A square of hard-board, approx. 0.5 metres square, painted white, and a portable lamp are all that are needed. The species collected are not usually nocturnal, but are disturbed when the white board is placed close to the vegetation or to the edge of the dune slack. They fly to the light and usually alight on the board where they may be taken. A white board is more convenient than a white linen sheet as it may be easily cleaned, moved to a new site and is impervious to water.

Some larger and more mature dune systems have ideal 'rides' between the constituent dunes in which Malaise traps may be erected. It is unwise to place traps in exposed areas unless the wind conditions are calm (also vandalism can be a particular problem near holiday beaches). Under particularly windy conditions, all collecting is best confined to the leeward side of the dune ridge or any very large tussocks, where the eddies formed around the projection deposit most of the flies that have attempted to take the wing. Hollows in hummocky dunes also provide useful sheltered spots. Such collections are often a mixture of littoral, dune and casual species and little biological information concerning specific habitats can be obtained from them.

Further Investigations

Almost all aspects of the biology and life-histories of the stenotopic dune species require further investigation and this is an important field for future research by the amateur. As discussed previously, the factors that confine some species to dunes or to specific areas are not understood and the distribution of all but the most common species are poorly recorded. It is of particular importance that further researches are carried out on our dune fauna as soon as possible as dunes form part of the coastal habitat most under pressure from the tourist and leisure-holiday trade.

Further Reading

Ardö, P., 1957. Studies in the marine shore dune ecosystem with special reference to the dipterous fauna. *Opusc. ent.* (Suppl.) 14:1-255. 82 figs.

THE SEA SHORE AND CLIFFS
By Alan E.Stubbs

Caution: always check the tide times if you are on any coast where your retreat could be cut off.

At the first sight the sea shore would seem inhospitable to Diptera, an impression reinforced by their omission from most books on sea shore life. However, there is considerable interest for the dipterist, the smallness of the fauna being more than recompensed by the interest of the species concerned. This account deals with the rocky shore and cliffs, as well as beaches and lagoons. Saltmarshes and sand dunes are considered separately though there is some overlap especially as regards the drift line fauna. Sea cliffs and rocky shores generally occur where high ground reaches the coast and tend to be absent along estuaries and shore adjoining coastal levels. Though poorly recorded, present information suggests that the south coast of England, especially Devon and Cornwall is likely to be the richest area but interesting faunas will probably be found on most coastlines. In general it is best to seek sheltered areas within bays rather than promontories exposed to the full force of waves and wind.

Rocky Intertidal Shores

The term littoral fauna is applied to those animals which live in the intertidal zone.

The cranefly *Limonia* (*Geranomyia*) *unicolor* (which has a long proboscis like a mosquito) has larvae which feed on lichens and algae, especially *Lichina pygmaea* and *Catenella repens* and possibly *Enteromorpha*, on the upper part of the shore. Adults are best found by sweeping over sheltered shaded rocks at the top of the shore in mid-summer.

There are several littoral chironomids. *Clunio marinus* has wingless females and the males are found skimming over the surface of rock pools. *Psamathiomya pectinata* has reduced wings in both sexes and is found on pools and running over rocks and algae in the *Fucus* zone at low tide. Fully winged *Thalassomyia frauenfeldi* may be found running over rocks and though its zonal occurrence is uncertain it has on occasion been found high on the shore. Various other chironomids may be found on the shore but are often strays; however, *Halocladius fucicola* is normally found in brackish pools in the splash zone where larvae live in tubes or crawl over the bottom. Ceratopogonids occur on the shore but little is known of their ecology.

On most rock shores there is a barnacle zone and this is the place to sweep over rocks or search for dolichopodids of the genus *Aphrosylus*. Certainly the larvae of some of the four species are predatory on barnacles, but limpets and other prey may also be concerned. *A.celtiber*, with a larval density of up to 218 per square metre, must have a significant ecological role since this is a reasonably large species. The adults are predatory on other small creatures. *Hydrophorus* spp. have been recorded as skimming over pools, suggesting a suitable line of further study. The shining black hoverfly, *Eristalinus aeneus*, is locally found on rocky shores and its rat-tailed maggot larvae probably live in small pools in the splash zone. Small acalypterates will also be found. Small ephydrids can be locally abundant but often must be regarded as strays from freshwater. It is possible that some Canacidae and Tethinidae are typically associated with rocky shores but very little is recorded about habitat; *Canace nasica* is recorded as breeding in *Enteromorpha*.

Sea Cliffs

Caution: Sea cliffs can be dangerous because of falling rock and are often unsafe to climb; it is best to wear a hard hat of the type used on building sites; on soft cliffs beware of mud flows.

There are often rocky sea cliffs behind a rocky shore and it can be difficult to be precise as to where a species is actually breeding. Apart from the sheltered crevices that adults of the littoral *Limonia unicolor* frequent, there may be little on a dry cliff face. The most important feature to seek out is a seepage in the cliff or a tiny stream which makes the rock face wet. This is the habitat of craneflies (e.g. *Limonia goritiensis*, *Gonomyia conoviensis*), Dolichopodidae (e.g. *Liancalus virens*) and many small flies, especially Ephydridae. A seepage often has a wet sludge with larvae in it or festoons of string-like algae may contain larvae and pupae, those of some ephydrids being especially characteristic because of their stout spines posteriorly.

Sea cliffs are not always sheer rock, they may be inclined or landslipped and have a clothing of herb rich grassland, scrub or woodland. Also there may be streams which reach the coast in a ravine or a broader valley. Thus a variety of terrestrial and freshwater habitats may be available and these should be worked in much the same way as an inland situation. The main problem can be getting out of the wind but on most coastlines it is possible to pick a spot which is sheltered. Whilst little can be said at present about the particular features of the Diptera fauna, such areas can on a good day provide very rewarding collecting. Landslips can provide a great variety of terrain, sometimes including freshwater pools and seepages, whilst bare clay or sand surfaces may be used by burrowing bees and wasps, some of the parasitic flies often being in attendance.

Lagoons

These features usually occur where a shingle bar has formed a barrier across a bay or at the mouth of an estuary where a spit has formed a constriction. The most notable examples are on the south coast of England and on the coast of East Anglia.

A special habitat type is the occurrence of stable intertidal gravel, combined with a variable brackish salinity of water. There may be a number of Diptera which will be shown to frequent this habitat including Ephydridae, Tethinidae and probably Canacidae. However, a striking example is the cranefly *Limonia (Geranomyia) bezzii* which is only known from behind Chesil Beach and Poole Harbour (Dorset), Langstone Harbour (Hants) and Shingle Street (behind Orfordness, Suffolk) where it is assumed that the larvae feed on *Enteromorpha*. The gravel substrate only occurs locally but areas of fine silt and sand can also be highly productive provided there is an element of stability. Sweeping a net over the surface can sometimes produce a good haul of acalypterates and Dolichopodidae.

Drift Line

A drift line can occur on both rocky and sandy shores as well as salt marsh. It is probable that a good deal of local variation in fauna occurs. Seaweed (wrack) can be a major component of the drift line but for the best results it is necessary to find areas where the drift is several inches thick so that it keeps moist, combined with a high position on the shore so that it does not get disturbed by normal tides. Small quantities of fairly dry seaweed have a small fauna, but this is the breeding site of the large grey acalypterate *Helcomyza ustulata* (the adult looks like a scathophagid). This dry wrack can support a few other wrack flies on occasion and even the fully terrestrial *Fannia canicularis* has been reared. However, the richest fauna is in thick moist wrack. This includes the three *Fucellia* spp. (Anthomyiidae), *Scathophaga litorea, S.calida* and *Ceratinostoma ostiorum* (Scathophagidae), *Coelopa pilipes, C.frigida, Malacomyia sciomyzina* (Coelopidae), *Heterocheila buccata* (Helcomyzidae), *Orygma luctuosum* (Sepsidae, looks more like a coelopid), *Leptocera zostera* and *L.brachystoma* (and other Sphaeroceridae) and *Chersodromia* spp. (tiny Empididae). Phorids can also occur, some possibly being parasites of the abundant larvae and pupae of other Diptera. There is certainly a marked geographical and seasonal pattern of occurrence which would reward further study; it should be noted that some species are apparently most active as adults during the winter.

It is often easy to obtain the smaller species by looking among drifted seaweed or throwing some drift on a sheet for sorting but the larger ones may require individual stalking. *Chersodromia* and *Leptocera* can occur under quite sparse drift, even where wood and other material is predominant. Such small flies often do not take to the wing and may be tubed direct. If the wind is strong, one technique for the more mobile species is to hold the net immediately downwind so that it billows like a wind sock over the surface of the beach and then to lift the drift material so that any flies underneath which attempt to fly will get blown into the net.

Though considerable rearing of certain species has been carried out, much work is left for original study. It is relatively easy to rear material and don't forget to look for larvae or pupae in the substrate underneath - sieving being a suitable means of approach. More needs to be found out about parasites, such as the staphylinid beetles which parasitise puparia. Carrion in the form of dead fish, birds, seals etc. may on occasion be found on the drift line. Again results are only likely to be good if the carrion has been thrown up above normal tidal range (see section on Carrion).

General

When there is a strong off-shore wind, large numbers of flying insects get blown to the coast and huge numbers must meet their end out at sea. However, where there is any cliff, sea wall, groyne or other sudden vertical edge, the wind is likely to form an eddy such that many flies settle in the sheltered lee and show little enthusiasm for getting up again to battle with the wind. Such spots can on occasion yield a great diversity of flies, usually a mixture of coastal and inland species from a variety of habitats. Ecological information is unavailable but some interesting species can be found this way. In conjunction with the above observation, the edge of the sea where it laps against the beach may contain huge numbers of drowned flies which can form a long rolled ribbon possibly for miles along the shore. Such conditions are sometimes also associated with on-shore migrations of such species as *Episyrphus balteatus*, the mortality rate before reaching land obviously being high.

To interpret the significance of large concentrations of Diptera on the coast you need to consider the prevailing weather conditions over the past 24 hours or so and the degree to which the species are likely to have bred where you found them. If there are large numbers of aphid-feeding hoverflies, but no marked build up of other types of Diptera, in conjunction with a prolonged period of on-shore winds from the south or east, a migration is likely to have occurred.

SALTMARSH
by Alan E.Stubbs

The term saltmarsh is applied to those parts of the inter-tidal coast where flowering plants (as opposed to algae) are regularly inundated by salt water. In order to establish themselves, these plants require a stable substrate suitable for penetration by roots. Such conditions are normally restricted to sheltered areas where mud is plentiful, so most saltmarsh is found in estuaries or behind spits and bars as on the north Norfolk coast. It is difficult to define the limits of the saltmarsh habitat since it grades into freshwater river marsh at the head of an estuary. At the upper tidal limit of a saltmarsh there are ill-defined zones where inundation by salt water is progressively infrequent and there may be an imperceptible merger with adjacent terrestrial habitats such as meadow or sand dune. Salt spray laden wind may have a marked effect on these landward habitats and freshwater ponds and ditches may be brackish. The lower tidal limit normally does not extend down the shore below mid-tide level. The true inter-tidal saltmarsh includes some entirely natural habitat, a rare commodity in Britain today.

True saltmarsh is variable in character both physically and botanically. As regards the latter, the richest areas are on the coastline of East Anglia and the Thames Estuary and these are likely to prove richest in Diptera because of the general pattern of richest faunas being in the south-east. Physically a salt marsh is usually dissected by a mini-river system of muddy creeks and on the upper part of the marsh there will often be permanent muddy puddles called salt pans.

As with all open habitats, a major factor affecting the results obtained is wind. Thus a relatively still warm day suitable for sweeping is ideal. Failing this, every advantage must be taken of finding small scale sheltered spots in creeks or clumps of vegetation. Whilst one must not become blinkered as to what is good or bad, the poorest saltmarshes are usually those with a uniform cover of sea meadow grass (*Puccinellia*), especially if grazing is intense so that the short turf gives little cover. The best sites are normally those which are ungrazed and in general it is the top part of the marsh which is richest in species.

The most productive spots are those where there are clumps of rushes near high tide level (*Juncus maritimus, J.gerardii, Scirpus maritimus*), especially if there are freshwater seepages. Sweeping will normally yield an abundance of Diptera including such craneflies as *Limonia sera* and *L.complicata*, dolichopodids and a variety of acalypterates. Bare patches of mud under or by these clumps will often provide good collecting. Out on the more open saltmarsh, one of the main plants to look for is *Aster tripolium* since the flowers attract salt marsh hoverflies such as *Eristalinus aeneus* and *Eristalis abusivus* (flowers growing along the sides of creeks are sheltered on windy days). *Aster* is the foodplant of the tephritid *Paroxyna plantaginis*, these flies often being swept almost anywhere on a salt-marsh. The rare ephydrid *Parydroptera discomyzina* has been found the base of salt marsh herbage; no doubt this and any other flies with similar habits are often overlooked.

An abundant but none the less interesting species is the cranefly *Erioptera strictica* which usually has fully developed wings on the upper part of the saltmarsh but has stunted individuals with short wings low on the saltmarsh where specimens are especially common along creek banks. Saltmarsh pools have a characteristic fauna, which may include dolichopodids (e.g. *Dolichopus diadema*), chironomids (*Halocladius*), and acalypterates. Bare mud often has large numbers of the dolichopodid *Hydrophorus oceanus* and acalypterates. Among the saltmarsh species are the empid *Hilara lundbecki*, the dolichopodids *Dolichopus sabinus, D.plumipes, Machaerium maritimae*, the horseflies *Chrysops relictus, Haematopota bigoti* and *H.grandis* and the stratiomyids *Nemotelus uliginosus* and *N.notatus.*

The upper margin of a saltmarsh often has a strand line of plant debris which may yield its own distinctive fauna. It is a common feature of saltmarsh that an artificial flood prevention bank has been constructed, with former saltmarsh on the landward side reduced to brackish or freshwater marsh, or more usually drained with a ditch (dyke) system crossing fields of grazing marsh or even ploughed land. Many previous records for the coast have not separated these very different habitats from natural saltmarsh. The banks may contain a rich flora which is often ungrazed and ideal for sweeping as well as providing opportunities for collecting flower visitors at *Senecio, Daucus,* and other attractive plants. The banks may also offer shelter on the lee side on a windy day and provide a rich haul of Diptera although the true habitat will often remain unknown.

The ditch system and ponds, where they are present behind the bank, are usually brackish and tend to support a rich flora of mixed salt and freshwater character. This is a very important area for collecting, especially by sweeping emergent vegetation as well as collecting off bare mud. The fauna in the south-east includes the craneflies *Erioptera bivittata, Limonia ventralis, Tipula solstitialis, Ptychoptera contaminata,* a variety of tabanids, the Stratiomyidae *Stratiomys longicornis* and *S.furcata,* hoverflies *Helophilus parallelus, Lejops vittata* and *Tropidia scita,* the picture-winged otitids *Ceroxys urticae* and *Melieria* spp, many sciomyzids, sepsids, sphaerocerids, ephydrids, chloropids, agromyzids and calypterates. If *Phragmites* is present, this brings in its own characteristic fauna (see Marshes). The ditch flora and fauna is often ruined either by excessive mechanical clearance and deepening or through enrichment by run off from agricultural chemicals applied to the meadows. A dense growth of filamentous algae indicates such enrichment and with it an impoverished fauna.

The coastal marshes offer plenty of scope for refining our knowledge of the composition of the dipterous fauna and of the habitat factors which govern the distribution of the various species. The aspects of seasonal patterns of occurrence remain largely unexplored and there is even scope for mid-winter investigation since the inter-tidal fauna rarely has to cope with freezing conditions. Anyone with the opportunity to study the fauna in detail would be best advised to select one or two micro-habitats and to work those thoroughly. In this way one's results will not risk becoming too generalised and there is a chance that you may be able to get help with identifying the more difficult small acalypterates and other Diptera if samples are small and highly specific as regards habitat.

CAVES
by Anthony M. Hutson

The insects found in caves can be considered in three groups: *troglobites* are those insects exclusive to the caves and usually with special adaptations for this environment; *troglophiles* are frequent cave dwellers, but also occur outside the caves; *trogloxenes* are regular users of caves for part of their lives (sometimes called subtroglophiles) or occasional inhabitants. The latter group may occur in caves to hibernate or aestivate (or both), occur by virtue of having a very broad ecological tolerance or a fairly specialised food source that may occur in caves, or their occurrence is presumed to be quite fortuitous. Added to this are parasites of vertebrates which do not readily fall into one of these categories.

The cave itself can be divided into three main areas: the entrance area, the area of decreasing light intensity (threshold zone) and the area of no light (dark zone). Within these zones a variety of aquatic or terrestrial habitats may be available. Natural caves are mainly localised to certain limestone areas in Britain but many mines, culverts and cellars offer similar opportunities for many of our cave dwellers.

The larvae of most Diptera generally shun the light and are thus indirectly pre-adapted to cave life, but the adults are usually less crepuscular and not adapted to the high humidities, so that their occurrence is much more restricted. There are no true troglobitic Diptera in British caves. In Britain the nearest we have to an exclusively cave-dwelling fly is the fungus-gnat, *Speolepta leptogaster*. This species breeds inside caves, including the dark zone, the larva living in a slime tube supported by lateral strands of webbing on the damp cave walls and ceiling. It forages from the tube to feed on algal and fungal matter. Because of its pale head-capsule it looks rather nematode-like, but a closer look at the animal itself and the structure of its web will quickly identify this characteristic insect. The pupa hangs down freely from the wall. This is an extremely common species in all kinds of British caves, but it may also occur in quite small rock crevices or in the larger burrows of mammals, since there are several records of it being collected away from cave-like habitats. *Macrocera* spp. (Mycetophilidae) have been recorded breeding in caves in Europe and North America where they build a web that might be confused with that of *Speolepta*, but there are as yet no records of these in Britain. Other species that are notably regular in caves at all times of year are *Trichocera maculipennis* (Trichoceridae), *Triphleba antricola* (Phoridae), *Leptocera racovitzai* (Sphaeroceridae), *Heleomyza serrata* and *Scoliocentra villosa* (Heleomyzidae). The first three are rare outside caves and so may be considered as troglophiles; the last two are very common in caves and appear to maintain colonies, but they are equally common outside cave systems.

All may be associated with the dung or carrion of mammals such as badger, rabbit, moles, etc. or of birds. *H.serrata* and *Sphaerocera* spp. have been found in a lost mine exposed by preparations for a motorway cutting. The evidence suggested that these species had been surviving in a cave that had long been sealed up, but it is possible that there was some small access point.

Probably the majority of flies to be found in caves are hibernating or aestivating. Many Mycetophilidae, particularly *Bolitophila* and some species of Exechiini, regularly hibernate in caves and can be found far from the entrance. The same can be said of the common mosquito, *Culex pipiens* (Culicidae). Various Chironomidae, Sciaridae, and other Trichoceridae, Phoridae, Heleomyzidae, Sphaeroceridae, etc. also hibernate in caves in small numbers. Some species of *Bolitophila* and *Rymosia* (Mycetophilidae) reach a peak population in caves in the summer months. The majority of the overwintering flies are females, but this is not true for all species and is probably not true for the aestivators.

The other major element in the fauna of British caves is the group of opportunists that will invade a cave if the preferred habitat is available, even if only temporarily. Thus water will attract Dixidae, Chironomidae, etc.; rotting plants or animals will attract Psychodidae, Sciaridae, Phoridae, Sphaeroceridae, Heleomyzidae, Calliphoridae, Muscidae, etc.; fungus will attract Psychodidae, Mycetophilidae, Sciaridae, Cecidomyiidae, Phoridae, etc.; dung (including bat guano) will attract Heleomyzidae, Sphaeroceridae, Psychodidae, Phoridae, etc. The occurence of large accumulations of bat dung is rare in British caves since few of our bat species breed in caves and these are all species of restricted distribution. Dung is a habitat that has a rich fauna associated with it in other temperate, but more particularly tropical caves. It is still important in British caves, but many of the common dung species of European caves are rare or absent in Britain. *Megaselia melanocephala* (Phoridae) is an egg parasite of the common cave spider, *Meta menardi* but it only enters caves in search of spiders and has also been recorded as breeding in dung.

A water course that enters a cave system after running on the surface may bring quantities of nutrients in the form of debris for flies in the cave, but will also carry many of the otherwise unexpected aquatic stages of insects with it. Thus the occurrence of Simuliidae must arise in this way and it would appear that they can gather in a normal larval colony inside the cave. One or two records suggest that adults emerging from such colonies may be able to breed and to maintain a colony within the cave system, but this is unlikely and requires careful observation for confirmation.

Also of regular occurence in caves are the wingless nycteribiid flies parasitic on bats (see Associations with Vertebrates). However, since they do not normally leave the host except to deposit offspring on the nearby substrate and this normally occurs during the breeding season of the bats, when most of them are away from caves in Britain, they cannot be considered as part of the cave fauna.

The richest fauna is, of course, near the entrance, particularly when well vegetated and damp. Many crepuscular species, particularly of such families as Tipulidae and Mycetophilidae, will shelter in the entrance to a cave. Tipulids such as *Limonia nebuculosa* and *Limnophila submarmorata* like the dark damp areas that a cave mouth may offer, but will rarely be found far from the threshold. Many hundreds of Mycetophilidae can be found resting just inside a cave entrance.

Many of the flies at the cave entrance are not really part of the cave fauna, but the distinctions are not clear. The relationship between the fauna of caves (with a more or less constant climatic regime independent of the ambient weather conditions) and smaller rock crevices, animal burrows and other underground cavities are not well documented. Much work has been published from the continent of Europe on the ecology and classification of Diptera occurring in caves; there is still plenty of scope for comparable work in Britain.

The Diptera associated with caves worldwide have been reviewed by Matile (1970). Records of insects from British caves compiled by the British Cave Research Association (formerly the Cave Research Group of Great Britain) are published in *Hypogean Fauna*. Many records here are accompanied by information on the position in the cave of the collection, temperature, humidity, air flow, activity, as well as details of date and locality. Records will continue to be assembled by the BCRA. Analysis of these records and others scattered through the literature would rapidly point to useful areas of research on the status of many of the common cave dwellers, on their periodicity, activity, sex ratios, habitat preferences, influences of the geology of the caves, etc. More careful rearing of larvae from caves will better establish which species breed there and on what medium. A high incidence of attack by entomophagous fungi has been demonstrated in some instances and this is a subject that we know little about.

Caution: Caving by the inexperienced can be dangerous. Anyone wishing to examine the fauna of caves should be properly prepared with a hard hat, a good light and reserve lighting, should ensure that someone on the surface knows where they are, should be particularly careful and should preferably be accompanied by an experienced caver. For further details see the National Caving Code available from the National Caving Association. Remember, too, that bats are very prone to disturbance and that two species of British bat (mouse-eared and greater horseshoes bats) are protected under the Conservation of Wild Creatures and Wild Plants Act, 1975 - both of these bats frequent caves at all times of year.

Further Reading

Matile, L., 1970. Les Dipteres Cavernicoles. *Annales de Speleologie* **25** (1): 179-222.

URBAN AREAS
by Alan E. Stubbs

Many entomologists live in urban areas and despite the longing to get out into the countryside, they often find that their limited time can only be deployed in their immediate surroundings. There are always those days when the weather forecast is poor but use could be made of an hour's sunshine while it lasts. It is almost impossible to generalise about the opportunities in any one urban area but some of the following hints may apply. Often there are more fragments of the former countryside emersed in urban areas than one might expect and these can be very rewarding. There are so many species of Diptera that even in an urban area there is plenty of interest for the dipterist.

In the House

Even the busiest among us occasionally get the chance to look out of the window and in so doing spot the occasional interesting fly on the glass. Other members of the household can also be trained to report any strange insects. Windows act as a sort of Malaise or Herting trap since most flies which enter a house go to a window expecting to escape. Various flies are frequently found in this way - *Scenopinus* (Scenopinidae) is named the window fly because it is more often found here than in the field; it can be predatory on household insects such as carpet beetle larvae. *Microchrysa* (Stratiomyidae) are frequent, and small acalypterates including *Drosophila* are common, the heleomyzid *Tephrochlamys* is of regular occurrence as is the anisopodid *Silvicola cinctus*. Calypterates, such as *Calliphora* and *Lucilia*, readily make their presence known by the buzzing against a window pane but various less obtrusive species are also to be found. The house fly, *Musca domestica*, is not all that common in many areas, the fly circling the lamp shade being *Fannia canicularis*. In the south, *Helina punctata*, a muscid with similar larval habits to *Scenopinus*, may appear. The large craneflies come into the house in the autumn including *Tipula paludosa*. Common mosquitoes in the house include *Culex pipens* (does this bite man or not?), *Culex modestus* and *Culiseta an-*

nulata. If house martins or other birds nest on the house, then hippoboscids may enter through the windows. *Pollenia rudis* (cluster fly) and *Thaumatomyia notata* (Chloropidae) sometimes hibernate indoors in large numbers.

The Garden

Gardens vary considerably in their potential for Diptera. A well kept garden is rarely as good as one with areas of rank grass and weeds and a great deal depends on the character of the gardens or other terrain in the general neighbourhood. For the more mobile insects, particularly hoverflies, it is possible to provide suitable flowers to attract Diptera into the garden. In general the flat daisy like flowers are good (not the double cultivars), allowing for a seasonal succession; golden rod is ideal in mid summer and michalmas daisy is one of the best autumn forms. Flowering trees and shrubs are also valuable. If there is a space, a sallow bush (especially male *Salix caprea*) is worth planting; laurel and other spring flowering shrubs are useful, as well as most fruit trees and hawthorn. In the autumn a wall or trellis with ivy blossom is a good attraction. In all cases a sunny aspect is essential and the most sheltered spots are especially valuable for spring and autumn flowers when temperatures are likely to be low.

Both vegetable garden and the flower beds should yield a variety of phytophagous larvae and adults of such flies. Syrphids include *Merodon* and *Eumerus* which attack bulbs; the scathophagid *Norellia spinipes* is on *Narcissus*. Leaf mines include the agromyzids *Phytomyza aquilegiae* on *Aquilegia* and *P.syngenesiae* on *Chrysanthemum* and other plants. Your vegetables may be attacked by *Psila rosae* (carrot fly), *Delia brassicae* (cabbage root fly) and other pests (see Higher Plants). Aphid colonies on beans, roses, etc. should be searched for predaceous syrphid larvae (also eggs and pupae). It may be possible to study parasitic flies by rearing them from caterpillars, woodlice and other invertebrates.

A compost heap can provide an interesting fauna and there is the opportunity to breed out larvae. A range of species may be involved, such as stratiomyids (*Sargus, Microchrysa*), syrphids (*Syritta*), numerous acalypterates (drosophilids, sphaerocerids, etc.), muscids, fanniids, etc. Undoubtedly these species will show preferences for different parts of the compost heap - grass cuttings, general plant debris, dead leaves, fruit debris from the house - all are likely to have distinct larval faunas.

A garden pond may provide considerable interest. The large dolichopodid *Poecilobothrus nobilitatus* frequents such situations and there are almost bound to be some ephydrids and in the shallows perhaps some rat-tailed maggot larvae of *Eristalis* (recognisable by the small depression in the meniscus where the transparent breathing tube reaches the surface). Chironomid larvae are almost bound to occur in the bottom sediment. Failing a pond, a water butt or any other standing water may have a variety of mosquito larvae. A bird bath or a long standing bowl of water may become the breeding site of *Dasyhelea* (Ceratopogonidae), the larvae living in the sediment in the bottom.

A garden is a convenient place to try out bait traps, water traps, Malaise traps, etc. Bait traps for Calliphorids have shown seasonal and locality differences which can readily be studied with advantage. If the garden shed or the garage has a window, the door can be left open so that flies may be caught as in a Herting trap. If an old tree dies, leave the stump and retain some large logs to rot in the shade. Some interesting species may be found this way.

Waste Ground

Most urban areas have waste ground, though to the entomologist these can be paradises rather than waste. The neglected building site, the unmanaged corner of a park, derelict allotments and the local rubbish dump all have potential. Neglected quarries also provide good terrain in some urban areas. Here one may find rank vegetation which is conducive to sweeping, an abundance of flowers gives good potential and often there are trees and shrubs to diversify the range of habitats. There may even be old hedgerows and small copses within this type of ground. The commoner hoverflies, an abundance of calypterates and a range of small acalypterates typify waste ground. There is often the chance to find some of the tephritid larvae, such as *Phagocarpus* in hawthorn berries, *Rhagoletis alternata* in rose hips, *Euleia cognata* mines in coltsfoot leaves and *Urophora cardui* galls on thistle stems.

Recording

It is usually possible to pursue one's studies in and around the home in a more leisurely fashion than is possible on forays into the countryside. This gives you the chance to work out a system of recording, to get to know some of the commoner species and in particular to study the behaviour of flies, so that forays further afield can be put to best advantage. And remember, many of the life cycles and breeding sites of the species on your doorstep remain unknown and undescribed.

GLOSSARY OF SELECTED ECOLOGICAL TERMS

aphidophagous	feeding on aphids (= aphidivorous).
arboricolous	living on trees (= arboreal).
autecology	the ecology of a single species.
basic	water, soil or rock with a high pH (opposite of acid).
benthic	living on the bed of a water body.
benthos	the environment on the bed (bottom) of a water body.
biocoenose	an ecological assemblage (community) of species.
bog	an area of wet acid peat.
calcareous	water, soil or rock with a high calcium content.
canopy	the upper storey of a tree (especially the foliage).
carr	wet or swamp woodland on peat.
commensal	occupying the nest or body of another organism, without any adverse effect (cf. inquiline).
coprophagous	feeding on dung.
coprophilous	living in or on dung (= stercoricolous).
diapause	a resting period, usually of a larva or pupa.

drift (geology)	superficial surface deposits which mask the underlying solid rock (e.g. river alluvium, river terrace sand or gravels, glacial deposits such as boulder clay).
dystrophic	water bodies with high levels of suspended vegetable matter, e.g. peat.
ectoparasite	external parasite living on the surface of the host.
emergent vegetation	plants rooted below water but with leaves and flowers rising above the water surface.
endoparasite	internal parasite, living inside the host.
eutrophic	water bodies that are rich in plant nutrients.
facultative	opportunist (applied to parasite or predator) as opposed to obligate.
field layer	all plant growth between 6 ins. and 6 ft. (15cm – 2m).
fen	an area of wet base-rich peat.
flush	a seepage (often marked by lush vegetation).
forage	the act of searching for and gathering food.
fungicolous	inhabiting fungi (not necessarily feeding on fungi, termed fungivorous or myc(et)ophagous).
ground layer	all plant growth (or litter) up to 6 ins. (15cm) in height.
herbaceous	non-woody flowering plants (herbs).
honeydew	a sugary substance secreted by aphids, attractive to Diptera when coating leaves.
host	the victim of a parasite or food-plant of a phytophagous species.
hydrophilous	water loving.
inquiline	a species living harmlessly in the home (nest, gall etc.) of another animal.
larviparous	the adult female deposits young larvae rather than eggs.
larvoviviparous	the adult female gives birth to fully mature larvae.
lignicolous	living on wood.
littoral	intertidal sea shore, also the margins of lakes.
macrophytes	larger flowering plants growing in water
marsh	an area of wet ground with a mineral soil, with or without some peat.
mesotrophic	water bodies intermediate between oligotrophic and eutrophic.
myiasis	larval infection of living tissue, applied to man and other vertebrates.
myrmecophilous	living with ants.
nidicolous	living in nests (of birds and mammals).
obligate	can live in no other way (applied to parasitic or predatory relationships or to plant feeders).
oligotrophic	water bodies which are poor in plant nutrients.
oviparous	laying eggs.
ovoviviparous	eggs hatch immediately after being laid.
parasite	an organism that consumes another slowly without resulting in its death, or feeds in gut.

parasitoid	an organism that starts life as a parasite but completes its development by killing the host and consuming it, sometimes then becoming a predator.
phoresy (phoretic)	the habit of hitch-hiking a lift on another animal, usually as a means of dispersal.
phytophagous	feeding on living plant tissue.
planktonic	living suspended in water.
predator	captures and consumes living prey.
puparium	the higher Diptera, Cyclorrhapha, pupate inside the hardened larval skin, which forms the puparium; inside this is the true pupa.
riparian	river bank habitat.
saprophagous	feeding on decaying vegetable matter.
sarcophagous	feeding on carrion.
seepage	groundwater coming to the surface over a diffuse area (see spring).
shrub layer	all plant growth between 6 and 15 ft (2-5m).
shrubs	all flowering plants with a woody stem (e.g. heather up to large bushes of tree species).
spring	groundwater rising at a specific point.
stenotopic	confined to a particular habitat type.
stercoricolous	living in dung.
swarm marker	a physical feature (e.g. branch of a tree, the top of reeds, top of a mountain, a lamp shade in a house, a man standing in a field) used as an assembly point for individual flies or for a swarm.
symbiotic	an association of mutual benefit between two species.
synanthropic	living around man's habitation.
vernal	occurring in the spring (season).
wetland	embraces both water and wet ground such as a fen, marsh and bog (sometimes also used to include salt-marsh and other coastal habitats).

Further Reading

Fitter, R., 1967. *Dictionary of British Natural History.* Penguin, London.
Jackson, B. D., 1971 (Rep.) *A Glossary of Botanic Terms.* Duckworth, London.
Leftwick, A. W., 1975. (Rep.) *A Dictionary of Zoology.* Constable, London.

Chapter 5

Association with other animals and micro-organisms

Only twenty years ago the life histories of Sciomyzidae were virtually unknown - today it is almost proved that the entire world fauna consist of larval parasites and predators of molluscs. This is but an example of our ignorance of the way Diptera live yet it shows dramatically how our knowledge of Diptera can make major strides forward given the right lead. Are we on the verge of another stride forward in finding that some members of that vast phorid genus *Megaselia* are parasites of other Diptera? Whilst some associations between flies and other animals are well known, the literature is full of half facts and, in all probability, many outright errors. The sheer number and diversity of Diptera, viewed against what is known, suggests that naturalists are still only at the beginning of understanding the scope of the influence and ecological role of Diptera in their many intricate and complex relationships with other creatures.

FLIES AND MAN
by Kenneth G. V. Smith

Flies can affect man in many ways - they can attack his crops (both in the field and as stored food) and domestic animals, and they can attack his person directly by the transmission of disease or by actual tissue invasion (myiasis). The medical importance of Diptera is of course much more apparent abroad where mosquitoes transmit such diseases as malaria and yellow fever or in Africa where the infamous tsetse fly transmits sleeping sickness (trypanosomiasis), and throughout the world several other families transmit disease. The reduction of man/mosquito contact by improved standards of hygiene and the reduction by drainage of potential breeding areas has eliminated malaria in this country although the anopheline mosquitoes capable of transmitting the causative *Plasmodium* are still present. Malaria occurred as the 'ague' until about 1870 and there were local minor outbreaks from returning infected troops after both world wars.

However, we should not rule out the Diptera as disease transmitters in the United Kingdom as many undoubtedly mechanically transmit enteric and other infections. Diptera that live in close association with man, such as Muscidae and Calliphoridae, are known as synanthropic and can be important factors in hygiene. Often the evidence for the dissemination of disease by non-biting Diptera is largely circumstantial and much work remains to be done in establishing direct connections.

Many dung frequenting flies are probably common transmitters of enteric infections by the contamination of food, and the decline of the number of horse-drawn vehicles in London early this century has been directly correlated with a reduction in the incidence of infant mortality from summer diarrhoea. In Hawaii and in England work has shown that many synanthropic Diptera frequent dog excrement, an ubiquitous pabulum and this is clearly a problem that needs further investigation in the interests of public health. Open refuse tips are another potential source of infection from synanthropic Diptera.

Flies have been suspected of the mechanical transmission of poliomyelitis. The stools of patients suffering from this disease contain the virus, which is also found in corpses and sewage. Visiting houseflies carry the virus (on their bodies), which can persist and multiply there for three weeks.

The arboviruses (arthropod-borne) animal-human ultraviruses are transmitted by bloodsucking Diptera. Work on the vectors of arboviruses proceeds apace throughout the world but almost certainly many more Culicidae, Ceratopogonidae and Tabanidae occurring in Britain will be found to be vectors of disease to man and his domestic animals.

Cases of myiasis involving flies that invade the living tissues of man are fortunately few but abroad these are not uncommon. In Britain invasions of the human eye by young larvae of *Oestrus*, *Gasterophilus* and *Hypoderma* are recorded, and there was an unusually high number in 1976. Fortunately *Oestrus* larvae die before they damage the eye, but *Hypoderma* can be more serious. *Lucilia* has been involved in aural myiasis in the U.K. The commonest occurrence of myiasis is of the intestinal (enteric) kind where larvae of such genera as *Eristalis*, *Piophila*, *Drosophila*, *Calliphora* or *Musca* may be involved. The larvae of *Fannia canicularis*, *Musca domestica* and *Sylvicola fenestralis* have been involved in urinogenital myiasis.

Finally Diptera, especially Calliphoridae, Muscidae and Phoridae, can be involved in the decomposition of man's body after death when there is a distinct faunal succession which can have considerable forensic and medico-legal value by aiding in the establishment of the time of death.

Further Reading

Busvine, J.R., 1966. *Insects and Hygiene. Methuen. 467 pp.*

Greenberg, B., 1971-1973. *Flies and Disease.* Princeton University Press, New Jersey. 2 vols. 856 + 447 pp.

Leclercq, M., 1969. *Entomological Parasitology.* Pergamon Press. 158 pp.

Smith, K. G. V., (Ed.) 1973. *Insects and other Arthropods of Medical Importance.* British Museum (Natural History), London. 561 pp.

Zumpt, F., 1965. *Myiasis in man and animals in the Old World.* Butterworths. 267 pp.

ASSOCIATIONS WITH VERTEBRATES, THEIR NESTS, ROOSTS AND BURROWS

by Anthony M. Hutson

At the outset, readers should be reminded that there are many restrictions applicable to the handling of birds and some other vertebrates and to the interference with the occupied nests of birds and roosts of some bats. The laws pertaining to birds are covered by the Protection of Birds Act, 1967, and those to other animals are included in the Protection of Wild Creatures and Wild Plants Act, 1975. The otter was added to this latter act in 1977. Further animals are partially protected by other national and local laws. In all cases every effort should be made not to create too much unnecessary disturbance to their life.

There are, however, many ways in which dipterists can study the fauna associated with vertebrates: the examination of birds is most effectively done by contact with a qualified bird ringer (in this country bird-ringing is co-ordinated by the British Trust for Ornithology, Beech Grove, Tring, Herts); nests can be collected after the birds have vacated them (but remember that birds may still use a nest as a roost for several days after the young have fledged and that they may return to produce another brood); the Mammal Society and the British Deer Society provide useful contacts; there is a large number of organisations that consider the killing of birds and mammals as sport and contact with these may produce useful material; and there are official bodies that "manage" populations of many animals.

Do not use a pooter when collecting from nest material or off dead or live animals - there is a strong risk of lung infections. Bites and scratches inflicted by animals can also result in infection.

Blood-feeders and Sweat-feeders as Free-living Adult Flies

The families Ceratopogonidae, Culicidae, Simuliidae, Tabanidae and Muscidae all include species that bite vertebrates, but their food preferences are poorly known. In all except the Muscidae it is only the females that bite and many require flower sugars as well. Much more careful observation, experiment on host preferences, height and time of biting and blood-meal analysis of fed adults is necessary to obtain a better picture of their biting activity. Present knowledge is very restricted apart from where it affects man and his domestic animals. While many species may be opportunist feeders and may be more habitat or behaviourally specific than host specific, they certainly should have preferences as well. It is only recently that man and his domestic animals have ousted or restricted many wild animals, particularly larger mammals, and introduced others, perhaps obscuring true host preferences. The present boom in rural Wild Life Parks might provide an opportunity for study in this field! The endoparasites and diseases of birds and mammals and their vectors is a subject that is only beginning to receive attention in Britain (see under micro-organisms).

In the Ceratopogonidae, the only bloodsucking genus in Britain is *Culicoides*, which feeds on mammals, birds and possibly snakes. *Forcipomyia (Lasiohelea) velox* feeds on frogs - it occurs as near as France and could occur here. These flies are a great irritant to man and domestic animals, especially in upland areas. They are recorded in Britain as vectors of *Onchocerca cervicalis*, a filarial nematode found in horses, and are a potential problem as vectors of other diseases.

Since Marshall's Monograph of British mosquitoes in 1938, only 3 species have been added and little has been added to the knowledge of the biology of British mosquitoes. Both sexes feed at flowers or on juices of fruits and the females of all British species feed on the blood of vertebrates; some species are capable of completing at least one generation without a blood-meal, but they do not normally do so unless forced. Most of the British species have been recorded as biting man, a few have been recorded as biting domestic animals. The common *Culex pipiens* is thought to feed mainly on birds but has also been seen feeding on frogs, lizards and snakes; little else is known of the relationship of mosquitoes to wild animals, although several species will bite caged rabbits.

In the Simuliidae, the females feed on birds and mammals. Some may be primarily bird feeders, particularly in the subgenus *Eusimulium*, while others are recorded as primarily feeders on man and domestic animals. Analysis of blood-meals of light-trap caught black flies in Scotland has revealed a small number of "rodent" feeders in two of six species examined. There is no reason to rule out other small mammals (from badgers downwards) as possible sources of blood for some black fly species. In Canada some blackflies have been shown to have distinct preferences for certain species of bird.

Current increased interest in the larger Brachycera may improve the understanding of Tabanidae, recorded as biters of man and large domestic animals, particularly horses and cattle, but also pigs and sheep. Deer have been recorded as hosts and there are records from abroad of *Chrysops* feeding on birds down to the size of thrushes as well as reptiles and amphibians. From present knowledge there are important differences in the choice of site on the host animal, time of biting and location of the host. As these are relatively large day-flying species that are fairly readily identified, direct field observation on feeding activity should be more practical.

The Muscidae include one subfamily of biting flies, the Stomoxyinae. Three species occur in Britain and are mainly recorded as biting man and his domestic animals. Their attacks may be painful and persistent, but *Haematobia irritans* rarely bites man. A few other muscids are closely associated with animals, such as *Musca autumnalis*, *Morellia simplex*, *Hydrotaea irritans* and *Trichopticoides decolor* which are all attracted to sweat; *M.autumnalis* and *Hydrotaea irritans* are also attracted to seepages from eyes, nose and open wounds. While they may be a considerable nuisance to domestic animals in farms where their numbers are allowed to build up, Muscidae are probably of minor importance to wild animals. For most of these groups, the species may be generalised feeders on a wide variety of hosts rather than showing specific relationships, equivalent to Diptera that visit a variety of flowers depending on their availability and visual and olfactory impact. The reaction of the host to the presence of biting flies may limit the choice of hosts. Other aspects of adult behaviour, such as courtship and larval ecology, may be very important and should be investigated. Nevertheless, while the choice of host may not be too important for many species, the flies can be of great importance to the host in their attentions by force of numbers, viciousness or as agents in the spread of diseases.

Parasites of Mammals, Birds and Amphibia

In Britain the adults of two small families of Diptera (Hippoboscidae and Nycteribiidae) are strict ectoparasites of birds and mammals. The dipterous parasites of British mammals are confined to the large mammals (domestic animals and deer) and bats. The Hippoboscidae are almost permanent parasites of birds and larger mammals and the Nycteribiidae occur exclusively on bats. They are larviparous, producing fully grown larvae (or prepupae) which immediately pupate. Hence the only active phase is the adult and this lives in close association with the host. They all feed entirely on the blood of the host. In two other families (Oestridae and Gasterophilidae) the larvae are internal parasites of larger mammals and the larvae of some species of two other families (Calliphoridae and

145

Neottiophilidae) are parasitic on mammals, birds and amphibians. Colyer and Hammond (1968) outline the life histories and details may be found in Zumpt (1965).

(i) Mammals

In all associated groups of flies there is plenty of scope for additional work on host preferences, life cycle and current distribution. It is probable that further species of Nycteribiidae, which are ectoparasites of bats, could be added to the three on the British list. With Hippoboscidae further studies are needed on infestation rates, seasonality, site preferences and distribution of the species occurring on wild ponies (is *Hippobosca equina* really now confined to the New Forest?) and on deer. The present status of the sheep ked, *Melophagus ovinus*, is unknown to dipterists (though possibly known to vets). The present distribution of the Gasterophilidae is very poorly known and better techniques for finding the adults and pupae need defining - all are parasites of horses and perhaps the differences in life cycle could be supplemented by observations on habitat and seasonal data. The Oestridae are mostly parasites of deer and may not be as scarce as the infrequent sightings of adults would suggest. With the various introductions of deer this century and the increasing numbers of the long established species, the status, ecology and host distribution of these flies needs updating. Little seems to be known of the current status of the nasal bot fly of sheep, *Oestrus ovis* in relation to the effectiveness of the treatment for its control. It has been noted that male Oestridae form mating swarms away from the immediate vicinity of hosts and more information on this behaviour would be welcome. The three species of warble fly, *Hypoderma*, need study since there is a current programme to eradicate *H.bovis* and *H.lineata* which attack cattle. *H.diana* which parasitises deer (in particular roe) is poorly known.

The above families of flies are entirely specialised to a parasitic life cycle. However, several other families of flies have species which have become totally or occasionally parasitic. In the Calliphoridae, *Lucilia sericata* is well known for causing sheep strike, the larvae causing myiasis of the flesh under wet or soiled fleece. Cattle, horses and humans can also suffer "sheep-strike"! Other calliphorids, such as *Protophormia terraenovae* and *Calliphora vicina* can be involved but usually as secondary agents, although *P.terraenovae* has been recorded as the primary cause in Scotland,from May to July, while *L.sericata* becomes more important later in the year.

(ii) Birds

Several calliphorids are parasites of nestling birds. *Lucilia richardsi* has once been recorded as the agent of traumatic myiasis in the nightjar in Finland. Other blowflies, such as *Protophormia terraenovae* may attack nestling birds, but this needs confirmation. *Protocalliphora azurea* is recorded in Britain from a wide range of birds' nests, particularly hole-nesting birds or birds with a covered nest. The larvae feed on the blood of the nestlings and if present in large numbers can kill them. If this happens they are not averse to turning carrion feeder. The wide range of hosts recorded for this species may be incorrect, as much recent work on the genus encourages the idea that other species may occur and that some of the early material may have been misidentified. Other species may be added from nests such as crows, sand martins and possibly some tits.

One other larva that is a blood-sucking parasite of nestling birds is that of *Neottiophilum praeustum*. This also has a wide range of hosts, but usually small passerines in more open nests. Unlike *Protocalliphora* it is wholly dependent on blood and cannot complete its development if the nestlings die too soon. The only other species of the family Neottiophilidae is *Actenoptera hilarella*, which also occurs in Britain, but its larva is unknown.

The only other dipterous parasites of birds are members of the family Hippoboscidae, the general facies of which have already been discussed. Five species are indigenous to Britain on birds and at least three others might occur. One of these occurs on ospreys. The other two are largely tropical species which occur on a wide range of hosts and are frequently carried outside their normal range by migrant birds. Five other accidental species have been recorded, including some quite unlikely species on vagrant birds, but common migrants have equally brought unexpected parasites. In Britain swallows are very rarely host to hippoboscids, but in Europe, two species occur including the species that is common in Britain on house martins. Of our resident species *Crataerina hirundinis* is restricted to house martins, *C.pallida* to swifts, *Ornithomya avicularia* to larger passerines (from blackbird upwards) and many non-passerines, *O.fringillina* to small passerines (mainly finches and warblers) and *O.chloropus* on birds of all sizes in more open, barren areas such as moorland. In the case of the *Crataerina* spp. the flies are brachypterous and the pupae are deposited in and around the nests, presumably an adaptation to the fact that these birds return to the same nest site to breed. More work on the infestation rates, relationships between the breeding cycle of host and parasites, comparisons between occurrence in natural (tree and cliffs) and artificial (buildings) breeding sites and effects on the hosts, particularly the young, would be interesting. Pupae of the other species may be found in the nests of hole-nesting birds, but rarely in other nests. They are assumed to be deposited at random, but this is unlikely: birds in reed beds are frequently infested where random deposition of pupae would result in heavy losses of flies with a low fecundity. While the general host range is recorded, little is known of the degree of host selection, to what extent flies move between hosts, whether they try to move to a host of the same species, and the role this might play in the dispersal of certain kinds of lice which are frequently phoretic on these flies.

(iii) Amphibians

The calliphorid, *Lucilia bufonivora* is well known as an obligate parasite of toads and sometimes frogs. It needs to be confirmed whether some carrion feeders such as *Lucilia silvarum* and *Calliphora vomitoria* can occasionally be primary parasites. Some species of *Sycorax* (Psychodidae) are known to attack frogs.

Inhabitants of Nests, Roosts and Runs

The Diptera associated with birds' nests are well documented in the bibliography by Hicks (1959, supplements 1962, 1971). Doubtless there are many records missed by him but the bibliography is extremely valuable and it is hoped that supplements will continue to be published. No such bibliography exists for Diptera associated with mammals. On the other hand, the literature on the fauna of birds' nests consists almost entirely of rearing records, very little ecological work has been done, while there are several important papers discussing the ecology of the fauna associated with small mammal runs and nests (see Hackman, 1963 et seq; Baumann, 1977).

(i) Mammals

No attempt has been made to synthesise the scattered literature on flies associated with mammals except for a few species of rodents and ecologically similar mammals. Many British mammals use a nest throughout the year although the winter nest may be different from the summer nest. For instance the dry aerial summer nests of the dormouse and harvest mouse have a very limited fauna, their winter-nests are much more productive, but little studied. The voles, shrews, moles and to a lesser extent mice and rats also have permanent runways or burrows which have a fauna associated with them. Most work has been done on the mole, voles and squirrels, very little on the larger mammals such as badger, other carnivores or rabbits and hares. The more aquatic species, such as water vole and coypu have also been largely neglected. There is considerable scope for further work on all mammals.

The more ecologically biased work on the fauna associated with small mammals has attempted to attach to the flies degrees of dependence on the mammals. Thus species very closely associated with mammal nests and their burrows are termed *eucoenic*. These would include *Leptocera talparum* and *L.pseudonivalis* (Sphaeroceridae), *Eccoptomera microps* (Heleomyzidae) and possibly *Camilla* spp. (Camillidae). Species with a strong association with this habitat but well able to occur elsewhere are termed *tychocoenic*. Some species of this group show some adaptations to this environment such as reduced eyes and wings and in acalypterates, elongate aristae. This group includes other *Eccoptomera* spp., *Crumomyia* (Sphaeroceridae), some species of Phoridae, other Heleomyzidae and Sphaeroceridae and possibly some Sciaridae and Mycetophilidae. There is then a great variety of species that have been recorded from this habitat, but some are only temporary or occasional visitors. These species include further representatives of those families mentioned above as well as many others including Trichoceridae, Empididae, Drosophilidae, Calliphoridae and Muscidae. These casual species are termed *xenocoenic*. The similarity between the criteria for these categories and those used in discussion of cave fauna are obvious and reinforced by the considerable overlap of species. No substantial work has been published on this field in Britain.

The study of bat guano in caves is included in general cave studies but is a limited resource in Britain. Again Heleomyzidae and Sphaeroceridae dominate. Accumulations of bat guano at roosts in buildings are much larger and more widespread. Often these accumulations are very dry and unsuitable for many flies, but there are frequently deposits of fresher, damper guano and these may have a rich and individual fauna. Similarly bat roosts in trees have barely been examined and it will be interesting to see what fauna will associate with bats using bat-boxes.

(ii) Association with Birds' Nests

Species from nearly fifty of the families that occur in Britain have been reared from birds' nests. The first species that should be discussed is one that might well have been dealt with as a parasite. This is *Carnus hemapterus* (Carnidae) which is ovoviviparous or even larviparous and the larvae live in a wide range of aerial nests of birds, usually birds that nest in fairly sheltered places, particularly hole-nesting birds. Nests in exposed situations, such as wood pigeon have also been used. The larvae feed on debris in the nest and overwinter as pupae. Many of the nests in which the larvae develop are not re-used in the following year, so the emerging adults fly to an occupied nest. On arrival at a suitable nest the wings are shed and the abdomen becomes greatly distended (physogastric). Even in this condition it is barely 2mm long and lives on the unfeathered nestlings and sometimes on feathered young and adults. Its food has been the subject of much debate. Some authors insist that it is a blood feeder, but its mouth parts do not seem suitable for this and others suggest that it feeds on fatty secretions from the bird's skin. Confirmation should not be difficult.

The rest of the Diptera fauna of birds' nests consists of a mixture of coprophagous, saprophagous, sarcophagous, predaceous and parasitic species, all with a varying degree of reliance on this habitat. Apart from the different opportunities that different kinds of nests offer to Diptera at the time of the birds' occupation, there is also a succession of fauna in most bird's nests. After the birds have left different species of Diptera may move in to breed and other species will simply occupy the nest to pupate or as adults to hibernate. The frequent use of old nests by small mammals and bees may encourage yet other species to occupy. In this way even the loose dry aerial nests of birds such as reed warbler may start as poor habitat for flies, but can accumulate debris and be used by other occupants, such as harvest mouse and so become a habitat worthy of investigation. At the same time, some species that occupy the nest early in its history may leave it to pupate in the soil or in nearby bark, etc. Thus nests should be collected at various times; probably the best two periods to collect are soon after the young have left the nest and at the turn of the calendar year. If you wish to collect nests soon after the young have fledged, don't forget that many species of birds and their young will continue to use the nest as a roost for several days. Record the position of nests, since the nest of a blackbird on the ground may contain quite different species from one higher in a bush or on a building. The fauna of nidifugous birds (young leave nest soon after hatching) varies from those such as many waders and terns that do not really build a nest and hence have a very limited associated fauna, to those such as moorhens and coots that build a solid nest providing habitat for a variety of insects. Colonial nidifugous birds, such as many of the seabirds, produce a general accumulation of guano that attracts certain flies, such as Sphaeroceridae and Heleomyzidae. Similarly, heavily used roosting areas of thrushes or starlings provide a good substrate for Chyromiidae, etc.

The vile nests of cormorants and shags may have a special fauna, but little has been recorded from them. The equally unpleasant nests of shearwaters, fulmar and petrels (Procellariidae) may also contain interesting species. Large compact nests that are built on year after year, such as heron, are rich in species. Hole-nesting birds can produce a rich fauna and the sand martin has a rather special fauna including rare species of *Meoneura* (Carnidae) and the brachypterous *Nostima semialata* (Ephydridae).

Collecting Techniques

Contact with bird-ringers and other groups examining birds and mammals has been mentioned in the introduction. For finding Hippoboscidae on live birds it is usually sufficient to blow through the feathers and pick off any flies seen. A more sophisticated technique that will also collect other ectoparasites is the use of a Fair Isle apparatus (Cogan & Smith, 1974). In experienced hands it is perfectly safe to treat a bird in this way, but it should not be attempted by anyone inexperienced in handling birds. In all cases make sure the apparatus is perfectly cleaned of ectoparasites before using it for another bird.

The technique described above will not work for mammals. There is no satisfactory apparatus for collecting from live mammals. Bats must be searched painstakingly, and often painfully (for the searcher), and any ectoparasites picked off with fine forceps or paint brush dipped in chloroform or alcohol. The same applies to the large mammals that carry ectoparasites. Endoparasitic larvae can only be collected by dissection, except that skin bot-fly larvae can sometimes be squeezed out or can be encouraged to eject by smearing vaseline over their spiracles. All the specimens so far mentioned in this section should be stored in alcohol; for the rest it varies from group to group and has been discussed in an earlier chapter.

Free-flying blood-feeders and adult Oestridae and Gasterophilidae can be collected with a net when visiting their prey. A smaller net than is usually used for sweeping may be useful here.

For the fauna of nests, the nests should be searched in the field and any active flies collected. The nest can be put in a container from which any emerging flies can be extracted or which contains a funneling system that will catch them automatically. Make sure that the nest is ventilated but retains the humidity that it had in the field and in the case of ground nests also take the top layer of the soil directly under the nest. Take care, particularly with mammal nests which are used all year, that you are not removing the only shelter of an animal during inclement circumstances. The fauna of runs and burrows can be sampled by direct pooting or by various traps. Most of the traps used have been variations on a funnel leading into a collecting chamber. At least part of the system should be of gauze to allow a good airflow. Natural baits, such as dung or animal food-stuffs can be used; artificial baits, such as cheese, should be used with caution as they may give misleading results. The funnel should fill the run or burrow, but will frequently be rejected by the mammal. In burrows they can be set to collect fauna moving into the burrow, out of the burrow or simply along it. Insect pitfall traps can be used but the major problem is to prevent the trap filling up with debris. Barber's trap (Hackman,

1963) is fairly successful in this respect. A replaceable section of turf can be removed to gain access to burrows away from their entrance.

It should be noted that in the special effort involved in collecting these Diptera, the dipterist will find representatives of other groups of arthropods. These should not be wasted and may be welcomed by another specialist.

Flies as Food

Apart from the many ways in which vertebrates provide food for Diptera, it should not be forgotten that a large number of Diptera will end up as food for vertebrates. Observations of the food of insectivorous animals are rarely recorded but are an important part of the ecology of prey and predator. There is no review of the widely scattered literature on insects as food of vertebrates.

With dead animals, stomach analysis can give valuable indicators of a predator's food preferences and feeding behaviour. But stomach analysis is by no means the only method of collecting such information. Direct observation in the wild is difficult but possible with some birds, hedgehogs and amphibians, but is not very practical with many mammals. Collecting insect debris from around nests and at sites where certain bats, such as long-eared bats, hang up to dismember larger prey can provide identifiable remains. A polythene sheet can be hung under the nests of birds such as hirundines and roosts of bats to enhance such samples. Most insectivorous birds produce pellets of the larger indigestible insect remains, but it involves very careful observation to see the ejection of these pellets and to collect them. Swifts collect large balls of food in the mouth to take to their young and these can sometimes be collected; in this case the contents are in good conditon. Identifiable remains can be found in droppings. The identification of the fragmentary remains obtained by most of these methods can be absorbing and challenging work for an entomologist.

Further Reading

Baumann, E., 1977. Investigations on the dipterofauna of burrows and nests of voles *(Microtus, Clethrionomys)* on meadows in the mountainous region of the nature reserve 'Hoher Vogelsburg'. *Zool. Jb. Syst.* **104**: 368–414. [in German]

Cogan, B.H. & Smith, K.G.V., 1974. *Instructions for Collectors* No. 4a. Insects. 5th. ed., British Museum (Natural History), London.

Hackman, W., 1963. Studies on the dipterous fauna in burrows of voles *(Microtus, Clethrionomys)* in Finland. *Acta zool. fenn.* **102**: 1–64. [and later papers in *Notul. ent.]*

Hicks, E.A., 1959. *Check-list and bibliography on the occurrence of insects in birds' nests.* State College Press, Iowa, 681pp. [and supplements: 1962, *Iowa St. J. Sci.* **36**: 233–348; 1971, *Ibid* **46**: 123–338]

Maa, T.C., 1971. An annotated bibliography of batflies (Diptera: Streblidae; Nycteribiidae). *Pacif. Insects Monogr.* **28**: 119–211.

Rothschild, M. & Clay T. 1952. *Fleas, flukes and cuckoos.* A study of bird parasites. Collins (New Naturalist), London, 304 pp. [also published in Arrow paperback].

Thompson, G.B., 1969. Deer Keds: notes and records. *Deer* **1**: 317.

Woodroffe, G.E., 1953. An ecological study of the insects and mites in the nests of certain birds in Britain. *Bull. ent. Res.* **44**: 739–810.

Zumpt, F., 1965. *Myiasis in Man and animals in the old world.* Butterworths, London., 267 pp.

FLIES ASSOCIATED WITH FLIES (DIPTERA)
by Dr. Henry Disney

It appears that few flies parasitise other flies. However, the habit may be more widespread than has been realised.

The tachinid genera *Trichopareia* and *Siphona* parasitise larval Tipulidae (leatherjackets). .*Siphona* has been reared from terrestrial cranefly larvae and also from an anthomyiid *Pegomya* sp. and from Lepidoptera, while *Trichopareia* specialises in wood breeding tipulids *(Ctenophora, Tipula irrorata, T. flavolineata). Lypha dubia* has been bred from a syrphid *(Merodon sp.).*

It is in the Phoridae that growing evidence suggests not only that the parasitic habit is widespread but that other Diptera may frequently serve as hosts. *Borophaga incrassata* has long been known to parasitise the larvae of *Bibio marci.* More recently, *Megaselia paludosa* have been reported parasitising *Tipula paludosa* larvae without killing the host. Likewise *Megaselia flavicoxa* parasitises *Bradysia bicolor* (Sciaridae) and *M.obscuripennis* selects larval Sciaridae of the genus *Trichosia. Megaselia rufipes* has been reported parasitising tipulid larvae but the evidence suggests that it probably does not oviposit until the 'host' has died. Some early records of *Megaselia* as parasites of Diptera larvae require confirmation of the identity of the Phoridae.

In large colonies of *Simulium* larvae and pupae, the larvae of the chironomid genus *Cardiocladius* has been observed preying on them. Often larvae of *Eukiefferiella* can be found living beside the *Simulium* pupa within the cocoon. A wide range of adult flies are predatory and very often their prey consists of or at least includes other Diptera. The various predatory groups are discussed in the section on Studying Behaviour. Often the prey is likely to be non-specific within an acceptable size and behaviour range. However, in some cases the prey is highly specific e.g. the empids *Rhamphomyia sulcata* and *Empis femorata* nearly always carry the bibionid *Dilophus febrilis* even though it may be otherwise unobtainable. Ceratopogonidae of the genus *Bezzia* are predatory on the smaller midges of the genus *Culicoides*; abroad some *Culicoides* and *Lasiohelea* spp. are known to suck body fluids from mosquitoes much larger than themselves. Predation by larval Diptera is much commoner than by adults; some are specific such as the cecid genus *Lestodiplosis* which preys on other cecid larvae.

There are records of adult Diptera sucking the juices from the bodies of dead flies. Such scavenging habits are known among *Pegomya, Helina* and Lauxaniidae. Pallopteridae may have the same habit since *Palloptera saltuum* has been found on dead Lepidoptera larvae. This behaviour may be concerned with obtaining moisture rather than food but further critical observation is required.

BUTTERFLIES AND MOTHS (LEPIDOPTERA)
by Kenneth G. V. Smith and James Dear

The major dipterous parasites of Lepidoptera are Tachinidae of the subfamilies

Tachininae and Goniinae. Not many Tachinidae are polyphagous but a few may attack many hosts; *Phryxe nemea* attacks at least 15 families of Lepidoptera, but the record must surely be held by *Compsilura concinnata* for which over a hundred host species are known from three orders. Some are more or less specialist in their choice of host such as *Wagneria, Lydella, Gonia* and *Voria* which attack the larvae of Noctuidae. More specialist species include *Cyzenis albicans* from the winter moth *(Operophtera)* and *Phryxe magnicornis* from burnet moths *(Zygaena)*.

The method of entering the host in the tachinids can be divided into six main types.

1. Larviparous or oviparous; larvae or eggs are laid apart from the host on leaves or soil. The resultant searching larvae (as in Dexiinae) are often modified for spending some time in exposed conditions with sclerotized plates forming a continuous shield in contraction. Larvae are sometimes deposited near the host (Macquartiini). Egg production in this group is about 400 to 1000 by an individual female.

2. Larviparous or oviparous; larvae or eggs laid directly on to the host's body (Macquartiini and Tachininae). Egg production about 100 to 200.

3. Eggs deposited on foliage and hatch only when ingested by the host (Goniinae). The eggs are viable for up to six weeks and are very small, i.e. less than 0.2 mm. Egg production about 2000 to 6000.

4. Oviparous species that lay large eggs on the host, sometimes attached by stalks *(Carcelia)* or flattened basally (Phasiinae and Tachininae). Egg production about 100 to 200.

5. Oviparous species that insert their thin shelled eggs into the host by piercing ovipositors (most Phasiinae). Egg production 100 or less.

6. Larviparous or oviparous species that introduce larvae through damage caused to the host's cuticle by piercing apparatus (some Goniinae and Tachininae). Egg production about 100 or less.

Each subfamily in the Tachinidae appears to have a method of host-selection which is related to the overall phylogenetic evolution of the family and this is shown by the information on the family under the various host subsections in this chapter. Further detailed information on the biology of Tachinidae will be found in Askew (1971), Clausen (1940), van Emden (1954), Herting (1960) and Shaw and Askew (1976) and rearing records since Audcent's (1942) host list are given by Hamm (1942), Parmenter (1953) and Hammond & Smith (1953-1960). A world catalogue of hosts is given by Thompson (1943-1960).

The establishment of new parasite-host relationships, by rearing, is work which amateurs can easily undertake, provided great care is taken. Many erroneous records have crept into the old literature from careless observations and records of parasites from lepidopterists' rearing cages, perhaps containing mixed foodplants, mixed larvae and even other unnoticed insects which have been the real hosts from which the parasites have emerged. It is as well to persuade lepidopterist colleagues that the disappointment felt when a carefully reared rarity yields a parasite instead of an adult moth or butterfly can be partly alleviated by passing the offending insect on to an appropriate specialist and thereby perhaps establishing a new host record.

Most Calliphoridae and Sarcophagidae are scavengers (saprophagous) on decaying organic matter, especially of animal origin. Some have become parasites of insects and other invertebrates and are dealt with in other sections of this chapter, but none are truly parasitic on Lepidoptera although there have been records claiming this from time to time. *Sarcophaga albiceps, S. aratrix* and *S.exuberans* have been reared from larvae of *Lymantria* and other moths.

Phoridae is another family regarded as largely saprophagous but some are obligate parasites as discussed elsewhere. Some species of *Megaselia* reared from Lepidoptera are probably occasionally facultative parasites (see Hammond & Smith 1955).

Lepidoptera are frequently taken as prey by the larger Asilidae and Empididae. It has been suggested that in years of great abundance *Tortrix viridana*, the green tortrix moth has been partly contolled by *Empis livida*. Predaceous Syrphid larvae sometimes take small caterpillars.

Adults of the ceratopogonid *Forcipomyia (Trichohelea) papilionivora* may sometimes be found clinging onto the wings of butterflies, with the mouthparts piercing the veins to feed on the internal fluid. *F. (Microhelea) fuliginosa* has a similar relationship with Lepidoptera larvae.

Further Reading

Askew, R.R., 1971. *Parasitic Insects*, London.
Audcent, H., 1942. A preliminary list of the hosts of some British Tachinidae (Dipt.). *Trans. Soc. Br. Ent.* **8:** 1–42.
Clausen, C.P., 1940. Entomophagous Insects. New York & London. [Reprinted New York 1972]
Emden, F.I. van., 1954. Diptera Cyclorrhapha Calyptratae (1) Section (a) Tachinidae and Calliphoridae. *Handbk Ident. Br. Insects* **10** (4a): 1–133 (Royal Entomological Society).
Ford, T.H. 1973. Some records of bred Tachinidae. I. *Ent. Rec. J. Var* **85:** 288-290; 1976. 2. *Ibid.* **88:** 6871.
Hamm, A.H. 1942. Records of bred Tachinidae (Dipt.) chiefly from the Oxford district. *Entomologist's mon. Mag.* **10:** 191–192.
Hammond, H.E. & Smith, K.G.V., 1953—1960. On some parasitic Diptera and Hymenoptera bred from lepidopterous hosts. *Entomologist's Gaz.* **4:**273–279; **6:** 168–174; **8:** 181–189; **11:** 50–54.
Herting, B. 1960. Biologie der Westpalaarktischen Raupenfliegen. Dipt., Tachinidae. *Mon. Z. Agnew. Ent.* **16:** 1–188.
Parmenter, L., 1953. Some records of bred Tachinidae. *Entomologist's Rec. J. Var.* **65:** 29-31.
Shaw, M.R. & Askew, R.R., 1976. Parasites (pp. 24–56) in Heath, J. *et al.* (eds) *The Moths and Butterflies of Great Britain and Ireland.* Vol. 1. Oxford and London.
Thompson, W. R., 1943–1958. *A catalogue of the parasites and predators of insect pests..* Belleville & Ottawa. [In several parts]

BEETLES (COLEOPTERA)

by James Dear and Kenneth G. V. Smith

Present information indicates that there are some strong associations between flies and beetles, including parasitism in both directions.

Flies as Parasites of Beetles

Three British families of Diptera parasitise Coleoptera, viz. Tachinidae, Sarcophagidae and Phoridae (Emden 1950) and possibly Asilidae (Knutson 1972). Published records of parasitic Calliphoridae are erroneous or refer to genera now placed in other families. Abroad *Villa* (Bombyliidae) have been reared from tenebrionid beetles and the genus would repay attention in Britain. Pyrgotidae and Nemestrinidae are non-British families which parasitise Coleoptera.

Tachinidae are the commonest parasites of Coleoptera. Two subfamilies (Dufouriinae, Dexiinae) are exclusively beetle parasites as are most species of the tribes Microphthalmini, Macquartiini (Tachininae) and Blondeliini (Goniinae). Of 39 potential species, 33 are probably regular beetle parasites and there are definite records for 26 of them. The subfamily Dufouriinae parasitise larvae and adults of *Cassida* and *Plagiodera* (Chrysomelidae), adult weevils (Curculionidae) and adult ground beetles (Carabidae). The Dexiinae all deposit eggs or young larvae in the vicinity of beetle larvae expecially those of chafers or dung beetles (Scarabaeidae). The young larvae search for a host which they probably enter through a spiracle and when fully developed they leave before the host pupates. In the Tachininae *Macquartia* lays in a similar way but near chrysomelid larvae, and sometimes the parasite emerges after pupation of the host In the Goniinae the tribe Blondeliini contains genera which parasitise Coleoptera, mostly adult Chrysomelidae but adult Carabidae in *Zaira*. The common earwig parasite *Triarthria setipennis* has been recorded from timber beetles such as Cerambycidae and Scolytidae but these records are almost certainly errors and probably came from earwigs sharing the beetles' tunnels. This is mentioned as a warning of how careful one must be in seeking to establish parasite-host relationships. Brief information on the biology of Tachinidae is given under Lepidoptera above, and the works of Askew (1971), Clausen (1940), Emden (1954) and Herting (1960) cited there should be studied. The host list which follows is based largely on continental records but is restricted to British Coleoptera; British records are indicated (B); L, P, A, = larva, pupa, adult.

Phasiinae: Phania spp., possible, foreign sp. ex Carabidae *(Amara, Harpalus)*. **Dufouriinae: Anthomyiopsis nigrisquama**, L. *Plagiodera* (Chrysomelidae); **Campogaster exigua**, A *Sitona* (4 spp.), *Hypera* (Curculionidae); **Dufouria chalybeata, D. nigrita**, L/P/A *Cassida* spp. (Chrysomelidae) (B);**Freraea gagatea**, A *Carabus, Harpalus* (Carabidae); **Rondania fasciata**, probable (other spp., Curculionidae). **Dexiinae: Billaea irrorata**, L *Saperda populnea* (Cerambycidae); **Dexia rustica**, L *Melolontha, Serica, Amphimallon, Phyllopertha* (Scarabaeidae) (B); **D. vacua**, *Melolontha*; **Dinera grisescens**, L *Harpalus* (Carabidae) (B); **Estheria** spp., probable; **Phorostoma carinifrons**, L *Aphodius ater* (Scarabaeidae) (B); **Prosena siberita**, L *Anomala, Serica, Melolontha* (Scarabaeidae); **Trixa** spp., indet. L Scarabaeidae, also possibly *Hepialus* (Lepidoptera). **Tachininae: Dexiosoma caninum** L *Melolontha*; **Macquartia praefica**, L *Chrysomela* (Chrysomelidae); **M. dispar** L *Chrysomela sanguinolenta*; **M. grisea**, L *C. fastuosa, C. sanguinolenta* **M. nudigena**, probably; **M. pubiceps**, L *Chrysomela aurata*; **M. tenebricosa**, L *Chrysomela varians, C. graminis* (B), several other spp.; **M. tessellum**, L *Phytodecta olivacea* (Chrysomelidae) (B); **Leiophora innoxia**, A *Haltica* (Chrysomelidae) (B); **Medina collaris**, A *Lochmaea* (B), *Galerucella* (Chrysomelidae); **M. luctuosa**, A *Plagiodera, Agelastica, Haltica* (Chrysomelidae); **Meigenia dorsalis**, L *Phytodecta*; **M. mutabilis**, L *Phaedon, Phytodecta* (B), other genera of Chrysomelidae; **M. majuscula**, probable; **Policheta unicolor**, A *Chrysomela* spp. (B) (? also a sawfly). **Zaira cinerea**, A *Carabus* (B), *Broscus, Harpalus, Amara, Calathus, Feronia*; **Stomatomyia acuminata**, L *Blaps, Opatrum, Pedinus* (Tenebrionidae), also Lepidoptera (records of *Nemorilla floralis, Winthemia quadripustulata* and *Thelymorpha marmorata* (Goniinae), which are predominantly parasites of Lepidoptera require confirmation).

Sarcophagidae are mostly feeders on dead flesh, but a few have been recorded as parasites of beetle larvae. *Sarcophaga nigriventris* has been reared from a *Carabus*, a *Blaps* and a moribund *Necrophorus*; *S. aratrix* from *Prionus coriarius* (Cerambycidae) and *S. albiceps* from Scarabaeidae and the cerambycid *Saperda*. Probably these flies are never regular true parasites of insects but are probably attracted to dead or moribund hosts.

In the Phoridae the genus *Phalacrotophora* is specifically parasitic upon the pupae
of ladybirds (Coccinellidae). The life-histories of the British species of this genus
have been reviewed by Colyer (1952, 1954) but the biology and taxonomy of the
genus needs further elucidation in Britain.

It is likely that many more parasitic associations with beetles remain to be recorded.
In order to emphasise this point, the larval feeding habits of British Asilidae are
almost unknown, yet in regions of the world outside Europe the scant information
indicates that parasitism of scarabaeid larvae, or sometimes of other beetles, is a
normal mode of life. Certainly there is some reason to believe that *Laphria flava*
larvae are predators (or parasites?) of large wood boring beetles. Here is a lead for
a coleopterist or an asilid man to follow up.

Adult Beetles as Prey of Adult Flies

Adult Coleoptera are understandably not popular as the prey of adult Diptera due
to their tough cuticle. However, adults of the ceratopogonid *Atrichopogon
meloesugans* feed on the body fluids of *Meloe* and *A. oedemerarum* is found on
Oedemera. Also the more powerful Asilidae and Empididae will take Coleoptera
as prey, the former more frequently.

Beetle Larvae as Prey of Fly Larvae

Beetle larvae are more vulnerable than adults and are taken as prey by fly larvae;
Cecidomyiidae may take larvae of scolytid bark beetles, strawberry weevil
(*Otiorrhynchus* spp.) and pine weevil (*Hylobius*); Asilidae may take scarabaeid
grubs; Therevidae take various larvae; Scenopinidae take carpet beetle larvae;
Medetera (Dolichopodidae) take larvae, pupae and adults of bark beetles;
Lonchaeidae take bark beetle larvae. The Pallopteridae include several species
which inhabit bark beetle burrows as larvae, but they are assumed to be
commensals (see discussion under Higher Plants); several Odiniidae have
associations with specific wood boring beetles (see Dead Wood) but the
relationship requires further study.

Beetles as Predators of Flies

It is probable that beetles are more important as control agents of Diptera than
the converse. Nearly 2000 species of British Coleoptera are predatory, in most
cases as both larva and adult. One of the major food resources is flies, especially
larvae, and even the present incomplete evidence points towards flies being the
exclusive or predominant prey for many beetles. Such predators as staphylinids
and silphids are abundant in carrion and clerids in dry carrion, where fly larvae
often form the main diet. In fungi, dung and leaf litter the same strong relationship
between beetles and flies is almost certainly true.

The staphylinid *Aloconota gregaria* may be a significant biological control agent
against wheat bulb fly, *Delia coarctata*, and it seems likely that similar
relationships with other phytophagous flies exist. Some beetles probably specialise
in eating fly eggs, others the larvae.

Beetles as Parasites of Flies

One of the most interesting relationships between beetles and flies is that some staphylinid larvae are parasites of fly puparia. *Aleochara*, which has 29 British species, is recorded as parasitising chiefly calypterates, expecially Anthomyiidae, including species of economic importance. It is probable that the beetles are more habitat specific than dependent on certain fly species – for instance *A. algarum* is a parasite of seaweed flies such as *Coelopa* and *Orygma*. A major study by Welch (1965) includes references to the literature. It is possible that some related genera of Staphylinidae may have parasitic associations with Diptera.

Acknowledgement

Peter Hammond has advised on staphylinid associations.

Further Reading

Colyer, C.N., 1952. Notes on the life-histories of the British species of *Phalacrotophora* Enderlein (Dipt., Phoridae). *Entomologist's mon. Mag.* **88**: 135–139, 1954 *ibid*, **90**: 208-210

Crowson, R., (In Press). *The Biology of Beetles*, Sidgwick & Jackson, London.

Emden, F.I. van, 1950. Dipterous parasites of Coleoptera. *Entomologist's mon. Mag.* **86**: 182–206.

Knutson, L.V., 1972. Pupa of *Neomochtherus angustipennis* (Hire), with notes on feeding habits of robber flies and a review of publications on morphology of immature stages (Diptera: Asilidae) *Proc. Biol. Soc. Wash.* **85**; 163–178.

Welch, R.C., 1965. The biology of the genus *Aleochara* Grav. (Coleoptera, Staphylinidae), Ph.D. Thesis, London.

ANTS, BEES AND WASPS (ACULEATE HYMENOPTERA)
by Christopher O'Toole

Flies interact with aculeates in a variety of ways. The adults of some species are simply predators and may occasionally feed on ants, wasps and bees. The life-histories of others are closely intertwined with those of aculeates: their larvae are scavengers in aculeate nests or are parasites of aculeate eggs or larvae. The adults of such flies frequent the nest sites of the hosts and are more often encountered by hymenopterists than by dipterists. Thus, the dipterist who would collect these flies must become an honorary hymenopterist and develop an eye for the likely nest sites of ants, wasps and bees.

Mining wasps and bees prefer to make their nests in light, sandy well-drained soils. Sandpits, dunes, sandy heaths and open, dry woodland are suitable places to explore. Many wasps and bees also nest in ready-made cavities such as old beetle borings in dead wood, log piles and old fence posts. One local solitary bee *Hylaeus pectoralis* is known to nest only in the vacated galls of the chloropid *Lipara lucens;* the large, cigar-shaped, galls are made on the reed *Phragmites*.

Many species of ant live in light soils, usually under flat stones; decaying logs are also used. The wood ants (*Formica rufa* group of species) are hosts to a variety of Diptera and these ants make conspicuous nest mounds of pine needles or other litter, while some, such as *F. fusca* and *F. lemani*, nest under stones and logs. The records of interactions between flies and aculeates are widely scattered in the literature and are often inaccessible to entomologists who do not live close to a good library. The published records for the British Isles are therefore gathered together in Appendix 1 (Predators), Appendix 2 (Nest scavengers), Appendires 3-5 (Parasites) and Appendix 6 (commensals). Good general accounts of the biology of parasitic flies are given in Clausen (1940) and Askew (1971) (see Lepidoptera). Good accounts of the flies associated with social wasps and bumblebees are given by Spradbery (1973) and Alford (1975) respectively.

Adult Flies as Prey of Aculeates Flies are the exclusive prey of four genera of solitary sphecid wasps —*Oxybelus, Crabro, Ectemnius* and *Mellinus*. Three other genera, *Crossocerus, Rhopalum* and *Lindenius* prey on flies as well as on other small insects. Detailed prey records are given in Hamm & Richards (1926, 1930). The flies are caught, stung and paralysed by the female wasp and are stored in the nest as food for the wasp larvae. An egg is laid on one of the flies in each cell.

Predatory Adult Flies — Asilidae — Empididae — Scathophagidae (Appendix 1) No British predatory flies specialise in hunting aculeates. The published records show that aculeates form only a small proportion of the prey taken by these flies. More records are needed and there is much the amateur can do by following asilids, empids and scathophagids and noting what insects are taken as prey. Asilids are most often seen in sandy areas such as heaths and dunes. Species of *Dioctria* are best sought in hedgerows, woodland clearings and the lush vegetation along the sides of streams. These habitats are also frequented by empids. Scathophagids (dung flies) are voracious predators. The commonest species, *Scathopaga stercoraria* spends much of its time at dung pats, where males find mates and both sexes seek mainly dipterous prey. A solitary fly-hunting sphecid wasp, *Mellinus arvensis* also seeks prey at dung pats and is frequently attacked by *Scathophaga stercoraria*. All too often the flies themselves end up as stung and paralysed prey, to be stored by the wasps as food for their larvae.

Fly Larvae as Nest scavengers — Ceratopogonidae — Sciaridae — Scatopsidae — Milichiidae — Phoridae — Syrphidae — Sphaeroceridae — Fanniidae — Muscidae (Appendix 2) Flies which scavenge in the nests of social Hymenoptera (ants, paper-making wasps and bumblebees) are normally tolerated by the workers and are presumably recognised as harmless. The larvae of these flies feed on vegetable debris, dead nest occupants and possibly the faeces of the host.

Insects which spend part or all of their life-cycles in association with ants are called *myrmecophiles*. Scatopsids such as *Colobostema nigripenne* and *Holoplagia richardsi* spend their entire life-cycle in the host nest and adults, as well as larvae and puparia, are found in the nest galleries. Milichiids of the genera *Phyllomyza* and *Milichia* are also closely associated with ants.

Other species, such as those of the syrphid genus *Microdon,* spend their larval and pupal life in the ant nest and the adults live and mate outside, the females entering the nest only to lay eggs. *Microdon* larvae are strange, slug-like creatures, with a tough, reticulately ridged dorsal surface and were originally described as molluscs! So long as the larvae remain upright, the ants ignore them, but if they accidentally expose their soft undersides, the ants attack and often kill them.

To collect the smaller scavengers in ant nests, it is necessary to dig up several handfuls of nest material and take it home in suitable containers such as plastic sandwich boxes. The nest material can then be sifted for dipterous larvae and puparia. Adult sciarids, scatopsids, phorids and sphaerocerids can be collected in this way, using a pooter. Puparia should be segregated and stored individually in tubes in a cool, dry place, such as a garden shed. Remember to mount each puparium on a card beneath the emerged adult when this is staged. Adult ceratopogonids and phorids can also be collected by sweeping gently over the nest mounds of wood ants (*Formica* spp.). Donisthorpe (1927) gives a good account of the dipterous 'guests' of British ants.

The larvae of the syrphid genus *Volucella* live, according to species, in the nests of social wasps and bumblebees. Eggs are laid on the nest envelope and the larvae usually drop down into the nest cavity, where they scavenge. Some larvae remain in the comb and migrate to cells, where they feed on faecal and salivary matter extruded from mature aculeate larvae and are known to be partly predatory. Adult *Volucella* are well-known mimics of wasps (*inanis, zonaria*) and bumblebees, (*bombylans*). They can be found at flowers, especially brambles (*Rubus* spp.) and hogweed (*Heracleum*). Males can often be seen hovering at between five and seven feet above the ground in woodland clearings. Larval *Volucella* can be taken in nest debris in early autumn when the wasp or bumblebee colonies have died out. It is a good idea to mark the nest entrance in some way before the colonies have declined, so that they can easily be found in autumn when there is no activity to betray their presence. Pupation does not occur until the spring.

Many species found in wasp's nests are not specific. For instance the long list of published records summarised by Spradbery (1973) includes many flies with generalised scavenging habits and some which are specific to the surroundings of the nest, e.g. the record of *Ctenophora bimaculata* (larvae eat dead wood) and *Protoclythia modesta* (feed on fungi growing on dead wood). This demonstrates how careful one must be in describing the fauna of a nest. Apart from the syrphids already discussed, there are relatively few Diptera specific to wasp nests – *Fannia vesparia* and *Achanthiptera rohrelliformis* are the best examples, these rarely being seen as adults but the larvae are on occasion abundant. There is a similar need to reassess the significance of ant nest associates.

Parasites – Bombyliidae – Phoridae – Conopidae – Drosophilidae – Tachinidae – Sarcophagidae – Anthomyiidae (Appendices 3–5)

The dipterous parasites of aculeate Hymenoptera can be divided into three main groups.

(i) **Larvae as Internal Parasites of Adult Aculeates.** The phorid genera *Pseudacteon* and *Megaselia* and the Conopidae comprise the only British flies in this category. There are two British species of *Pseudacteon, brevicauda* and *formicarum*, the latter being the commonest. Female *Pseudacteon* lay their eggs in the abdomens of living worker ants. A female is attracted to an ant nest by smell and hovers over the workers before landing on one and inserting an egg between two of the abdominal tergites with its long, pointed ovipositor. Although this has been observed many times, no-one has yet bred *Pseudacteon* from ants and so the larvae and puparia are undescribed. This gap in our knowledge could be filled if large numbers of recently dead ants were collected from nests and kept under observation. Adult *Pseudacteon* can be collected by sweeping over and around ant nests, especially those of the common black ant of gardens, *Lasius niger*. The chances of catching adults can be increased by exposing some of the ant nest so that the workers rush out, emitting their characteristic scent. The flies can be best seen if the collector squats down so that the area immediately above the exposed nest appears above the sky line. A *Megaselia* species has been reared from larvae parasitising a queen *Bombus terrestris*.

Female conopids also lay their eggs in living, adult hosts, namely solitary wasps and bees, social wasps and bumblebees. Smith (1969) outlines the biology of the British species and gives a summary of prey records. Adult conopids are wasp-like in appearance, with an elongate abdomen. Both sexes frequent flowers, the males in search of mates and the females in search of hosts. At the generic level, conopids are fairly host-specific. A female conopid, having found a suitable host, follows it closely and in some cases mimics the host's flight pattern. Eventually the conopid closes in and, while still in flight, lays an egg in the abdomen of the host; the egg is injected into the membrane between two tergites or sternites with a specially adapted ovipositor. The larva remains in the abdomen, feeding on body fluids. The host is not killed immediately and the infected aculeate may carry on foraging for some time before death ensues. Pupation takes place within the body of the host.

(ii) **Fly Larvae as Parasites of Aculeate Eggs** (Appendix 4). The eggs of aculeates are relatively large and it is not surprising that other insects exploit this rich food source. Two species of the sarcophagid genus *Ptychoneura* have adopted this life-style and have been bred from stem-nesting solitary wasps.

(iii) **Fly Larvae as Parasites of Larval and Pupal Aculeates** (Appendix 5). Flies in this category can be further subdivided into those in which the larvae are external parasites and those in which the larvae feed on food stored in the host's cell. This latter habit is often called *cleptoparasitism*.

Females of the sarcophagid *Brachicoma devia* larviposit (i.e. lay living larvae) in the nests of bumblebees. The larvae feed externally on the full-grown bumblebee larvae and pupae. They pupate in the nest material (summer generation) or in the soil (overwintering generation). Puparia can be collected from nest material or from the soil around nests. Adults can be collected by watching at the entrance of bumblebee nests, which occur in such places as hedgerow banks, compost heaps, under rubble on waste ground and often in bird nest boxes.

The larvae of some species of Bombyliidae are external parasites of the larvae of solitary mining bees. The adults of the genus *Bombylius* are aptly called 'bee-flies', for in shape and colour these furry flies resemble the orange-coloured species of bumblebee. They have a characteristic, rapid, darting flight and can be found hovering at flowers. *Bombylius major* is the commonest British species and appears in spring, in open woodland, where it visits primroses, bugle and violets. The females spend much of their time flying over dry, sunny banks where there are host nests. Eggs are laid in mid-flight over the nest site, or the female hovers low, dipping her abdomen until it touches the ground when she releases her eggs. The eggs hatch almost immediately and the worm-like first instar larvae migrate into the nest burrows of the host, usually a species of *Andrena*. There the larva seeks an open cell and remains inactive until the host larva is nearly full-grown.

160

The *Bombylius* larva then sucks the body fluids of the bee larva and eventually pupates within the host's cell. Neither the larva nor the adult of *Bombylius* is equipped to break out of the sealed cell of the host and it is the remarkably active pupa, with its coronet of three pairs of tough spines, which performs this task and then migrates to the surface of the soil. Here the anterior part of the pupa protrudes out of the soil and the adult fly emerges very soon afterwards.

There is considerable doubt as to the British hosts of *Villa*, though a parasitic relationship with Lepidoptera larvae is thought possible. However, *V. modesta*, a denizen of sand dunes from June to September, has been bred from the cells of the solitary bee *Osmia aurulenta* nesting in empty snail shells (O'Toole, unpubl. data). *Thyridanthrax fenestratus* has been seen 'shadowing' females of the large hunting wasp *Ammophila sabulosa* in the New Forest.

The cocoons of wood ants (*Formica* spp.) are parasitized by two species of phorid, *Aenigmatias brevifrons* and *A. lubbocki*. The females of these flies are wingless, flattened in shape and resemble small cockroaches. Both sexes can be found in the galleries of *Formica* nests, though the two species are quite rare.

The remaining families in this section have in common the larval habit of feeding on the host's food store, either paralysed insect prey in the case of sphecid wasps, or honey and pollen in the case of solitary bees. The drosophilid *Cacoxenus indagator* is typical. It lives in the nests of solitary bees, especially species of *Osmia*. Both sexes frequent the immediate area of the host's nest. The female waits around until the female bee leaves the nest and then enters and lays one or more eggs in the cell that is currently being provisioned. It has been noted that when the *Cacoxenus* leave the nest of *Osmia rufa*, the tips of their abdomens are often dusted with pollen, indicating that they oviposit directly into the host's food store. Up to 28% of *O. rufa* nests may be infested with *Cacoxenus*.

The females of Sarcophagidae and Anthomyiidae which parasitise wasps and bees also loiter in the nest sites of the hosts, waiting for the female wasps or bees to leave on foraging trips. Some species such as the sarcophagid *Amobia signata* specialize in parasitising solitary wasps, while others, such as the anthomyiid *Leucophora personata* restrict themselves to solitary mining bees (Appendix 5). There are two sub-families of the Sarcophagidae specializing in aculeates, the largest being the Miltogramminae (*Amobia, Miltogramma, Senotainia, Pterella, Metopia* and *Ptychoneura*), with most species associated with ground-nesting aculeates as considered below. In the Macronychiinae, *Macronychia griseola* has been recorded from the ground-nesting *Oxybelus*, but *M. ungulans* has been reared from the fly-hunting wasp *Ectemnius cavifrons* which is wood-nesting and *M. polyodon* has been associated also mainly with wood-nesting aculeates.

Two species of sarcophagid, *Miltogramma punctatum* and *Metopia argyrocephala* are remarkable in that they readily parasitise both wasps and bees, so that the larvae must be capable of coping with either insect prey in wasps' nests, or pollen and honey mixtures in the nests of bees. It would be interesting to check if the larvae really do feed on the food store or whether they feed on the host larvae. With the exception of one species, all the sarcophagids which parasitise aculeates are larviparous. The exception is *Senotainia conica* which lays its eggs on an adult female wasp as it carries its prey back to the nest. Presumably the larva of the fly detaches itself from the wasp and lives on the stored insect prey. Aculeates have been found with Diptera eggs attached to their bodies, usually the sides of the thorax. All but two of the species were crabronine wasps and most were female. The identity of the Diptera eggs was uncertain but possibly they belonged to *Senotainia conica*, one of two species of sarcophagid frequenting one of the sites concerned.

The anthomyiid *Eustalomyia*, with four attractive grey and black species, may be found near the entrances of solitary wasp nests in dead wood. The larva consumes the host's prey, which is often adult Diptera.

Flies as Commensals of Aculeates —Braulidae — Milichiidae (Appendix 6)

The Braulidae comprises one genus, *Braula*, with two species, both of which are associated with bees. *B. caeca* is a cosmopolitan commensal of honeybees and the louse-like, wingless adults are often found attached to worker and queen bees. There are no claws, but the bristles of the tarsal combs are well-adapted for clinging to the body hairs of bees. Previously thought to be parasites, braulids are now known to be commensals, the adults feeding on honey as it is regurgitated by worker bees. The eggs are laid in the brood comb of the bee and the larvae feed on the food presented to the bee larvae. Little harm seems to be done to the bees and pupation takes place in a small burrow excavated in the wall of the host's cell. *Desmometopa sordidum* (Milichiidae), which is phoretic on hive bees, consumes the collected pollen.

Further Reading

Alford, D.V., 1975. *Bumblebees*, Davis-Poynter, London.

Donisthorpe, H. St. K., 1927. *The Guests of British Ants: Their Habits and Life–histories*, Routledge, London.

Hamm, A.H. & Richards, O.W., 1926. The Biology of the British Crabronidae. *Trans. ent. Soc. Lond.* **74**: 297–331.

Hamm, A.H. & Richards, O.W., 1930. The Biology of the British Fossorial Wasps of the families Mellinidae, Gorytidae, Philanthidae, Oxybelidae and Trypoxylidae. *Trans. ent. Soc. Lond.* **78** : 95–131.

Hobby, B.M., 1931. The British species of Asilidae (Diptera) and their prey. *Trans. ent. Soc. S. England.* **6**: 1–42.

Latter, O.H., 1931. Observations on the insect enemies of the British bee *Osmia rufa* (L.) (Hym. : Megachilidae). *Proc. ent. Soc. Lond.* **5** : 58.

Smith, K.G.V., 1969. Conopidae. *Handbk. Ident. Br. Insects* **9** (3a) : 18pp.

Spradbery, J.P., 1973. *Wasps*, Sidgwick & Jackson, London.

APPENDIX 1. RECORDS OF DIPTERA PREDATORY ON ACULEATE HYMENOPTERA.
ASILIDAE: **Asilus crabroniformis,** *Vespula germanica, Andrena fulva, Apis mellifera;* **Dysmachus trigonus,** *Pompilus cinereus;* **Eutolmus rufibarbis,** *Lasius niger;* **Machimus atricapillus,** *Myrmica rubra, M. ruginodis, Lasius niger, Ancistrocerus trifasciatus, Lasioglossum smeathmanellum;* **Pamponerus germanicus,** *Lasioglossum calceatum;* **Philonicus albiceps,** *Formica fusca, Andrena* sp., ; **Laphria marginata,** *Myrmica ruginodis, Formica rufa;* **Dioctria baumhaueri,** *Diodontus minutus, Entomognathus brevis, Lasioglossum fulvicorne;* **D. linearis,** *Lasius niger, Formica fusca;* **D. oelandica,** *Andrena minutula, Lasioglossum lativentre;* **D. rufipes,** *Formica fusca;* EMPIDIDAE: **Empis opaca,** *Nomada marshamella;* SCATHOPHAGIDAE: **Scathophaga stercoraria,** *Lasius flavus, Mellinus arvensis.*
APPENDIX 2 RECORDS OF DIPTERA SCAVENGING IN THE NESTS OF ACULEATE HYMENOPTERA N.B. The larvae of **Volucella** (Syrphidae), **Fannia** (Fanniidae), **Achanthiptera** and **Muscina** (Muscidae), although primarily scavengers, may occasionally feed on larvae, pupae and weakened adults of their hosts, expecially towards the end of the season.

TRICHOCERIDAE: **Trichocera hiemalis, T regulationis,** *Vespula;* TIPULIDAE: **Ctenophora bimaculata,** *Vespula;* CERATOPOGONIDAE: **Forcipomyia braueri,** *Formica fusca;* **F. myrmecophila,** *Formica rufa,* *F. exsecta;* **Atrichopogon lucorum,** *Lasius brunneus;* MYCETOPHILIDAE: **Docosia gilvipes,** *Vespula;* SCIARIDAE: **Plastosciara brachyptera,** *Lasius alienus;* **P. vanderwieli,** *Vespula.* **Scatopsciara vivida,** *Vespula;* SCATOPSIDAE: **Colobostema nigripenne,** *Lasius fuliginosus, Formica rufa;* **Holoplagia richardsi,** *Lasius fuliginosus;* **Scatopse notata,** *Vespula;* PHORIDAE: **Megaselia longicostalis,** *Lasius fuliginosus, Formica fusca;* **M. pulicaria,** *Formica rufa;* **M. giraudi,** *Formica exsecta, Dolichovespula norwegica;* **M. minor,** *Lasius fuliginosus;* **M. rufipes,** *Vespula;* **M. aequalis,** *Lasius fuliginosus, L. brunneus;* **M. ciliata,** *L. fuliginosus, L. brunneus;* **M. conformis,** *Myrmica laevinodis;* **M. fungivora,** *Lasius fuliginosus;* **Conicera pauxilla,** *Vespula germanica;* **Diploneura concinna,** *Vespula germanica;* **D. funebris,** *Vespula;* **Triphleba lugubris,** *Vespula vulgaris;* **Gymnoptera longicostalis,** *Vespula;* **G. vitripennis,** *Bombus;* **Phora aterrima,** *Lasius fuliginosus;* PLATYPEZIDAE: **Protoclythia modesta,** *Vespula;* SYRPHIDAE: **Microdon devius,** *Lasius fuliginosus, Formica rufa, F. sanguinea, F. fusca;* **M. eggeri,** *Lasius niger;* **M. mutabilis,** *Myrmica ruginodis, Lasius niger, Formica fusca, F. lemani;* **Volucella bombylans,** *Vespula vulgaris, V. germanica, Bombus;*V. **inanis,** *Vespula vulgaris;* **V. pellucens,** *Vespula vulgaris, V. germanica, V. rufa;* **V. zonaria,** *Vespula vulgaris, V. germanica;* HELEOMYZIDAE: **Tephrochlamys laeta, T. rufiventris** var. **canescens,** *Vespula;* SEPSIDAE: **Themira lucida,** *Vespula vulgaris;* SPHAEROCERIDAE: **Leptocera caenosa,** *Vespula germanica;* **L. claviventris,** *Vespula vulgaris;* **L. clunipes,** *Lasius brunneus;* **L. flavipes,** *Vespula;* **L. fungicola,** *Lasius fuliginosus, Formica rufa, Vespula germanica;* **L. heteroneura,** *Vespula;* **L. moesta,** *Vespula germanica;* **L. palmata,** *Vespula vulgaris, V. germanica;* **L. rufilabris,** *Formica fusca;* MILICHIIDAE: **Phyllomyza equitans,** *Lasius fuliginosus;* **P. formicae,** *Formica rufa* (as *donisthorpei), Lasius fuliginosus;* **Milichia ludens,** *L. fuliginosus;* FANNIIDAE: **Fannia canicularis,** *Vespa crabro, Vespula germanica, Bombus;* **F. coracina,** *Vespula;* **F. fuscula,** *Vespula vulgaris,* **F. hamata, F. scalaris,** *Vespula;* **F. vesparia,** *Vespula germanica;* MUSCIDAE: **Achanthiptera rohrelliformis,** *Vespula vulgaris, V. germanica;* **Muscina pabulorum,** *Vespula rufa;* **M. stabulans,** *Vespula germanica;* **Phaonia populi,** *Vespula.*

APPENDIX 3. RECORDS OF DIPTERA WITH LARVAE PARASITIC ON ADULT ACULEATE HYMENOPTERA.

PHORIDAE: **Pseudacteon brevicauda,** *Myrmica ruginodis;* **Pseudacteon formicarum,** *Myrmica lobicornis, Tapinoma erraticum, Lasius fuliginosus, L. niger, L. alienus, L. flavus, Formica sanguinea;* **Megaselia** sp., *Bombus terrestris;*CONOPIDAE: **Conops ceriaeformis,** *Bombus muscorum;* **C. flavipes, C. quadrifasciatus,** *Bombus lapidarius;* **Leopoldius brevirostris,** *Vespula;* **Physocephala nigra,** *Bombus muscorum;* **P. rufipes,** *Bombus terrestris, B. lucorum, B. lapidarius, B pratorum, B hortorum, B. ruderarius, B. sylvarum, B. pascuorum;* **Zodion cinereum,** *?Halictus rubicundus;* **Thecophora atra, T. fulvipes,** *Halictus, Lasioglossum;* **Sicus ferrugineus,** *Bombus terrestris, B. lapidarius, B. hortorum, B. pascuorum.*

APPENDIX 4.RECORDS OF DIPTERA WITH LARVAE PARASITIC ON THE EGGS OF ACULEATE HYMENOPTERA

SARCOPHAGIDAE: **Ptychoneura cylindrica,** *Pemphredon lugubris, Crossocerus capitosus;* **P. rufitarsis,** *Rhopalum coarctatus, R. clavipes.*

APPENDIX 5. RECORDS OF DIPTERA WITH LARVAE PARASITIC ON LARVAL ACULEATE HYMENOPTERA

BOMBYLIIDAE: **Bombylius major,***Andrena labialis, A. bicolor, A. chrysosceles, A. clarkella;* **B. minor,** *Colletes daviesanus;* **Thyridanthrax fenestratus,** *Ammophila sabulosa;* **Villa modesta,** *Osmia aurulenta;*PHORIDAE: **Aenigmatias brevifrons,** *Formica rufibarbis;* **A. lubbocki,** *Formica fusca, F. transkaucasica;* DROSOPHILIDAE: **Cacoxenus indagator,** *Anthophora acervorum, Osmia rufa, O. aurulenta;* TACHINIDAE: **Gonia divisa,** *Anthophora, Bombus terrestris;* **G. picea,** *Anthophora retusa, A. acervorum, B. terrestris;* SARCOPHAGIDAE: **Amobia signata,** *Odynerus spinipes, Ancistrocerus nigricornis, Pemphredon lugubris, Trypoxylon figulus, T. attenuatum, Ectemnius lapidarius;* **Miltogramma germari,** *Anthophora bimaculata;* **M. punctatum,** *Podalonia viatica, Trypoxylon figulus, Colletes succinctus, C. fodiens, C. daviesanus, C. halophilus;* **Senotainia conica,** *Tachysphex unicolor, Oxybelus uniglumis, Crabro peltarius, Mellinus arvensis, Argogorytes fargeii, Philanthus triangulum;* **Pterella grisea,** *Cerceris rybyensis, C. arenaria;* **Metopia argyrocephala,** *Ammophila sabulosa, Oxybelus uniglumis, Crabro peltarius, Philanthus triangulum, Cerceris rybyensis, Colletes succinctus, C. daviesanus, Andrena barbilabris;* **Macronychia griseola,** *Oxybelus uniglumis;* **M. polyodon,** *Crossocerus elongatulus, C. capitosus, Ectemnius lapidarius, E. rubicola, Bombus terrestris;*M. **ungulans,** *Ectemnius cavifrons;* **Brachicoma devia,** *Dolichovespula sylvestris, Bombus terrestris, B. lucorum, B.*

pratorum, B. ruderatus, B. hortorum, B. ruderarius, B. muscorum; ANTHOMYIIDAE: **Leucophora cinerea,** *Diodontus tristis, Lasioglossum nitidiusculum;* **L. grisella,** *Cerceris arenaria, Andrena tarsata;* **L. obtusa,** *Andrena fulva;* **L. personata,** *Andrena nigroaenea, A. trimmerana, A. labialis;* **L. sericea,** *Andrena haemorrhoa, A.fulva;* **L. unistriata,** *Andrena labialis;* **Eustalomyia festiva,** *Crossocerus leucostomus;* **E. hilaris,** *Trypoxylon figulus, Ectemnius cavifrons, E.lapidarius, E. rubicola;* **E. histrio,** *Crabro;* **E. vittipes,** *Crossocerus megacephalus.*

APPENDIX 6. ADULT DIPTERA AS COMMENSALS OF ADULT ACULEATES
BRAULIDAE: **Braula caeca,** *Apis mellifera;* MILICHIIDAE: **Desmometopa sordidum,** *Apis mellifera.*

HYMENOPTEROUS PARASITES OF DIPTERA (Hymenoptera Parasitica)
by Dr. Mark R. Shaw and Dr. Richard R. Askew

It seems that Diptera came to be an important host group for parasitic Hymenoptera only at a comparatively late stage in the evolution of both groups. This is suggested by the patchiness in the occurrence of hymenopterous parasitism of Diptera, as well as from the nature of the associations that have arisen. Thus parasitism by Hymenoptera is virtually confined to those Diptera which have specialised in particular directions and many of the Hymenoptera obligatorily associated with them are considered to be among the most recently evolved of the parasitic Hymenoptera. It is, however, possible to find evidence for coevolution between the hosts and their parasites within some of these highly specialised groups.

In general parasitic Hymenoptera attack the immature stages of insects and therefore explanations for the unsuitability of many Diptera might reasonably be based on the biology of their larvae. The earliest Diptera larvae probably lived in semi-liquid environments, to which the host-seeking adults of parasitic Hymenoptera are quite unsuited; unlike parasitic Diptera, Hymenoptera rarely make use of planidium larvae or speculative egg placement. The primary evolution of many Diptera has resulted in their larvae adopting more fully aquatic existences, and these have continued to be generally free of parasitism by Hymenoptera. A number of Hymenoptera do manage to succeed as specialist parasites of the early stages of more-or-less aquatic insects, including some Diptera which will be mentioned later, but it is significant that in most of these cases the host's aquatic habit is probably a relatively late evolutionary development, occurring after the parasite's ancestor was already attacking a more terrestrial ancestral host. Many of those Diptera larvae which have not become primarily aquatic have retained the primitive habit of living in wet substrates such as mud, manure or other rotting organic remains, or they live concealed beneath the surface of the soil. Although some of these larvae are elusive and poorly known it is certain that they are little parasitised, and the range of Hymenoptera able to attack them is severely limited. Indeed, it is noteworthy that the parasites which do attack Diptera larvae living in decomposing plant and animal matter near ground level seem to belong chiefly to the very advanced families Diapriidae (Proctotrupoidea), Eucoilidae and Figitidae (both Cynipoidea), suggesting that colonisation by Hymenoptera of this ancient habitat is relatively recent. Other insects living in such places, where predation may be high, seem also to suffer less parasitism by Hymenoptera than their relatives inhabiting living vegetation.

The Diptera larvae most attacked live in situations where the great majority of Hymenoptera search for hosts and, in practice, these tend to belong to groups which are associated with living plants. The aphidivorous Syrphinae, for example, live freely exposed on plants and are attacked by a wide range of parasitic Hymenoptera. Diptera larvae whose presence is advertised by leaf-mines, galls, or some other sign of plant damage, suffer high levels of parasitism comparable with those of other insects having similar larval habits.

The systematic position of a host is often of far less importance than its feeding habit in determining which parasites attack it. Leaf-mining Diptera, for example, are found in about a dozen widely-separated families, yet their parasite complexes are closely similar and generally include species such as the eulophid *Pnigalio soemius* and the braconid *Colastes braconius* which are simply parasites of leaf-miners and regularly attack respectively four and three orders of insects having this habit in Britain. Another example is provided by the pteromalid *Habritys brevicornis* which, although it normally parasitises sphecoid wasps nesting under bark, has been reared as a solitary parasite from puparia of the stratiomyid *Pachygaster orbitalis* found beneath bark.

Environmental clues are important to prospective parasites and parasitism of Brachycera, for example, may be low partly because these larvae are often relatively mobile and leave no consistent traces. Among the Nematocera it is noteworthy that parasitism is virtually confined to the families Mycetophilidae and Cecidomyiidae. Many members of the former are easy targets since their larval existences are, although cryptic, sedentary in the localised fruiting bodies of fungi. The habit of spinning silken cocoons, and in some cases larval webs, is also likely to attract parasitism. Similarly, parasitism of Cecidomyiidae is most severe in the gall-formers, not quite so heavy in the remaining phytophagous species, and it appears to be virtually non-existent in the relatively mobile predatory species. Certain Tipulidae would look to be good targets for parasitic Hymenoptera but, again, fairly high mobility may be what is saving them from regular attack. It is true of other orders, too, that hosts which are relatively static are usually the most heavily parasitised by Hymenoptera.

Successful parasitism may also be prevented in certain substrates owing to the different ways in which Diptera and Hymenoptera emerge from their pupation sites. For this, Hymenoptera depend almost entirely on their legs and powerful mandibles and emerge with wings already expanded, while in the Diptera orthorrhaphous pupae can often wriggle, using their backwards projecting spines, to the boundary of the medium before emerging, and many adult Cyclorrhapha (i.e. Schizophora) use the ptilinum to ease their way from the pupation site to the air before expanding their wings. Emergence from, say, a sloppy medium may thus present more problems to an adult hymenopteron than to a dipteron.

In addition to the above are more obvious factors tending to exclude parasitism in certain cases, of which the rapid development and dispersal of ephemeral colonies is sufficiently frequent to deserve mention. All of these constraints operating in concert seem to account reasonably well for at least the gross pattern of parasitism found with the order.

In the following sections no attempt has been made to give an exhaustive account of the hymenopterous parasites of Diptera at a specific level, but rather to present a broad perspective of what is known. In most families of Diptera there is such a diversity in larval biology that generalisations merely from the view-point of host taxa would be confusing, and for this reason a brief treatment under host groups is followed by some supplementary information about the the principle families of parasitic Hymenoptera involved.

Nematocera Tipulidae seem to have no regular hymenopterous parasites although curiously, several of the very few dipterous parasites of Diptera are associated with them. These include species of *Siphona* and *Trichopareia* (Tachinidae), and the phorid *Megaselia paludosa*. Mycetophilidae (host records of which perhaps apply also to Sciaridae) are evidently attacked by various groups of parasitic Hymenoptera, but in few cases are the associations well documented or understood. The majority of the diapriid subfamily Belytinae is thought to parasitise Diptera and the scanty host records mostly refer to Mycetophilidae living in fungi. Most of the very few rearing records of the ichneumonid subfamilies Oxytorinae (= Microleptinae *sensu* Townes) and Orthocentrinae have also been from Mycetophilidae, of which fungivorous species certainly seem to be the main hosts of Oxytorinae, at least. An example of apparent specialisation in this subfamily is provided by *Proclitus edwardsi* which may be specific to *Brachypeza radiata*, a mycetophilid developing only in *Pleurotus cornucopiae* which is itself confined to *Ulmus*.

Some species of Cecidomyiidae have been better studied biologically because of their economic importance and consequently more is known of their parasites. Although it is true that the gall-making species have been most worked, it nevertheless seems that this habit really does attract most parasitism by Hymenoptera. The most celebrated parasites of Cecidomyiidae are the Platygasteridae (Proctotrupoidea), almost all of which attack this host group. Many early insights into the biology of parasitic Hymenoptera resulted from studies on Platygasteridae (references in Clausen, 1940; see Lepidoptera). Most species are 'egg-pupal' parasites — that is, they oviposit into the host egg but delay final destruction of the host until it has pupated — although these extremes are not always reached. Many are gregarious, and polyembryony occurs in several species of *Platygaster;* in extreme cases up to about 20 individuals may result from a single egg laid. Although Platygasteridae are not entirely restricted to the gall-causing species, some parasites of Cecidomyiidae are. Most of the chalcidoid family Torymidae, for example, is parasitic on the various insects living in galls, an ecological specialisation which has resulted in several genera (e.g. *Torymus)* having extraordinarily wide host ranges in a systematic sense, although at a specific level a good deal of extreme specialisation has arisen. Another biologically diverse chalcidoid genus, although this time without such obvious ecological specialisation, is *Tetrastichus* (Eulophidae) which has a profound although by no means exclusive association with cecidomyiid galls. Various Pteromalidae, especially the tribes Ormocerini and Pirenini, are also important parasites of Cecidomyiidae. For papers on parasitism in Cecidomyiidae see Clausen (1940) and Askew and Ruse (1974).

Brachycera On the whole the larval habits of the Brachycera have remained rather generalised and most species inhabit the ground layer, be it mud, dung, soil, or compost. Although most of these larvae have never been reared, they will almost certainly prove to be generally free of parasitism. A rather bizarre example of parasitism of Brachycera is practised by species of the chalcidid genus *Chalcis*.

These oviposit into the fully grown larvae of *Stratiomys*, presumably during the brief time between their leaving the water and finding a pupation site. Although species of *Chalcis* are extremely local in Britain, this example of opportunism once again demonstrates that host accessibility is an all-important criterion.

Cyclorrhapha Among the Aschiza, parasitism by Hymenoptera is best known in the family Syrphidae and, in particular, the subfamily Syrphinae whose exposed aphidivorous larvae are not only highly susceptible but also economically important and easy to study. Parasites include the megaspilid (Ceraphrontoidea) *Trichosteresis glabra*, which is a larva-pupal endoparasite of aphidivorous syrphids and of interest in that certain related genera are also associated with aphids, in which they are hyperparasites. A less differentiated condition exists in the pteromalid genus *Pachyneuron*, which includes regular parasites of Syrphinae as well as parasites of similarly aphidivorous Chamaemyiidae, and apparently also parasites of the aphids themselves. Perhaps the best known parasites of Syrphidae are the entire ichneumonid subfamily Diplazontinae, many of which are abundant in Britain. Emergence is from the syrphid puparium but oviposition is into the host larva or even, in some cases, the egg. The occurrence of egg-pupal parasites in the subfamily suggests the possibility that a wide range of syrphids may be open to attack by Diplazontinae, although published rearing records relate only to the aphidivorous Syrphinae. Other parasites attacking Syrphinae include the encyrtid (Chalcidoidea) genus *Syrphophagus* and the figitid (Cynipoidea) subfamily Aspicerinae. The presence of such a diverse assemblage of parasites attacking this ecologically specialised host group provides a good example of colonisation of an accessible niche by parasitic Hymenoptera, since it can be seen to have happened so many times. Syrphids of saprophagous habits are often parasitised by *Rhembobius*, an ichneumonid genus of the subfamily Phygadeuontinae (= Gelinae *sensu* Townes = Cryptinae *auctt.)* which oviposits into the puparium.

Although the biology of the Conopidae may appear unsuitable for parasitism by Hymenoptera, the pteromalid *Habrocytus conopidarum* which is an isolated species within a large and biologically diverse genus, develops gregariously inside conopid puparia.

The beginning of the Schizophora is a convenient place to mention a major influence on the parasites of Diptera, namely the evolution of the puparium that arose in this group of predominantly terrestrial flies. The puparium is, to a parasite, a source of both food and protection from the external environment, and consequently something of a boon. Hymenoptera make use of the puparium in two ways: either they oviposit into it in which case they usually develop as ectoparasites on the pupa itself, or else oviposition is into the larva but the development of the endoparasite is completed only after the host has pupated. Apart from some Diapriidae and several genera of phygadeuontine ichneumonids, which are often abundant parasites of the litter layer but biologically poorly understood, most of the parasites which oviposit into Diptera puparia seem to be pteromalids. In this family genera which are completely specialised to this way of life include *Spalangia, Muscidifurax* and the well studied *Nasonia*, other common species occurring in the more polyphagous genera *Dibrachys* and *Eupteromalus*. Some of these seem to attack chiefly Calyptratae. Endoparasites of cyclorrhaphous Diptera are virtually always larva-pupal (or egg-pupal in some extreme cases) and many of them are known to cause premature pupation of their hosts (Clausen, 1940). This interesting phenomenon is induced by several widely separated families of Hymenoptera, but the physiology of the process has not been fully investigated. It is worth mentioning that the arguably less specialised habit of killing the larva before it has pupated, so notably absent among endoparasites of Diptera, is a feature of many of the parasites which attack Lepidoptera.

Among the several groups of parasites that attack only Cyclorrhapha are two important subfamilies of Braconidae, namely Opiinae and Alysiinae. Adult Opiinae have sharply-pointed, thin mandibles which meet in front, while those of the Alysiinae are multidentate, blunt, and bent so strongly outwards that they project beyond the sides of the head when opened. Both have to do the same job − that is, tear open the host puparium so that the adult parasite can emerge − but there is clearly more than one way to do this effectively! These braconid parasites of Diptera are known to attack most of the Schizophora but for both subfamilies it seems that leaf-mining hosts are of prime importance, or at least best known. As expected, Schizophora seem to be parasitised more or less according to the availability of their larvae, although our knowledge of their parasites is largely dependent on the economic importance of the hosts. In the Tephritidae, in which the larvae are restricted in movement, usually either in galls or in the flowering or fruiting parts of plants, parasitism often reaches high levels and is practised by a wide range of parasitic Hymenoptera. Among the Chalcidoidea the pteromalid genus *Habrocytus* has a large species-group tied to Tephritidae, and the families Eurytomidae and Torymidae are characteristic parasites of the gall-causing species. Varley (1947) has made a detailed study of the parasites and population dynamics of *Urophora jaceana* galling *Centaurea* flowerheads. Tephritid larvae inhabiting fruit are often of economic importance and are known to be attacked by various parasites, including Opiinae and Alysiinae.

Diptera breeding in seaweed cast up on the shore are often parasitised, and broods of 60-70 individuals have been recorded for the diapriid *Platymischus dilatatus* developing in the puparia of the sepsid *Orygma luctuosa*.

The family Ephydridae is certain to have interesting parasites and, indeed, a thorough knowledge of these may prove to be helpful in understanding evolutionary trends within the host family. The larvae of *Hydrellia* species endophytic in submerged vegetation are attacked by the opiine braconid *Ademon decrescens*. This species is reputed to be amphibious as an adult, using its long legs and hairs for swimming, and attacking its host underwater. Another remarkable parasite of an ephydrid is the pteromalid *Urolepis maritima* which emerges from the puparia of *Ephydra riparia* after they have floated to the surface of the brackish water inhabited by the larvae.

Among the parasites of Drosophilidae, the eucoilid *Pseudeucoila bochei* is an increasingly well-known laboratory animal through the researches of van Lenteren, Bakker and others. Perhaps their most appealing finding is that females of this solitary larva-pupal endoparasite need to experience both parasitised and unparasitised larvae of *Drosophila* before they can learn to avoid laying superfluous eggs in hosts already attacked. Leaf-mining Drosophilidae are frequently attacked by species of *Halticoptera* (Pteromalidae), but other leaf-mining and similarly endophytic Diptera are also attacked by this genus.

The impressive analysis of Griffiths (1964-8) on the Alysiinae parasitising Agromyzidae and several other leaf-mining Diptera demonstrates the value of examining natural relationships of host groups in concert with their parasites. The highly specialised alysiine tribe Dacnusini is a principal enemy of Agromyzidae; most species are exceedingly host specific although just a few are equally remarkably polyphagous. Various Opiinae, and in particular the genus *Opius,* are possibly rather less host specific but also numerous as parasites of Agromyzidae and other leaf-mining Diptera. Several groups of chalcidoids have also rather fully exploited these endophytic hosts. Among these, parasites of leaf-mining Diptera occur chiefly in the eulophid subfamilies Eulophinae and Entedontinae, and in the pteromalid tribes Miscogasterini and Sphegigasterini. It is noteworthy that Eucoilidae (Cynipoidea) attack only those Agromyzidae boring stems or causing galls (*Melanagromyza* and *Hexomyza),* which may be seen as a link with other Eucoilidae known to attack root-inhabiting Diptera larvae such as *Delia brassicae* and *Psila rosae.* Information on the parasite complexes of individual agromyzid species is given by Cameron (1939), Askew (1968) and Dye (1977).

Chloropids are parasitised by various Dacnusini (e.g. *Coelinidea* and *Coelinius* species) and the pteromalid genus *Stenomalina* is also associated with them. Large hosts have large parasites; thus *Stenomalina liparae* and the dacnusine *Polemochartus liparae* are specific to the genus *Lipara.* Parasites listed for economically important species, such as *Oscinella frit,* include Diapriidae and Eucoilidae. Tachinidae developing as larvae in other insects are prone to attack from hyperparasitic chalcidoids of the family Perilampidae, and ichneumonids of the subfamily Mesochorinae which are also obligatory hyperparasites. Otherwise the parasites of the Calyptratae are best treated together. The relatively few leaf-mining and plant-inhabiting species have parasites similar to those of ecologically related groups, but many larvae of the Calyptratae live in protein-rich, messy environments, which are often not the sites chosen for pupation. This may help to explain why the ichneumonid and pteromalid parasites of puparia are such prominent elements, although in an ecological study of Diptera associated with dead snails Beaver found that the phygadeuontine ichneumonid *Mesoleptus* is a larva-pupal parasite. A considerable number of Alysiinae, which are also larva-pupal parasites of cyclorrhaphous Diptera, similarly manage to attack species whose larvae inhabit various decaying animal remains. The small species, including Phoridae, are attacked by genera such as *Aspilota,* while the large calliphorids and sarcophagids are parasitised by *Alysia* and *Aphaereta.* Some figitids and eucoilids also attack blow-fly larvae and many of the parasites of Diptera inhabiting carcasses are known to be attracted to the smell of decaying meat in much the same way as their hosts. Much interesting information about the role of parasites in controlling populations of various synanthropic muck-breeding Diptera is given by E.F. Legner and co-workers in a series of papers published from about 1965 onwards, mostly in *Annals of the Entomological Society of America.* No information appears to be available on the parasites, if any, of Diptera obligatorily parasitising vertebrate animals, although the pteromalid genus *Bairamlia* is a specific parasite of fleas.

Additional information on the chief groups of parasites which attack Diptera is summarised below:

Ichneumonoidea. Rather few groups parasitise Diptera: Ichneumonidae of the subfamilies Phygadeuontinae (apart from isolated cases such as *Rhembobius* the relatively few genera known to parasitise Diptera puparia are grouped round *Phygadeuon* and round *Mesoleptus,* although quite possibly some of the many genera of unknown biology will also turn out to be parasites of Diptera); Oxytorinae (perhaps entirely associated with Mycetophilidae but otherwise biology obscure); Orthocentrinae (parasites of Diptera near the ground, but host affinities and biology unclear); and Diplazontinae (parasites of Syrphidae, perhaps confined to the aphidivorous Syrphinae). Braconidae of the subfamilies Opiinae (parasites chiefly of Schizophora feeding in plant tissues); and Alysiinae (more generally associated with Cyclorrhapha, although hosts of Dacnusini are mostly endophytic and it may be significant that this subfamily seems not to parasitise Syrphidae); a few species of *Blacus* (Helconinae) are also said to attack Diptera but the subfamily is otherwise endoparasitic upon Coleoptera. All the ichneumonoids which attack Diptera are strictly solitary parasites.

Chalcidoidea. Almost every large family in this diverse and important superfamily contains species, genera, or tribes which attack Diptera, but none of the families is particularly associated with this order. Pteromalidae and Eulophidae are the most important families in which species attacking Diptera are found. Solitary development is the more usual but a few species are habitually gregarious.

Ceraphrontoidea. This superfamily, recently split from the next, contains few known parasites of Diptera although the biology of many genera is unknown.

Proctotrupoidea. The families Platygasteridae (associated especially with Cecidomyiidae) and Diapriidae are each predominantly parasitic upon Diptera. In the Diapriidae most, at least, of the Belytinae seem likely to attack Mycetophilidae, while in the subfamily Diapriinae are species which parasitise cyclorrhaphous Diptera puparia occurring near the ground. Wright and co-workers (1947) seem to suggest that some are larva–pupal parasites, but others oviposit into the puparium. Both solitary and gregarious development are known. The family Scelionidae comprises minute insects which, along with the two chalcidoid families Trichogrammatidae and Mymaridae, develop entirely within insect eggs. It is true of all these egg parasites that their best known hosts are in other orders, yet there are a few records of each from various dipterous eggs (especially Syrphidae and Tabanidae, but also Cecidomyiidae, Rhagionidae and others) which suggest that eggs of Diptera laid in accessible sites will be attacked. This may conceivably have some bearing on larviparity and also on the habits of certain Diptera, such as asilids, which conceal their eggs.

Cynipoidea. Two families, Eucoilidae and Figitidae, are associated with Diptera and, if the dubiously-placed Anacharitinae are excluded from the Figitidae, both probably attack cyclorrhaphous Diptera exclusively. The figitid subfamily Aspicerinae may attack only syrphids but otherwise host relations in the two families are far from clear. On the whole figitids are larger insects than eucoilids and the hosts of both seem mostly to be found somewhere near ground level or below. Biological data given by James (1928) are probably fairly typical, in which case both would be solitary larva-pupal parasites which oviposit into very young hosts.

Further study

In looking for information on parasites of Diptera one repeatedly comes across statements to the effect that most species of such-and-such a group seem likely to be parasites of Diptera, but their habits and biology are poorly known. This just about sums it up – far more biological information is needed before the parasites of Diptera, and the effect they have on their hosts, can be properly understood' and this will only come about if the value of even chance rearings of parasites is appreciated by dipterists. On a rather grander scale, the work of Griffiths (1964-8) leaves no doubt as to the value of having really large collections of reared parasites from a particular host group, and anyone engaged in studying the larvae of Diptera should include a quantitative account of parasitism, even (or especially!) if none is found.

Biological data should be collected cautiously and any doubts as to host or other details should be expressed in a permanent way on data labels etc. Ideally the data with a reared parasite should include, besides locality and name of host, date and stage of host when collected, substrate from which host collected, date of parasite emergence, and stage of host killed. Other relevant information, such as ectoparasite or endoparasite, should also be recorded if available. The parasite should be mounted together with its exuviae and host remains; pin only really big specimens, but mount others on triangular card points, gluing one mesopleuron to the tip with the wings extended outwards (above the thorax like a butterfly at rest) and the legs towards the pin. Always use a water-soluble glue, and use it sparingly.

Acknowledgements: We are grateful to P.J. Chandler, M.I. Crichton, M. Drake, N.D.M. Fergusson, T. Huddleston, G.E.J. Nixon and J. Quinlan for helpful discussions of various points.

Further Reading

Askew, R.R., 1968. A study of leaf-miners and their parasites on laburnum. *Trans. R. ent. Soc. Lond.* **120**: 1–37.

Askew, R.R. & Ruse, J.M., 1974. The biology of some Cecidomyiidae (Diptera) galling the leaves of birch (*Betula*) with special reference to their Chalcidoid (Hymenoptera) parasites. *Trans. R. ent. Soc. Lond.* **126**: 129–167.

Cameron, E., 1939. The holly leaf-miner (*Phytomyza ilicis* Curt.) and its parasites. *Bull. ent. Res.* **30**: 173–208.

Dye, P.M., 1977. A study of *Phytomyza ranunculi* (Schrank) (Dipt., Agromyzidae) and its insect parasites. *Entomologist's mon. Mag.* **112**: 155–168.

Fulmek, L., 1962. *Parasitinsekten der Blattminierer Europas*, 203 pp., The Hague.

Fulmek, L., 1968. Parasitinsekten der Insektengallen Europas. *Beitr. Ent.* **18**: 719–952.

Griffiths, G.C.D., 1964-8. The Alysiinae (Hym. Braconidae) parasites of the Agromyzidae (Dipt.). In six parts, *Beitr. ent.* **14–18**.

James, H.C., 1928. On the life histories and economic status of certain cynipid parasites of dipterous larvae, with descriptions of some new larval forms. *Ann. app. Biol.* **15**: 287–316.

Varley, G.C., 1947. The natural control of population balance in the knapweed gall–fly (*Urophora jaceana*). *J. Anim. Ecol.* **16**: 139–187.

Wright, D.W., Geering Q.A. & Ashby, D.G., 1947. The insect parasites of the carrot fly, *Psila rosae* Fab. *Bull. ent. Res.* **37**: 507–529.

SAWFLIES (HYMENOPTERA SYMPHYTA)

Thirteen genera of Tachinidae are known to be casual parasites of caterpillar-like sawfly larvae. Some genera of tachinids, such as *Blondelia, Compsilura, Meigenia, Voria, Bessa* and *Diplostichus*, are believed to parasitise sawfly larvae

171

as freely as Lepidoptera. There is a need for further work to clarify more precisely the role that Diptera play in parasitisation of sawflies. Since so few hymenopterists in Britain have paid serious attention to rearing sawfly larvae, the field is still wide open for study.

Adults of the ceratopogonid *Forcipomyia (Microhelea) fuliginosa* have been observed on both sawfly and Lepidoptera larvae.

LACEWINGS (NEUROPTERA)

Adults of the ceratopogonid *Forcipomyia (Trichochelea) eques* are recorded attached to the wing veins of lacewings.

HETEROPTERAN BUGS (HETEROPTERA)

Heteroptera, usually known as 'true' bugs are parasitised by tachinid flies belonging to the subfamily Phasiinae. The biology of this group of flies was monographed by Dupuis (1963) and rearing records are largely confined to the continental literature. The female fly either attaches her egg to the integument of the host (all British genera except *Alophora* and possibly also *Leucostoma* and *Cylindromyia*) or injects the egg through the host's integument by means of a piercer (*Alophora, Leucostoma?, Cylindromyia?*). The parasite larva develops within the abdominal cavity of the nymphal or adult host. Generally, both sexes are attacked. Parasitised bugs may eventually be recognised by their swollen abdomens. Parasitism may also bring about a reduction in overall size and even a change in colouration. As a rule, parasitised female *Aelia acuminata* (Pentatomidae) are unable to lay eggs, and even if they are able to do so, the number of eggs is reduced. Continental work reported that tachinid larvae parasitising *Eurydema oleracea* (Pentatomidae) leave female hosts via the 'anus', and male hosts via the intersegmental membrane joining abdominal segments seven and eight. The tachinid larva usually kills the host at the time of its emergence, although adult bugs may sometimes live for several days afterwards. After leaving the bug, the larva pupates, presumably in the soil or leaf litter. Parasitism of *Aelia acuminata* often reaches a high figure. At present, there are insufficient data to allow any conclusions to be drawn regarding host specificity of Phasiinae. Very little information on host associations, of parasitisation or habitat relationships has been gathered in Britain. Of the 19 British species, 13 are certainly parasites of Heteroptera but there are British rearing records for only three of them. Southwood & Leston (1959) mention a parasitised *Acanthosoma haemorrhoidale* (Acanthosomatidae) but no tachinids have been reared from this species.

The following host list is restricted to genera and species of Heteroptera occurring in Britain; it is based largely on continental records, those of British origin are indicated (B): **Alophora hemiptera**, *Palomena prasina, Pentatoma rufipes* (Pentatomidae); **A.obesa**, *Leptopterna dolabrata* (B), *Lygus* (Miridae), *Zicrona caerulea* (Pentatomidae), *Beosus* (Lygaeidae), *Myrnus* (Rhopalidae); **A.pusilla**, *Anthocoris nemoralis* (B), *A.sarothamni* (B), *Lyctocoris* (Cimicidae), *Nysius*,

Chilacis, Kleidocerys (Lygaeidae), *Cymus* (Berytinidae), *Aethus* (Cydnidae);
Gymnosoma globosum, *Aelia acuminata, Neottiglossa* (Pentatomidae); **G.nitens,**
Sciocoris cursitans (Pentatomidae); **G.rotundatum**, *Palomena prasina, Pitedia
juniperina* (Pentatomidae); **Subclytia rotundiventris**, *Elasmucha grisea* (B),
Elasmostethus interstinctus, Cyphostethus tristriatus (Acanthosomatidae),
Piezodorus lituratus (Pentatomidae); **Cylindromyia brassicaria**, *Dolycoris
baccarum, Palomena prasina* (Pentatomidae); **Evibrissa vittata**, *Troilus luridus*
(Pentatomidae); **Lophosia fasciata**, *Aelia acuminata* (Pentatomidae); **Cinochira atra**,
Eremocoris plebejus (Lygaeidae); **Labigastera forcipata**, *Enoplops scapha*
(Coreidae), *Dicranocephalus agilis* (Stenocephalidae); **Leucostoma simplex**, *Aptus
mirmicoides* (Nabidae).

The other group of Diptera which parasitises heteropteran bugs is the family
Cecidomyiidae. On the Continent, Kieffer has reared a single male *Endopsylla
endogena* from a dead nymph of *Stephanitis pyri* (Tingidae). Pupation took place
inside the tingid, and the adult emerged through a circular hole cut in the dorsal
surface of the host. Certain species of Cecidomyiidae act as predators upon
heteropteran bugs (see Barnes, 1930). Tachinid and cecidomyiid parasites of
Heteroptera may be reared in the same way as Pipunculidae (see below). Predatory
host species may require an insect food source. The adult Phasiinae occur at
flowers (see Flower-visiting Flies) but most (except *Alophora* spp) are scarce and
southern in Britain. *Elachiptera brevipennis* (Chloropidae) is recorded as egg-
laying under the wing pads of *Nabis subapterus* (Nabidae), but it is not clear
whether this is a regular association.

Further Reading

Barnes, dae H. F., 1930. Gall midges (Cecidomyiidae) as enemies of tachinid the Tingidae, Psyllidae,
Aleurodidae and Coccidae. *Bull. Ent. Res.* **21:** 319-329.
Dupuis, C., 1963. e Essai monographique sur les Phasiinae. *Mem. Mus. Nat.* **26:** 461 pp.
Southwood, T.R.E. & Leston, D., 1959. Land and water Bugs of the British Isles. Warne, London.

LEAF HOPPERS (HOMOPTERA: AUCHENORHYNCHA)
by Mark Jervis

The group of flies which usually comes to mind when considering parasitism of
bugs is the family Pipunculidae, the members of which are exclusively parasitic on
leafhoppers and their relatives. Pipunculids are recognised by their large eyes,
semi-globular and extremely mobile heads, and by their habit of hovering
stationary above or amongst plant foliage. They are on the whole quite small flies,
although *Nephrocerus flavicornis* is reasonably large (wing length 7-9mm). The
group is taxonomically quite difficult and although 77 species are in the check list,
it is quite clear that a good many more await discovery. Some species may be
adequately distinguished only on the basis of larval characteristics.

The general biology of Pipunculidae has been covered by Coe (1966); studies on
the biology and life histories of certain British species have been carried out by
Rothschild (1964), Whittaker (1969), Waloff (1975) and Benton (1975).

Due to the inconspicuousness of adult Pipunculidae, very few observations have

173

been made on the searching and oviposition behaviour of the female flies; however available accounts show that this involves a large visual component. For example, female *Verrallia setosa* will hover about two centimetres away from birch leaves and twigs whilst searching for nymphs of *Oncopsis flavicollis*. Before seizing nymphs, the female parasites orientate themselves and make distinct pouncing movements onto the host, and may even pounce onto birch buds and bud scales, which *Oncopsis* nymphs closely resemble. In fact, out of 12 "ovipositions" (i.e. in which the ovipositor was clearly used), 4 were into *Oncopsis* nymphs, and 8 were into birch buds and bud scales (Benton, 1975). Depending on the species of parasite, the host may either be hoisted into the air by the ovipositing female fly, jump forward carrying the parasite with it, or remain upon the plant. A single egg is laid at each oviposition by means of the female's piercer. Generally oviposition takes place in third, fourth and fifth instar nymphs. However, *Verrallia* attacks only the adults of Cercopidae; Coe reports that searching female *Verrallia* avoid the spittle which surrounds froghopper nymphs.

As the pipunculid larva develops it increases in size, and so causes the host's abdomen to distend. Parasitised male hosts are more easily recognised compared to female hosts, since it is difficult to determine whether the abdomen of a female leafhopper is swollen due to parasitism, or due to the presence of its own eggs. Parasitised individuals of some leafhopper species sometimes undergo a change in overall body colouration; this is especially true of *Kybos* spp. and *Empoasca vitis* (Typhlocybinae), adults of which may change from a brilliant green colour to an orange/yellow colour. Even in the absence of such colour changes it is possible, with a little practice to recognise parasitised hosts. Pipunculid larvae cause parasitic castration in their hosts, in which the gonads become reduced and non-functional. Also, the external genitalia of hosts may be affected through parasitism; this can make identification of hosts difficult. Again, with a little practice, it is often possible to identify even badly affected host individuals.

Depending on the species of pipunculid, and possibly also the species and size of host, the larva completes its development in (a) the host nymph, (b) the host adult, or (c) either of these host stages. In *Chalarus* spp., development may be completed only in the host adult. The mature larvae of pipunculids emerge by rupturing the host's integument, which is all that remains of the host; the larvae consume all other tissues.

After emerging from the host, larvae of most species crawl or drop to the ground where pupation takes place, either in the soil or leaflitter. A number of *Dorylomorpha* spp. have been shown to pupate upon vegetation. Benton reports that certain of the host species attacked by *D.haemorrhoidalis* and *D.xanthopus* live in wet grassland where *Juncus* is growing; he suggests that these species pupate upon vegetation as an adaptation to living in wet habitats liable to flooding. Most species of British Pipunculidae overwinter as pupae. *Cephalops semifumosus*, *Cephalops curtifrons* and *Eudorylas obliquus* are unusual in that they overwinter as first instar larvae within hosts. Even more unusual is *Chalarus parmenteri* which overwinters either as a first instar larva or as a pupa, depending upon the species of host that is attacked. Each species has a characteristic adult emergence time (i.e. flight period). That is, each species of parasite is synchronised in its emergence with the particular host species and host stages that it attacks.

Various methods may be employed in collecting adult Pipunculidae. Malaise traps obtain quite reasonable numbers of adults but hand netting is the usual collecting method. Bramble in hedgerows and nettle patches are good places to look for adults, especially adults of *Chalarus*. Where brambles or briars prevent the use of a net, hovering flies may be pooted in flight.

The host relations of Pipunculidae may be broadly summarised as follows (from Benton (1975) which differs from Coe (1966):–

Chalarus, Typhlocybinae (Cicadellidae); *Verrallia*, Cercopidae and Macropsinae (Cicadellidae); *Tomosvaryella*, Cicadellidae; *Pipunculus*, Cicadellidae; *Cephalops*, Delphacidae and Cixiidae; *Eudorylas*, Cicadellidae and Flatidae; *Dorylomorpha*, Cicadellidae.

Rearing records for 30 of the 77 + species of British Pipunculidae have been obtained so far. The majority attack more than one species of host; although they may be described as "unspecific", several clearly show a "preference" for a particular set of host species. All available evidence suggests that in *Chalarus* the "preference" of each species is determined by the behaviour of the female parasite. The majority of *Chalarus* spp. have been reared from hosts taken from a variety of foodplants. The species of foodplant therefore appears to be unimportant in influencing their choice of hosts. More information is required on the host characteristics which influence host selection by female pipunculids, e.g. coloration, morphology, behaviour, ecology or a combination of such factors. The following methods can be employed in rearing Pipunculidae:

1.) This is similar to the method employed by Waloff (1975). The apparatus used in this case consists of a 7.0×2.5cm glass tube. At one end is inserted a perforated cork bung; at the other end is inserted a bored cork which is pressed onto a 3×1cm glass tube. Both corks are covered in gauze. The small glass tube is kept almost full of water to maintain high humidity in the rearing tube. Parasitised leafhoppers are placed individually in these rearing tubes and are provided with a piece of foodplant. The tubes are then placed in an outdoor shed. After the parasite larva has emerged from the host, and has pupated, the foodplant and host remains should be removed and the host remains stored in a safe place. During the winter, the rearing tubes should be partly covered with peat in order to prevent the water from freezing. This method is unsuitable for small, delicate leafhoppers such as Typhlocybinae and the following method is recommended for these hosts:

2.) The apparatus used in this case consists of a 2.5×7.0cm glass tube, partly filled with plaster of paris. A small amount of "Vermiculite" (this is available from most horticulturists) is placed upon the plaster of paris and a few drops of water are added to provide a humid atmosphere for the leafhoppers (moistened acid-washed sand may be used instead of plaster of paris and "Vermiculite"). The parasitised leafhopper is placed in the rearing tube, along with a piece of foodplant; the tube is then capped with a perforated plastic stopper and placed in an outdoor shed. Once the parasite has emerged from the host and has pupated, remove the foodplant and host remains, and cap the tube with a cork bung.

When using either of these methods, it may be necessary to replace the foodplant daily as this may rapidly wilt. During the summer, check the tubes daily for emerging adults. If you wish to keep the adult flies alive, provide them with either a small ball of cotton wool dipped into dilute sugar solution or half a soaked raisin placed on the end of a pin which is inserted into the cork bung of the rearing tube. It is important to label the rearing tubes and collect the following data: 1) date of collection of parasitised host leafhopper and instar; 2) foodplant of host; 3) sampling locality; 4) date when mature larva emerged and pupated and instar of host; 5) date when adult fly emerged. It is essential that the puparia are kept with reared adults since the former may be useful for developing a larval taxonomy. Leafhoppers occur in a variety of habitats ranging from grassland to woodland canopy. In fact it is possible to begin your rearing studies almost anywhere. Even the rose bushes in the garden may support a population of leafhoppers (*Edwardsiana rosae*). Nettles and brambles also support a number of leafhopper species. Parasitism may be quite high; as many as 60% of adults of one of the nettle-associated species, *Eupteryx urticae*, may be parasitised. It is worth noting that in several bivoltine species of leafhoppers, the second generation of adults tends to be more heavily parasitised compared to the first generation. Leafhoppers are best collected using a sweep-net and pooter. It is important not to sweep too vigorously, otherwise the leafhoppers may be injured. In the later stages of parasitisation, hosts are recognised by their sluggish behaviour, swollen abdomens and altered colouration (see above).

For information on host plant preferences and habitat distribution of leafhoppers, see Waloff and Solomon (1973) (grassland leafhoppers), Claridge and Reynolds (1972) and Claridge and Wilson (1976) (woodland leafhoppers).

Further Reading

Benton, F.P., 1975. *Larval taxonomy and bionomics of some British Pipunculidae.* Unpublished Ph.D.thesis, University of London.

Claridge, M.F. & Reynolds W.J., 1972. Host plant specificity, oviposition behaviour and egg parasitism in some woodland leafhoppers of the genus *Oncopsis* (Hemiptera Homoptera : Cicadellidae). *Trans. R. ent. Soc. Lond.* **124** (2) : 149-166.

Claridge, M.F. & Wilson, M.R., 1976. Diversity and distribution patterns of some mesophyll-feeding leafhoppers of temperate woodland canopy. *Ecological entomology* **1** : 231-250.

Coe, R.L., 1966. Diptera ; Pipunculidae. *Handbk. Ident. Brit. Insects.* 10 (2c).

Rothschild, G.H.L., 1964. The biology of *Pipunculus semifumosus* (Kowarz) (Diptera : Pipunculidae), a parasite of Delphacidae (Homoptera) with observations on the effects of parasitism on the host. *Parasitology* **54** : 763-769.

Waloff, N. & Solomon M.G., 1973. Leafhoppers (Auchenorrhyncha : Homoptera) of acidic grassland. *J.appl.Ecol* **10** : 189-212.

Waloff, N., 1975. The parasitoids of the nymphal and adult stages of leafhoppers (Auchenorrhyncha : Homoptera) of acidic grassland. *Trans. R.ent. Soc. Lond.* **126** (4) : 637-686.

Whittaker, J.B., 1969. The biology of Pipunculidae (Diptera) parasitising some British Cercopidae (Homoptera). *Proc. R.ent. Soc. Lond.* (A) **44** (1-3) : 17-24.

APHIDS AND THEIR ALLIES (HOMOPTERA: STERNORHYNCHA)
by Ian McLean

The evolution of aphidophagous larvae, probably from phytophagous ancestors, has occurred chiefly in three families of Diptera, the Cecidomyiidae, Syrphidae and

Chamaemyiidae. The prey principally belong to the various families of aphids within the super-family Aphidoidea. A chloropid is also recorded as preying on aphids. In addition, the other three super-families of the Sternorhyncha have a few records of fly associations. Thus certain Coccoidea (scale insects) are attacked by Chamaemyiidae and Aleyrodoidea (whiteflies) by a drosophilid, whilst some Psylloidea (jumping plant lice) are parasitised by Cecidomyiidae.

There is much useful and interesting research the amateur dipterist can do on this subject as no special or expensive equipment is required only patience in searching for the larvae and a certain amount of daily attention for successful rearing. Many aphids are found on garden plants or weeds, so interesting material for study can close at hand. Collection of early stages associated with aphids (and allied bugs) is often the best way of obtaining many of these Diptera as the adults may be inconspicuous and difficult to collect by sweeping. Many eggs, larvae and pupae are undescribed, and if the adult females of these flies are caught it is possible to obtain eggs and rear the larvae using the techniques described below. In addition to obtaining information on life histories, the variation of adult morphology within a species in taxonomically difficult genera, such as *Paragus* or *Pipiza*, can be studied by examining a series of the offspring reared from a single known female.

The three main groups of larvae are readily separated. Larvae of Cecidomyiidae lack conspicuous posterior respiratory tubes. The other two families have such tubes; in Syrphidae the pair of tubes is fused in the third (final) instar. The tubesare separated in all instars of Chamaemyiidae and in early instars of Syrphidae, but the latter larvae will normally be larger.

Many aphids excrete a sugary substance termed honeydew, which can form a sticky coating on leaves where aphids are abundant (providing the rain does not wash it off). A wide range of flies will feed on honeydew, their sucking mouth parts probing the leaf for an alternative source of energy to the nectar of flowers. It is well worth searching and sweeping foliage covered with honeydew.

Cecidomyiidae

Predators: although the larvae of the majority of species in this family are phytophagous, two British genera are known to have larvae which are predatory upon aphids, namely *Aphidoletes* and *Monobremia*.The commonest species is *Aphidoletes aphidimyza* for which Harris (1973) lists 61 species of aphid which have been recorded as prey, including both tree and herb layer species. The adults first appear about May and there are several generations through the summer with larvae being found until the end of September. These later larvae overwinter in cocoons in the soil (and pupate the following spring). *Aphidoletes urticariae* is less common than the preceding species, and it has been recorded in association with 12 species of aphid, all but one of which have also been recorded as hosts for *A. aphidimyza*. The last species in this genus, *Aphidoletes abietis* has only been recorded from the adelgid *Adelges abietis* on *Picea* (spruce) and it may be a specialised predator of this woolly aphid. Finally, *Monobremia subterranea* is an uncommon species for which Harris (1973) records five aphid species as prey, with two known hosts in England.

As the larvae are only 3—4 mm long when full grown, the smaller early instars are easily overlooked when searching through dense aphid colonies in the field. Therefore, aphid colonies on their host plants should be collected in polythene bags and brought back for rearing, even when larvae are not detected. Rearing of aphidophagous Cecidomyiidae is complicated by the requirement for soil where the larvae can spin their cocoon and pupate (though sometimes they will spin up on plants). Rearing is probably best carried out in small cylinder cages (see fig. 'A') with aphids kept alive on their host plant with a daily light spray of water to prevent desiccation. It is sometimes difficult to get a high rate of rearing success with these species.

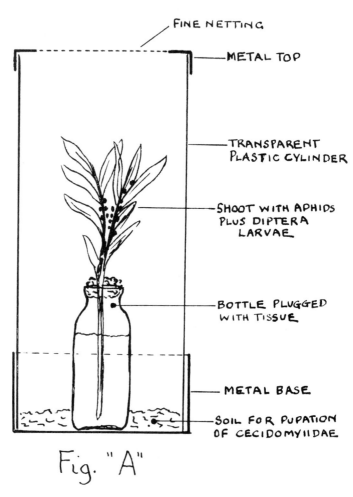

FINE NETTING

METAL TOP

TRANSPARENT PLASTIC CYLINDER

SHOOT WITH APHIDS PLUS DIPTERA LARVAE

BOTTLE PLUGGED WITH TISSUE

METAL BASE

SOIL FOR PUPATION OF CECIDOMYIIDAE

Fig. "A"

Cylinder cage for rearing Aphidophagous Diptera larvae.

Parasites: The cecidomyiids *Endaphis* and *Endopsylla* are endoparasites of aphids and psyllids respectively.

The female of *Endaphis perfidus* lay its eggs on or near aphids. As the reddish-coloured parasite larvae develop they can be easily seen within the body of the aphid. When fully grown, the larva makes its exit via the anus of the host, and 'jumps' to the ground where it pupates. A species of *Endaphis* is known to attack a species of aphid living on rest-harrow (*Ononis repens*) in N.E. England.

Larvae of *Endopsylla* are endoparasites of nymphal and adult psyllids. Lal (1934) has studied a species of *Endopsylla* which parasitises *Psylla mali* living on hawthorn. The female lays its egg upon the forewing of the host psyllid. The basal stalk of the egg is inserted in the wing membrane alongside one of the veins. The larva hatches and crawls from the wings to the body of the host. There, it usually feeds for 3 to 4 days as an ectoparasite, and then it burrows through one of the intersegmental membranes into the haemocoel of the psyllid. When fully grown, the larva leaves the host by piercing the abdomen at its base; it then drops to the ground to pupate. *Endopsylla agilis* has been reared from adult *Psylla foersteri* living on alder.

No doubt additional species remain to be discovered. Our present knowledge of the taxonomy and biology of cecidomyiids is brought together by Harris (1973), and larvae of *Aphidoletes aphidimyza*, *A. urticariae* and *Monobremia subterranea* can be identified from his drawings. Hodkinson (1974) gives a very useful review of the biology of the Psylloidea and references to work on their natural enemies.

Syrphidae

The larvae of hoverflies in the subfamily Syrphinae have been found to be aphid predators for all those species reared until now. There are possible exceptions with the genera *Chrysotoxum* and *Xanthogramma* as *C. verralli* and *X. pedissequum* have been found in the nests of the ant *Lasius niger* (Dixon, 1960). These may have become associated with ants via the relationship of ants tending aphids; it is possible that the syrphid larvae are facultative predators of root aphids. In addition, the known larvae of the tribe Pipizini (subfamily Milesiinae) are also aphidophagous.

The larvae of aphidophagous Syrphidae have been described by Dixon (1960) and Goeldlin (1974) and the species they describe are listed in an appendix. Those descriptions based on American material in Dixon (1960) are omitted as they are not conspecific with the British species (Goeldlin, 1974). Because a species is listed here as being described it does not necessarily mean that the description is sufficiently detailed for separating a larva from other closely related undescribed larvae. The key given by Dixon (1960) enables the commoner species to be identified from third instar larvae. Further detailed studies are needed as altogether less than half the species of Syrphinae and Pipizini have any larval description published.

There is little published information on the range of aphid species preyed upon by the different syrphid larvae. Some apparently specific associations have been discovered, while other species have been recorded from a number of aphid hosts, though much work remains to be done before the true range of prey taken in the field is reliably worked out. The relationship between predator and prey is complicated by the large variation in the relative abundance of different aphids from year to year. The habitat preference of the adult hoverfly is also important. That hoverflies have strong habitat preferences was clearly shown by Pollard (1971). Working with the aphid *Brevicoryne brassicae* he showed that species such as *Leucozona lucorum* and *Epistrophe eligans* laid eggs on infested brussel sprouts planted in woodland and hedge habitats, while in open fields *Episyrphus balteatus* and *Platycheirus peltatus* were the species which laid on the plants. It is therefore desirable to record the habitat, host plant and aphid prey when collecting eggs and larvae of hoverflies from aphid colonies.

A number of interesting life histories are known for aphidophagous Syrphidae, and some of these are summarised here.

Association with root aphids: *Pipizella varipes* has been shown by Dixon to have larvae which feed on the root aphid *Anuraphis subterranea* which was found on the umbellifer *Pastinaca sativa* during August. The eggs are laid above soil level on the stem of the plant near colonies of the aphid which are frequently ant attended.

Association with aphid galls: *Heringia heringi*, *Pipizella virens*, *Pipiza festiva* (not British) and *Neocnemodon latitarsis* have been reared from the petiole galls of the aphid *Pemphigus spirothecae* on Poplar *(Populus nigra* var. *pyramidalis). H. heringi* has been bred from an aphid gall on *Salix*. The larvae of *H. heringi* and *P. festiva* develop by feeding on the aphids inside the closed galls and then hibernate in the soil as fully developed larvae before pupating the following spring and emerging during the summer.

Association with woolly aphids (Adelgidae) on conifers: In addition to feeding on aphids in poplar galls, *N. latitarsis* has been recorded feeding on the adelgid *Adelges piceae* on *Abies. Neocnemodon vitripennis* has been reared from and as predator of the aphid *Eriosoma lanigerum* on *Malus*. These two species of *Neocnemodon* are therefore apparently adapted to feeding on those members of the Aphidoidea which produce large amounts of waxy covering material.

Association with psyllids: There are few records of Diptera larvae as predators on psyllids. Larvae of *Melanostoma mellinum* have been found feeding on *Psyllopsis fraxini* which forms galls on ash leaves. Other syrphid larvae may feed on psyllid nymphs; further rearing from known hosts is required.

Rearing of syrphid larvae is best carried out in 3" × 1" tubes. Syrphidae are the largest dipterous predators of aphids (full grown they are 10-20 mm. long) and consequently they require more aphids than do Cecidomyiidae or Chamaemyiidae in order to complete their development successfully. This should be kept in mind when collecting larvae and it should always be ensured that an adequate supply of aphids is available.

Hoverfly eggs can often be found laid on plants near to aphid colonies. They are about 1 mm. long, white in colour and are laid singly or in small batches. Ladybird eggs (Coleoptera: Coccinellidae) also found near aphid colonies are, in contrast, yellow to orange in colour and are laid in larger batches of 10-50. Chandler (1968) describes the chorionic sculpturing of the eggs of 35 of the common aphidophagous Syrphidae, which can be identified, using his key, under the high power of a microscope.

Chamaemyiidae Adult Chamaemyiidae are often found in large numbers in a variety of habitats. Sweeping grass in wet or dry habitats is a good way of finding *Chamaemyia* while *Leucopis* species may be swept from adelgid infested conifers, from coastal dunes and slacks or more rarely in other habitats. The larvae of Chamaemyiidae are exclusively predators on aphids, adelgids and coccids. Those species of *Leucopis* which feed on aphids are best obtained by rearing as they are seldom found as adults.

Chamaemyiinae: *Chamaemyia* (11 British species). The larvae of members of this genus are predators on coccids which feed on the roots and within the leaf sheaths of grasses (Tanasijtshuk, 1970). Searching at the base of grasses in an area where *Chamaemyia* are common should result in the discovery of larvae. *Parochthiphila* (2 British species) which is closely related to *Chamaemyia*, also has larvae which feed on coccids in leaf sheaths. *P. spectabilis* has been swept from tussocks of *Molinia caerulea* so possibly the larvae feed on coccids at the base of this grass. The other British species *P. coronata*, last found at Walton-on-Naze, Essex in July 1912, has been reared abroad from the scale *Pseudococcus aberrans* in the leaf sheath of *Agropyron repens* but this scale has not yet been recorded from Britain. *Acrometopia wahlbergi*, which has been swept from sedges *(Carex)*, has an unknown life history.

Leucopinae: *Leucopis* sens. strict. (6 British species) are all predatory on aphids. The larvae may be found feeding in dense colonies of aphids during the summer. Like the hoverflies, the true host ranges of the different species are imperfectly known at present. *Leucopis griseola* has been bred from *Schizoneura ulmi* leaf galls on elm; other species have been bred from a variety of aphid hosts. *Leucopis (Leucopomyia) silesiaca* has been bred from the ovisacs of a number of species of scale insect. In *Leucopis (Lipoleucopis) praecox* adults emerge in March-April and they may be swept from pines *(Pinus sylvestris)* infested with the woolly aphid *Pineus pini* on which the larvae feed. *Leucopis (Neoleucopis)* (3 British species) are predators as larvae of Adelgidae on conifers. Sweeping *Adelges* infested *Abies* and *Pineus* infested *Pinus* throughout the spring and summer will enable the adults to be collected, while larvae can be reared from the infested twigs.

Rearing of the larvae of this family can be carried out in 3" × 1" tubes for most species, though *Neoleucopis* can be reared from adelgid infested twigs placed in plastic boxes, polythene bags or by using the cylinder cage method (fig. 'A'). As with the other families the host plant, host and habitat should be recorded when collecting larvae. The larvae of *Leucopis* species found in dense aphid colonies are inconspicuous when feeding in the midst of the aphids, and they frequently hide at the base of petioles on herbaceous plants.

Drosophilidae The larvae of *Acletoxenus formosus* have been recorded as predators of whiteflies (Aleyrodoidea).

Chloropidae *Thaumatomyia* larvae are predatory on root aphids, e.g. *T. notata* on *Pemphigus bursarius* at the roots of grass.

Techniques: Where to look. Aphids may be found throughout spring and summer predominantly on actively growing plant tissue (young shoots and developing inflorescences) but also on mature leaves and stems. The number of species and their hosts is too great to be discussed in detail here and only a few selected examples can be given. Blackman (1974) and Stroyan (1976) should be consulted for further information on aphids.

Predatory Diptera larvae often hide during the day in curled up leaves and syrphids sometimes leave a black tar-like excrement on leaves and shoots to betray their presence. It can be difficult finding larvae even where they must be present so it is possible that a search at night with a torch would be worth trying. Occasionally larvae fall onto a beating tray. The occurrence of aphids on a given plant can be very seasonal but some of the more easily found ones are on sloe, *Prunus spinosa* (spring); sycamore, *Acer pseudoplatanus* (summer); elder, *Sambucus niger* (summer); nettle, *Urtica dioica* (early summer); thistle, *Cirsium* (summer); as well as in the garden on rose and cabbages. The adult hoverflies are most plentiful in May and June, and it follows that these months are best for searching out larvae. However, some species occur later in the year and hibernating larvae may be found among woodland leaf litter in mid-winter.

The woolly aphids (Adelgidae) on conifers are described in detail by Carter (1971). *Pineus pini* is common on scots pine, *Pinus sylvestris*. Diptera larvae may be difficult to find on infested branches as they can be hidden by the waxy secretions of their prey.

Rearing Techniques. When the cylinder cage method is used (Fig. 'A') for Cecidomyiidae and Chamaemyiidae the aphids should remain alive long enough for the larvae to complete their development. The water level in the bottle must be kept topped up to prevent the plants wilting and the top should be tightly plugged to prevent the larvae drowning. When the larvae are reared in tubes fresh aphids should be provided daily. Plaster of Paris is set at the base of the tube and must be kept damp to prevent larvae desiccating. Muslin at the mouth provides air. Alternatively a corked tube with a piece of moist paper inside can be successful but muslin rather than cork may be preferable. Cleanliness is essential for success with this method; tubes and larvae must be kept free from dead aphids by frequent washing.

Those species which overwinter in the early stages can be offered moist leaf litter or damp moss on top of soil in a flower pot with the mouth covered by muslin. The flower pot should be placed outside in a sheltered position. It should be noted that many aphidophagous syrphids overwinter as fully fed larvae and many failures in rearing have been due to not making provision for this habit.

Data must be kept associated with reared material and preserved aphids at each stage, starting with labelling of polythene collecting bags and ending with permanent records for predators and aphids kept conveniently as card indexes.

Further Reading

Blackman, R. 1974. *Aphids*. Ginn & Co. London.

Chandler, A.E.F., 1968. A preliminary key to the eggs of some of the commoner aphidophagous Syrphidae (Diptera) occurring in Britain. *Trans. R.Ent. Soc. Lond.*, **120**: 199-218.

Dixon, T.J., 1960. Key to and descriptions of the third instar larvae of some species of Syrphidae (Diptera) occurring in Britain. *Trans. R. ent. Soc. Lond.* **112**: 345-379.

Goeldlin De Tiefenau, P. 1974. Contribution a l'etude systematique et ecologique des Syrphidae (Dipt.) de la Suisse occidentale. *Mitt. Schweiz. Ent. Ges.* **47**: 151-252.

Harris, K.M., 1973. Aphidophagous Cecidomyiidae (Diptera) taxonomy, biology and assessments of field populations. *Bull. ent. Res.* **63**: 305-325, plates X-XI.

Lal, K.B. 1934. Insect parasites of Psyllidae. *Parasitology*. **26**: 325-334.

Pollard, E., 1971. Hedges VI. Habitat diversity and crop pests: a study of *Brevicoryne brassicae* and its syrphid predators. *J. app. Ecol.* **8**: 751-780.

Stroyan, H.L.G., 1976. Homoptera Aphidoidea pt. 1. *R.E.S. Handbooks for identification of British Insects.* **X**: 4 (a). London.

Tanasijtshuk, V.N., 1970. Palaearctic species of the genus *Chamaemyia* Panzer (Diptera, Chamaemyiidae) from the collection of the Zoological Institute, USSR Academy of Sciences. *Ent. Rev. Wash.* **49**: 128-138.

APPENDIX:

List of described British Aphidophagous Syrphid Larvae. D = Dixon (1960) (* = not illustrated), G = Goeldlin 1974. Arrangement in alphabetical order

SYRPHINAE: *Baccha elongata* (D*,G), *Chrysotoxum verralli* (D), *Dasysyrphus albostriatus* (D.G), *D. tricinctus* (D), *Epistrophe eligans* (D), *E. euchroma* (G), *E. grossulariae* (D*), *E. nitidicollis* (D*G), *Episyrphus balteatus* (D,G), *Leucozona lucorum* (D*), *Megasyrphus annulipes* (G), *Melangyna guttata* (D), *M. lasiophthalma* (G), *M. triangulifera* (D.G.), *M. umbellatarum* (D*), *Melanostoma scalare* (D*), *Meliscaeva auricollis* (D*), *M. cinctella* (D), *Metasyrphus corollae* (D,G), *M. lapponicus* (G), *M. latilinulatus* (D*), *M. luniger* (D.G), *Parasyrphus lineolus* (G), *P. vittiger* (G), *Platycheirus ambiguus* (G), *P. albimanus* (D), *P. clypeatus* (D), *P. immarginatus* (G), *P. manicatus* (D,G), *P. peltatus* (G), *P. scutatus* (D), *Scaeva pyrastri* (D.G), *S. selenitica* (D), *Sphaerophoria scripta* (D*,G), *Syrphus ribesii* (D,G), *Syrphus vitripennis* (D), *Xanthogramma pedissequum* (D).

MILESIINAE: (PIPIZINI) *Pipiza austriaca* (G), *P. noctiluca* (D*), *Pipizella varipes* (D). '

DRAGONFLIES (ODONATA)

Adult ceratopogonids *Forcipomyia (Pterobosca) paludis* have been recorded feeding on adult Odonata, usually with the mouth parts penetrating the wing veins from which they probably imbibe fluid.

GRASSHOPPERS (ORTHOPTERA)

In Europe there are a number of Tachinidae known to parasitise grasshoppers of the family Acrididae. The only such record in Britain is that of *Meigenia mutabilis* parasitising *Chorthippus*. One may also note that the calliphorid *Stomorhina* from southern Europe (which on rare occasions is blown into Britain) has larvae which develop in locust eggs. Non-British records exist for rhagionid larvae preying on locust egg capsules. *Sarcophaga nigriventris* and *S. incisilobata* have been reared from grasshoppers but the details are obscure. The sarcophagid *Blaesoxipha gladiatrix* parasitises *Chorthippus brunneus, C. parallelus* and *Omocestus viridulus*, restricting attention almost entirely to females. The female fly has been recorded selectively shadowing female *C. parallelus*. Other relationships with Orthoptera probably await discovery.

EARWIGS (DERMAPTERA)

It is perhaps surprising that as many as three genera of tachinids should parasitise our very small fauna of earwigs; *Triarthria, Ocytata* and *Zenillia* have been recorded from the common earwig, *Forficula auricularia*, although the record of *Zenillia nemea* (a Lepidoptera parasite) is probably erroneous. The easiest way to start the search is to look under bark or in broken hollow stems frequented by earwigs and seek the dumpy pupa with a short two-pronged tail which belongs to *Triarthria*.

BITING LICE (MALLOPHAGA)

Some bird lice are phoretic on hippoboscids as a means of dispersing from one host to another.

MAYFLIES (EPHEMEROPTERA)

by Peter Cranston

The nymphs of the may fly *Ephemera danica* may carry larvae of the Orthoclad chironomid *Epoicocladius flavens* (= *ephemerae*) on the abdomen or beneath the wing buds. In Europe the genus *Rhithrogena* may carry the larvae of the chironomid *Symbiocladius rhithrogenae*, a species which has not yet been found in Britain. In both Australia and America Chironomidae are known to have obligate phoretic associations with Ephemeroptera, predominantly those living in flowing waters. Although simuliid larvae are recorded in phoretic relationships with mayfly nymphs in Africa it is thought unlikely that any such associations exist in Britain.

The ceratopogonid *Palpomyia semifumosa* has been observed piercing the thorax of the may-flies *Rhithrogena semicolorata* and *Centroptilum luteolum*, while in flight. In the latter instance, feeding lasted 55 minutes, involving fourteen separate punctures and resulting in the death of the may-fly. In these cases, the may-fly is only twice the length of its attacker, but *P. flavipes* has been recorded as piercing the eye of a *Baetis* species, much larger than itself.

STONEFLIES (PLECOPTERA)

A *Palpomyia* species (Ceratopogonidae) has been recorded as sucking juices from an unnamed perlid.

SPIDERS (ARANEAE)

by Dr. Anthony G. Irwin.

Spiders, the arch-enemies of flies, do not go unpunished for their misdeeds, for Diptera have sought their revenge in every conceivable way. Predation and parasitism of eggs and adults, the stealing of prey and the impudent use of webs for resting and mating are the means by which flies redress the traditional balance.

Predation on Eggs by Fly Larvae

Species of several families of flies have been recorded as developing in egg cocoons of spiders, where the larvae are partially protected from predation and parasitism while they eat the eggs. **Phoridae:** *Megaselia pulicaria* and *M. tenebricola* have been bred from egg cocoons found under logs. In North America, *Phalacrotophora epeira* regularly breeds in *Araneus* cocoons. **Ephydridae:** *Trimerina madizans* has been reared from *Micryphantes* cocoons. **Chloropidae:** Several genera of Oscinellinae (*Oscinella, Oscinisoma, Mimogaurax* and *Siphonella*) are recorded as egg predators abroad, though in Britain most species that have been reared were from other media, including plant hosts. Only *Conioscinella halophila* has been reared from a spider egg cocoon in Britain.

Rhinophoridae: *Melanophora roralis* has been reared once from the egg cocoon of *Araneus cornutus*, but some authors doubt the accuracy of this observation. **Sarcophagidae:** *Sarcophaga clathrata* has often been bred from the egg cocoons of *Araneus cornutus*. It seems likely that other species of *Sarcophaga* may have similar habits.

Predation on Spiders by Adult Flies

In the tropics, species of the asilid subfamily Leptogasterinae regularly catch spiders, even those sitting on their webs. In Britain, *Leptogaster cylindrica* has been observed catching a small spider. Other Asilidae tend to catch flying insects and are unlikely to be attracted to a spider. The only other British record of a fly catching a spider was when a *Platypalpus pallidiventris* (Empididae) was observed catching a female *Erigone dentipalpus*, of which many were airborne at the time.

Parasitism of Spiders by Fly Larvae

The Acroceridae are alone among the Diptera in being obligate parasites of spiders. Eggs are laid, sometimes in masses, on vegetation. The newly-hatched larva is mobile, crawling like a 'looper' caterpillar or jumping by means of the posterior tail bristles and sucker, until it contacts a spider, to which it clings using posterior hooks. Entry is effected through a leg joint, whence the larva enters the spider's abdomen, there to mature. A foreign species is known to attach its posterior spiracles to the lung-books of the host, to assist respiration. Overwintering occurs within the spider which appears to behave normally until the mature larva emerges to pupate. The few breeding records indicate that Acroceridae are not host-specific but wolf spiders (Lycosidae) seem to be preferred. The British breeding records include *Ogcodes pallipes* from *Alopecosa accentuata* and *Pardosa amentata*, *Ogcodes gibbosus* from *Pardosa pullata* and *Trochosa* sp. and *Acrocera globulus* from *Pardosa* spp. and a drassid. With the exception of the last, all the known British hosts are in the Lycosidae.

Certain Phoridae have been bred from spiders which were probably unhealthy and dying when attacked. Further observations are required to confirm phorids as facultative parasites of spiders.

Sphaerocera pusilla (Sphaeroceridae) has been found as a possible external parasite of a *Clubiona* sp.

Cleptoparasitism on Spider Prey of Solitary Wasps by Fly Larvae

Certain sarcophagid flies *(Miltogramma, Metopia* and *Senotainia)* are known to breed on the paralysed stores of spider-hunting wasps.

Scavenging on Spiders' Prey by Adult Flies

Microphorus crassipes (Empididae) is known to feed on tipulids and other flies entangled in spiders' webs. *M. holosericeus* has been observed sucking a *Cricotopus* (Chironomidae) in a spider's web. An anthomyiid and *Scathophaga stercoraria* (Scathophagidae) have also been seen engaged in this activity.

Desmometopa and *Phyllomyza* (Milichiidae) are known to ride on crab-spiders (Thomisidae), from where they have easy access to the spiders' prey which they help consume. It is doubtful if the spiders derive any benefit from these scavenging passengers.

Resting on Webs by Adult Flies

Cecidomyiidae of many genera regularly rest in large numbers on old spider's webs and associated web-lines. Abroad, many species of limoniine Tipulidae are known to habitually rest and even perform mating dances on the stay lines of spiders' webs. A common feature of these species is the possession of strikingly white tarsi. The British species, *Dolichopeza albipes* (Tipulinae), has been observed hanging from spiders' webs, though the habit has not yet been recorded in this country.

Techniques

Keeping spiders is easy if you do not allow them to desiccate. It is best to feed them on live food. They will often eat their own weight of food in a week. If the abdomen looks shrivelled, the spider may be thirsty, so give it a drop of water to drink.

Further Reading on Spiders

Bristowe, W.S., 1958. *The World of Spiders*. New Naturalist, Collins, London.
Locket, G.H., and Millidge, A.F., 1951-1974. *British Spiders*. Ray Society, London. 3 Vol. (with Merrett, P. in Vol. 3).

PSEUDOSCORPIONS (PSEUDOSCORPIONES)

These are well known 'hitch-hikers' on Diptera. Pseudoscorpions live in leaf litter, compost heaps, under stones, in the soil and in dead wood. Being tiny animals without wings, and having relatively large crab like pincers for grasping prey and other objects, they are able to hang onto flies and other insects and obtain a free lift from one site to another. The flies often acquire their phoretic passengers when they emerge from pupae at a breeding site and the chances are that the fly will move to another spot of similar ecological nature which will suite the pseudoscorpion. There may be several pseudoscorpions on a single fly. It remains an uncommon event for the dipterist to find attached pseudoscorpions but this may largely be a question of getting one's eye in for the best opportunities.

MITES (ACARI)

by Anthony M. Hutson

Mites are frequently attached to adult flies and experience in the field soon shows that certain species of fly are much more commonly infested than others. There is remarkably little known about the true nature of many of these associations between flies and mites, the difficulties being compounded by the problems of identifying the mites, especially the immature stages, and the different kinds of associations that are possible. A general account of associations between mites and insects and an extensive bibliography is given by MacNulty (1971). This paper demonstrates a fascinating variety of interactions between mites and their hosts. Evans, Sheals & Macfarlane (1961) give an excellent introduction to mites and include a very useful section on insect/mite associations.

Insect/mite associations are found in three of the four orders of mites found in Britain: the Mesostigmata, Astigmata and Prostigmata. The normal development of a mite is from an egg to a 6-legged larva, followed by at least one 8-legged nymphal stage and then the 8-legged adult. In the mesostigmatid mites it is the second nymphal and adult stages that attach to insects. Among the Astigmata, insects carry the adults of Epidermoptidae and the specialised non-feeding 2nd nymphal stage (hypopus) of such families as Acaridae and Anoetidae. In the Prostigmata it is usually the larvae that are carried. With the Diptera, mites occur on the outside of the host, but mites are known to invade the spiracles of bees and to hide themselves beneath overlapping sclerites and in the genital cavity of other groups of insects. While some of these associations are parasitic, the most common function is probably phoretic. Phoresy is the transportation of one organism by another - 'hitch-hiking' - and is almost the only method available for relatively immobile mites to utilise isolated temporary habitats, such as dung, small pools and birds' nests. In recent years this subject has been discussed in some detail by authors such as Binns and Costa in journals such as *Acaralogia*.

In the Mesostigmata the adults of the common *Macrocheles muscaedomesticae* and *M. glaber* develop in dung and the adult females are dispersed by attaching to various dungflies and beetles. All stages of these mites feed mainly as predators in the dung, *muscaedomesticae* on the eggs and larvae of Diptera, *glaber* more on such animals as enchytraeid worms. A similar situation occurs with the two species of mites transported by the mushroom sciarid, *Lycoriella auripila*; one species, *Arctoseius cetratus*, is polyphagous including being an important predator on the larvae of its host. while the other, *Digamasellus fallax*, feeds largely on nematodes. Both these species tend to select female flies as hosts. Other species of *Macrocheles* live in decaying animal and vegetable matter and the identification of the mites on flies of genera such as *Microsania* may give some lead to their as yet unknown larval medium.

Members of the astigmatid mite genera *Strelkoviacarus*, *Microlichus* and *Myialges* commonly occur on Hippoboscidae *(Ornithomya* spp.) from birds.The life history of only one species is at all well known: *Myialges macdonaldi* develops on the bird host where it feeds as a skin parasite. After mating the adult females change in form and attach themselves to a hippoboscid. The female lays a large number of eggs on long stalks around herself and soon after hatching the larvae presumably return to the bird. The adult female *Myialges* attaches to the abdomen of the fly and is parasitic, but those of the other genera, which usually attach to the wings, head or thorax, do not appear to feed while on the flies. Hill, Wilson & Corbet (1967) have discussed the British species.

The hypopial stage of members of mite families such as Acaridae and Anoetidae are attached to the host by suckers. Little work has been done on these mites on Diptera, perhaps partly because they need to be reared through to the adult to ensure positive identification.

Many of the more obvious terrestrial mites found on British Diptera are prostigmatid mites of the families Trombidiidae and Erythraeidae. As examples,

Evans et al. (1961) quote *Rohaultia* (= *Johnstoniana*), *Atomus* and *Leptus* as parasites of respectively Tipulidae, Muscidae and Tabanidae. Smith (1951, 1955) looked at *Limonia tripunctata* and found that the mites on the thorax were *Calyptostoma* and those on the abdomen were *Johnstoniana*. However, similar mites on the thorax of *Tipula luna* were *Johnstoniana*, though perhaps of a different species. This again demonstrates how important it is to record the location of the mites on the host's body, noting also whether, and where, the mouthparts are penetrating the host's cuticle. As these mites are larvae it is important to try to rear them through to the nymph or even the adult.

Better known are the water-mites found on many adult Diptera with aquatic larvae. Chironomidae are particularly involved, but other Nematocera with aquatic larvae (Tipulidae, Chaoboridae, Culicidae, Simuliidae and Ceratopogonidae) are frequently affected; Empididae and Ephydridae are also recorded. Even apparently terrestrial species, such as certain Mycetophilidae, have been recorded carrying water-mites; perhaps they pick them up when drinking. The larvae of a wide variety of water-mites are found with the mouthparts embedded in the host fly, usually in the abdomen. When the fly returns to the water (e.g. to lay eggs) the mite larvae drop off, so that the presence of the mites on mosquitoes has been used as an indication that the fly has not yet laid any eggs. Whilst the larval stages of these mites are certainly parasitic and phoretic on insects, the nymphs and adults are free-living predators which may occasionally attach to insects. Smith & Oliver (1976) have reviewed the available information on the water-mite/insect associations, with particular reference to Chironomidae, and provide a good base-line for further studies. Five of the seven superfamilies of water-mites include species associated with Diptera.

There are many mite/fly associations, some loose, some casual or occasional and hence not very important, but many which still require investigation to ascertain their importance to both parties.

Fly Larvae as Predators of Mites

Larvae of two species of Cecidomyiidae, namely *Therodiplosis persicae* and *Feltiella tetranychi*, are specialised predators on mites, feeding almost exclusively on red spider mites (Tetranychidae). Both species occur in glasshouses and outdoors and *T. persicae* has some potential as a possible biological control agent for use against glasshouse red spider mites *(Tetranychus urticae* and *T. cinnabarinus)*. Larvae of *Lestodiplosis* and *Arthrocnodax* also feed on some tetranychids, eriophyids and other groups of mites.

Further Reading

Evans, G.O., Sheals, J.G, & Macfarlane, D., 1961. *The terrestrial Acari of the British Isles. Vol. I, Introduction and Biology.* British Museum, London, 218 pp.

Hill, D.S., Wilson, N.& Corbet, G.B., 1967. Mites associated with British species of *Ornithomya* (Diptera: Hippoboscidae). *J. med. Ent.Honolulu* **4**(2): 102-122.

MacNulty, B.J., 1971. An introduction to the study of Acari-Insecta associations. *Proc. Brit. ent. nat. Hist. Soc.* **4:** 46-70.

Smith I.M. & Oliver, D.R., 1976. The parasitic associations of larval water mites with imaginal aquatic insects, especially Chironomidae. *Canad. Ent.* **108:** 1427-1442.

Smith, K.G.V., 1951. Acarine larvae on *Limonia tripunctata* F. (Dipt., Tipulidae) and on a species of

Chironomidae (Dipt.). *Entomologist's mon. Mag.* **87**: 63.

Smith, K.G.V., 1955. Further notes on Acari in association with *Limonia tripunctata* F. and other Tipulidae (Dipt.). *Entomologist's mon. Mag.* **91**: 51-52.

WOODLICE (ISOPODA)

by Alan E. Stubbs

Since no tachinids are known as parasites of woodlice, it is something of a surprise that seven species of Rhinophoridae have this association, indeed it is the predominant way of life in this group (*Angioneura* and *Melanomya*, placed in Calliphoridae in the Nearctic check list, probably attack snails). A useful review is given by Sutton (1972), and the bizarre larvae of the parasites may be identified from Bedding (1973). Only four species of woodlice have yet yielded rhinophorid parasites. Of these *Porcellio scaber* seems most prone to attack, with 5 species of fly involved, followed by *Oniscus asellus, Armadillidium vulgare* and with *Trachelipus rathkei* least parasitised. The first three species of woodlice are very common and some *P. scaber* populations have up to 30% parasitised. Woodlice make ideal subjects for study since they are easy to find and keep. There is thus plenty of opportunity to carry out further studies to increase our knowledge of the inter-relationships between the various species of fly and the various woodlice − surely more woodlice species will yield parasites. The percentage parasitisation by different species of flies may vary according to habitat.

The easiest species to find should be *Phyto discrepans* since this occurs in gardens, *Paykullia maculata* attacks woodlice under loose bark so may also locally occur in gardens and *Melanophora roralis* has been found high on the sea shore. Further observations on the behaviour of these species would be of interest since *P. maculata* has been seen running over the ground or dead wood in short jerky sprints with wings waving to show off the dark apical markings; the jerky running makes it look like a mimic of a spider hunting wasp (the arboreal *Dipogon*).

Further Reading

Bedding. R.A., 1965. *Parasitism of British terrestrial Isopoda by Diptera*, Ph.D. Thesis, London.

Bedding. R.A., 1973. The immature stages of Rhinophorinae (Diptera : Calliphoridae) that parasitise British woodlice. *Trans. R. ent. Soc. Lond.* **125 (1):** 27-44.

Sutton, S., 1972. *Woodlice*, Ginn, London.

Thompson, W.R., 1973. The tachinid parasites of woodlice. *Parasitology* **26** : 378-448.

WATER FLEAS AND CYCLOPS (CLADOCERA AND COPEPODA)

Larvae of most aquatic Diptera are adapted to feed on easily captured food, such as detritus and micro-organisms. Larger active food usually involves a parasitic or commensal relationship with a large host. Aquatic Diptera larvae have not got the mobility to chase large active prey as predators. An exception is the phantom midge larva of *Chaoborus* which is planktonic and has large grasping 'jaws' with which it catches waterfleas, cyclops and similar prey.

CENTIPEDES AND MILLIPEDES (MYRIAPODA)

The tachinids *Loewia foeda* and *Helocera delecta* have been recorded as parasites of *Lithobius*, a common genus of large fast centipedes (Chilopoda). One wonders how the fly succeeds in parasitising such a difficult sort of host. Possibly other tachinids and centipedes are also involved in such a relationship. The phorid *Megaselia elongata* parasitises millipedes (Diplopoda).

SLUGS, SNAILS AND BIVALVES (MOLLUSCA)

by Peter Chandler, Peter Cranston, Dr. Henry Disney and Alan E. Stubbs

Mollusca are almost ubiquitous, slow moving and available throughout the year. Potentially they provide endless scope for exploitation by Diptera but seemingly this is a specialist job. It is noteworthy that no tachinids attack live molluscs. The major role has been adopted by the Sciomyzidae, with 65 species in Britain, the entire family being specialist on attacking live Mollusca. There is in addition a scattering of species from other families which are known to exploit live or dead Mollusca and it seems probable that there is considerable opportunity for proving further associations.

Over the last 15 years the early stages of many British Sciomyzidae have been described and the basic details of hosts and ecological setting elucidated mainly through the work of L.V. Knutson. There remains considerable refinement of our knowledge to be worked out but it is clear that the Sciomyzidae can act as a significant ecological control on some mollusc populations. The eggs are either laid on the host or in the vicinity of hosts. Depending on the species of fly and the size of host, the larva utilises one or several molluscs in the course of its development. The young larva penetrates the host and becomes an internal parasite but the mollusc dies and the larva finishes its meal as a predator (the term for this life style is parasitoid). The larva may then need to move off in search of further hosts which it consumes as a predator - an *Elgiva* larva has been known to consume 23 snails. Pupation may be within a snail shell (resulting in a curious twisted puparium), sometimes after having sealed the shell with a calcareous plate (some *Pherbellia* and *Colobaea*), or the larva may leave the host to pupate elsewhere. Some puparia or infected shells will float as an adaptation to habitats which flood. Knutson (1970) gives a good general account of sciomyzid biology and references to earlier work. Examples of sciomyzid life styles are as follows:- predators of snails that float or forage on emergent vegetation *(Sepedon)*; exposed egg masses of aquatic or hydrophilous snails *(Antichaeta)*; pea shell bivalve molluscs *(Knutsonia lineata* and *Renocera striata)*; non-operculate aquatic and hydrophilous snails (many *Pherbellia, Pteromicra)*; terrestial snails *(Tetanura, Coremacera)*; slugs *(Tetanocera elata)*. A wide range of snails, slugs and sphaeriid bivalves are utilised as hosts. Among the more frequently used aquatic and emergent snails are *Limnaea, Physa* and *Succinea* and terrestrial snails include *Cochlicopa, Retinella* and *Discus*. Pond sides, marshes and woods are the most favoured terrain but even dry grassland and sand dunes have a few specialist species of these snail killing flies.

Flies with larvae which attack living snails crop up sporadically in other families of Diptera. Within the Phoridae, *Megaselia aequalis* and *M. ciliata* larvae attack slug eggs. A few species of Sarcophagidae parasitise snails, notably *Sarcophaga nigriventris*, and also a few calliphorids are recorded as being parasitic on snails; *Melinda* is a parasite, expecially on *Helicella virgata; Eggisops* is parasitoid on snails and slugs.

Chironomids have developed an association with aquatic mollusca in a few instances. Aquatic snails, including *Physa fontinalis* and *Limnaea* species, are often found to contain the larvae of *Parachironomus varus* within the mantle cavity of the living snail. Infestation of these snails may be as high as 70 % in *Physa* and 40 % in *Limnaea*. The larvae are believed to feed on the mantle and also on detritus grazed from the mantle and shell surface. The same species, although possibly a different sub-species, may be found on the outer shell, grazing on diatoms etc. from the surface. *Anodonta cygnea*, the swan mussel, has been found to contain larvae of *Glyptotendipes* on the outer surface of the mantle. Lesions on the mantle suggest that this larva is parasitic on the mussel, but in all likelihood this is a case of facultative (opportunist) parasitism. Larvae of the genus *Metriocnemus* were found within the mantle of the freshwater mussel *Dreissenia* which had been experimentally damaged, but here it is suggested that the larvae were casual visitors.

Dead molluscs and avaiare exploited by a wide range of Diptera: Psychodidae *(Philosepedon; humeralis)*, Empididae *(Crossopalpus curvipes)*, Phoridae); *(Spiniphora maculata, Megaselia brevicostalis, M. tenebricola)*, Piophilidae *(Piophila vulgaris)*, Ephydridae *(Discomyza onincurva)*, Heleomyzidae *(Neoleria maritima)*, Sphaeroceridae *(Copromyza pedestris, Leptocera luteilabris, L. nana, L. palmata, L. fontinalis, Sphaerocera pusilla)*, Sarcophagidae *(Sarcophaga hirticrus, S. teretirostris)*, Fanniidae *(Fannia canicularis)*, Anthomyiidae *(Subhylemyia longula Lasiomma licopa, octoguttatum, Craspedochocta pullula)* and several others have been recorded. In most cases the exploitation of dead molluscs is part of a spectrum of polyphagous or saprophagous habits. In a few *(e.g. Copromyza pedestris, Discomyza incurva, Spiniphora maculata)* it appears to be obligatory. Some muscids *(Muscina assimilis, Hydrotaea occulta)*, with larvae predatory on other fly larvae, also occur in dead snails.

There is considerable scope for the amateur to fill in many gaps in the knowledge of the natural history of the mollusc-exploiting Diptera. For example the hosts or prey of some Sciomyzidae are still not known. Also there is reason to believe that *Melanomya nana* and *Angioneura* spp. (Rhinophoridae in British list but placed in Calliphoridae in the Nearctic Catalogue) may be associated with snails since several species in these genera have this habit in N. America, yet nothing is recorded on the life histories in Britain. In addition there is an almost complete lack of quantitative data on the frequency of exploitation of molluscs (dead or alive) by Diptera in the field in normal circumstances.

Rearing of flies from molluscs is not difficult. Many of the sciomyzid life histories have been gained by bottling up female flies with a selection of live molluscs and rearing through from the egg stage (the range of molluscs accepted at home may not be the same as in the field). It should also be possible to locate infected molluscs in the field but a good deal more needs to be learnt about the necessary field craft. The fauna of dead molluscs can be studied by killing molluscs in boiling water, or by crushing, and placing them in the field for flies to lay their eggs; alternatively bring suitable female flies home in the hope that they will lay. Live molluscs are easy to keep providing sufficient humidity is maintained but dead molluscs will turn bad very quickly. Thus all material being reared should be kept in jars with a muslin top to allow ventilation, overcrowding should be avoided and a close watch kept.

Further Reading

Beaver, O. 1972. Notes on the biology of some British Sciomyzid flies (Diptera: Sciomyzidae) I. Tribe Sciomyzini. *Entomologist*, **105**: 140-143; II. Tribe Tetanocerini. *Entomologist* **105**: 284-299.

Beaver, R.A., 1969. Anthomyiid and muscid flies bred from snails. *Entomologist's mon. Mag.* **105**: 25-26.

Beaver, R.A., 1972. Ecological studies on Diptera breeding in dead snails I. Biology of the species found in *Cepaea nemoralis (L)*. *Entomologist* **105**: 41-52.

Deeming, J.C. & Knutson, L.V., 1966. Ecological notes on some Sphaeroceridae reared from snails and a description of the puparium of *Copromyza (Apterina) pedestris* Meigen. *Proc. Ent. Soc. Wash.* **68**: 108-112.

Knutson, L.V., 1970a. Biology and immature stages of *Tetanura pallidiventris*, a parasitoid of terrestrial snails (Dipt.Sciomyzidae). *Ent. Scand.* **1**: 81-89.

Knutson, L.V., 1970. Biology of snail-killing flies in Sweden (Dipt., Sciomyzidae). *Ent. Scand.* **1**: 307-314.

Knutson, L.V.,J.W., Stephenson & C.O. Berg. 1970. Biosystematic studies of *Salticella fasciata* (Meigen), a snail killing fly (Diptera: Sciomyzidae). *Trans. R ent. Soc. Lond.* **122**: 81-100.

Robinson, W.H. & Foote, B.A., 1968. Biology and immature stages of *Megaselia aequalis*, a phorid predator of slug eggs. *Ann. Ent. Soc. Amer.* **61**: 1587-1594.

Stephenson, J.W. & Knutson, L.V., 1966. A resume of recent studies of invertebrates associated with slugs. *J. Econ. Ent.* **59**: 356-360.

APPENDIX: Summary of life histories of British Sciomyzidae

Totally aquatic predators (i) **Bivalves** *(Pisidium):* - *Knutsonia lineata; Renocera striata.* (ii) **Gastropods** (non-operculate aquatic snails): -*Dictya; Elgiva* spp.:*Knutsonia albiseta; Sepedon* spp.; *Tetanocera ferruginea, T. hyalipennis; T. punctifrons; T. robusta.*

Amphibious predators (normal food either aquatic or emergent snails):-*Colobaea pectoralis; C. punctata; Pherbellia argyra; P. brunnipes; P.dorsata; P. griseola; P. grisescens; P. nana; P. ventralis; Pteromicra* (all spp.); *Sciomyza simplex; Hydromya; Limnia paludicola; Pherbina; Psacadina verbekei (= punctata); P. zernyi; Tetanocera arrogans; T. silvatica; T. unicolor.*

Parasitoids on emergent snails *Colobaea bifasciella* (on exposed *Lymnaea*); *Pherbellia schoenherri (Succinea); Sciomyza dryomyzina (Oxyloma* in America).

Terrestrial predators (usually initially parasitoid) (i) **Snails in dry open habitats:** -*Salticella fasciata* (Helicidae on dunes, initial parasitoid but may become saprophagous and has been reared on woodlice and earthworms); *Pherbellia cinerella* (also in marshes); *P. knutsoni* (dunes); *Coremacera tristis* (dry grassland). (ii) **Snails in Woodland:** - *Pherbellia albocostata; P.annulipes; P. dubia; P. scutellaris; Euthycera fumigata; Tetanocera phyllophora; Trypetoptera punctulata* (iii) **Slugs** - *Tetanocera elata.*

Terrestrial parasitoids *Tetanura pallidiventris* (woodland snails).

Amphibious egg predators (on snail egg masses) *Antichaeta analis (Lymnaea); A.brevipennis (Succinea).*

Life history unknown (i) **Probably aquatic or amphibious:** - *Colobaea distincta; Pherbellia fuscipes; Ectinocera borealis; Psacadina vittigera; Renocera fuscinervis; R.pallida* (carr); *Tetanocera freyi.*

(ii) **Probably terrestrial:** - *Pelidnoptera* spp. (woods); *Pherbellia pallidiventris* (dune and grassland); *Dichetophora* sp. (chalk grassland); *Limnia unguicornis* (separation from *paludicola* not firmly established).

EARTHWORMS (ANNELIDA)

The genus *Pollenia* (Calliphoridae) is parasitic on earthworms. The eggs are laid on the soil and the newly hatched larva searches out a worm which it enters to become an internal parasite. The greatest opportunity of finding a host is with those earthworms which live in the leaf litter and surface layers of the soil rather than the deeper burrowing species. Despite the frequent abundance of adult flies, little work has been published in Britain on the relative importance of parasitisation to earthworm populations. The ecological differences between the

5 cytoplasmic polyhedrosis viruses and 2 poxviruses. Undoubtedly, many more insect viruses await discovery.

Bacteria

Bacteria growing in the haemolymph of an insect may accumulate to a level where the haemolymph becomes milky white. Such bacteria, sometimes referred to as 'milky disease bacteria' are usually members of the genus *Bacillus*, which consists of spore-forming bacteria. The milkiness can be readily observed through the almost transparent cuticle of a larva like *Tipula*; in this instance the appearance of the larva is similar to that of an NPV-infected larva, but the haemolymph is a 'whiter white' in the latter. The presence of bacteria in haemolymph can be shown if a drop of the haemolymph is smeared on a microscope slide, heat-fixed, stained (e.g. Gram-stained) and examined microscopically.

The best known sporing bacterium in insects is *Bacillus thuringiensis* which has a wide host range. In addition to the endospore the vegetative cell also produces a protein crystal which is toxic to many insects, causing a lowering of the gut pH. This creates conditions favourable for the germination of the spore, and the resulting vegetative cell invades the moribund insect. Spore and crystal mixtures of *B.thuringiensis* constitute the most widely-used microbial control agent; hundreds of tons are produced annually to control pest insects. The growth of Diptera in the dung of cattle and chickens can be controlled by incorporating this organism in the animal feedstuffs.

Many non-sporing bacteria, such as members of the families Enterobacteriaceae and Pseudomonadaceae, are also found in association with insects. Some of these can cause disease, but many live harmlessly on the cuticle or in the gut, only invading the insect when it becomes moribund or when it dies. The presence of bacteria in the tissues of a dead insect should therefore not be taken as evidence that these bacteria are the cause of death.

Fungi

Most fungi grow by producing long strands of hyphae and reproduce by forming spores. Insect-parasitic fungi usually invade the host through the cuticle. The infection may be confined to the cuticle, or may spread to other tissues. Infected insects may sometimes be recognised by a powdery growth, often green or white, on the cuticle where the fungus is sporulating. Killed insects may be 'mummified' due to extensive growth of fungus in the tissues, and there may be melanisation resulting in blackening, both on the cuticle surface and in the insect's tissues. The most frequently observed entomogenous fungus affecting Diptera in Britain is *Entomophthora* (= *Empusa) muscae*. Epizootics (epidemics) of this species result in large numbers of mummified flies (usually *Scathophaga* or small syrphids) on herbage in small areas. The dead flies usually have the wings outstretched and the legs tightly clinging to the vegetation (and probably attached by fungal rhizoids). The intersegmental membranes of these flies are usually very pronounced because of spores of entomogenous fungi, but in this situation infection may rely more on humid conditions, e.g. rain after a dry period or local humid conditions in marshy woodland. The permanently humid environment of caves may extend the viability of spores of entomogengous fungi, but in this situation infection may rely more on contact than on airborne spore dispersal. *Heleomyza* spp. in caves are frequently affected by fungus, such as *Hirsutella dipterigena* producing a few large fruiting bodies from dead flies, similar to the common *Cordyceps* on a wide range of arthropods.

Many species of *Cordyceps* are parasitic on beetle larvae, some on their pupae or adults and the rest on a variety of other insects (including a few on Diptera), other arthropods and a few on other fungi. *Metarhizium anisopliae* causes the Green Muscardine disease of many insects, including Diptera. Other hyphomycetous fungi, such as *Beauveria, Aspergillus, Cephalosporium, Aegerita, Hirsutella*, etc. are facultative parasites ranging from some that are normally saprophytic, such as *Aspergillus*, to some, such as *Hirsutella*, that would seem to be primarily parasitic. Species of *Coelomomyces* occur mainly in the larvae of mosquitoes, but do not seem to have been recorded in Britain yet.

One of the most characteristic groups of entomogenous fungi is the Laboulbeniales. Between 1890 and 1931 Roland Thaxter published many beautifully illustrated papers on this group of fungi, but there is still plenty of scope for study. Apart from their host specificity, many species show remarkable specificity of position on the host − they may be restricted to certain small sclerites, may occur only on, say, the right side of the host, and may occur only on one sex. Up to 16 species have been associated with one species of beetle. In Britain, Laboulbeniales of the genus *Arthrorhynchus* occur on Nycteribiidae.

The effect of many of these fungi is not always obvious and some fungi, such as the Laboulbeniales, are very small. Leatherdale (1970) lists 33 species in 18 genera (excluding Laboulbeniales) from British Diptera, but the host identifications of many are unrecorded (16 families are mentioned). The taxonomy of these fungi is difficult and so they have been largely neglected. Most work on the biology concerns *Entomophthora* spp. that occur on aphids and much of the work in Britain has been published by N. Wilding of Rothamsted Experimental Station. Steinhaus (1963) includes several sections on various entomogenous fungi. Ferron (1978) discusses the systematics and ecology of entomogenous fungi in reviewing the biological control of pests.

Protozoa

Protozoa, including trypanosomes, amoebae, gregarines, coccidia and haplosporidia, are common in the gut lumen and/or beneath the peritrophic membrane of many insects. These organisms can be easily observed if insect guts and their contents are squashed in saline under the low-power of the microscope. The larger ones are visible with the naked eye.

Many of these intestinal protozoa are apparently harmless commensals, although some can invade the host and cause disease. Gregarines are very common in the guts of tipulid larvae. They occur in a variety of sizes and morphological forms. Most of these organisms have not been properly characterised. Some gregarines occur in the haemocoel of the host, although still attached to the gut. They appear as large white or pale orange structures on the surface of the midgut, and may be visible through the host's cuticle if it is transparent.

Ciliates have been found infecting the haemolymph of aquatic larvae, and amoebae attacking the winter gnat, *Trichocera hiemalis*.

The microsporidia constitute a large group of protozoa, many of which cause disease in insects. The presence of a microsporidian infection might be indicated by, for example, white areas in the haemocoel of a mosquito larva or the enlargement of some nerve ganglia in a *Tipula* larva; the infection can be confirmed by the demonstration of spores and/or other stages of the life-cycle in a Giemsa-stained preparation.

Some protozoa which infect a mammalian host have part of their life-cycle in a dipteran host. The best known of these is the malaria parasite in the mosquito. In some cases an insect feeding on a mammal infected with a protozoan can be damaged by the ingestion of a large mass of the protozoa, e.g. the sheep parasite, *Trypanosoma melophagium*, can block the midgut of the sheep ked, resulting in the deaths of large numbers of keds on infected sheep.

Nematodes

Nematodes infect larvae, pupae and adults. Some, such as a tylenchid which parasitises the non-British sciarid, *Bradysia paupera*, usually kill their host in the larval stage, while others, such as a tylenchid which parasitises the mushroom-infesting phorid, *Megaselia halterata*, renders its host sterile.

Mermithid nematodes usually invade the host through the cuticle and may grow to a large size at the expense of the host. There is usually only one or a few parasitising an individual host insect, in contrast to some of the other insect-parasitic nematodes, large numbers of which may be present in a single host. Mermithids emerge by penetrating the host's cuticle and the host usually dies soon afterwards. They are found in larvae and/or adults of Culicidae, Simuliidae, Chironomidae, Muscidae, Sciaridae, Tipulidae and Tabanidae.

Flies can also be important in transporting eggs of nematodes, including those that are parasitic in animals and presumably also those in plants.

Cestodes and Trematodes

The eggs of tapeworms have been reported in the gut of adult and larval Diptera. Adults of *Musca domestica* have been studied in particular and in some cases they will feed selectively on the proglottids (tapeworm segments full of eggs). The ingested eggs can survive in the gut for several days. Other flies have also been found to ingest eggs. It would thus seem that Diptera can be an important intermediate host particularly in crowded confined animals. This is the case with *Musca domestica* and the cestodes *Choanotaenia infundibulum, Raillieta asticillus* and *R.tetragona* – the first two are parasites of fowl and turkey and the latter of pigeon, peafowl and guineafowl. Under artificial conditions, it has been shown that *Sarcophaga* could transmit both internally and externally the eggs of *Echinococcus granulosus* from dog dung. These examples are from domestic animals in Britain, but there could be relationships between Diptera and native vertebrates since in many cases the details of the cestode life histories are uncertain. Eggs can also be ingested by Diptera larvae. They can survive in the larva for several days, but rarely survive the metamorphosis to adults.

Trematode eggs have also been found in Diptera. Such cases are very rarely recorded and their significance is uncertain.

Effects of Disease on the Host Population

It was stated earlier that the majority of micro-organisms infecting insects have probably yet to be discovered. For most of those that have been found little is known about how widespread they are in the host population or about what effect they have on that population. It is likely that insect/pathogen relationships will be found to parallel vertebrate/pathogen relationships, with a small proportion of the host population infected most of the time (in which case the disease is said to be enzootic), with occasional large outbreaks (epizootics - the equivalent of epidemics in human populations), which, in the case of a lethal disease, may result in significant reductions in host population numbers. This situation is known to occur with the iridescent virus of *Tipula* spp. larvae.

Infectious disease is one of several possible mortality factors, including predators, environmental factors and limited food supply. Most insect species suffer heavy mortality due to a combination of these factors, with only a few individuals surviving to reproduce the next generation.

Acknowledgement

A.M.Hutson has provided much of the information on fungi and cestodes and trematodes.

Further Reading

Burges, H.D., 1973. Enzootic diseases of insects. *Annals of the New York Academy of Sciences,* **217** : 31-49.

Cantwell, G.E., 1974. *Insect Diseases,* 2 vol., Marcel Dekker, New York.

Carter, J.B., 1976. A survey of microbial, insect and nematode parasites of Tipulidae (Diptera) larvae in north-east England. *J.anim.Ecol.* **13** : 103-122.

David, W.A.L., 1975. The status of viruses pathogenic for insects and mites. *Ann.Rev.Ent.* **20** : 97-117.

Ferron, P., 1978. Biological control of insect pests by entomogenous fungi *Ann. Res. Entomol.,* **23**: 409-442.

Leatherdale, D., 1970. The arthropod hosts of entomogenous Fungi in Britain. *Entomophaga.* **15** : 419-435.

Smith, K.A., 1976. *Virus-Insect Relationships,* Longman, London.

Steinhaus, E.A., 1963. *Insect Pathology, an Advanced Treatise.* 2 vol. Academic Press, London 689pp.

Chapter 6

Associations with Plants

FUNGI

by Peter Chandler

Fungi are an important food source for dipterous larvae, especially in woodland where they attain the greatest variety. Many fungi grow on wood, sometimes of particular trees, while terrestrial species often form mycorrhizal associations with specific trees and are confined to their vicinity. Most Diptera developing in fungi (fungicolous) are woodland insects but fungi growing in pasture or dune are not neglected. Fungus associations are known for about 375 species in thirty-five families of British Diptera although potentially more than 600 may be fungicolous; at least twenty families include some obligate fungicoles. A systematic list of the Diptera involved is provided in an appendix. Many flies require living or at least comparatively fresh fungi; this applies to most Tipulidae, Mycetophilidae, Phoridae, Platypezidae, Heleomyzidae, Anthomyiidae and some Drosophilidae. As a fungus fruiting-body matures and decays other flies will invade it and may accelerate decomposition, e.g. *Fannia, Psychoda, Forcipomyia, Drosophila* and Sphaeroceridae and a definite succession may be discerned. The predatory muscid larvae may begin development while the fungus is alive but complete it during decomposition. Tougher fungi (usually lignicolous) have their own special fauna but if they dry out or decay will be unproductive of flies although still inhabited by beetles; some bracket fungi when fallen to earth may become damp and then attract the same flies as do deliquescent species.

Most fungicolous Diptera restrict their choice of fungus but this is less true of those which develop in decaying fungi and some of the latter may have a wide range of other larval habitats. Some which attack fresh fungi are polyphagous, affecting fungi in many different groups although the choice may be restricted in some of these groups. More base their choice on texture and develop only in soft fungi or only in tougher species. Some are restricted mainly to fungi growing on wood (lignicolous), others to terrestrial fungi.

Many flies are apparently restricted to one or a few species of fungi but this may be due to insufficient data. Where a fly has been reared repeatedly from a single genus or species and not from any others, this may indicate true oligophagy (a few usually related hosts) or monophagy (a single host species). The common mycetophilids *Brachypeza radiata* and *Mycetophila cingulum* have been repeatedly reared from *Pleurotus* (chiefly *cornucopiae*) and *Polyporus squamosus* respectively and are probably confined to these fungi.

The polyphagous species have been reared most frequently and the many probably fungicolous flies which have not been reared, especially in the Mycetophilidae, may be restricted to a few species or to groups of fungi which have been little studied. The inhabitants of most common fungi are relatively well known thanks to the efforts of many workers, especially Buxton (1960), Trifourkis (1977) and in the case of the Mycetophilidae, Edwards, Eisfelder (1954-5) and Plassmann. Many groups of fungi, especially of smaller species have not been sampled although efforts to include them in rearing programmes have been disappointing. Nevertheless, Buxton's rearing from *Peziza* of three *Allodia (Brachycampta)* spp., from *Calocera* of *Trichonta vernalis* and *Phronia siebeckii,* also the recent rearings of *Anatella* spp. from *Helotium* and *Exidia* illustrate the need to diversify the fungi investigated. Some fungi which have been well studied, however, have a limited fauna, e.g. *Auricularia, Clavaria* and many smaller agarics.

Daldinia concentrica, a hard black fungus commonest on ash wood, is not much favoured by Diptera. Atypical stromata of this fungus, however, occur on burnt birch, oak and gorse; they are small and light brown with a hollow interior containing gelatinous material. Hingley (1971) found that the larvae of the small black drosophilid *Amiota alboguttata* develop in the gelatinous contents from July onwards. Much searching of typical fungi has failed to reveal larvae but more observations are desirable. The fly is uncommon but has been swept around decaying trees and at sap runs. Several other scarce *Amiota* of unknown habits have been recorded from Britain. Investigation of other similar Ascomycetes may throw light on them. Another drosophilid, *Steganina coleoptrata,* often swept around decaying beeches, develops in the tough Ascomycete *Hypoxylon fragiforme* on beech bark.

Hypoxylon rubiginosum is the host of the cecidomyiid *Mycocecis ovalis* which forms a canopy of silk and frass over a galled area of the fungus. This is the only certain British dipterous gall on a fungus, although gall-like formations have been suggested for *Mycetophila blanda* on *Lactarius* and *M. lunata* on *Coniophora.* In Europe, a platypezid *Agathomyia wankowiczi* forms galls on *Ganoderma applanatum* but there is no evidence that it occurs in Britain.

Ganoderma, however, is common here; the large brackets, conspicuous on beech trunks, are tough and not affected by many Diptera but when fresh several *Drosophila confusa* are often seen at rest beneath the brackets among droplets of moisture coloured reddish by the spores. *Odinia boletina,* which probably develops in beetle borings in Polyporaceae, may alight on this or other polypores (but not *Boletus* as implied by its name). *Mycetophila tridentata* has been reared from *Ganoderma* and may be specific.

The birch bracket fungus *Piptoporus betulinus* is not very attractive to Diptera when fresh although invaded by sphaerocerids and sciarids during decomposition. *Mycetophila forcipata* is, however, specific to it and a few other Mycetophilidae have been recorded. The chloropid *Botanobia (= Gaurax) dubia* has been reared from *P. betulinus;* the fly is not often found but has occurred at rest under brackets of *Coriolus* and *Bjerkandera.* The scarce tipulid *Scleroprocta pentagonalis* has been recorded as case bearing larvae in rotting *P. betulinus* when it has fallen from the tree in the spring − it is not clear whether this is a specific relationship.

The soft pore fungi of family Boletaceae (*Boletus* sensu lato) support a large dipterous fauna. Apart from many flies which also attack other Agaricales, there are some mycetophilids, several *Pegomya* (Anthomyiidae), *Fannia melania* and syrphids of the genus *Cheilosia* which select them preferentially. Hackman (1976) found that several *Pegomya* were highly specific within the Boletaceae, especially favouring *Leccinum*. Where the same fungus was attacked by several species, there were specific differences in the affected part of the fungus (cap, pores or stipe). *P. zonata* deposits eggs in a cluster through a hole in the cap, *P. winthemi* singly in the pores while *P. incisiva* oviposits in the stipe where the larvae remain. The field mushrooms (*Agaricus* spp.) are curiously not attractive to Mycetophilidae, but nevertheless have a varied fauna including several *Pegomya* (especially *calyptrata*), the platypezid *Plesioclythia dorsalis* and several phorids. Some phorids and cecidomyiids have been reared only from cultivated mushrooms and it is not known whether they are normally associated with *Agaricus* in the field. The grassland habitat is sparse in Mycetophilidae but they utilise other grassland fungi, e.g. *Lepiota procera* and coprophilous *Coprinus* spp. The swarms of *Pseudexechia trivittata* which Edwards noted about horse dung were probably interested in *Coprinus* as confirmed by recent observations. The silvery grey anthomyiid *Delia albula*, common on sand dunes, develops in *Psathyrella ammophila* a fungus specific to decaying marram grass (*Ammophila arenaria*) and may attack other fungi. The glistening white caps of *Oudemansiella mucida*, common on old beech trunks, attract females of *Pegomya transversa;* larvae may be observed through the translucent gills, burrowing at the bases. The fly has also been reared from *O. radicata* and *Armillaria mellea*, the 'honey fungus', which grows on the wood of many trees in which it develops tough black rhizomorphs. The latter are probably too hard for Diptera but the fruiting-bodies are attacked by most polyphagous agaric feeders and by at least five spp. of *Platypeza* and *Protoclythia* (Platypezidae) of which larvae feed between the gills. Buxton's rearing of two of them from *Lycoperdon pyriforme* has not been repeated and requires confirmation. Platypezidae, where the life history is known, appear to be oligophagous or monophagous. The occurrence of closely related species in the same fungus as with *A. mellea* is a common feature; both *Polyporivora* develop in *Coriolus* and at least two *Agathomyia* in *Bjerkandera*. The discovery that *Paraplatypeza atra* develops in *Pluteus cervinus* was interesting as a north american *Paraplatypeza* had previously been reared from it.

If soft fungi which have begun to decay are observed closely, very small shining dark brown to black flies may be seen hovering nearby or alighting. These may be *Leiomyza* or *Anthomyza albimana;* they are not very specific but may require the fungus to be relatively fresh. Decaying fungi may attract, amid the swarms of Drosophilidae, the rather small grey fly *Acartophthalmus nigrinus*, which has not been reared but presumably develops in fungi, the uncommon *Piophila bipunctata* and many Sphaeroceridae (especially *Copromyza (Fungobia)* species) most of which have not been reared.

Stinkhorns (Phallales)

The common stinkhorn *Phallus impudicus* attracts many flies when it bears the strongly smelling grey green sticky spore mass on its cap. Several studies have been carried out on the range of flies involved (e.g. Smith, 1956; Nielsen, 1963) which are principally those attracted to carrion (*Calliphora, Lucilia*) or dung (muscids such as *Phaonia variegata, Polietes lardarius* and *Muscina* species;

Scathophaga, Dryomyza) but also include the mycophagous *Suillia, Drosophila* and *Fungobia* species. Both flies and slugs play a part in spore dispersal. Several other Phallaceae *(Mutinus, Dictyophora)* and Clathraceae *(Clathrus)* are attractive to flies but no work has yet been done on the Diptera involved probably because of the relative infrequency of the fungi.

By contrast, *Phallus* is poorly utilised for larval development. Smith (1956) mentions several species but all are polyphagous; in North America the platypezid *Melanderomyia kahli* appears specific to Phallaceae. There is no evidence, however, that *Atelestus*, considered to be a near relative by some authors, is a fungus feeder.

Truffles (Tuberales)

These underground fungi have been little studied by entomologists, apart from the early work in France by Dufour and Laboulbene, who reared most of the Diptera noted here from these plants including *Cheilosia* and *Suillia* spp. Collin mentioned that Joy had reared *Suillia humilis* and *S. pallida* from truffles and Edwards referred to the common fungus gnat *Brevicornu crassicorne* from truffles, these being the only British rearing records from these fungi, which will certainly merit closer study.

Several mycologists have referred to small swarms of flies hovering a foot or so above the spot where truffles are concealed a short distance below the soil surface. Truffle hunters lie on the ground to better observe the flies. The fungi can also be detected by the scorched appearance of herbaceous vegetation or by a cracked surface in bare soil so it is not essential to employ trained animals.

Beechwoods on the Chalk are the most productive situations to seek truffles in Britain although they occur in other woods also. Rearing records are presumed to refer to *Tuber* but study of other genera of Tuberales e.g. *Choiromyces* (Terfeziaceae), Plectascales *(Elaphomyces)* or the subterranean Gasteromycetes (Hymenogastraceae) would be desirable.

One other British *Suillia, ustulata*, a frequent beechwood fly and several non-British species were reared from truffles in France. Some common *Suillia* have not been reared and investigation of subterranean fungi may provide the answer. The identity of the *Cheilosia* in truffles is in doubt but the puparia have been described as distinct from those in *Boletus.*

Epichloe typhina (Clavicipitales) (a common grass parasite)

This ascomycete commonly attacks many grasses from May to September, sheathing the stem for up to 5 cm. as a whitish growth, darkening on maturity to golden yellow. Affected shoots do not flower and it may kill the grass. Anthomyiids of the *Pegohylemyia phrenione* group specialise in this fungus; their elongate white eggs are laid on it in early summer. The larvae burrow in the fungus but pupate in soil. An account of this association was given by Williams (1971) on the assumption that only one fly, 'Anthomyia spreta' was involved. Ackland *(ibid.)* corrected this and found two distinct types of larval behaviour not identified to species by rearing; in one case the larva on hatching made a silk tube to which the egg shell remained attached and it fed by scraping the fungus around this, in the other it burrowed away from the egg before forming a long silk tube.

Slime Moulds (Myxomycetes = Mycetozoa)

Slime moulds are not strictly fungi but many live on rotten wood and the Diptera associated with them have affinities with the fungicoles. Buxton (1954) covered flies reared from these organisms, noting that only a very small number of British Myxomycetes have been studied by dipterists. Most species reared were either polyphagous or associated by chance. Three Mycetophilidae *(Mycetophila vittipes* and *Platurocypta* spp.) however have been reared more than once from Myxomycetes and never from fungi and the association appears regular. *M. vittipes* is the commonest of a species group including five other British species of unknown life history and it seems possible that they too are Myxomycete feeders. Recently *Manota unifurcata* has been reared from rotten wood bearing an undetermined Myxomycete but confirmation is required.

The Range of Fungi Inhabited by Diptera Larvae

Most Diptera developing in fungi select the larger species. Interesting results have been obtained from some smaller fungi especially when those outside the two main groups of large fungi (Agaricales, Aphyllophorales) have been studied but in general smaller and more delicate fungi are not chosen, even some of the colonial small agarics often being ignored.

There are well over 2000 species of fungi in Britain of sufficient size to support dipterous larvae and even microscopic rusts (Uredinales) and mildews (Erysiphaceae and Peronosporales), parasitic on higher plants, provide food for some cecidomyiid larvae *(Mycodiplosis)* while others *(Peromyia)* consume moulds on decaying agarics. *Forcipomyia radicicola* feeds on moulds on decaying roots of Umbelliferae and this may be the preferred food of other larvae living on such materials.

Most flies discussed here develop in the conspicuous fruiting-bodies of the fungi. Some dipterous larvae may feed on the branching thread-like mycelium permeating the substrate but little information is available. Mycetophilidae, Sciaridae and Cecidomyiidae which develop in rotten wood may be feeding on mycelium and examination of gut contents of some wood feeding mycetophilids, e.g. *Boletina flaviventris* by Trifourkis (1977) has shown fungal material to be present. Some cecidomyiids which infest cultivated mushrooms (e.g. *Mycophila)* develop principally in mycelium rather than fruiting bodies.

The terms agarics, boleti and polypores cover most of the fungus hosts and are used here for convenience. 'Agarics' refers to all fungi with the spore bearing layer (hymenium) on radiating gills or folds, i.e. all Agaricales (except the Boletaceae) and some Aphyllophorales (Schizophyllaceae and Cantharellaceae). 'Boleti' was used by early authors to cover all fungi with the spore bearing layer in pores leading to much confusion in entomological literature; it is now restricted to the Boletaceae of which nearly all British members are soft terrestrial fungi with a cap and stipe. The remaining pore-bearing fungi (Polyporaceae, Scutigeraceae, Fistulinaceae, all in Aphyllophorales), mostly lignicolous, are termed 'polypores'.

Fungal taxonomy has till recently been in a state of flux but the greater emphasis now placed on microscopic characters has led to some degree of stability. The classification and nomenclature adopted here follows the arrangement in the *British Fungus Flora - Agarics & Boleti: Introduction* (Henderson, Orton & Watling, 1969) for these groups. The generic nomenclature is in most cases as *Collin's Guide to Mushrooms and Toadstools* (Lange & Hora, 1963) which is followed for most other groups except Polyporaceae where the more natural arrangement in *The Polyporaceae of the European USSR and Caucasus* (Bondartsev, 1953; translation, 1971, Jerusalem) is adopted. For Ascomycetes, *British Cup Fungi and their allies* (Dennis, 1960) has been followed.

Collecting and Rearing

While much has been achieved in assessing the range of flies dependent on fungi and the range of fungi involved, there is considerable scope for original observation.

Some workers have collected many different fungi to record any flies subsequently emerging, while more usually fungi obviously containing larvae have been selected. Buxton (1960) employed the first method and noted that his results were therefore different, especially in producing relatively few Mycetophilidae. Another factor noted by him was that many larvae, especially fungus gnats, require living fungal tissue. Since soft fungi die more rapidly after removal from the mycelium it is preferable to collect them when larvae are nearly mature. Otherwise, large numbers of immature mycetophilid larvae may emerge and quickly die.

Rearing records are only of value if the fungus is correctly identified; the literature is full of records where no identification or an incorrect one has been made. It is important to isolate each sample (e.g. in a self sealing polythene bag) when several are collected on one day to avoid cross-contamination. Each identified fungus should be examined to ascertain the stage of development of larvae and to establish the range of species present. Some examples of each species should be killed and expanded in hot water ($70°$ − $80°C$), temporarily fixed in Pampel's fluid and preserved in alcohol (70 per cent.); this procedure ensures minimal retraction. Larvae required for rearing may be transferred with part of the fungus to transparent plastic rearing boxes kept at a temperature of $22 \pm 2°C$. The floor of these containers is covered with a shallow layer of fine, sterilised peat to absorb the decomposition products of deliquescent fungi, but a high humidity should be maintained by frequent spraying with dechlorinated water. Inclining the peat layer to provide a moisture gradient offers a choice of pupation sites; damp pieces of cardboard have been found a suitable pupation site for some species. Adequate ventilation should be provided by air holes in the lid; these holes should be covered with fine silk to exclude small flies from entering and to prevent oviposition by muscids. Early removal of the fungus after emergence of larvae is desirable to prevent mould growth.

Two or more species of Mycetophilidae and more often flies of several other families may be reared from a single fungus. To correlate larvae with respective adults, pupae should be carefully isolated and the final larval exuviae should be examined wherever possible. The larval mouth-parts or head capsule (in the case of Nematocera) are usually intact in the exuviae. Permanent mounts of these parts may then be prepared for comparison with preserved larvae.

Fungicolous flies may have several generations in summer and autumn and generally overwinter in the larval or pupal stage, although some mycetophilids overwinter as adults (e.g. in caves, leaf litter or within hollow plant stems). Development in most cases is rapid and larval and pupal stages may be passed in a few days especially when the fungus is ephemeral. Some flies, however, pass through fewer or only one generation per year, e.g. some Platypezidae which have a short autumn flight period and pass most of the year in a larval or pupal diapause; *Platypeza consobrina* has survived a second winter in this stage. When rearing from fungi it is therefore necessary to retain material collected in summer at least till late autumn and that collected in autumn until the following summer or even longer to ensure that all flies present have emerged. Saprophagous species, e.g. Sciaridae and *Sylvicola cinctus* may pass several generations in the same fungal material.

The best season for most fungi is autumn and it is then that both adults and larvae of fungus flies are best sought. The quantity of fruiting bodies appearing varies annually according to the amount of early autumn rain. A mild humid autumn is best but when rain has been too heavy fungi become waterlogged and are then unsuitable for larvae. Some fungi, however, typically produce fruiting bodies earlier in the year. In spring several agarics appear, e.g. *Calocybe gambosa*, from which several Mycetophilidae have been reared and some polypores are most productive then. In summer *Pleurotus cornucopiae* and *Polyporus squamosus*, which both grow principally on elm, support a wide range of Diptera and the terrestrial *Paxillus involutus* may occur from early summer onwards although more abundant in autumn. *Pleurotus ostreatus*, which usually occurs in late autumn and winter has produced few Diptera in comparision to its close relative; this also applies to other winter fungi e.g. *Flammulina velutipes*.

One problem which awaits solution concerns the manner in which many fungus flies pass the summer when fruiting bodies are few, especially those species which pass several generations in summer and autumn. Adults of many (including the hibernaters) emerge in spring and some are presumably longer lived as adults than as larvae although adult feeding is unrecorded in most. The aggregations of Mycetophilidae which occur in damp refugia in woodland, nevertheless, have a somewhat different species composition in summer, with a bias towards those developing in rotten wood, encrusting fungi or polypores, while in autumn those developing in agarics come to the fore at least in numbers. Trifourkis (1977) studied the life cycle of *Bolitophila hybrida* of which adults may be found throughout the year; he found that prolonged mild spells in winter may induce early pupation and adult emergence of overwintering larvae in the top soil, but emerging adults hibernate and do not oviposit.

Recognition of Early Stages of Fungicolous Diptera

Mycetophilid larvae are usually slender white maggots with a distinct dark head capsule. The larvae of Keroplatinae and Sciophilinae which inhabit webs on the surface of the fungus are usually more slender. Bolitophiline larvae, gregarious in soft fungi, have distinct short antennae. Most larvae of Mycetophilinae are internal feeders with prominent ventral creeping welts and black head capsules sharply contrasting with the body which harmonises with fungal tissue, i.e. usually white but sometimes brightly coloured; the common *Mycetophila fungorum* has the head capsule light brown. The larvae of *Phronia* which feed at the surface of encrusting fungi are broad ovate, sometimes covered with slime or even with limpet-like protective cases like those of *Epicypta*.

The web formers often pupate in the web, sometimes without a cocoon. Species in soft fungi normally pupate in soil, usually with a loose white cocoon. Some species regularly pupate in a tougher cocoon within the tissue of non-deliquescent fungi, e.g. *Mycetophila alea* in *Russula nigricans* (where the cocoon bears a papery cap for adult emergence, near the surface of the fungus) and *M. ornata* in *Polypilus giganteus;* many cocoons may be found together.

Other Nematocera usually have a slender body, again with a distinct head capsule, partly retractile in the Tipulidae which are usually larger. Some e.g. *Limonia bifasciata* reside within a compact mucilaginous tube within the fungus tissue, in which they pupate. *Ula* larvae, which pupate in soil, may emerge in large numbers from soft fungi. Cecidomyiid larvae, very small and often numerous when found, may be brightly coloured (orange, red or yellow) like other cecid larvae, irrespective of the colour of the fungus.

Cyclorrhaphous larvae have no sclerotised head capsule. Most are white cylindrical maggots tapered anteriorly but easy recognition of most families is not yet possible; many have been described inadequately or not at all. Medium sized larvae occurring to the exclusion of others may be *Suillia* or *Pegomya;* larger larvae of similar type in smaller numbers with other dipterous larvae will probably be the carnivorous muscids. *Muscina assimilis* has been reared in large numbers, having decimated other larvae but usually other flies will also be reared in numbers. Fanniid larvae are rather different, flattened, darker coloured with a more chitinised cuticle and bearing long often branching lateral processes on all segments. Some platypezids *(Platypeza, Protoclythia, Plesioclythia, Paraplatypeza)* are superficially similar but usually less flattened and with shorter, unbranched or only slightly branched processes. Larvae of both groups occur on the surface of gills rather than within fungus tissue but fanniid larvae are more active and usually only appear when decomposition has begun. Platypezid larvae have a wide range of form: *Callomyia* which feed on the surface of encrusting fungi are oval, strongly flattened with 48 branched lateral processes while those which tunnel through the tissue of polypores *(Orthovena, Polyporivora, Agathomyia)* are more cylindrical and white with reduced processes. The latter pupate in the fungus, *Polyporivora* forming a silk cocoon.

Cheilosia larvae are robust, cylindrical white maggots with the syrphid character of the posterior spiracles united in a short tube. Drosophilid larvae and puparia are best distinguished from other small Cyclorrhapha by the pair of short processes bearing the spiracles at each end of the body. Phorid larvae are small and rather featureless but may have short processes resembling those of Platypezidae.

Acknowledgement

The information on rearing was provided by Dr. Stephen Trifourkis, who also permitted use of the data in his thesis (1977) and commented on other aspects.

Further Reading

Buxton, P.A., 1954. British Diptera associated with fungi. II. Diptera bred from Myxomycetes. *Proc. R. Ent. soc. Lond.* (A) **29:** 163-171.

Buxton, P.A., 1960. British Diptera associated with fungi. III. Flies of all families reared from about 150 species of fungi. *Entomologist's mon. Mag.* **96:** 61-94.

Buxton, P.A. & Barnes, H.F., 1953. British Diptera associated with fungi. I. Gall midges (Cecidomyiidae) reared from the larger fungi. *Proc. R. ent. Soc. Lond. (B)* **22:** 195-200.

Colyer, C.N., 1954. Notes on a new species of *Megaselia* (Dipt., Phoridae) from Britain; notes on British fungicolous Phoridae. *Entomologist's mon. Mag.* **90:** 108-112.

Eisfelder, I., 1954. Beitrage zur Kenntnis der Fauna in hoheren Pilzen. *Zeitschrift fur Pilzkunde.* **16:** 1-12, 1955. *ibid.* 18: 1-15, 19: 12-20.

Hackman, W., 1976. De som larver i haltsvamper levande anthomyiidernas biologi (Diptera). *Notulae Ent.* **56:** 129-134.

Hingley, M.J., 1971. The Ascomycete fungus *Daldinia concentrica* as a habitat for animals. *J. Anim. Ecol.* **40:** 17-32.

Nielsen, B.O., 1963. Om forekommen af Diptera pa Alm Stinkvamp *(Phallus impudicus* Pers.). *Saertryk af 'Flora og fauna.'* **69:** 126-134.

Smith, K.G.V., 1956. On the Diptera associated with the stinkhorn *(Phallus impudicus* Pers.) with notes on other insects and invertebrates found on this fungus. *Proc. R. ent. Soc. Lond.* (A) **31:** 49-55.

Trifourkis, S., 1977. The bionomics and taxonomy of the larval Mycetophilidae and other fungicolous Diptera. I: 1-393, II: 394-792. N.E.L.P. Faculty of Science, Ph. D. Thesis, University of London.

Williams, C.B., 1971. Notes on a fungus eating Anthomyiid fly in North Britain and in North America. *Entomologist* **104:** 1-3; (note by D.M. Ackland, 1972. *ibid.* **105:** 231-232).

APPENDIX: Known Fungus Associations of British Diptera

References are to rearing unless otherwise indicated.

TRICHOCERIDAE: some **Trichocera (annulata, hiemalis, regelationis, saltator)** are polyphagous in fresh and decomposing fungi but develop in many other media.**TIPULIDAE:** the few tipulid fungicoles are mainly obligate and usually polyphagous. **Limonia (Metalimnobia) bifasciata,** agarics, boleti, *Phlebia, Scleroderma,* soft polypores. *Ganoderma;* **L. (M.) quadrimaculata,** recorded from *Phaeolus schweinitzii* but may be monophagous in *Inonotus hispidus;* **L. (M.) quadrinotata,** *Amanita, Clavaria;* **L. (Limonia) nubeculosa,** agarics and soft polypores, usually leaf mould; **L. (Atypophthalmus) inusta,** decaying *Merulius tremellosus;* **L. (Rhipidia) uniseriata,** *Russula nigricans,* usually rotten wood; **L. (Achyrolimonia) decemmaculata,** polyphagous in Polyporaceae, Meruliaceae, Thelephoraceae; **Ula mollissima,** softer Polyporaceae, Boletaceae, *Hydnum, Scleroderma,* some agarics - mostly lignicolous; **U. sylvatica,** many agarics – mostly terrestrial, boleti, *Scleroderma;* **Scleroprocta pentagonalis,** *Piptoporus betulinus.* **PSYCHODIDAE:** a few **Psychoda (cinerea, phalaenoides)** develop in decaying agarics as well as other media; **P. lobata** has been reared only from decaying fungi *(Armillaria, Amanita, Coprinus)* but more work is required on the species involved and degree of dependence. **CERATOPOGONIDAE: Forcipomyia (F) ciliata,** decaying agarics, polypores, other media; **F. (F.) radicicola,** moulds on decaying Umbelliferae roots; **Culicoides (Avaritia) scoticus,** polyphagous in agarics, boleti and soft polypores. **CHIRONOMIDAE: Bryophaenocladius furcatus,** indet. polypore, other media; **B. ictericus,** *Xylosphaera, Lycoperdon;* **Metriocnemus atratulus,** old *Chrondrostereum.* **ANISOPODIDAE: Sylvicola cinctus,** soft decaying fungi, decaying wood; **S. fenestralis,** *Piptoporus, Russula,* usually other decaying materials. **MYCETOPHILIDAE:** it is uncertain how many species are fungicolous but there are definite associations for more than 130 spp. and probably most other species of the genera concerned are also fungus feeders. Others develop in rotten wood but the family also includes inhabitants of bird's nests, caves, mosses, liverworts and carnivorous web formers on various substrates.

Bolitophilinae: larvae are gregarious and develop internally in soft fungi; **Bolitophila (B.) cinerea,** mainly *Hypholoma,* also *Collybia, Lacrymaria, Hebeloma, Pholiota, Armillaria, Flammulina;* **B. (B.) saundersi,** mainly *Hypholoma,* also *Hebeloma, Lepista,* visiting *Pholiota aurivella;* **B.(B.) tenella,** *Cortinarius, Pholiota, Armillaria, Hypholoma;* **B. (Cliopisa) fumida,** *Xeromphalina campanella;* **B. (C.) glabrata,** *Clitocybe* species especially *nebularis;* **B. (C.) hybrida,** mainly *Paxillus involutus,* also *Clitocybe, Tricholoma, Rozites, Lepista, Coprinus, Suillus* (some of latter records dubious); **B. (C.) maculipennis,** *Boletus, Paxillus* and Tricholomataceae; **B. (C.) occlusa,** *Tyromyces lacteus, T. caesius, T. stipticus;* **B. (C.) pseudohybrida,** *Lepista nuda, Ripartites, Paxillus, Clitocybe, Russula;* **B. (C.) rossica,** *Boletus;*

Diadocidiinae: **Diadocidia ferruginosa,** *Peniophora* spp. usually rotten wood. (larvae in long dry silk tubes); Ditomyiinae: **Ditomyia fasciata,** polyphagous in polypores; **Keroplatinae:** mainly carnivorous larvae singly in webs, often on rotten wood. **Keroplatus testaceus,** under brackets of polypores or on encrusting fungi, forms a dense white cocoon; **Cerotelion lineatus,** encrusting fungi and rotten wood, pupa in slimy threads; **Orfelia (O.) fasciata,** moulds under wet bark; **O. (O.) unicolor,** under brackets of *Coriolus.* Sciophilinae: most form webs on the surface of fungi, probably feeding on spores. **Mycomya** species, webs on encrusting fungi; **M. cinerascens** on *Stereum;* **M. duplicata** on *Auricularia;* **M. marginata** on many fungi; **M. wankowiczi** on *Stereum* (but also *Hypholoma, Phallus); **M. winnertzi** on *Ganoderma, Phellinus;* **M. wrzesniowskii** on *Xylodon* (= 'Poria'); **Leptomorphus walkeri,** *Xylodon versipora,* several times; **Sciophila buxtoni,** Polyporaceae *(Daedaleopsis, Pseudotrametes, Coriolus);* **S. hirta,** polyphagous, especially Polyporaceae, *Cantharellus, Lactarius, Armillaria, Pholiota, Collybia, Auricularia, Bulgaria;* **S. interrupta,** *Hydnum repandum;* **S. lutea,** polyphagous, many polypores, agarics, boleti, *Hydnum, Ustulina, Stereum;* **S. ochracea,** probably *Phellinus pomaceus* ('*Fomes*' sp. on plum; cocoons on cherry); **S. rufa,** *Fomes fomentarius* on birch in Scotland, large strong papery cocoons; **Monoclona rufilatera,** '*Poria*' sp.; **Apolephthisa subincana,** *Xylodon versipora, Phlebia merismoides* and underlying bark, indet. mycelium beneath bark, in tube of mucilage; **Coelosia tenella,** *Stereum hirsutum;* **Coelophthinia thoracica,** *Leccinum scabrum, Hydnum repandum;* **Rondaniella dimidiata,** polyphagous, polypores. *Stereum, Sparassis, Boletus, Pholiota, Russula;* **Leia bimaculata,** decaying *Russula* spp., *Collybia, Hebeloma, Calocera viscosa;* **Tetragoneura sylvatica,** slight slimy web on *Xylodon versipora;* **Ectrepesthoneura hirta,** *Coriolus,* indet. encrusting fungi, rotten wood; **Docosia gilvipes,** polyphagous, polypores, agarics, boleti, *Ustulina, Scleroderma, Auricularia, Peziza;* **Manotinae: Manota unifurcata,** rotten wood bearing indet. myxomycete. **Mycetophilinae** (Exechiini): all known larvae develop internally in soft fungi. **Anatella flavomaculata,** *Helotium aciculare;* **A. lenis,** *Exidia glandulosa;* **Rymosia affinis,** stipes of *Russula* & *Amanita;* **R. fasciata,** *Tricholoma, Galerina, Morchella, Clavaria;* **R. virens,** *Laccaria amethystina;* **Tarnania fenestralis,** many large agarics and boleti; **T. tarnanii,** several Tricholomataceae & Cortinariaceae; **Allodiopsis (Gymnogonia) excogitata,** visits *Coprinus* spp; **A. (Myrosia) maculosa,** *Cortinarius* spp., *Coprinus atramentarius;* **A. (A.) domestica,** Tricholomataceae *(Tricholoma, Clitocybe, Marasmius);* **A.(A.) rustica,** Tricholomataceae *(Clitocybe, Lepista);* **Exechia bicincta,** *Gomphidius viscidus;* **E. confinis,** *Lactarius piperatus;* **E. contaminata,** *Hypholoma, Lactarius* (especially *turpis);* **E. dorsalis,** many agarics (especially *Collybia maculata),* boleti; **E. fusca,** polyphagous, many agarics, boleti, *Clavaria,* soft polypores *(Polyporus, Pseudotrametes);* **E. lucidula,** *Inocybe patouillardii, Collybia dryophila;* **E. lundstroemi,** *Collybia, Hydnum;* **E. nana,** *Suillus luteus;* **E. nigroscutellata,** *Russula, Lactarius;* **E. parva,** Tricholomataceae & *Russula;* **E. pseudocincta,** *Lactarius deliciosus;* **E. separata,** mainly Boletaceae, *Cortinarius, Gomphidius;* **E. seriata,** *Leucopaxillus, Amanita, Russula, Lactarius, Boletus;* **E. spinuligera,** *Hygrophorus, Amanita;* **Exechiopsis fimbriata,** Tricholomataceae including *Laccaria;* **E. indecisa,** Boletaceae (records from *Tricholoma, Amanita, Russula* require confirmation); **E. intersecta,** *Tricholoma saponaceum;* **Pseudexechia trivittata,** visits *Coprinus* spp.; **Allodia (A.) anglofennica,** *Collybia butyracea;* **A.(A.) lugens, A.(A.) ornaticollis,** many agarics, boleti; **A.(A.) truncata,** *Marasmius androsaceus;* **A. (Brachycampta) alternans,** several large agarics, boleti; **A. (B.) barbata, A. (B.) silvatica, A. (B.) triangularis,** *Peziza repanda;* **A. (B.) grata,** many agarics including *Paxillus;* **Brevicornu (Stigmatomeria) crassicorne,** *Tuber;* **B. (B.) griseicolle,** Cortinariaceae *(Hebeloma crustuliniforme, Cortinarius elatior, Inocybe* sp).; **B. (B.) sericoma,** *Amanita rubescens;* **Brachypeza bisignata,** visiting *Pleurotus ostreatus;* **B. radiata,** *Pleurotus* (usually *cornucopiae,* also *ostreatus);* **Cordyla brevicornis,** mainly *Boletus, Russula,* also *Amanita, Lactarius, Lepiota, Rozites;* **C. crassicornis,** *Russula azurea, R. emetica;* **C. murina,** *Lactarius torminosus, Scleroderma verrucosum;* **C. fasciata, C. flaviceps, C. fusca, C. nitidula,** Russulaceae *(Russula, Lactarius).*
Mycetophilinae (Mycetophilini): **Trichonta** and **Phronia** are usually surface feeders on encrusting fungi, while **Mycetophila** always develop internally. **Trichonta atricauda,** *Corticium* sp.; **T. terminalis,** *Corticium, Peniophora cinerea, P. incarnata;* **T. falcata, T. stereana,** *Stereum hirsutum,* under mucilage and frass; **T. melanura,** *Stereum hirsutum, Pholiota mutabilis;* **T. venosa,** *Lycoperdon* sp.; **T. vernalis,** *Calocera cornea,* larvae bright yellow like fungus, feeding internally; **T. vitta,** *Xylodon* spp.; **Phronia biarcuata** (= **johannae),** **P. strenua,** case-bearing larvae on encrusting fungi (conical black cases in **strenua). P. braueri,** larvae slug like (coat of black slime) on encrusting fungi; **P. conformis, P. fusciventris** (= tarsata), **P. tenuis,** larvae in thin white mucilage on encrusting fungi; **P. humeralis,** *Corticium* sp.; **P. siebeckii,** *Calocera viscosa* (larvae like **Trichonta vernalis); Dynatosoma fuscicorne,** many Polyporaceae, large larvae at base of tube layer, *Merulius;* **Mycetophila alea,** usually *Russula nigricans* (tough cocoons with papery cap embedded in fungus), also other *Russula, Lactarius, Amanita, Hygrophorus, Clitocybe,*

Leucopaxillus; **M. blanda,** *Lactarius* (especially *deliciosus),* cocoons in fungus; **M. britannica,** *Armillaria, Hebeloma, Hypholoma, Russula, Polyporus squamosus;* **M. cingulum,** common in *Polyporus squamosus;* **M. confluens,** Boletaceae; **M. czizeki,** *Lactarius helvus;* **M. finlandica,** *Tricholomopsis rutilans;* **M. forcipata,** *Piptoporus betulinus,* larvae at base of tubes, pupa in soil; **M. formosa,** *Phlebia;* **M. fungorum,** polyphagous, many agarics, boleti, *Phallus, Polyporus squamosus;* **M. ichneumonea,** *Lactarius, Russula, Lepista, Stropharia, Xeromphalina;* **M. luctuosa,** polyphagous, agarics, boleti, *Piptoporus, Coriolus, Chondrostereum, Ustulina;* **M. lunata,** *Coniophora puteana;* **M. marginata,** polyphagous, mainly lignicolous agarics, polypores, *Stereum, Xylosphaera,* also *Tricholoma, Phallus;* **M. ocellus,** polyphagous on lignicolous fungi (especially Meruliaceae and Thelephoraceae, also *Xylodon, Sparassis, Pleurotus ostreatus);* **M. ornata,** lignicolous fungi (*Stereum, Pleurotus,* polypores, commonly *Polypilus giganteus*), cylindrical cocoons in fungus; **M. pictula,** *Xylodon versicora,* slight silky cocoon; **M. pumila,** indet. polypore; **M. ruficollis,** *Collybia fusipes;* **M. sepulta,** *Hypholoma elongatum;* **M. sigillata,** *Boletus, Russula, Hygrophoropsis;* **M. signata,** Boletaceae (*Suillus variegatus);* **M. signatoides,** Boletaceae (*Boletus, Leccinum* spp.), records from *Russula, Lactarius, Paxillus* require confirmation; **M. spectabilis,** *Lactarius piperatus, Tricholoma* sp.; **M. tridentata,** *Ganoderma applanatum;* **M. trinotata,** lignicolous fungi (*Coriolus, Stereum, Bjerkandera);* **M. vittipes,** myxomycetes (*Arcyria incarnata, A. denudata);* **Epicypta aterrima,** case-bearing larvae on indet. mycelium on wood; **Platurocypta punctum,** myxomycetes (*Lycogala, Reticularia);* **P. testata,** myxomycetes (*Reticularia, Lycogala, Tubifera).*

SCIARIDAE: most sciarids develop in decaying vegetable matter, some in rotten wood and there are many dubious records from fungi and myxomycetes. **Lycoriella (L) agraria,** cultivated *Agaricus;* **L. (L.) auripila,** cultivated *Agaricus* & encrusting fungi; **L. (L.) solani,** polyphagous, especially polypores (from which it may emerge in large numbers), *Stereum, Phlebia,* several agarics, also generally saprophagous (?); **Bradysia umbratica,** cultivated *Agaricus;* **Scatopsciara quinquelineata,** *Suillus luteus;* **S. tricuspidata,** wood encrusted with *Stereum;* **S. vivida,** cultivated *Agaricus,* indet. lignicolous fungus, myxomycete *Fuligo septica,* also recorded from wasp's nest; **Ctenosciara hyalipennis,** *Bjerkandera adusta;* **Zygoneura sciarina,** *Auricularia mesenterica,* also rotten wood. **SCATOPSIDAE: Coboldia fuscipes,** polyphagous in decomposing fungi, *Fuligo;* **Scatopse notata,** *Leccinum scabrum,* many other habitats; **Apiloscatopse flavicollis,** *Tricholoma pessundatum;* **A. scutellata,** *Bjerkandera adusta.* **CECIDOMYIIDAE:** cecids in fungi have been little studied apart from those attacking cultivated mushrooms. Probably many develop in polypores and those feeding on microscopic fungi require closer study; some other cecids are known to be predatory as larvae on the latter and **Lestodiplosis** are probably predatory on the mites in fungi. **Lestremia cinerea,** *Chondrostereum,* orange larvae on stipe of cultivated mushrooms; **Mycophila barnesi,** *Scleroderma verrucosum,* cultivated muchrooms, many other media; **M. speyeri,** cultivated mushrooms, other media; **Peromyia fungicola,** mould on *Lactarius* sp.; **Winnertzia** sp., *Stereum* and soft polypores, possibly strayed from rotten wood; **Brittenia fraxinicola, Henria psalliotae, Heteropeza pygmaea,** cultivated mushrooms (first and last, *Daldinia);* **Camptodiplosis auriculariae,** *Auricularia auricula-judae,* pink saltatorial larvae; **C. boleti,** possibly *Polypilus giganteus,* recorded in Europe in 'milk' exuded from cap of *Scutiger confluens;* **Lestodiplosis polypori,** *Polyporus squamosus;* **L.** spp., many polypores, *Boletus, Pholiota, Collybia, Pleurotus, Daldinia;* **Mycocecis ovalis,** *Hypoxylon rubiginosum* (galls); **Mycodiplosis** species, rusts and mildews on many plants including **M. coniophaga** (rust on *Rosa),* **M. saundersi** (rust on thistles), **M. tremulae** (*Melampsora* on *Populus).*

STRATIOMYIDAE: Sargus bipunctatus, visits decaying *Polyporus squamosus,* usually dung. **SCENOPINIDAE: Scenopinus fenestralis,** *Inonotus hispidus,* feeds on microlepidopterous and coleopterous larvae in many habitats. **EMPIDIDAE:** these records are probably chance strays from other habitats; larvae are probably all carnivorous. **Tachypeza nubila,** *Bjerkandera, Amanita, Paxillus, Hypholoma, Daldinia,* normally bark; **Crossopalpus nigritellus,** young plasmodium of *Fuligo septica,* normally dung; **Empis vitripennis,** *Lycoperdon* sp. **DOLICHOPODIDAE:** some rotten wood breeders (**Systenus scholtzii, Medetera** spp.) have been reared from lignicolous fungi, probably due to pupation in this medium.

PHORIDAE: a few polyphagous scavengers occur in decaying fungi and other media but most fungicolous phorids are confined to fresh fungi. Metopininae: **Megaselia (Aphiochaeta) armata, M. (A.) woodi,** indet. fungi; **M.(A.) buxtoni,** *Pleurotus cornucopiae, Polyporus squamosus, Bjerkandera fumosa;* **M. (A.) frameata,** *Hypoxylon, Polypilus, Plicaturopsis;* **M. (A.) fungicola,** indet. lignicolous fungus; **M. (A.) hyalipennis,** *Polypilus;* **M.(A.) imberbis,** *Pleurotus cornucopiae, Polypilus giganteus;* **M. (A.) pumila,** indet agaric; **M. (M.) berndseni,** *Amanita, Russula, Stropharia;* **M. (M.) bovista,** cultivated mushrooms; **M. (M.) cinereifrons,** *Merulius corium;* **M. (M.) flava,** *Peziza, Amanita, Tricholomopsis;*

M. (M.) flavicans, many agarics, boleti, *Morchella;* **M. (M.) halterata,** cultivated mushrooms, *Amanita, Russula;* **M. (M.) hirtiventris,** *Agaricus campestris, Pholiota* sp.; **M. (M.) impolluta,** *Pluteus umbrosus;* **M. (M.) lata, M. (M.) nigrescens, M. (M.) pygmaeoides, M. (M.) scutellariformis, M. (M.) scutellaris,** many agarics and boleti; **M. (M.) lutea,** many agarics, boleti, *Scleroderma;* **M. (M.) lutescens,** *Russula foetens;* **M. (M.) maura,** *Gymnopilus, Pholiota, Hypholoma;* **M. (M.) nigra,** *Agaricus* (field and cultivated), ? *Russula, Boletus;* **M. (M.) plurispinulosa,** *Pleurotus cornucopiae, Coprinus micaceus,* other media; **M. (M.) pygmaea,** *Agaricus, Amanita, Pluteus, Rozites;* **M. (M.) rufipes,** several agarics, boleti, polypores, usually other decomposing matter; **M. (M.) spinicincta,** *Gymnopilus, Hypholoma, Coprinus;* **M. (M.) sylvatica,** *Coprinus radians.* **Phorinae: Conicera pauxilla,** *Pluteus cervinus* (a record of *C.* atra from *Boletus bulbosus* requires confirmation); **Diplonevra concinna, Hypocera mordellaria,** visiting indet. fungi; **Triphleba minuta,** *Gymnopilus junonius,* apparently monophagous; **T. trinervis,** rotten indet. fungi.

PLATYPEZIDAE: the development of the Opetiinae is unknown but it seems certain that all other platypezids are fungus feeders. **Platypezininae: Callomyia amoena,** *Corticium* sp., external; **Agathomyia antennata,** ? *Coriolus,* ? *Bjerkandera;* **A. falleni, A.** unicolor: *Bjerkandera adusta.* **Platypezinae: Protoclythia modesta, P. rufa, Platypeza consobrina, P. fasciata, P. hirticeps,** *Armillaria mellea* (? **modesta, fasciata** from *Lycoperdon pyriforme,* **fasciata** from *Boletus); Plesioclythia dorsalis,* *Agaricus* spp., *Calvatia gigantea, Boletus edulis;* **Paraplatypeza atra,** *Pluteus cervinus;* **Orthovena furcata,** *Polyporus squamosus;* **Polyporivora infumata, P. picta,** *Coriolus versicolor.*

SYRPHIDAE: a few **Cheilosia,** a large phytophagous genus, develop in fungi; the record of **Ferdinandea cuprea** from *Fistulina* is probably due to choice of pupation site by this sap run feeder. **Cheilosia longula,** Boletaceae *(Boletus luridus, Suillus bovinus);* **C. scutellata,** Boletaceae *(Boletus edulis, B. erythropus, B. satanas),* indet agaric and non-British *Amanita caesarea;* **C.** sp. ? **mutabilis** or **soror,** *Tuber.*

PLATYSTOMATIDAE: Platystoma seminationis, (? by chance) *Tricholomopsis rutilans.* **DRYOMYZIDAE: Dryomyza anilis,** decaying *Phallus,* generally saprophagous. **HELEOMYZIDAE:** possibly all Suilliinae develop in fresh fungi but only a few Heleomyzinae have this habit, these few being usually saprophagous. **Suilliinae: Suillia affinis,** *Lactarius deliciosus;* **S. bicolor,** polyphagous, many agarics, boleti, *Hypoxylon, Lycoperdon;* **S. collini,** ?*Lactarius* sp.; **S. fuscicornis,** polyphagous, many agarics, boleti, *Phallus, Cantharellus;* **S. humilis, S. pallida, S. ustulata,** *Tuber* **(ustulata** also from dead elder stem); **S. notata** var. **hilaris,** many agarics, *Clavaria;* **S. variegata,** polyphagous, many agarics, boleti, *Peziza, Auricularia, Scleroderma,* soft polypores *(Polyporus, Polypilus)(*also recorded from roots of *Aster);* **Allophyla atricornis,** several agarics. **Heleomyzinae: Heteromyza oculata,** indet. lignicolous fungus; **Tephrochlamys flavipes,** several agarics, soft polypores *(Polyporus, Laetiporus, Fistulina),* *Tuber,* also bird and mammal nests; **T. rufiventris,** *Hypoxylon ragiforme,* many other media; **T. tarsalis,** several agarics, *Boletus, Polypilus, Clavaria, Lycoperdon,* also bird's nests; **Neoleria ruficauda,** visits fungi, also carrion; **N. ruficeps,** *Russula, Amanita, Armillaria, Cortinarius, Polypilus;* **Heleomyza serrata,** *Fistulina,* usually other media. **SEPSIDAE: Nemopoda nitidula,** plasmodium of indet. myxomycete, general scavenger. **LAUXANIIDAE: Lyciella pallidiventris,** *Phlebia merismoides,* also under bark. **SPHAEROCERIDAE:** fungicolous species usually occur only in fungi in an advanced state of decomposition; a few are possibly obligate fungus feeders. **Sphaerocera (S.) monilis,** visits decaying fungi; **S. (Ischiolepta) pusilla,** *Coprinus atramentarius,* cultivated mushrooms, other media; **Copromyza (Olinea) atra,** visits decaying fungi; **C. (Fungobia) fimetaria,** common on decaying fungi, also carrion; **C. (F.) nitida,** visits fungi but normally other media; **C. (F.) roserii,** *Armillaria,* visits decaying fungi; **C. (Borborillus) vitripennis,** *Boletus edulis;* **Leptocera (Limosina) appendiculata, L. (L.) palmata, L. (L.) setaria, L. (L.) silvatica,** visit decaying fungi; **L.(L.) moesta,** on indet. fungus; **L. (L.) claviventris,** *Pleurotus, Coriolus, Chondrostereum,* other media; **L. (L.) clunipes,** many agarics and boleti; **L.(L.) flavipes,** *Boletus edulis;* **L. (L.) fungicola,** *Boletus edulis, Piptoporus betulinus;* **L.(L.) heteroneura,** cultivated mushrooms. **L. (L.) parapusio,** several agarics, also visits carrion; **L. (Coproica) ferruginata,** many agarics, boleti, other media; **L. (L.) fontinalis,** myxomycete *Fuligo septica.* **LONCHAEIDAE: Lonchaea chorea,** twice from fresh plasmodium of *Fuligo septica,* other media; **L. fumosa,** *Amanita, Phallus* egg stage, plant stems; **L. laticornis,** *Coriolus,* probably strayed from under bark. **PIOPHILIDAE:** most feed in carrion but **Piophila (Mycetaulus) bipunctata** develops in decaying fungi. **ODINIIDAE: Odinia** species develop in beetle orings, usually in wood but a few evidently associate with beetles in lignicolous fungi. **Odinia boletina,** visits Polyporaceae *(Ganoderma, Bjerkandera, Polyporus),* Meruliaceae *(Phlebia);* **O. maculata,** visiting indet. polypore. **ACARTOPHTHALMIDAE: Acartophthalmus nigrinus,** visits decaying fungi *(Polypilus).* **ANTHOMYZIDAE: Anthomyza albimana,** *Boletus* sp., visits *Polyporus, Hypholoma, Tricholoma.* **ASTEIIDAE: Leiomyza dudai,** several agarics, chiefly lignicolous; **L. laevigata,** *Pleurotus cornucopiae;* **L. scatophagina,** several agarics, chiefly lignicolous, *Polyporus squamosus.***DROSOPHILIDAE: Leucophenga** and several **Drosophila** are obligate but polyphagous fungus feeders. Other genera are possibly monophagous but most **Drosophila** are saprophagous and feed in many fermenting materials. **Steganina coleoptrata,** *Hypoxylon fragiforme;* **Amiota (A.) alboguttata,** *Daldinia concentrica;* **Leucophenga maculata,** several agarics *(Pleurotus, Amanita, Russula),* boleti, polypores *(Polyporus, Coriolus, Inonotus, Ganoderma), Ustulina;* **Drosophila (D.) cameraria,** various agarics, *Inonotus, Polypilus, Phallus;* **D. (D.) confusa,** agarics, boleti, soft polypores, visits *Ganoderma;* **D. (D.) funebris,** decaying fungi, many other media; **D. (D.) histrio,** *Boletus, Amanita, Polypilus;* **D. (D.) kuntzei,** *Polyporus squamosus, Amanita rubescens;* **D. (D.) phalerata,** many agarics, boleti, *Polyporus, Phallus, Clavaria, Chondrostereum;* **D. (D.) repleta,** *Lactarius, Paxillus, Fuligo,* many fermenting media; **D. (D.) transversa,** several agarics, boleti, *Ustulina, Peziza;* **D. (Dorsilopha) busckii,** decaying agarics, boleti, other media; **D. (Sophophora) melanogaster,** *Polyporus squamosus,* many fermenting media; **D. (S.) obscura,** agarics, boleti, *Inonotus, Phallus,* tree wounds; **D. (S.) subobscura,** *Phallus, Boletus, Hypholoma, Inonotus,* many other media. **CHLOROPIDAE: Tricimba cincta,** *Bjerkandera, Chondrostereum, Russula foetens;* **T. lineella,** *Lycoperdon gemmatum;* **Botanobia dubia,** *Piptoporus betulinus,* visiting *Coriolus, Bjerkandera.* **TACHINIDAE: Elfia cingulata, Actia bicolor, Elodia ambulatoria,** parasites of tineid larvae in Polyporaceae *(A. bicolor* also in non-fungicolous Lepidoptera). **ANTHOMYIIDAE:** although most have phytophagous larvae, only **Pegomya** (of which at least half are higher plant feeders) has many fungicolous species, but the **Pegohylemyia phrenione** group is notable for its specialised habits. **Pegohylemyia dissecta,** P. **laterella,** *Epichloe* on grasses; P. **silvatica,** many agarics, boleti, *Phallus;* **Anthomyia pluvialis,** several agarics, boleti, *Phallus;* A. **procellaris,** *Pleurotus ostreatus,* also bird's nests; **Delia albula,** *Psathyrella ammophila;* D. **antiqua,** several agarics *(Russula, Amanita, Tricholoma, Armillaria)* in France, normally plant roots - fungus association requires confirmation; **D. frontella,** *Suillus bovinus;* D. **platura,** young plasmodium of *Fuligo,* also saprophagous and in plant roots; **Hylemya latifrons,** *Boletus subtomentosus;* **Pseudonupedia setinerva,** *Suillus granulatus;* **Pegomya (P.) calyptrata,** *Agaricus;* P. **rufina,** *Agaricus* including cultivated mushrooms and Lepiotaceae; P. **geniculata,** many agarics but not boleti; P. **maculata,** *Lactarius deliciosus;* P. **pulchripes,** several indet. fungi; P. **transversa,** Tricholomataceae *(Oudemansiella, Armillaria);* P. **ulmaria,** Bolbitiaceae *(Agrocybe aegerita),* ? *Boletus;* P. **winthemi,** Boletaceae *(Boletus, Leccinum),* various agarics (Cortinariaceae, Tricholomataceae, Cantharellaceae); P. **deprimata,** Boletaceae *(Boletus, Suillus);* P. **tenera,** P. **zonata,** Boletaceae *(Boletus edulis* group, *Leccinum);* P. **fulgens,** P. **furva,** P. **incisiva,** P. **pallidoscutellata,** P. **tabida,** P. **vittigera,** Boletaceae *(Leccinum* spp.); **Mycophaga testacea,** 'carnivorous larvae in many fungi' (Canzanelli, 1941), fly frequent near fungi but no other rearing records. **FANNIIDAE:** most are saprophagous, although often in specialised situations and fungicoles include several general scavengers but a few apparently specific to fungi. **Piezura boletorum,** indet. fungus; P. **graminicola,** *Coprinus micaceus,* visiting another *Coprinus* sp.; **Fannia aequilineata,** *Inonotus dryadeus,* normally sap runs, wood detritus; F. **canicularis,** many decaying fungi, other media; F. **difficilis,** *Lactarius, Boletus,* bird's nests; F. **immutica,** indet. fungus, visiting *Pleurotus ostreatus;* F. **incisurata,** indet. fungus, other media; F. **manicata,** *Amanita, Laetiporus,* several boleti *(Boletus, Suillus),* other media; F. **melania,** several boleti, *Armillaria, Lactarius, Tricholoma, Phallus;* F. **monilis,** *Pleurotus cornucopiae, Polyporus squamosus,* visits *Hypholoma, Fistulina, Bjerkandera;* F. **mutica,** indet. fungus; F. **scalaris,** *Boletus, Polyporus, Laetiporus,* other media. **MUSCIDAE:** larvae are carnivorous, at least in the final instar; most consume other dipterous larvae, some always in fungi, others also in other media. **Azelia aterrima,** visiting *Armillaria, Hypholoma,* carrion; **Alloeostylus diaphanus,** agarics, boleti; **Dendrophaonia querceti,** *Phallus,* under bark or nests of birds and mammals; **Hydrotaea dentipes,** *Boletus edulis, Armillaria mellea,* also dung; H. **occulta,** *Boletus chrysenteron,* carrion, other media; **Muscina assimilis,** agarics, boleti, *Polyporus,* wide range of decaying materials; M. **pabulorum,** indet. fungi, other media; M. **stabulans,** agarics, boleti, polypores, truffles, many other media; **Phaonia gobertii,** *Inonotus hispidus,* usually under bark; P. **pallida,** *Amanita rubescens,* under bark; P. **populi,** *Russula, Lactarius, Cantharellus, Bjerkandera,* also under bark and wasp's nest; P. **variegata,** many agarics, boleti, *Polyporus, Inonotus,* rotten wood, carrion, etc.; **Mydaea discimana,** *Suillus bovinus;* M. **electa,** indet. agarics, Boletaceae, *Phallus;* M. **maculiventris,** *Polyporus squamosus;* M. **setifemur,** indet. fungus; M. **tincta,** agarics, boleti, *Morchella;* M. **urbana,** *Polyporus squamosus,* also dung; **Stomoxys calcitrans,** *Boletus edulis, Russula foetens,* normally dung.

MOSSES, LICHENS AND LIVERWORTS
By Alan E. Stubbs

Relatively few Diptera are dependent on these lower plants. Possibly some associations have been overlooked but there seems to be remarkably little information.

Mosses

Three species in the tipulid subfamily Cylindrotominae have larvae which are adapted to living in moss. The larvae are green and have fleshy lobes which aid camouflage. *Phalacrocera replicata* lives in aquatic mosses in acid pools (especially *Sphagnum* and *Hypnum fluitans*); *Triogma trisulcata* has semi-aquatic larvae in mosses on moorland (such as *Hypnum cuspidatum*) whilst *Diogma glabrata* larvae occur in mosses on stones and on the soil in woodland. This is a rather neat ecological separation between the species.

A number of *Tipula* spp. have larvae which are frequently found under terrestrial mosses but often they are living in the small amount of soil under the moss rather than within it. However, they presumably include at least the decaying parts of the moss in their diet. This habit is particularly strong in the sub-genus *Savtshenkia*, including *T.(S.) pagana* of mossy lawns as well as the woodland and upland species. Semi-aquatic mosses are the larval site of *Savtshenkia macrocera*, *S.subnodicornis* (on boggy ground) and *S.cheethami*, as well as of *Prionocera turcica* and *Tipula melanoceros*. A European species of *Gnoriste* (Mycetophilidae) has been reared from moss and this association may occur with the two British species. The green larvae of *Ptiolina obscura* (Rhagionidae) have been found amongst damp moss in woodland.

A variety of other Diptera larvae and pupae may be found under terrestrial moss but these are usually more associated with the substrate, such as dead wood or soil. A variety of adult Diptera may also sometimes be found by searching in moss; in most cases they will simply be sheltering within the moss or are there because the underlying substrate forms their breeding site. Many non-specialist dipterous larvae are found amongst aquatic and semi-aquatic mosses.

Lichens

No Diptera feeding on terrestrial lichens have come to attention during the preparation of this handbook. However, adults of the mycetophilid genus *Docosia* are usually found on lichen covered tree branches so it is possible the larvae feed on lichens or at least live beneath them. The tipulid *Geranomyia unicolor* feeds on marine littoral lichens.

Liverworts

Larvae of the tipulid *Dolichopeza albipes* are recorded as living among liverworts such as *Pellia*. The rhagionid *Spania nigra* mines the leaves of *Pellia neesiana* and this habit is shared with certain lestremiine Cecidomyiidae. Larvae of the mycetophilid *Boletina dubia* were found in a slime tube on the liverwort *Reboulia* and also accepted *Pellia* as food.

HIGHER PLANTS

by Raymond Uffen and Peter Chandler

The relationship of flies with higher plants is a subject which merits much closer study than it has hitherto received but a considerable amount of information is nevertheless available and an attempt is made to synthesise this here and in the accompanying appendix which gives more detailed information on some of the families involved.

The phytophagous habit has been evolved several times in the Diptera from saprophagous ancestors. Only ten families include a high proportion of higher plant feeders, but the two largest groups, Cecidomyiidae (gall midges) and Agromyzidae (mainly small leaf miners) include more than 800 plant feeding species, while more than 300 species dependent on plants are distributed among 24 other families. Other than the cecids, few Nematocera feed in plants; hardly any Brachycera and few Aschiza are involved. In the Calyptratae, only the Anthomyiidae and Scathophagidae have developed in this direction. It is in the Acalyptratae that a tendency towards phytophagy has occurred many times and either facultative or obligate plant feeding has evolved.

Many dipterous larvae are aquatic or live in a semi-liquid medium. Terrestrial larvae mostly live in and are protected by a medium of great bulk compared to themselves. Life open to the air and the risk of desiccation and easy predation is exceptional. The cranefly *Cylindrotoma* is the only phytophagous, caterpillar-like dipterous larva to be found away from water in Britain. The concealed, burrowing habit of dipterous larvae confines the larger species to boring in shoots, stems, roots and catkins or fruits. The surface of subterranean parts may be channelled (e.g. Anthomyiidae).

The mobile, cryptically coloured larvae so often found on plants are aphid-hunting syrphids. Some (e.g. *Pipizella varipes*) attack root aphids. Phytophagous acalypterate larvae are cylindrical, colourless maggots and are usually helpless when removed from the support of their surroundings.

Primitive dipterous larvae have chewing mandibles and can ingest quantities of not very nutritious pabula (e.g. *Tipula* in moss, grass roots, decayed wood). The reduction in mouthparts in more advanced Nematocera is accompanied by a change of food to fungi (especially Mycetophilidae), more fungus-infested wood and living green plant tissues in the case of gall-midges. From Brachycera onwards only scraping mouth hooks are available and some form of saprophagy is usual.

By no means all the larvae living in degraded plant tissues, such as rotten wood, sap flows or decaying leaf litter obtain nourishment directly from the medium inhabited. The food may be obtained from associated fungi or micro-organisms or the Diptera may be predatory. Most rearing records are quite uninformed about this. Roberts (1969, 1970) shows how to deduce the kind of food ingested from the structure of the mouthparts and foregut and gives references to earlier papers. As predaceous larvae of higher Diptera suck out their prey after external digestion with saliva and those saprophytic on large particles evolve crushing mills in their foreguts, examination of stomach contents is not likely to be fruitful. Direct observation of items ingested is rarely reported. Chemical precipitation tests have been used to test specific hypotheses as to food. Melin's discussion (1923, reference under Behaviour) of the evidence for animal versus vegetable food for asilid larvae typifies the pitfalls in establishing larval diets.

Specialisation in attacking living plant cells is sporadic and widespread in Diptera. It may occur in odd species or an isolated genus (probably reflecting little more than a change in oviposition responses) or in a complete tribe or higher unit (usually with pronounced morphological adaptation of fly or larva).

The Range of Phytophagous Diptera

The reported associations with higher plants are of a casual nature in the Ceratopogonidae, Anisopodidae, Bibionidae, Phoridae, Otitidae, Lauxaniidae, the subfamily Tipulinae and most of the Sciaridae involved, where saprophagous species may sometimes invade living plant tissue. The two recorded associations in the Heleomyzidae are of normally fungivorous species and require confirmation. The Lonchaeidae and Muscidae have predatory larvae and only a few species occur in plants where they feed on other larvae. The nature of the association in the Chironomidae (several genera), Dolichopodidae (*Thrypticus* only) and Ephydridae (at least 24 spp. probably involved, 12 reared) requires further study; these groups are leaf miners of aquatic plants and have evolved this habit from free living aquatic ancestors. One species, *Hydrellia griseola*, which is highly polyphagous, has invaded terrestrial plants in marshy areas in addition to its normal subaquatic hosts.

Another group requiring further study on the nature of their association with plants is the Pallopteridae. Several *Palloptera* spp. are commensals of bark beetles while at least five certainly develop only in flowerheads, stems or leaf sheaths of higher plants but it is not clear whether they are primary feeders or only present in the borings of other larvae. Two species, *P.umbellatarum* and *P.usta*, have been reported from both bark beetle burrows and flower heads of Compositae; it is possible that the latter records are due to confusion with *P.parallela*.

Scaptomyza spp. are leaf miners of diverse herbaceous plants in the largely saprophagous and fungivorous family Drosophilidae. *Cheilosia, Portevinia, Merodon* and *Eumerus* are plant-feeding genera of the saprophagous subfamily of Syrphidae; few *Cheilosia* larvae are yet known, but they attack stems, basal rosettes and rootstocks of herbaceous plants such as *Primula, Scrophularia* and cynareine Compositae while one is a leaf miner of Crassulaceae.

Most Chloropidae (in excess of 100 species) and Anthomyzidae (15 spp.) are primary plant feeders, mainly in monocotyledons, but a few in each case are inquilines in galls of other phytophagous insects, and the Chloropidae include a few genera with fungivorous or predaceous habits. The few associations with dicotyledons in these families are mostly in need of confirmation.

The Tephritidae (associations with dicotyledons especially Compositae and one with a monocotyledon, *Asparagus*, are known for 70 of the 76 British spp.), Psilidae (27 spp. but only 10 reared, many in monocotyledons, but one *Chyliza* and most *Psila* in dicotyledons especially Umbelliferae), Opomyzidae (14 spp., only 6 reared, all in Gramineae) and Agromyzidae (320 spp. in monocotyledons, dicotyledons and pteridophytes) probably all develop in higher plants. Many Anthomyiidae also develop in higher plants, attacking all parts of angiosperms, also gymnosperms and pteridophytes, although (as discussed in the Appendix) there are many other life styles including more than 30 spp. in fungi; of the 219 British spp., at least 110 are probably higher plant feeders, the relationship having been definitely established for nearly 60 of them.

The Scathophagidae have a curious range of larval food sources (Chandler & Stubbs, 1967); about half of the 53 British species probably develop in higher plants but definite associations are established for only eleven of which ten are phytophagous while *Cleigastra* is predatory on other larvae within plant tissue. Most associations are with monocotyledons but a few attack dicotyledons (Polygonaceae, Nymphaeaceae, Scrophulariaceae).

The largest group of plant feeding Diptera are the gall midges (Cecidomyiidae) but a satisfactory account cannot yet be given of them. Plant feeders belong to the Cecidomyiinae (some fungus feeders occur in the other sub-families) and most known associations involve gall formation. Study of the adult insects has not, however, kept pace with description of many forms based on differences in the galls. Probably 500 of the 637 species in the Check List are associated with plants but it is not clear how many of these are good species. Most are associated with herbaceous plants, both monocotyledons and dicotyledons, while a good number are gall causers on woody plants including gymnosperms.

The Range of Plants attacked by Diptera

Pteridophytes. These support the anthomyiid genera *Chirosia* and *Acrostilpna*, which develop in stems or rolled up fronds. Several spp. develop in bracken *(Pteridium)* as well as other ferns and it is not clear whether there is any host specificity. A few Cecidomyiidae develop in ferns and six species of Agromyzidae attack ferns and horsetails; *Pteridomyza hilarella* is common on bracken.

Gymnosperms. These are affected by few Diptera but some Anthomyiidae *(Lasiomma)*, Chloropidae *(Siphonella, Hapleginella)* and Lonchaeidae *(Earomyia)* develop in the cones, the last being predatory on other larvae in this situation. There are a few cecid gall causers, e.g. *Taxomyia taxi* on yew *(Taxus)*.

Monocotyledons. Gramineae are attacked by many Diptera including Cecidomyiidae, *Palloptera quinquemaculata*, all Opomyzidae, some Anthomyzidae, *Hydrellia griseola*, many Agromyzidae, most Chloropidae, *Nanna* spp. (Scathophagidae) and a few Anthomyiidae *(Phorbia* spp. and *Delia coarctata*, while some *Pegohylemyia* develop in *Epichloe* fungus on grasses). Cyperaceae support *Cordilura* spp. (Scathophagidae), some Chloropidae, a few Agromyzidae, *Psila fimetaria* and in subaquatic situations some Chironomidae. Juncaceae have a rather specialised Diptera fauna including *Thrypticus bellus* (Dolichopodidae), *Loxocera* spp. (Psilidae), *Palloptera scutellata*, possibly some *Phorbia* and a few Agromyzidae. Apart from the rather unspecialised chironomid and ephydrid miners in aquatic species, few Diptera attack other monocotyledons. Examples are the syrphids *Portevinia, Eumerus* and *Merodon* on the subterranean parts of Liliaceae, Amaryllidaceae and Iridaceae, *Chyliza* spp. (Psilidae) in the stems and roots of Orchidaceae, *Anthomyza bifasciata* on the reedmace *Typha*, the agromyzid *Metopomyza ornata* on flowering rush *(Butomus)* and a few others on Liliaceae, Juncaginaceae and Iridaceae, the scathophagids *Norellia spinipes* in

Narcissus and the genera *Parallelomma* and *Delina*, which are leaf miners of Orchidaceae and Liliaceae. In the Anthomyiidae, a few species such ás *Delia antiqua* are associated with *Allium*.

Dicotyledons. Most Diptera feeding in plants attack dicotyledons; most groups are affected but some families (Compositae, Umbelliferae, Cruciferae, Caryophyllaceae, Chenopodiaceae, Ranunculaceae, Polygonaceae and in the case of Agromyzidae, Scrophulariaceae, Boraginaceae and Papilionaceae) are especially favoured.

Compositae are attacked by many Agromyzidae, Cecidomyiidae, Anthomyiidae, some *Psila* spp., *Palloptera parallela*, a few *Cheilosia* spp. and at least 59 species of Tephritidae are confined to this family. The Umbelliferae are strongly represented among the foodplants of Agromyzidae, Cecidomyiidae, Psilidae and Pallopteridae. The tephritids *Euleia heraclei* and *Cryptaciura rotundiventris* and the anthomyiid *Pegomya versicolor* are also leaf miners of this family. The decaying stem bases and tap roots of the larger umbels also support *Sylvicola zetterstedti* (Anisopodidae) and *Forcipomyia radicicola* (Ceratopogonidae), while *Pachygaster* larvae (Stratiomyidae) occur here as well as in rotten wood. The Cruciferae, Chenopodiaceae and Caryophyllaceae are heavily attacked by drosophilids and anthomyiids; the latter family also well utilise the Polygonaceae and Solanaceae. Some families are attacked only sporadically by dipterous larvae. Some larvae, e.g. *Cylindrotoma* (Tipulidae) and *Phytosciara* (Sciaridae) are generalised feeders on low growing dicotyledons in shaded marshy places. Some noteworthy associations in groups not much affected by Diptera are of *Cheilosia semifasciata* with Crassulaceae, *C.variabilis* and *Gimnomera* with Scrophulariaceae, *Pegomya seitenstettensis* with *Oxalis* and that of the psilid *Chyliza extenuata* and the agromyzid *Phytomyza orobanchia* with the stem bases of broom-rapes (Orobanchaceae). Apart from the many cecidomyiid galls, living trees and shrubs are not much affected by Diptera although several Agromyzidae develop in their leaves and younger stems (see Appendix) and the fruits of some trees (especially Rosaceae) are attacked by tephritid "fruit flies", while *Conioscinella gallarum* (Chloropidae) and *"Sciara" tilicola* are recorded as inquilines in galls on *Quercus* and *Tilia* respectively. *Egle* spp (Anthomyiidae) are associated only with the catkins of Salicaceae.

Leaf Mines

Leaf mines are a common way of life for many insects; like galls, they usually result in obvious damage and have therefore been more studied than species developing in other parts of the plant. The Diptera with this habit include most Agromyzidae, *Phytosciara halterata* (Sciaridae), *Thrypticus* (Dolichopodidae), some *Cheilosia* (Syrphidae), a few Tephritidae (*Cryptaciura, Euleia, Trypeta* spp.), *Scaptomyza* (Drosophilidae), a few Anthomyzidae (*Anagnota, Paranthomyza*), many Anthomyiidae (especially *Pegomya*) and in subaquatic situations, Ephydridae and Chironomidae. Agromyzidae, by restricting their size, have been enabled to make specialised mines in leaves. Dipterous leaf mines, particularly the gallery mines of Agromyzidae, may be distinguished from those of other insects by the alternating rows of frass grains near the edges of the mines, resulting from the larvae having to lie on their sides to use their vertically

216

operating mouthparts. An arcuate pattern of residual dead tissue is also commonplace. Other leaf miners are mainly larger larvae of Tephritidae and Anthomyiidae. These are often communal feeders. Their mines usually end up as distended blotches with patches or random dots of frass. The damage extends more deeply and results in browning of the mine area.

Hering's Keys to the Leaf Mines of Europe is written in clear German with a minimum of consistently applied vocabulary. With Spencer's Handbook on British Agromyzidae the new student should be well placed. On leaf mines in general, Hering's textbook, translated by Spencer, is the classic.

Dipterous leaf miners nearly always feed up very fast (not *Euleia cognata*, Tephritidae). Mines can therefore be kept in clean plastic bags to prevent desiccation. Puparia can be removed and kept on damp sand in corked glass tubes. Cleanliness is essential to prevent attack by moulds, unless the fly is due to emerge quickly. *Hydrellia* can be reared by collecting their aquatic hostplants, with root if possible, and standing or floating in clean water as appropriate.

Plant Galls

Galls formed by Diptera do not present any single feature for recognition. Cecidomyiid galls may be simple distortions such as are also made by aphids, or nearly closed single cells or multilocular aggregations much like those caused by mites. Rosette galls at the tips of shoots where the growing point has been stunted are frequent. Many cecid galls are new structures of value to the fly larva.

Galls made by larger Diptera are only infrequently new structures, though quite striking distortions occur, e.g. the aborted growing points of *Phragmites* caused by the chloropid *Lipara*. Shoot galls may be operculate during the whole of their growth (e.g. the tephritid *Paroxyna misella*) or thick-walled and closed until the mature larva makes a thin window through which the fly can emerge (e.g. *Urophora cardui*).

If a fly larva quits its gall to pupate, it normally leaves the exuviae of the first and second instars behind it. These remains can be retrieved and used for at least approximate identification of the gallcauser. In the case of some larger species patience is essential in searching through frass and damaged plant tissue under a stereomicroscope. For rearing techniques see under Cecidomyiidae in Appendix.

Other Forms of Phytophagy

Other Diptera live in more concealed situations - stems, roots, flowers, seeds and fruits and less is generally known of these unless they attack crop plants. There is much to be learned about the associations between Diptera and monocotyledons. Chloropidae feed mainly between the leaf sheaths of grasses and Anthomyzidae are reported to do the same. The tabulated data hint at many more species than have yet been reared attacking the stems of rushes and sedges (Psilidae, Scathophagidae, Pallopteridae, etc.). Liliaceae and Orchidaceae also invite closer study of the Diptera associated with them.

Plant seeds are attacked by cecids, phorids, tephritids, scathophagids and anthomyiids. Germinating bean seeds have their growing points destroyed and their cotyledons burrowed by the anthomyiid *Delia platura*.

Large herbs, such as *Scrophularia, Arctium,* thistles, etc. have tough stems and rootstocks that give similar habitats to living and decaying wood. This probably accounts also for the peculiar fauna of umbelliferous stem bases discussed above. The elaborate structure of the flowerheads of Compositae provides excellent concealment for fly larvae. Orange Cecidomyiidae often occur. Tephritidae are dominant amongst the larger larvae, galling or channelling the receptacle or eating the green seeds. The ecology of the interacting species of Tephritidae in flowerheads is a suitable subject for the amateur. Partial double broods occur in several species, suggesting poor adaptation to British climatic conditions and flowering periods. Comparative observation on continental colonies could be informative.

Other Associations with Plants

The most frequent association with plants of non-phytophagous Diptera is visiting flowers for nectar and pollen; this is dealt with in detail below.

Many flies feed on honeydew on leaves. A sweeping motion of the front legs facilitates detection of sugars by the chemoreceptors on the tarsi. The habit is commonplace in Rhagionidae and may be seen in other families, through to calypterates, e.g. Tachinidae.

Female agromyzid flies are known to puncture the leaves of their foodplants with their ovipositors and then to lick up the exuding sap. This can be an important source of food in winter and may be a link in the ritual of recognizing the correct plant for oviposition. In general adult flies are not closely associated with the plants upon which they have fed as larvae, so that the discovery of the foodplants of many phytophagous Diptera is still to be achieved.

Melin (1923) showed that several genera of Asilini lay their eggs in plant tissues and that the newly hatched larvae drop to the ground. *Leptarthrus brevirostris* oviposits on heads of *Dactylis* on chalk grassland. *Atherix* and *Atrichops* lay their eggs in batches, often using the leaves of trees, and the larvae drop into the river beneath. Many mud-dwelling Syrphidae also oviposit beneath leaves overhanging pond margins and the use of aquatic plants for oviposition by *Notiphila* (Ephydridae) is described in the Appendix. Larvae of *Chrysogaster* (Syrphidae) tap the air-spaces in the submerged parts of aquatic plants for respiration.

Many flies prefer to rest on particular plants. When it rains or turns cold some flies rest beneath leaves well above the ground, whilst others crawl down into tussocks or leaf litter. Such field knowledge rarely gets recorded.

Further Reading

Barnes, H.F., 1946-1956. Gall midges of economic importance, 7 vols. Crosby Lockwood, London.

Buhr, H., 1964-1965. Bestimmungstabellen der Gallen (Zoo - und Phytocecidien) an Pflanzen Mittel - und Nordeuropas. Band I, II, 1572 pp., 25 pls. Jena, Gustav Fischer.

Chandler, P.J., 1975. Observations on plant associations of the Psilidae (Diptera). *Ent.Rec.J.Var.* **87** : 13-17.

Chandler, P.J. & Stubbs, A.E., 1967. A species of *Norellia* R-D. (Diptera, Scathophagidae) new to Britain. *Proc. Brit. Ent. Nat. Hist. Soc.* **2** : 120-124. (Reviews plant records in family).

Collin, J.E., 1951. The British species of *Palloptera* Fallen (Diptera) *Entomologists' Rec. & J.Var.,* **63** : Suppl. 1-6.

Darlington, A., 1968. The pocket encyclopaedia of plant galls in colour. 191 pp. London, Blandford.

Hering, E.M., 1957. Bestimmungstabellen der Blattminen von Europa. (3 vols.). Junk., S-Gravenhage.

Niblett, M., 1956. The Flies of the London area, 3. Trypetidae. *Lond. Nat.* **1955** : 82-8.

Nijveldt, W., 1969. Gall midges of economic importance. Vol. VIII : Gall midges - miscellaneous. 221 pp., 14 pls. London, Crosby Lockwood.

Roberts, M.J., 1969. Structure of the mouthparts of the larvae of the flies *Rhagio* and *Sargus* in relation

Roberts, M.J., 1970. Structure of the mouthparts of syrphid larvae in relation to feeding habits. *Acta Zoologica* **51** : 43-65.

Seguy, E., Faune de France, vol 28. Muscidae, Acalypterae et Scatophagidae. Paris 1934.

Spencer, K.A., 1972. Diptera Agromyzidae. *Handbk. Ident. Brit. Ins.* **10** 5 (g). 136 pp.

Stubbs, A.E., 1969. Observations on *Palloptera scutellata* Mcq. in Berkshire and Surrey and a discussion of the larval habitats of British Pallopteridae (Dipt.). *Entomologists' mon. Mag.* **104** : 157-160.

APPENDIX: Known Higher Plant Associations of British Diptera

Information is given for all species where higher plant associations are known in all families except the Agromyzidae (where a good account is already available) and the Cecidomyiidae (where only a summary can at present be attempted). The information in this appendix has been compiled by Raymond Uffen (Tephritidae), Dr. Anthony Irwin (Ephydridae), Dr. John Ismay (Chloropidae), Michael Ackland (Anthomyiidae), Keith Harris (Cecidomyiidae), Alan E. Stubbs (Tipulidae, Anisopodidae, Bibionidae, Pallopteridae, Scathophagidae), Peter Cranston (Chironomidae) and Peter Chandler (other families).

The following abbreviations are used: B-British; F-foreign; fh-flowerhead; fr-fruit; k-catkin; l-leaf; lm-leaf mine; lst-leaf stalk; m-mine; r-root; sd-seed; st-stem.

TIPULIDAE: It is possible that many *Tipula* and *Nephrotoma* spp. will eat the roots of living plants as well as decaying plant material. This is the case in some of the grassland species which are regarded as pests, principally **Tipula paludosa** and **T.oleracea**; **Limonia ornata** is always found at *Petasites hybridus* and may possibly have a relationship with live or dead plant tissue; **Cylindrotoma distinctissima** is unique among British Diptera in having a green caterpillar-like larva eating the leaves of *Caltha, Viola, Stellaria, Anemone, Petasites* and *Chrysosplenium.*

CERATOPOGONIDAE: **Forcipomyia radicicola,** *Arctium,* Umbelliferae (*Aegopodium, Angelica, Anthriscus, Conium, Heracleum*) (r); **Atrichopogon pollinivorus** and several unnamed species, adults consume pollen of *Lonicera, Crataegus, Prunus, Iris,* etc. (? specific); **Dasyhelea dufouri,** *Dipsacus* (axils), *Filipendula* (r), other habitats; **D.versicolor,** *Arctium* (r), elm sap.

CHIRONOMIDAE: some chironomids are known to feed on aquatic plant tissue but further clarification is required on the species involved. A few are leaf miners, others are half miners (they cut a groove in a leaf and cover a tube with debris, but they are not true plant eating species). Many chironomids graze on the surface of aquatic plants (ingesting epiphytes etc.); these are not considered here. **Cricotopus brevipalpis,** *Potamogeton natans;* **C.sylvestris,** *Scirpus* (also sponges etc.); **C.tricinctus,** *P.natans, Glyceria;* **C.trifasciatus,** *P.natans, Polygonum amphibium* (half m); **C.** spp (likely to be more); **Polypedilum** (probably some); **Pentapedilum** (probably some); **Glyptotendipes** (most); **Endochironomus** (most); **Stenochironomus fascipennis,** *Carex, Scirpus;* **Psectrocladius** (several spp. form galleries on leaf surfaces and some may graze on the leaf). **ANISOPODIDAE: Sylvicola zetterstedti** larvae are found in or on the outside of the stem bases of *Angelica sylvestris* in the spring when the plant is dead - whether the association begins when the plant is alive is unknown. **BIBIONIDAE:** there have been reports of the gregarious soil-living larvae damaging grass roots but it is not clear whether this is a primary form of feeding or incidental. **SCIARIDAE:** several species (e.g. **Plastosciara perniciosa, Bradysia praecox, B.tritici, Ctenosciara hyalipennis, Pnyxia scabiei**) have been reported as damaging seedlings of various cultivated plants but apparently not specific; "**Sciara**" **tilicola**, cecid galls on *Tilia;* **Phytosciara halterata**, *Adoxa, Caltha, Chrysosplenium, Menyanthes, Myosotis, Ranunculus, Senecio, Tussilago* (lm)(F).

CECIDOMYIIDAE (gall midges): larvae of most feed directly on living plants, often inducing characteristic plant galls. Leaves, stems, buds, flowers and fruits are commonly affected and the associations between species and their plant hosts are often (but not invariably) highly host-specific, with gall midge species restricted to a single plant species, genus or group of related genera. There are, however, many species, especially in the subfamilies Lestremiinae and Porricondylinae, which feed on fungi, in leaf litter, soil, rotting wood, etc. and there are also a few Cecidomyiinae with zoophagous larvae feeding as predators on mites, aphids, other cecidomyiids and other small invertebrates and a few which are endoparasites of aphids and psyllids.

Identification of gall midges based on galls alone is feasible but should generally be confirmed by collecting larvae and rearing adults. Larvae of most Cecidomyiidae are easily recognised, being yellow, orange or red and bearing a chitinised sternal spatula mid-ventrally on the thorax. The larval head capsule is very small and inconspicuous; the body is usually elongate-cylindrical, slightly to moderately depressed dorso-ventrally and tapered or rounded anteriorly and posteriorly. Collect larvae by dissection of infested tissues and organs or by keeping samples of plant material in thin polythene bags until larvae appear in water films on the insides. Record details of galls, supported by drawings, photographs and dry or pickled specimens, and ensure that host plants are accurately identified. Preserve some larvae in 70 - 80% alcohol and rear adults from the remainder. Full-grown larvae, which are usually about 3 - 5 mm. long, should be selected for rearing since feeding will usually cease once the plant material has been collected. Species that pupate in galls or in buds, fruits, flowers and other plant organs are easily reared by keeping samples of infested material in polythene bags for a month or so. Species that pupate in soil should be confined in tubes, jars or cages containing about 2.5 cm of a 50:50 mixture of sterile washed sand and sphagnum peat. Plant material may be placed directly on the sand/peat mix so that larvae can find their own way into the medium or larvae may be introduced separately with a soft wet fine brush. Larvae of many species overwinter in cocoons in soil and larval diapause may continue for months or years (the record is at least 13 years for the orange wheat blossom midge, *Sitodiplosis mosellana*!) so it is advisable to keep material for at least 1 - 2 years, preferably in a cool, moist, shaded environment outdoors or in a garden shed or outbuilding.

During periods of adult emergence, which generally last from a few days to a few weeks, examine containers daily, if possible. Collect adults at least an hour after emergence either by killing first with ethyl acetate or other killing agent or by catching them directly with a fine brush moistened in 70 - 80% alcohol. Store in small tubes or vials containing 70 - 80% alcohol and avoid breakages of antennae and legs by handling gently during collection and preservation. Large species may be staged on pins and points or may be stored dry in containers or papers but are then much more susceptible to damage.

Some specimens from each series should be mounted on microscope slides for detailed examination and identification using high-powered bright-field and phase-contrast microscopy. Standard techniques using either canada balsam or gum-chloral mountants may be used and the latter, especially Swan's or Stroyan's modified Berlese fluids, give best results. Prepare specimens by dissecting off one wing, the head and the abdomen, leaving the thorax with legs and one wing attached. Mount each of the four parts under separate small cover-slips (6 - 9 mm.) on the same slide, taking care to display the frontal aspect of the head and antennae and the dorsal side of the abdomen and genitalia. Recently collected specimens may be transferred directly into gum-chloral mountant from ethanol but older specimens may have to be softened in cold 10% alcoholic KOH for a few hours before processing through glacial acetic acid to the mountant. No single publication covers either the British or the Western European Cecidomyiidae and much taxonomic research and field collecting is required before workable keys to genera and species can be provided. A key to European plant galls (Buhr, 1964 - 1965) includes all known British species and a selection of common galls is dealt with by Darlington (1968). Much biological and other information is given by Barnes (1946 - 1956).

The list below gives some gall inducing species. The numbers relate to the figures in Darlington (1968). This list is but a small fraction of the total British fauna but a complete list is not felt practical until a major revision is implemented.

Taxomyia taxi, *Taxus* (32 - 33); **Contarinia tiliarum,** *Tilia* (62 - 64); **Didymomyia tiliacea** (= **D. reamuriana),** *Tilia* (65 - 71); **Lasioptera rubi,** *Rubus* (92); **Dasineura rosarum** (= **Wachtliella rosarum),** *Rosa* (95); **D. crataegi,** *Crataegus* (111 - 112); **D. urticae,** *Urtica* (133 - 134); **Hartigiola annulipes,** *Fagus* (153 - 154); **Mikiola fagi,** *Fagus* (155 - 156); **Rhabdophaga rosaria,** *Salix* (233 - 234); **Dasineura fraxini,** *Fraxinus* (249 - 250); **Geocrypta galii,** *Galium* (266 - 267); **Cystiphora sonchi,** *Sonchus* (286).

DOLICHOPODIDAE: Thrypticus bellus, *Juncus* (lm) (F.) (probably all *Thrypticus* mine aquatic plants). **PHORIDAE: Megaselia rufipes,** *Tragopogon, Sonchus, Silene, Picris* (fh); cecid gall on *Silaus,* omnivorous. **SYRPHIDAE:** probably most *Cheilosia* (apart from a few fungus feeders) develop in stems or roots of higher plants but very few life histories are known. *Eumerus* and *Merodon* are pests of cultivated bulbs. **Cheilosia albipila,** *Cirsium palustre* (st); **C. antiqua,** *Primula* (r); **C. grossa,** *Cirsium palustre, Carduus crispus* (st); **C. semifasciata,** *Sedum telephium, Umbilicus* (1m); **C. variabilis,** *Scrophularia* (r); **Portevinia maculata,** *Allium ursinum* (? bulb, 1st); **Eumerus strigatus,** *Amaryllis, Allium cepa* (bulbs), *Iris, Pogonurus* (rhizome); **E. tuberculatus,** *Narcissus, Sprekelia* (bulbs), *Iris* (rhizome); **Merodon equestris,** *Narcissus, Hippeastrum, Sprekelia* (bulbs).

TEPHRITIDAE: picture-winged flies of this family are superficially attractive and their phytophagous larvae have fascinating habits, yet few people study them. This is partly because their adult morphology does not easily yield reliable diagnostic characters, whilst the variability of wing markings and their complexity, makes these tricky to use in a key directly to species. Hendel's key is the most reliable. Wing maps are given by Hendel and by Seguy. The several incompatible life cycles attributed to many species in the 19th century are testimony to frequent misidentifications. Much verification is required.

Two warm temperature species are imported in the fruits upon which they feed. These are *Ceratitis capitata* and *Rhagoletis cerasi*. Other exotics may be expected from time to time. The Tephritinae and Urophorinae are particularly attached to Compositae and feed in specific ways. All accessible parts may be attacked. *Paroxyna misella* is so far unique in having a gregarious, gall-making larva in the spring generation and a solitary, seedhead-eating larva in the summer brood. In times of failure of synchronisation between host plant and insect, shoot-tip feeders like *P.misella* may channel the growing tissue externally, though tephritid larvae usually feed in well concealed sites. The larvae are bluntly rounded and with no external elaboration. Few have been described, though the food of many is known. Some Trypetinae attack the flesh of fruits of Rosaceae, with some overspill to other plant families. Most other species attack Compositae, especially the seedheads of knapweeds and thistles, while *Trypeta* and related genera are leaf miners.

Most tephritids on Compositae restrict their attacks to a single tribe but a few attack any composite. Some species cause conspicuous galls on stems or roots, others make concealed galls in flowerheads or distort the whole structure. Some leave no external sign of attack. Except for leaf miners and fruit feeders nearly all tephritids pupate in the feeding site. The plant may, however, disintegrate during the winter and scatter the puparia. Species that pupate in spring normally have more durable feeding sites, in stems or in galls. This literature is often very inexact about the stage of development of flowerheads at the times of oviposition and larval feeding. Seedheads should be kept in a sheltered place outdoors for the winter, either hung up in nylon stockings or other easily ventilated material, or in flower pots with raised glass covers. The latter treatment is good for puparia in soil and for rootstocks.

Data are based on Niblett (1956 etc.), other British sources, R.W.J. Uffen's personal data, with gaps filled from Hering (1957) and, more cautiously, from Hendel's 1927 references to older continental work.

CERATITINAE: Ceratitis capitata, imported in apples, apricots (fr); **TRYPETINAE: Phagocarpus permundus,** *Berberis, Cotoneaster, Crataegus, Pyracantha* (fr); **Cryptaciura rotundiventris,** *Aegopodium, Angelica, Pimpinella* (1m),? *Arctium* (F); **Platyparella discoidea,** *Campanula latifolia* (st); **Platyparea poeciloptera,** *Asparagus officinalis* (st, the asparagus fly); **Myoleja caesio,** ? *Silene dioica* (1m) or ? *Sambucus or Lonicera* (fr), requires further study; **Euleia cognata,** *Tussilago, Petasites* (1m); **E. heraclei,** *Angelica, Heracleum, Pastinaca, Smyrnium, Apium* (1m, the celery fly) (B), many other Umbelliferae (F), ?*Cirsium arvense* (B); **Trypeta artemisiae,** *Artemisia, Chrysanthemum vulgare, Senecio, Eupatorium, Achillea ptarmica* (1m, can change leaf); **T. cornuta,** *Eupatorium, Petasites, Tussilago, Senecio* (1m) (F); **T. immaculata,** *Taraxacum* (B), *Crepis, Hieracium, Hypochoeris, Lapsana, Leontodon, Mycelis, Sonchus* (F) (1m); **T. spinifrons,** *Solidago virgaurea, Aster* (garden sp.) (1m); **T. zoe,** *Artemisia, Chrysanthemum, Eupatorium, Senecio, Petasites, Tussilago, Aster* (garden), *Chrysanthemum maximum* (1m); **Rhagoletis alternata,** *Rosa* (flesh of fr); **R. cerasi,** imported in cherries *(Prunus cerasus), P. avium, Lonicera, Berberis* (fr) (F); **R.**

meigeni, *Berberis* (sd kc); **Goniglossum wiedemanni,** *Bryonia dioica* (fr); **Chaetostomella onotrophes,** *Centaurea, Cirsium, Serratula, Arctium, Carduus* (fh); **Chaetorellia jaceae,** *Centaurea scabiosa, C. nigra* (fh); **Cerajocera ceratocera,** *Centaurea scabiosa* (fh); **C. microceras,** *C. scabiosa* (st); **Terellia longicauda,** *Cirsium eriophorum* (fh); **T. serratulae,** *Carduus crispus, C. nutans, Cirsium vulgare* (fh); **Orellia colon,** *Centaurea scabiosa* (fh, cocoons of chaff); **O. falcata,** *Tragopogon* spp. (r, st, solitary); **O. ruficauda,** *Cirsium arvense, C. palustre, C. pratense* (fh); **O. tussilaginis,** *Arctium* (fh, amongst sd, yellow puparia); **O. vectensis,** *Serratula tinctoria* (fh); **O. winthemi,** *Carduus crispus* (B), *Cirsium* spp. (F) (fh); **Xyphosia miliaria,** *Cirsium palustre, C. arvense, C. eriophorum, Arctium* spp. (fh); **UROPHORINAE: Urophora cardui,** *Cirsium arvense* (st gall); **U. cuspidata,** *Centaurea scabiosa* (fh gall); **U. jaceana,** *Centaurea nigra* (fh gall); **U. quadrifasciata,** *Centaurea nigra* (fh on sd); **U. solstitialis,** *Carduus nutans, Cirsium vulgare* (fh); **U. spoliata,** *Serratula tinctoria* (fh); **U. stylata,** *Cirsium vulgare, C. arvense, Carduus nutans* (fh); **Myopites blotii,** *Pulicaria dysenterica* (fh hard gall); **M. frauenfeldi,** *Inula crithmoides* (earliest fh, hard gall); **Ensina sonchi,** *Hypochoeris radicata, Aster tripolium, Leontodon, Picris, Sonchus, Tragopogon* (B), *Carduus nutans, Crepis, Senecio* (F)(fh); **TEPHRITINAE: Dithryca guttularis,** *Achillea millefolium* (r, unilocular spindle-shaped gall); **Oplocheta pupillata,** *Hieracium murorum, Picris hieracioides* (swollen fh); **Icterica westermanni,** *Senecio jacobaea, S. erucifolius* (r); **Oxyna flavipennis,** *Achillea millefolium* (r, spherical gall); **O. parietina,** *Artemisia vulgaris, A. absinthium,* ? *Aster tripolium* (st); **O. proboscidea,** *Chrysanthemum leucanthemum* (r, 5 mm. gall, uni-or multilocular); **Campiglossa argyrocephala,** *Achillea ptarmica* (withered tips) (F); **C. grandinata,** *Solidago virgaurea* (st gall); **Sphenella marginata,** *Senecio jacobaea, S. vulgaris, S. aquaticus* (swollen fh, forcing up group of pappus hairs); **Paroxyna absinthi,** *Artemisia vulgaris, A. maritima* (fh, leaves to pupate); **P. bidentis,** *Bidens* spp. (fh, unripe sd); **P. lhommei,** ? *Cirsium arvense* (adults on fh); **P. loewiana,** *Solidago virgaurea* (fh); **P. misella,** *Artemisia vulgaris* (fh spring brood 1-20 in open topped gall stopping growth, summer brood solitary on one sd, passing to receptacle); **P. plantaginis,** *Aster tripolium* (fh); **P. praecox,** ? *Filago gallica,* ? *Senecio* or *Chrysanthemum* sp. (F) (fh); **P. tessellata,** *Sonchus, Hypochoeris, Crepis, Taraxacum, Leontodon* (F)(fh); **Tephritis bardanae,** *Arctium* (fh within sd black puparia); **T. cometa,** *Cirsium arvense* (fh, unripe sd, surface of receptacle); **T. conjuncta,** *Chrysanthemum leucanthemum, C. maximum* (fh); **T. conura,** *Cirsium heterophyllum, C. vulgare, C. pale* (F)(fh hard gall); **T. dioscurea,** *Chrysanthemum* sp., ? *Achillea millefolium* (fh) (F); **T. formosa,** *Hypochoeris radicata, Sonchus arvensis, Crepis capillaris* (fh slightly swollen)(F); **T. hyoscyami,** *Carduus nutans, C. crispus* (fh); **T. leontodontis,** *Chrysanthemum leucanthemum, Leontodon autumnalis, L. hispidus* (fh, pupates in top of stem); **T. ruralis,** *Hieracium pilosella* (fh, slightly expanded)(F); **T. vespertina,** *Hypochoeris radicata* (fh); **Trypanea amoena,** *Lactuca* spp., *Picris hieracioides, Sonchus oleraceus* (fh)(F); **T. stellata,** *Hieracium murorum, Senecio jacobaea, S. erucifolius, S. squalidus* (B), both suborders and nearly all tribes of Compositae (F)(fh); **Achanthiophilus helianthi,** *Silybum marianum* (fh on young sd), ? *Centaurea, Cirsium* (galls on all parts) (F); **Heringina guttata,** *Hieracium, Anthemis, Chrysanthemum leucanthemum, Cirsium palustre* (fh)(F).

223

OTITIDAE: **Seioptera vibrans**, various plants (r) decaying veg.; **Tetanops myopinum**, *Ammophila* (? st. base). PSILIDAE: probably all breed in plants but many have yet to be associated with their hosts. **Loxocera albiseta, L. ichneumonea,** *Juncus effusus* (st base); **L. sylvatica,** ? *Luzula sylvatica* (adults on); **Psila fimetaria,** *Carex* (st); **P. bicolor,** garden *Chrysanthemum* (r), ? *C. vulgare,* ? *Artemisia vulgaris* (adults on); **P. humeralis,** ?*Myrrhis,* ?*Heracleum* (adults on); **P. limbatella,** *Chrysanthemum* (r); **P. nigricornis,** *Daucus, Chrysanthemum* (r); **P. nigromaculata,** *Succisa pratensis* (st); **P. pallida,** ?*Heracleum,* ? **Arctium** (adults on); **P. rosae,** *Daucus, Pastinaca, Apium, Anthriscus, Heracleum, Carum, Conium,* also *Brassica* (carrot root fly); **Chyliza vittata,** ?*Neottia nidus-avis* (r), *Epipactis, Orchis, Himantoglossum* (l/st, passing into r); **C. extenuatum,** *Orobanche elatior, O. rapum-genistae* (in swollen st bases, may be found in spring by pulling up dead flowering stems of previous year - look also for **Phytomyza orobanchia).** LAUXANIIDAE: **Calliopum aeneum,** *Viola,* (ovaries) *Trifolium,* (st. base) also saprophagous; HELEOMYZIDAE: **Suillia ustulata,** *Sambucus* (st); **S. variegata,** *Aster tripolium* (r)(both also fungi). PALLOPTERIDAE: probably most breed in plants but the larvae of some live solely or in part in dead wood, especially in the burrows of bark beetles Nomenclature follows Collin (1952), not the check list. **Palloptera parallela,** *Cirsium, Carlina, Centaurea scabiosa* (fh); **P. quinquemaculata,** *Arrhenatherum* (st base); **P. saltuum,** *Heracleum* (st); **P. scutellata,** *Juncus effusus* (1 base); **P. trimacula,** *Angelica sylvestris, Heracleum sphondylium* (st); **P. umbellatarum,** ?*Cirsium vulgare, Carlina vulgaris* (fh, also bark beetle burrows); **P. usta,** ? *Carlina vulgaris* (fh, F, also bark beetle burrows). LONCHAEIDAE: **Earomyia nigra,** *Verbascum, Angelica, Cirsium* (st); **E. schistopyga,** *Picea* (cones), ? predator of *Lasiomma melania* (Anthomyiidae); **E. viridana,** *Abies* (cones) (?other conifers); **Lonchaea chorea,** *Beta* (r), dung, bark, etc.; **L. fumosa,** *Hyoscyamus, Petroselinum, Asparagus* (st), *Pastinaca, Brassica* (r); **L. tarsata,** thistle (st), also under bark (probably all Lonchaeidae have predatory larvae). OPOMYZIDAE (probably all 14 spp. develop in stem bases of Gramineae): **Geomyza balachowskyi,** *Holcus;* **G. tripunctata,** *Lolium, Triticum,* etc.; **G. venusta,** *Bromus;* **Opomyza florum,** *Triticum;* **O. germinationis,** *Festuca, Lolium, Poa, Agrostis, Phleum, Alopecurus, Phalaris, Holcus, Triticum;* **O. petrei,** *Holcus, Anthoxanthum.* ANTHOMYZIDAE: **Anthomyza bifasciata,** *Typha* (st/1 sheath); **A. collini** (*gracilis* auct.), deformed *Phragmites,* galls of *Lipara* (Chloropidae) and mite *Steneotarsonemus;* **A. elbergi** (*sordidella* auct.), *Molinia, Deschampsia* (1 sheath); **Paranthomyza nitida,** *Silene* (1m); **Stiphrosoma sabulosum,** *Arrhenatherum, Lolium* (1 sheath), also mouse's nest; **Anagnota bicolor,** *Silene* (1m), also mole's nest.
EPHYDRIDAE: *Hydrellia* larvae may leave the host plant prior to pupation and enter another plant indiscriminately, there to form a pupation mine; there is thus need for caution in defining the true food plants and it is possible that some of the records below will need revision. **Clanoneurum cimiciforme,** *Atriplex, Beta, Halimione, Salicornia, Suaeda, Spergularia* (1m); **Notiphila brunnipes,** lay eggs in flowers of *Nymphaea alba,* submerged at night, getting eggs under water, without getting feet wet; **N. cinerea** as *brunnipes* but on *Potamogeton* spp.; **N. riparia,** inserts posterior spiracles into air-spaces of roots of emergent vegetation *(Glyceria maxima, Typha latifolia, Juncus effusus);* **Hydrellia albiceps,** *Alisma plantago-aquatica, Nasturtium officinale* (1m); **H. albilabris,** *Lemna minor, L. polyrhiza*

(1m); **H. chrysostoma,** *Alisma plantago-aquatica, Potamogeton lucens* (1m); **H. cochleariae,** *Callitriche* sp., *Hydrocharis morsus-ranae* (1m); **H. flavicornis,** *Alisma lantago-aquatica* (1m); **H. griseola,** many Gramineae, *Alisma plantago-aquatica, Sagittaria, Damasonium, Lychnis flos-cuculi, Stellaria media, Bellis, Nasturtium officinale, Carex, Cyperus, Scirpus, Hydrocharis morsus-ranae, Stratiotes aloides, Lamium purpureum, Trifolium, Lemna minor, Allium cepa, A. porrum, Polygonum, Veronica, Typha latifolia* (1m); **H. modesta,** *Hydrocharis* sp., *Potamogeton natans* (1m); **H. mutata,** *Alisma plantago-aquatica, Stratiotes aloides, Hydrocharis morsus-ranae, Lemna* sp. (1m); **H. nasturtii,** *Nasturtium officinale* (1m); **H. ranunculi,** *Nasturtium officinale* (1m); **H. thoracica,** *Glyceria aquatica* (1m). **DROSOPHILIDAE: Scaptomyza (S.) flava,** many Cruciferae, *Reseda, Tropaeolum, Papaver, Chelidonium, Hypochoeris,* 5 genera Papilionaceae (1m); **S. (S.) graminum,** *Nasturtium* (st/1m), *Stellaria media* (1m), some records as 1m, many Caryophyllaceae, Chenopodiaceae, *Antirrhinum, Montia, Amaranthus, Trigonella, Lupinus, Medicago* may refer to other spp.; **S. (S.) griseola,** *Stellaria media* (1m); **S. (S.) montana,** *Pisum, Brassica* (1m); **S. (Parascaptomyza) pallida,** *Allium* (1m).

AGROMYZIDAE: all species are associated with plants, chiefly as leaf miners (often with a characteristic pattern) in both angiosperms and pteridophytes, but all parts of the plant may be attacked. *Ophiomyia* and *Melanagromyza* are typically stem miners and some may occur in roots. There are also a few seed feeders (*Phytomyza* spp. in Scrophulariaceae, *Liriomyza lutea* in *Angelica*). Most attack herbaceous plants but some utilise woody plants, which are not much affected by other Diptera except Cecidomyiidae; there are leaf miners in *Ilex, Alnus, Betula, Populus, Salix, Fraxinus, Malus, Cornus, Laburnum* and Caprifoliaceae, cambium miners (*Phytobia* spp) in Salicaceae and Rosaceae and *Hexomyza* spp. form twig galls in Salicaceae and broom (*Sarothamnus*). A complete food-plant list is given by Spencer (1972), which gives detailed information on biology and rearing. Few species have been added to the British list since this work: **Metopomyza ornata,** *Butomus umbellatus* (1m); **Phytoliriomyza pteridii,** *Pteridium aquilinum* (1m); **Paraphytomyza cornigera,** *Lonicera periclymenum* (1m).

CHLOROPIDAE: larvae of most spp. live in plants, especially stems, galls or seeds of grasses (a few live in bird's nests, under bark and in beetle burrows, are predators of root aphids or have been bred from spider egg cocoons).

OSCINELLINAE: Lipara lucens, *Phragmites* (cigar shaped gall near top of st); **L. rufitarsis, L. similis,** *Phragmites* (smaller galls); **Calamoncosis aprica,** *Draba incana* (foliage); **C. glyceriae,** *Glyceria aquatica* (ensheathed inflorescences); **C. minima,** *Phragmites* (inquiline in galls of *Lipara lucens*); **Siphonella oscinina,** *Pinus* (cones); **Polyodaspis ruficornis,** *Castanea sativa* (imported nuts); **Oscinomorpha minutissima,** *Salvia scalare* (F); **Aphanotrigonum meijerei,** *Elymus arenarius* (F); **A. nigripes,** *Calamagrostris epigejos, Elymus* (F); **A. trilineatum,** *Festuca pratensis, Poa pratensis, Calamagrostris epigejos, Elymus, Eriophorum vaginatum* (F); **Oscinisoma cognata,** *Scirpus* spp., *Typha latifolia, T. angustifolia, Sparganium* (F); **Conioscinella frontella,** *Holcus lanatus* (st, B), *Anthoxanthum odoratum, Phleum pratense* (F); **C. gallarum,** *Quercus* (bred from cynipid galls - *Andricus, Biorhiza pallida*); **C. mimula,** *Anthoxanthum odoratum* (st, B), *Bromus* sp. (F); **Tricimba cincta,** *Colchicum autumnale;* **Dicraeus fennicus,** *Agropyron repens* (sd, F);

D. styriacus, *Elymus arenarius* (F, may not be breeding record); **D. tibialis,** *Bromus erectus, B. inermis, Helichotrichon pubescens* (sd, F); **Eribolus nana,** *Carex, Scirpus, Sparganium* (F); **Tropidoscinis albipalpis,** *Urtica dioica* (B), Gramineae (secondary invaders, F); **T. kerteszi,** *Deschampsia caespitosa* (F); **T. zurcheri,** *Phragmites* (inquiline in galls of *Lipara lucens* and *L. similis);* **Oscinella angularis,** *Phalaris arundinacea* (st); **O. frit,** Gramineae (many wild and cultivated grasses, st, sd,); **O. maura,** *Dactylis glomerata* (st); **O.nigerrima,** *Phleum pratense* (F); **O. nitidissima,** *Agrostis tenuis, A. stolonifera, A. canina* (st, B), *Poa pratensis, Festuca rubra, Anthoxanthum odoratum, Holcus lanatus, Dactylis glomerata, Lolium perenne* (F); **O. pusilla,** *Agropyron repens, Lolium perenne, Poa pratensis, P. trivialis, Festuca pratensis, Phalaris arundinacea* (F); **O. trochanterata,** *Phalaris arundinacea* (? st); **O. vastator,** *Lolium perenne perenne, L. p. multiflorum, Festuca rubra, F. pratensis, Phleum pratense;* **Lioscinella anthracina,** *Carex;* **L. atricornis,** *Eriophorum;* **Hapleginella laevifrons,** *Larix* (cones); **Elachiptera cornuta,** various cereals, ? *Oenanthe crocata* (and decaying vegetable matter); **E. megaspis,** ? *Nasturtium officinale* (st).**CHLOROPINAE: Camarota curvipennis,** barley and oat shoots (B), rye, wheat and barley ears, *Agropyron repens* (F); **Platycephala planifrons,** *Phragmites;* **P. umbraculata,** *Phragmites* (F); **Meromyza femorata,** *Dactylis glomerata* (F); **M. laeta,** *Agrostis vulgaris, Festuca rubra* (st, F); **M. nigriventris,** *Phleum pratense;* **M. pratorum,** *Bromus carinatus, Ammophila arenaria, Calamagrostis epigejos, C. stricta, C. canescens, Hierochloe odorata, Elymus arenarius* (F); **M. saltatrix,** *Poa pratensis, Festuca rubra* (st, F), *F. pratensis, Alopecurus pratensis, Agropyron repens;* **M. variegata,** *Dactylis glomerata* (st, B), *Phleum pratense* (st, F); **Eurina lurida,** *Phragmites;* **Cryptonevra consimilis,** *Phragmites* (inquiline in *Lipara similis* galls); **C. diadema,** *Phragmites* (inquiline in *Lipara similis* galls); **C. flavitarsis,** *Phragmites* (inquiline in galls of *Lipara lucens* and *L. rufitarsis);* **C. tarsata,** *Carex* (F); **Lasiosina cinctipes,** barley and oats (B), *Hordeum murinum, Calamagrostis epigejos, Glyceria maxima, Bromus inermis, Festuca, Agropyron* (F); **Cetema cereris,** *Poa trivialis, Alopecurus pratensis, Agrostis stolonifera* (F); **C. elongata,** *Agrostis tenuis, A. stolonifera, A. canina* (B), *Agropyron repens, Hordeum murinum, Poa pratensis* (F); **C. neglecta,** *Lolium perenne, Festuca pratensis, Poa trivialis, Agrostis* (st); **Anthracophaga frontosa,** *Carex;* **A. strigula,** *Brachypodium silvaticum, Agropyron* (F); **Chlorops brevimana,** *Phalaris arundinacea;* **C. gracilis,** *Calamagrostis epigejos* (F); **C. hypostigma,** *Dactylis glomerata* (F); **C. interrupta,** *Agropyron, Phragmites* (F); **C. planifrons,** *Carex* (F); **C. pumilionis,** wheat, barley, rye, *Agropyron repens* (st, B); **C. speciosa,** *Deschampsia caespitosa.*

SCATHOPHAGIDAE: at least half of the family are likely to feed on plants though many have yet to be reared and the host plants determined. Some other species breed in dung (*Scathophaga)* or have free living predatory aquatic larvae (*Spaziphora,* ? *Pogonota).* **Norellia spinipes,** *Narcissus* (1/st base); **Norellisoma spinimanum,** *Rumex aquaticus* (F), *R. triangulivalvis, R. obtusifolius* (B)(1st/st); **Cordilura impudica,** *Carex acutiformis* (st); **C. spp.** ? all in *Carex;* **Nanna armillatum, N. flavipes,** *Phleum, Secale* (fh) (records of *Chaetosa punctipes* from these grasses probably refer to *Nanna* spp.); **Cleigastra apicalis,** *Phragmites, Typha, Rumex* (not phytophagous but a predator in borings of moths and in *Lipara* galls on *Phragmites);* **Gimnomera tarsea,** *Pedicularis palustris* (sd pods), *P. sylvatica* (adults on); **Hydromyza livens,** *Nuphar, Nymphaea* (1m); **Parallelomma paridis,** *Paris quadrifolia* (1m); **P. vittatum,** Orchidaceae,*Polygonatum,* ?*Paris* (1m); **Delina nigrita,** Orchidaceae (1m).

ANTHOMYIIDAE: many Anthomyiidae are plant-feeders in the larval stage, as leaf-miners, or in stems, roots and flower-heads. Some are important agricultural pests with well-known life-histories. Those species which do not feed directly on living higher plants occur in a wide range of habitats, such as fungi (especially *Pegomya*), bird's nests (some *Lasiomma, Anthomyia*), excrement (*Calythea, Emmesomyia, Hylemya, Nupedia, Paregle*), dead snails *(Subhylemyia)*, nests of Hymenoptera *(Eustalomyia, Leucophora)*, rotting vegetable matter (numerous spp. from various genera) and decaying seaweed *(Fucellia)*. Not all species of a genus are confined to a single type of food material; for example most *Lasiomma* are associated with bird's nests, but *L. melania* and *infrequens* appear to be coniferous seed-feeders. Generally, however, in clearly defined small genera such as *Egle (Salix* catkins), *Chirosia* (ferns) and *Chiastocheta (Trollius* flowers) all species share the same type of food-plant. Very little is known about the life histories of some common and widespread species, e.g. *Pegohylemyia striolata, Craspedochaeta pullula, Nupedia infirma, Pseudonupedia intersecta;* probably these are rather generalised feeders in decaying matter. The adults are most usually found about the time that their respective host plants flower. Thus the *Salix* catkin species are out early in the season, and the peak activity for many species lies in the period May to July. A few species may still be found in the autumn and *Pegomya meridiana* only occurs in this period.

Chirosia aberrans, *Thelypteris palustris;* **C. albifrons,** *Pteridium;* **C. albitarsis,** *Pteridium* (r, st); **C. betuleti,** *Athyrium filix-femina* (rolled up apex of frond); **C. cinerosa,** *Pteridium, Struthiopteris* spp. (1); **C. crassiseta,** *Pteridium* (st, 1st); **C. histricina,** *Pteridium,* also other ferns (1); **C. parvicornis,** *Pteridium* (rolled up apex of frond); **Chiastocheta,** *Trollius,* adults on flowers, larvae sd, ? st; **Pegohylemyia brunneilinea,** *Centaurea* (?st base); **P. fugax,** *Sambucus, Dianthus, Spinacia* (st), *Meconopsis* (buds), cauliflower heads; **P. gnava,** *Lactuca sativa* (fh, sd); **P. jacobaeae,** *Senecio jacobaea, S. erucifolius* (fh); **P. pseudomaculipes,** *Solidago* (fh); **P. sanctimarci,** ? *Allium ursinum;* **P. seneciella,** *Senecio jacobaea* (fh); **P. sonchi,** *Sonchus oleraceus, S. arvensis* (fh); **P. spinosa,** *Achillea millefolium* (st); **Lasiomma infrequens, L. melania,** conifers, *Pinus, Larix* (sd, cones); **Acrostilpna latipennis,** *Athyrium filix-femina* (1st); **Phorbia securis,** grasses and cereals (r, st); **Delia antiqua,** *Allium* (the onion fly); **D. brassicae,** various Cruciferae (r, cabbage root fly); **D. cardui,** *Dianthus, Cheiranthus, Silene, Lychnis* (st/1m); **D. coarctata,** cereals and grasses (st base, r, wheat bulb fly); **D. coronariae,** *Lychnis flos -cuculi,* st(F); **D. echinata,** many Caryophyllaceae and Chenopodiaceae, occasionally Polemoniaceae, *Agrostemma, Arenaria, Cerastium, Dianthus, Gypsophila, Lychnis, Saponaria, Silene, Spergularia, Stellaria, Vaccaria, Viscaria, Atriplex, Chenopodium, Phlox* (1m); **D. flavifrons,** *Silene inflata* (sd); **D. floralis,** *Raphanus sativus,* also *Cochlearia armoracia, Brassica* spp., *Cichorium intybus* (r); **D. florilega,** *Brassica, Cerastium, Spergularia* (1m), also stem bases of maize, rotting potatoes etc. and excrement; **D. planipalpis,** *Brassica napus, B. rapa,* (r, turnip fly), *Sinapis arvensis* (st); **D. platura,** polyphagous on sprouting garden plants and seeds of legumes (bean seed fly); **D. quadripila,** *Honkenya peploides* (1m); **Heterostylodes**

congenerata, *Hieracium, Picris* (fh); **H. nominabilis,** *Hieracium pilosella* (fh); **H. pratensis,** *Leontodon hispidum, Hypochoeris radicata* (fh); **Egle minuta,** *Salix* (k); **E. muscaria,** *Salix, Populus tremula* (k); **E. parva,** *Salix caprea* (k); **E. rhinotmeta,** *Salix caprea, S. aurita* (k); **E. steini,** *S. pentandra* (k); **Pegomya albimargo,** *Stellaria, Malachium, Cerastium, Lychnis, Silene* and other Caryophyllaceae (1m); **P. argyrocephala,** *Euphorbia cyparissias,* ? *E. lathyrus,* ? *E. amygdaloides* (st gall); **P. bicolor,** *Polygonum, Rumex, Begonia* (1m); **P. dulcamarae,** *Solanum dulcamara* (1m); **P. esuriens,** *Beta, Chenopodium hybridum, C. urbicum* (1m); **P. genupuncta,** *Arctium lappa* (1m); **P. haemorrhoa,** *Rumex obtusifolius, R. acetosa* (1 m); **P.holosteae,** *Stellaria holostea, S. alsine, Cerastium triviale, C. holosteiodes* (1m); **P. hyoscyami,** many Solanaceae, Chenopodiaceae and Caryophyllaceae (1m, beet fly); **P. interruptella,** *Solanum, Chenopodium hybridum* (1m); **P. meridiana,** *Hypericum perforatum* (fh); **P. nigrisquama,** *Solidago virgaurea, Aster bellidiastrum* (1m); **P. nigritarsis,** *Rumex, Polygonum, Oxyria,* other Polygonaceae (1m); **P. rubivora,** *Rubus idaeus, Filipendula ulmaria* (st); **P. seitenstettensis,** *Oxalis acetosella* (1m); **P. setaria,** *Polygonum convolvulus, P. baldschuanicum* (1m); **P. steini,** *Carduus acanthoides, C. crispus, C. nutans, Cirsium arvense, C. eriophorum, C. palustre, Carlina vulgaris, Cynara* sp (1m); **P. versicolor,** *Heracleum sphondylium,* ?*Rumex* (st).

MUSCIDAE: **Muscina stabulans,** *Brassica* (st), predator of larva of *Ceuthorhynchus quadridens* (weevil); **Phaonia trimaculata,** *Brassica* (st, r), predator of *Delia brassicae* and of aphids.

DIPTEROUS PESTS OF CULTIVATED PLANTS
by Keith Harris

Some Diptera are pests of agricultural and horticultural crops and of garden plants. In almost all cases the primary damage is caused by larvae feeding on or in living plant tissues and the amount of damage is usually directly related to the numbers of larvae feeding. Secondary infections of damaged tissues by fungal and bacterial diseases are common and often extend initial lesions.

The most important dipterous pests are those that cause direct damage to harvestable produce or that interfere with normal growth to such an extent that the quantity and quality of harvestable produce is reduced. Most essentially phytophagous families contain a few important pest species and the main ones are Tipulidae (leatherjackets); Sciaridae (in mushrooms, seedlings of various plants); Cecidomyiidae (hessian fly, saddle gall midge, pea midge, swede midge, pear midge, raspberry cane midge, blackcurrant leaf midge etc); Syrphidae (narcissus bulb flies); Tephritidae (celery fly); Psilidae (carrot fly, chrysanthemum stool miner); Agromyzidae (cabbage leaf miner, chrysanthemum leaf miner, holly leaf miner, etc.); Chloropidae (frit fly of cereals, gout fly) and Anthomyiidae(bean seed fly, onion fly, wheat bulb fly, cabbage root fly, beet fly etc.).

Vegetables are particularly prone to attack by dipterous pests. The cabbage root fly, onion fly and carrot fly regularly cause appreciable losses and have been the subject of considerable research aimed at devising effective control methods. Species attacking cereal crops and grasses are also of general importance but most of the species that attack fruits and ornamental plants are sporadic or local pests of relatively minor importance. Cultivated mushrooms are attacked by a number of dipterous larvae belonging to species of Sciaridae, Cecidomyiidae and Phoridae, which are sometimes present in vast numbers and cause substantial losses of crop.

Further Reading

Becker, P. 1974. Pests of ornamental plants. MAFF Bull. 97, 175 pp., H.M.S.O. London.

Edwards, C.A. & Heath, G.W. 1964. The principles of agricultural entomology. 418 pp., Chapman & Hall, London.

Hussey, N.W., Read, W.H. & Hesling, J.J. 1969. The pests of protected cultivation. 404 pp., Edward Arnold, London.

Jones, F.G.W. & Jones, M.G. 1964. Pests of field crops. 406 pp., Edward Arnold, London.

Massee, A.M. 1954. The pests of fruits and hops. (3rd edition). xvi + 325 pp. Crosby Lockwood. London.

FLOWER-VISITING FLIES

by Dr. Martin C. D. Speight

Flies are the main pollinating agents of a wide range of flowering plants and are important in pollinating many others, but their purpose in visiting flowers is not to pollinate them but to acquire food, or find a mate, to lay eggs, or to find shelter and warmth or to carry out a combination of these and other activities.

Flowers as Sources of Food

Most visits to flowers by flies are carried out for the purpose of collecting food in the form of either pollen or nectar. Pollen has been available for more than 200 million years and the Nematocera were able to exploit this food source very early. The adoption of pollen as a food source by insects had a fundamental effect on angiosperm evolution, providing an alternative to wind to move pollen from plant to plant, so modifications of plant structure soon developed to increase the effectiveness of pollination by insects. Indeed, plants began to compete for the insects' attention, by developing showy flowers to advertise the presence and location of their pollen and producing nectar as a food for pollinators! Since some insects visited flowers only to consume nectar, many plants have evolved specialised flowers with hidden nectar stores which cannot be tapped without the visitor either getting dusted with pollen or brushing against the stigmata at the same time. As flower types radiated (evolved in different directions) so did the mouthparts of the flies exploiting them, so that today there are a significant number usable only by particular Diptera.

Flower colour, odour and behaviour have also diversified to ensure effective pollination and flowers of a certain colour, smell and form are recognised as food sources by the appropriate insects. Further, flowers signal their whereabouts at the time of day that their pollinators are on the wing, e.g. those pollinated by moths are frequently closed, scentless and without nectar during daylight hours.

The choice of flowers visited is determined by the fly's food requirements and preferences. Some flies will visit flowers primarily for their pollen some authors still ignore this fact), others will take both pollen and nectar and others nectar alone. Wind pollinated flowers do not produce nectar and are only visited by pollen feeding flies; these are mainly females which consume pollen more often than do males, because it is a source of protein needed for egg maturation. Because pollen is also rich in carbohydrates, lipids, vitamins and minerals and is also a useful energy source for male flies but nectar, which is composed almost entirely of sugars in solution, is even more attractive to them and both sexes are equally attracted to flowers which carry both pollen and nectar.

Although there is substantial information on flower visiting by flies, it is still difficult to determine the preferences of a particular family e.g. which flowers are visited, whether pollen or nectar is collected, whether both sexes visit flowers, etc. There is a need for simpler but accurate observation on flower visiting. However, some flowers are certainly visited more frequently and by a wider range of flies than are others and with the limited British flora it is possible to list these more popular plant species: Ranunculaceae: *Ranunculus* spp. (especially yellow petalled buttercups); *Caltha palustris* (marsh marigold). Cruciferae: *Cardamine* spp. (lady's smock); *Brassica* spp. Boraginaceae: *Myosotis* spp. (forget-me-not). Cistaceae: *Helianthemum* spp. (rock-rose). Caryophyllaceae:*Stellaria* spp. (stitchwort). Geraniaceae: *Geranium robertianum* (herb robert). Oxalidaceae: *Oxalis acetosella* (wood sorrel). Aquifoliaceae: *Ilex* (holly). Celastraceae: *Euonymus europaeus* (spindle). Aceraceae: *Acer pseudoplatanus* (sycamore). Papilionaceae: *Sarothamnus scoparius* (broom); *Ulex* spp. (gorse). Rosaceae: *Prunus laurocerasus* (cherry laurel); *P. spinosus* (blackthorn); *Filipendula* spp.; *Potentilla* spp., especially *P. erecta* (tormentil) *Rubus* spp. (blackberry, raspberry, etc.); *Dryas octopetala*; *Geum* spp.; *Rosa* spp. (dog rose, etc.);*Sorbus* spp. especially *S. aucuparia* (rowan); *Malus sylvestris* (crab apple),*Crataegus* spp. (hawthorn). Umbelliferae: * nearly all umbellifers. Araucaceae:*Hedera helix* (ivy). Caprifoliaceae: *Sambucus niger* (elder); *Viburnum* spp. Rubiaceae: *Galium* spp. (bed-straw). Valerianaceae: *Valeriana officinalis* (valerian). Dipsacaceae: *Succisa pratensis* (devil's bit scabious). Compositae:*most composites. Ericaceae: *Arbutus unedo* (strawberry tree); *Calluna* spp. (ling); *Erica* spp. (heather); *Rhododendron ponticum; Vaccinium myrtillus* (bilberry). Oleaceae: *Ligustrum vulgare* (privet). Buddlejaceae: *Buddleja* spp. Gentianaceae: *Blackstonia perfoliata* (yellow-wort). Convolvulaceae: *Calystegia* spp. (bindweed). Labiatae: *Mentha* spp. (mint). Plantaginaceae: *Plantago* spp. (plantains). Polygonaceae: *Polygonum* spp. (knotgrass and bistort). Euphorbiaceae: *Euphorbia* spp. especially *E. amygdaloides* (wood spurge). Salicaceae: *Salix* spp. especially *S. caprea* (goat willow), *S. repens* (creeping willow), *S. cinerea* (sallow). Alismataceae: *Alisma plantago-aquatica* (water plantain). Iridaceae: *Iris pseudacorus* (yellow flag). Liliaceae: *Allium* spp. (wild garlic etc.); *Narthecium ossifragum* (bog asphodel). Cyperaceae: *Carex* spp. (sedges); *Scirpus maritimus* (sea clubrush). Juncaceae: *Luzula* spp. (wood rush).

An * indicates those most frequently visited by flies. These flowers are mostly either white or yellow, with the yellow flowers predominating. Yellow flowers tend to be unspecialised, with easily available nectar. Red flowers, conversely, tend to be specialised, e.g. with a tubular corolla and their nectar is characteristically hidden in some way. Red flowers tend to be visited only by flies with specialised mouthparts (Knuth, 1906-9).

Flower-feeding Nematocera

Representatives of nearly all families have been recorded feeding at flowers. It has been suggested that the mouthparts of bloodsucking culicids and ceratopogonids evolved as flower-feeding devices to exploit hidden nectar stores reached only by a narrow tubular apparatus. Males of species in which the female sucks blood are known to collect nectar from flowers - *Theobaldia* (Culicidae) feeds at flowers during the night. Pollen is the protein source for females of some non blood-sucking *Atrichopogon* spp. (Ceratopogonidae) (Downes, 1955) which pierce pollen grains and suck out the contents. Even females of blood-sucking mosquitoes may gather nectar from small tubular blooms, usually after dark. A bizarre selection of flowers, e.g. moschatel (*Adoxa moschatellina)*, are patronised by simuliids but they do not use concealed-nectar flowers.

Non-biting Nematocera have unspecialised mouthparts, so flower-feeding is restricted to plants with more exposed nectar, like umbellifers. It might be expected that the elongate 'snout' of tipulids would be used for feeding at tubular flowers, but this is not as yet reflected in written accounts.There are a few records of *Nephrotoma* and *Tipula* feeding on umbels during daylight hours though night feeding may be more usual. The Bibionidae are frequently noticed at flowers (usually species with exposed nectaries) and long lists of plants visited by them could be compiled, most having exposed nectaries; the Scatopsidae, although less obvious, are very common on similar flowers. Flowers visited by cecidomyiids, mycetophilids and psychodids are mostly low-growing and found in damp and shady places, e.g. golden saxifrage (*Chrysosplenium).* Some Sciaridae and Keroplatinae, however, occur commonly on umbels and a few of the latter have elongate probosces adapted for flower-feeding, e.g. *Macrorrhyncha, Asindulum, Antlemon.* Most Chironomidae do not feed as adults, but a few imbibe nectar and in tundra environments *Smittia* spp. are important pollinators of saxifrages and *Salix* spp. The Saxifragaceae are probably more used by Nematocera than by other Diptera.

Flower-feeding Brachycera

In many Bombyliidae (beeflies), the proboscis is a long, rigid tube tipped by the labellae, which are blade-like (and able to pierce soft plant tissues) as opposed to the inflatable membranous flaps of many Diptera. They tap nectar sources in tubular flowers, e.g. primrose (*Primula vulgaris),* which cannot be tackled by most flies, while still in the air – they hover, humming-bird fashion, in front of the flower, enabling rapid escape when danger threatens. Some bombyliids are known to collect pollen but this has not been investigated in any detail.

Asilids, dolichopodids, empids and tabanids all feed at flowers, but according to Downes (1958) their greatly modified mouthparts have been developed primarily for blood-sucking or predation and are only secondarily used for flower-feeding. With the exception of some empids, none appears to collect pollen. Asilids make little use of flowers but are recorded from tubular flowers, e.g. *Knautia* (field scabious), *Vaccinium* (bilberry), Dolichopodid mouthparts differ markedly from those of most predatory flies, being short and rarely tubular; they are largely confined to flowers with well-exposed nectaries, e.g. buttercups (*Ranunculus).*

Flower-feeding among tabanids is frequent but poorly recorded. The non-blood-sucking males feed mainly at flowers but may also obtain sugar from honey-dew. Males of *Chrysops* spp. frequently visit ox-eye daisy *(Chrysanthemum leucanthemum)*, *Tabanus bromius* visits wild angelica *(Angelica sylvestris)* and wild garlic *(Allium)* and both sexes of *Hybomitra micans* visit *Heracleum* but no further precise records have been traced. Females are believed to feed on nectar for some days after emergence, moving on to blood meals after mating, when egg development demands protein; *Chrysops* and *Atylotus* females have been collected at flowers but information on other British species is lacking. The south European *Pangonius* are flower-feeders in both sexes; the female feeds at Labiatae and Scrophulariaceae while on the wing.

Many empids have an elongate, rigid proboscis and visit flowers with easily accessible nectaries and also long tubular flowers e.g. wild cherry *(Prunus avium)* and bog bean *(Menyanthes trifoliata)*. Willis & Burkill (1895-1908) list a wide range of plants visited by empids. These flies both suck up nectar and pierce plant tissues to suck the juices. Some empids, e.g. *Euthyneura*, definitely feed on pollen (ingesting entire grains) as well as nectar (Downes & Smith, 1969) and are apparently not predatory.

There are some records of Rhagionidae, Stratiomyidae and Therevidae feeding at flowers, usually composites or umbellifers with readily accessible nectar, but none of Scenopinidae, Xylomyiidae or Xylophagidae. The Acroceridae do not appear to be capable of feeding as adults.

Flower-feeding Cyclorrhapha Aschiza

The Syrphidae (hoverflies) are arguably the most important of all families in relation to pollination. Long lists of flowers visited by them are given in the writings of Kormann, Knuth, Parmenter and Willis & Burkill. Nearly all British species feed at flowers and in some genera the mouth-parts are greatly modified for this purpose. Both sexes are known to ingest pollen grains and nectar, though pollen consumption is documented for few species. Some, however, collect pollen from wind pollinated flowers, e.g. *Melangyna quadrimaculata* feeds from hazel *(Corylus)* catkins and van der Goot (1970) shows that *Melanostoma* and *Platycheirus* feed on pollen of grasses (Gramineae), sedges (Cyperaceae) and plantain *(Plantago lanceolata)*. *Melanostoma* is recorded as a pollinator of timothy *(Phleum pratense)* and cocksfoot *(Dactylis glomerata)*.

The typical syrphid proboscis (e.g. *Eristalis*) is largely membranous, hinged about half way along its length so that it may be folded back into the mouth opening; it is inflated into a tube for feeding, the fleshy labella enveloping and projecting beyond the horny syringe made by abbrum and hypopharynx. Nectar is mopped up by the labella, as in many Diptera. Pollen grains are also picked up by the labella and ingested. Hoverflies are thus able to probe hidden nectar sources in a wide range of flowers, the flies with longer probosces being able to reach the more deeply hidden nectaries. However, syrphids which specialise in feeding at tubular flowers (e.g. *Anasimyia, Rhingia, Sphegina, Volucella)* have a more sophisticated apparatus, in which the proboscis can become a very narrow tube, the labella being reduced to a pair of flexible, tongue-like structures which hug the sides of the feeding tube and hardly project beyond it and the head is elongated to accommodate it when folded. Thus *Rhingia* can feed from bluebell (*Endymion*), *Sphegina* from herb robert (*Geranium robertianum*), *Anasimyia* from bog-bean (*Menyanthes*) and *Volucella* from *Buddleja. Rhingia*, in particular, also feeds at a wide range of composites and umbellifers.

Holloway (1976) demonstrates that at least some hoverflies consume significant quantities of pollen away from flowers by eating grains combed out of their body hairs, while resting on foliage or even when in flight. Whether the thickness and disposition of the hair covering of flies like *Eristalis* has evolved as a pollen-collecting device as he suggests, is open to conjecture and closer observation is required of the activities of hairy hoverflies.

Conopidae also specialise in flower-feeding; the different genera have mouthparts modified to differing extents for flower-feeding and this is strongly reflected in the flowers visited. They are at least modified in *Leopoldius* which has a short stocky proboscis ending in large membranous labella. *L. signatus* is only recorded from ivy (*Hedera*) flowers, with well exposed nectar. In *Conops* and *Physocephala* the proboscis resembles that of *Rhingia* but when folded it projects forward beyond the head; they frequent flowers with exposed or concealed nectar and visit small tubular flowers like scabious (*Knautia*) and knapweed (*Centaurea*). *Sicus*, which collects nectar from long tubular flowers, e.g. clovers (*Trifolium* spp.) in addition to those visited by other Conopidae, has a remarkable thread-like semi-rigid proboscis almost as long as the body, with two joints that enable it to fold up like a collapsing letter Z; when folded its tip is left pointing backwards. The labella are here reduced to small blade-like flaps.

The Platypezidae are of interest in that they are not known to feed at flowers except for a single record of *Opetia* at *Pastinaca*. Lonchopteridae, Pipunculidae and Phoridae are all recorded as feeding from flowers with easily accessible nectar, e.g. celandines and buttercups (*Ranunculus* spp.) and certain composites. *Conicera* spp. (Phoridae) are common on umbels.

Flower-feeding Cyclorrhapha Schizophora

Flower-feeding is the exception rather than the norm among these Diptera, only becoming important in the calypterates. Chloropidae, Lauxaniidae, Psilidae, Sepsidae and Tephritidae also use flowers, chiefly Umbelliferae, as food sources but few have specialised in this habit. *Aphaniosoma* (Chyromyiidae) are closely associated with flowers in coastal habitats, *A. propinquans* on *Tripleurospermum*, *A. socium* on *Convolvulus*. The very small carrion-feeding *Meonura* spp. (Carnidae) occur on umbels (*M. vagans*), *Prunus spinosus* and *Aristolochia* (*M. flavifacies*).

Many calypterates including *Scathophaga* feed at flowers, consuming both pollen and nectar — these flower products are probably the sole source of food for many of them. Some have been seen collecting pollen from flowers with concealed nectar sources which they could not tap. Most do not have suitable mouth-parts to exploit tubular flowers, the exceptions being the dexiine and phasiine tachinids. The long probosces of the latter enable them to feed from Labiatae (Karczewski, 1967); only the labium is attenuated and the labella are reduced, stiff and blade-shaped.

Although they are unspecialised and largely confined to flowers with easily available nectar, the Muscidae are the next most important family to the Syrphidae as pollinators.

Other Uses of Flowers

Although few flies visit flowers without collecting pollen or nectar while there, their primary purpose in visiting is not necessarily to feed. Curiously, few predatory flies take advantage of the potential prey on flowers and only *Scathophaga* is noted for lying in wait for victims on or beside flower heads, although some empids certainly do likewise. However, the males of various flies, employ this tactic to locate females for mating, e.g. *Neoascia podagrica, Syritta pipiens* and various eristalines such as *Anasimyia* spp., *Eristalis arbustorum, E. nemorum* and *Helophilus pendulus*. The male patrols over a patch of flowers, diving onto any likely insect which settles and often settling to feed; where another male or an insect of a different species evokes this reaction it may be a territorial response. The behaviour of a patrolling male towards other males of its species is aggressive and each tends to keep to its own patch of flowers. In the rare species *Cheilosia nebulosa*, each male hangs poised in its own air space, beside a flowering bush of sallow (*Salix*) or blackthorn (*Prunus spinosus*) visited by the females. The males of *Platycheirus ambiguus* have a similar habit.

In some flies, flowers are visited for egg laying. Many Tephritidae lay their eggs in flower-heads of composites, where the larvae develop. Some cecidomyiids, including the agricultural pest *Mayetiola destructor*, which attacks wheat, oviposit in the flowers of grasses. At least one family, the Conopidae, visit flowers to lay eggs on other insects visiting them. Females of *Conops* spp. wait for bumble bees (*Bombus* spp.) at flowers darting after their hosts to lay eggs on them in mid-air. The prolonged spells some hoverflies (e.g. *Eristalis tenax*) spend on flowers are difficult to explain in terms of any of these needs and I consider that these flies find it advantageous to remain where bees are likely to occur because they are bee-mimics. Flowers can also provide good vantage points to watch for the approach of potential enemies or to shelter when the weather is cold, wet or windy. Large tubular flowers like those of bindweed (*Calystegia*), foxglove (*Digitalis*) and daffodil (*Narcissus*) provide excellent retreats from the rain. The warming influence of flowers is also quite important to many Diptera, e.g. in spring when a temperature of 10°C higher than the surroundings can be reached within the cup of a flower like *Anemone* and since many such flowers are heliotropic (i.e. turn to follow the sun during the day) they can maintain this higher temperature. Sun bathing within such flowers can thus confer upon the insect a higher metabolic rate.

All the flower-visiting activity mentioned above involves some benefit to the fly and often also to the plant. However, there are instances on which the plants benefit but the flies, far from obtaining something useful, may not escape. Flies attracted by the smell of carrion, dung or rotten fruit are usually involved, being enticed to flowers emitting similar odours. A British example is the cuckoo-pint (*Arum maculatum*) to which drosophilids, psychodids and sphaerocerids are attracted to effect pollination and remain trapped (Proctor & Yeo, 1973; see also

Mimicry). Many escape later to transfer pollen to other plants, entering oblivious of their previous experience. Sundews (*Drosera* spp.) attract, trap and devour small insects by means of the sticky exudation as do the Butterworts (*Pinguicula* spp.).

Collecting Flies from Flowers

Given reasonable weather the most important considerations in collecting are choice of area and location of spots where flies are congregating on flowers, so that these spots can be worked thoroughly and repeatedly during the day. Day excursions which cover the ground once only are not very rewarding. The best way to locate useful spots is rapid reconnaissance of the ground on arrival, preferably by mid morning, when flower visiting by many flies begins in earnest. Shelter, southerly aspect, presence of 'edge' and freedom from disturbance are important criteria. Edge is important because Diptera so often fly along the edges between vegetation types, e.g. paths, rivers, etc. so that appropriate flowers in such locations almost inevitably accumulate flies. A dense stand is usually more profitable than scattered plants but too large an area of flowers disperses the Diptera. The ideal is to find several stands separated by only a few metres so that successive visits may be made at about twenty minute intervals.

Another important consideration is time of day. After a prolonged period of inactivity in the night hours, flies need to warm up till metabolic rate is high enough to support flight and most do not visit flowers just after dawn has broken (see Time and the Living Fly). In the spring, when sun and showers alternate, slowing down feeding activity, flies arrive at flowers later and stay to feed longer than in the summer. Some hoverflies, e.g. many *Cheilosia* spp. can only be regularly found on flowers around midday. Others, such as *Scaeva selenitica*, feed at flowers early in the morning and briefly again in the evening, while *S. pyrastri* can be found at flowers throughout the day. *Ferdinandea cuprea* and *Myolepta luteola* will feed out in the open in the morning, but later in the day are only likely to be found in sheltered woodland glades. Visits are related to the timing of nectar availability or the period that flowers are in direct sunlight. The nectar store of many flowers is exhausted by early afternoon while the sun does not reach into small glades until it is high in the sky.

The collector should be selective when deciding which flowers to work for their fly visitors. Yellow or white non-tubular flowers are the most productive, but if flies belonging to a group specialised for flower feeding are sought, the flowers selected by them must be investigated. Among the hoverflies, *Pipizella heringi* and *Portevinia maculata* feed at flowers of wild garlic *(Allium ursinum)*, *Melangyna* spp. at alder *(Alnus)* and hazel *(Corylus)* catkins and *Cheilosia variabilis* at figwort *(Scrophularia nodosa)*, plants that are not generally attractive to flies. In early spring, sallow catkins *(Salix* spp.) may attract many flies when few other flowers are available. Ivy *(Hedera helix)* is important in the autumn.

Flies may be easily collected from flowers by means of pooter and handnet. The pooter is most effective for smaller flies which can be approached closely without taking to flight. Using a strong kite net to sweep stands of flowers can be very productive except for collecting larger species, which normally get frightened away by such action. It is best to approach flowers from such an angle that one's shadow does not fall across them and slowly enough to avoid disturbing one's quarry; it is also worth concentrating specifically on a desirable fly, ignoring its congeners, even to wait for a fly settled in an awkward position to move to a spot where a swipe with the net is easier.

Further Reading

Downes, J. A., 1955. The food habits and distribution of *Atrichopogon pollinivorus* sp. n. (Dipt., Ceratopogonidae). *Trans. R. ent. Soc.Lond.* **106:** 439-453.

Downes, J. A., 1958. The feeding habits of biting flies and their significance in classification. *Ann. Rev. ent.* **3:** 249-266.

Downes, J. A. & Smith, S. M., 1969. New or little-known feeding habits in Empididae (Diptera). *Can. Ent.* **101:** 404-408.

Holloway, B. A, 1976. Pollen-feeding in hover-flies (Diptera: Syrphidae). *N. Z. J. Zool.* **3:** 339-350.

Karczewski, J, 1967. The observations on flower-visiting species of Tachinidae and Calliphoridae (Diptera). *Fragm. Faun.,* Warsaw. **13:** 407-484.

Knuth, P., 1906-9. Handbook of flower pollination. Transl. J. R. Ainsworth Davies. 3 vols. Oxford.

Parmenter, L. 1956. Flies and their selection of the flowers they visit. *Ent. Rec. J. Var.* **68:** 242-243 (many earlier papers in *Ent. Rec. J. Var., Ent. mon. Mag., J. Soc. Brit. Ent.;* also 1961. *Ent. Rec. J. Var.* **73:** 48-49.

Proctor, M. & Yeo, P. 1973. The pollination of flowers. New Naturalist Series, No. 54, Collins, London. 418 pp.

Richards, A. J. (ed.) 1978. The Pollination of Flowers by Insects (Linn. Soc. Symp. No. 6) Academic Press, London. 214 pp.

van der Goot, V. S. & Grabandt, R. A. J, 1970. Some species of the genera *Melanostoma, Platycheirus* and *Pyrophaena* (Dipt., Syrphidae) and their relation to flowers. *Ent. Bericht.* **30:** 135-143.

Willis, J. C. & Burkill, I. H., 1895-1908. Flowers and insects in Great Britain. *Ann. Bot.* **9:** 227-273; **17:** 313-349, 539-570; **22:** 603-649.

Chapter 7

Behaviour and Adaptation

MIGRATION
by Alan E. Stubbs

Migration can be defined as purposeful movement from one geographic area to another. Whilst it can involve quite small distances and on an irregular basis, normally one is thinking in terms of large distances traversed by numbers of individuals on a fairly regular basis from generation to generation. Birds are the example which most obviously come to mind but the phenomenon is widespread among most of the groups of mobile animals including mammals, fish, butterflies and moths and ladybirds.

Not all animals migrate, the various species having adopted one of two basic strategies for survival, and even in a single species not all individuals necessarily follow one pattern. A species which does not migrate must be able to maintain viable population levels year after year on the resources of the home ground — a house sparrow stands a good chance of obtaining food all the year round in gardens. The other strategy is to move with the food supply — thus a swallow feeding solely on flying insects would starve to death during the winter if it stayed in Britain and therefore it must migrate. Of course the sparrow might be quite hard pressed during the winter too, but will it stand a better chance on the small piece of ground it knows intimately or should it risk the hazards of migrating hundreds or perhaps thousands of miles over land and sea in the hope of an easier life for a few months? Most sparrows decide to stay put.

Birds generally breed at only one end of the migration route. However, insects have the potential for breeding at a much faster rate, so continuous breeding can give an advantage outweighing the hazards of migration. If the insect's food is seasonal, it may be possible to extend the number of generations per year by migrating with the climatic belts so that food is always in suitable condition. Thus butterflies such as red admiral *(Vanessa atalanta)* feeding on nettle *(Urtica dioica)* and painted lady *(V. cardui)* feeding on thistle *(Carduus)* thrive in North Africa and the Mediterranean during the winter and move up into northern Europe as the summer advances and certainly some of their offspring fly south in the autumn. The Small Tortoiseshell *(Aglais urticae)* makes do with two generations at home and the Peacock *(Inachis io)* with one on nettle. The home based species are partly held in check by parasites so there is no fear of all the nettle being consumed by the natives.

As far as is known, no phytophagous Diptera have the same migratory strategy. There is, however, a group of flies which has a particularly unpredictable food supply — the aphidophagous Syrphidae. Aphids themselves provide numerous examples of local or regional migrants, both in order to find suitable host plants and also to get in and out of an area before the predators can fully exploit such an easy food supply. Possibly many of our aphid feeding hoverflies have to be very mobile, which in turn explains why they are so fond of flowers for building up their energy supply. Some species seem to have specialised habitats which would make anything more than local movement disadvantageous but at least half probably move about a great deal within a district. It is very difficult to prove long distance movement except in the full scale migrants, principally *Episyrphus balteatus, Scaeva* spp. and *Metasyrphus corollae*. These can sometimes arrive on the south and east coast of Britain in huge numbers, the sea and strand line being littered with those that did not succeed in finishing the journey. In an unconscious way they are obviously hoping that there will be more aphids here than in the lands they have come from − and if there has been an aphid population explosion that the local fauna has not been able to react to, then they are able to exploit the vacant niche. It is these migrant species which seem to pupate on completing larval development (certainly in the case of *M. corollae*) rather than overwintering as larvae, and this presumably enables an autumn emergence which flies south to carry on breeding for the winter. By recording the dates of the sudden appearance of large numbers of suspect migrant hoverflies, with enough recorders it should be possible to plot the migration front as it moves across Britain. Whether it will be practical to record movement south seems more questionable but with butterflies migration can be demonstrated by an observer logging the direction of flight of all individuals and thus analysing the predominant direction of migration, if any. More local movement of populations can be equally dramatic. The Coelopidae and other flies which feed on strand line wrack (washed up sea weed) on the sea shore can show mass migration though it is not clear how far these populations move. As with aphids, the availability of food supply can be unpredictable since so much depends on storms throwing up sea weed in the right quantity in the right place. The wider question of how to recognise a migration in coastal situations is discussed in the section on the sea shore.

Other forms of movement occur, though migration may not be the correct term. It is frequently noticed that various Diptera and other flying insects are to be found at the tops of hills and mountains, perhaps miles from the nearest potential breeding site. With the more powerful fliers, this behaviour may bring the sexes together at an assembly point but for the most part the phenomenon is not easily explained. In some cases these insects may have been carried beyond their normal terrain by the wind and they are simply hanging on to 'the end of the world'. Another feature of mountain areas can be the use of cols (passes) and it may be possible to log the fly past movement of Diptera. The main problem would be separating purposeful migration flight from passive 'blown with the wind'.

Whilst migration is scarcely a justified term, it is possible that in many species there are substantial movements of local populations on a daily rhythm. A species that spends the morning at ground level may spend the afternoon in the tree tops and in many cases the different sexes may be occupying quite different areas for much of the time. Very little is recorded on this subject.

MIMICRY

by Richard I. Vane-Wright

The similarity of the drone-fly *(Eristalis tenax)* to a honey-bee is an example of *the theory of mimicry*. Bees sting, and have an unpleasant taste. As a result, they are unacceptable to many birds, toads, and other insect-eating vertebrates. Through bitter experience, such predators come to recognize bees by their appearance and buzzing sound and learn to avoid them. The theory of mimicry attempts to explain the similarity of drone-flies to bees in the following way: if a predator which has learned to avoid bees mistakes a fly for a bee, and so declines to eat it, then the fly has gained some protection. Any fly which lives longer as a result will tend to leave more offspring. Selection for the most bee-like flies will occur at each generation. If the initial chance likeness to bees is variable, and at least partly inherited, then the species may eventually come to be very bee-like in appearance, sound and behaviour, as with the drone-fly. Mimicry, therefore, is a special case of Darwin's theory of evolution by natural selection. The theory of mimicry was originally proposed in 1862, by the English naturalist H. W. Bates, and gave rise to heated debates between those for and against Darwinism.

The structure of a Mimicry System

A mimicry system consists of two different signalling organisms, the *model* and the *mimic*, and a third, signal-receiving organism, the *operator*. The operator is not merely a passive receiver, but acts according to the message received from the model.

In our example, the bee is the model, the drone-fly is the mimic, and the potential predator is the operator. The model sends out a signal which informs the operator of its nature (in this case the signal says "I am nasty, so leave me alone"). The operator perceives this, and responds with an avoiding reaction. Any other organism which can produce a similar signal to that of the model is potentially in a position to take some advantage of this communication based interaction. Thus the drone-fly, by producing a similar signal to a bee, gains protection if a predator which dislikes bees is unable to distinguish the fly from a real bee. This type of mimicry is known as *Batesian* mimicry (named after H. W. Bates). Potentially there are many different types of mimicry (Vane-Wright, 1976), the subject being rather complex. However, it is possible to survey mimicry in the British Diptera under three main headings.

Flies as Mimics

Most cases of mimicry in the British Diptera probably fit the Batesian category, and appear to involve a deceptive resemblance by harmless flies to various stinging, warningly coloured social Hymenoptera. A number of assemblages are discussed by Brown (1951).

Bumble bee mimics. These tough, shaggy, brightly coloured bees can be divided into four colour groups: yellow or buff (e.g. *Bombus muscorum)*, mimicked by such Diptera as *Arctophila fulva, Criorhina floccosa* and *Laphria flava;* black with red tail (e.g. *B. lapidarius)*, mimicked by *Criorhina ranunculi;* banded with

239

white tail (e.g. *B. lucorum*) and banded with orange tail (eg. *B. pratorum*). *The last* three groups are all mimicked by various forms of one syrphid, *Volucella bombylans*. Another example of such remarkable polymorphic mimicry is *Merodon equestris*, which has been studied in detail by Conn (1972).

Hornet mimics. There are three dipterous mimics of *Vespa crabro* in Britain, *Asilus crabroniformis*, *Volucella inanis* and *V. zonaria*. When dead, they do not look convincing, but when alive the asilid certainly behaves sufficiently like a hornet to be deceiving. As in almost all cases of mimicry, behaviour is of great importance in completing the delusion.

Wasp mimics. Our dipterous *Vespula* mimics include some stratiomyids and many hover-flies, notably *Sericomyia silentis* and *Chrysotoxum festivum*. *Didea fasciata* is very wasp-like in flight, although it shows little resemblance when at rest. The yellow and black conopids may belong here, but see also below.

Honey bee mimics. In addition to *Eristalis tenax*, other syrphids such as *E. pertinax, Microdon mutabilis, M. eggeri, Mallota, Brachypalpus* and *Criorhina asilica* number amongst those species included in this assemblage.

Ichneumon wasps, although they do not inject poison, are apparently distasteful to many predators, and may form another group of models. Likely dipterous mimics include the large and brightly coloured *Ctenophora* crane-flies, *Megamerina*, and the micropezid *Rainieria*. The rhinophorid *Paykullia maculata*, with its fussy, jerking run, may be a mimic of the fiercely stinging spider-hunting wasps (Pompilidae).

Some of the Conopidae, the larvae of which are parasitoids of Hymenoptera, may be aggressive mimics of the cuckoo type. If close approach to the hosts by female conopids is helped by their wasp or bee-like behaviour, then they would fall into this category. The failure of hosts to detect the more deceptive conopids could certainly act as a selective agent promoting mimetic convergence. In this particular case, the brightly coloured species of Conopidae may also benefit simultaneously from a Batesian relationship. The investigation of Hymenoptera and vertebrates as potential operators in mimicry by conopids would be of great interest.

Flies as Operators

Proctor & Yeo (1973) have suggested that the similarity of certain flowers may have been caused through competition for pollinators. A possible example is eyebright *(Euphrasia)*, which may be a mimic of ling *(Calluna)*. The role of Diptera as pollinators in such systems would be a fascinating, but difficult study.

Flies as Models

Two possible cases in which generalised fly-like signals may act as models can be suggested. The cuckoo pint flower needs to lure insects inside for pollination. In addition to its foetid odour, the leaves are often adorned with fly-like dark spots which may be attractive to passing flies (Wickler, 1968). It would be interesting to know if there is any difference in response by particular flies to spotted and non-spotted *Arum* plants. Basic experiments should not be difficult.

A second case concerns the spider-eating spider *Ero*, which lures spiders to their doom by vibrating their webs like a trapped fly. This, of course, would appear to be an extremely generalised resemblance, but experiments could be conducted on the effects of different vibrations applied to a spider's web, and compared with the movements generated by trapped insects, including flies, and those made by *Ero* itself.

Investigations of Mimicry

It is all too easy to jump to conclusions about mimicry when a more rigorous analysis is really required. Indeed, few of the cases listed above have been the subject of experimental investigation. Often the real basis for a particular mimicry system may occur in another part of Europe, where the aculeate Hymenoptera fauna is so much larger – we may be seeing the edge of the range of the fly where the model is absent. And what is deceiving to us, or not deceiving to us, may not be so to the biologically relevant predators or other operators. However, the amateur can do much by noting mimetic behaviour in the field, thus paving the way for specialists to advise on or carry out more critical studies.

Further Reading

Brown, E. S., 1951 Mimicry as illustrated by the British fauna. *New Biology* **10**: 72-94, 6 pls.
Conn, D. L. T., 1972. The genetics of mimetic colour polymorphism in the large narcissus bulb fly, *Merodon equestris* Fab. (Diptera: Syrphidae). *Phil. Trans. R. Soc. Lond.* (B) **264**: 353-402, 1 pl.
Proctor, M. & Yeo, P., 1973. *The pollination of flowers.* London
Vane-Wright, R. I., 1976. A unified classification of mimetic resemblances. *Biol.J.Linn.Soc.* **8**: 25-56.
Wickler, W. 1968. *Mimicry in plants and animals* [translated from the German by R. D. Martin]. London.

STUDYING THE BEHAVIOUR OF DIPTERA
by Kenneth G. V. Smith

The late J. E. Collin once told a newspaper reporter at a "Verrall Supper" that a fly could be identified by the way it walked on the ceiling – well I think we can see what he meant. The experienced entomologist can identify many insects on the wing and when asked by a beginner how this is done he is often at a loss to explain exactly how. We make many such identifications on behaviour and it is instructive to ask ourselves how we do it and we may find that the answer is not well recorded in the literature. An obvious everyday example of flight behavioural differences is to be seen in our own homes where the house fly (*Musca domestica*) is the one that settles and the lesser house fly (*Fannia canicularis*) is the one that flies perpetually beneath the lamp-shade and never seems to settle. I have another example in an old ms key to adult Empidinae prepared by the Australian dipterist G. H. Hardy in which *Empis* and relatives were separated from *Hilara* by the charming couplet:

    1.   Flies low over water . . . . *Hilara*
    –   Flies high over land . . . . *Empis* etc.

A delightful help to the field observer but of limited use to a study bound taxonomist. Clearly it is sometimes possible to identify families or even genera by behaviour. If we take hovering we can think of Syrphidae in shafts of sunlight and Pipunculidae among the grass-stems or even within the folds of a net, or

Microsania (Platypezidae) in bonfire smoke. In Muscidae, *Fannia* and *Hydrotaea* males can be seen hovering under trees. Another aspect of behaviour is that of aggregating on crushed grass by *Hydrotaea (militaris, bimaculata)* although female *Fannia* will also do this and it would be interesting to know if other flies are attracted. Behaviour can also be linked to other phenomena such as mimicry and what dipterist has not been fooled by the wasp-like flight of *Chrysotoxum*. Other forms of behaviour are more enigmatic. Many Tipulidae bob or bounce on their long legs for no apparent reason. Attempts to associate this behaviour with egg laying or feeding have failed as the 'bobbing' continues when neither activity is being indulged. I once measured the rate of 'bobbing' of a tipulid as it sat in full sunlight one late afternoon on a garden wall in Oxford. As the sun sank and the temperature fell the rate of bobbing decreased, so perhaps it is directed at temperature control; clearly the problem needs further investigation.

Desperately little is known about territorial behaviour in Diptera, yet it is certainly widespread and important. Syrphidae are well-known as 'hover flies' and may certainly hover over 'markers' which delineate their territory and intruders are 'buzzed'. I have personally observed *Volucella zonaria* to mark territory by hovering over three or four particular leaves of shrubs within an area of some 25 square feet. Insects invading this territory even up to bumblebee size have been seen to be knocked out of the air by an aggressive male *zonaria*. The particular individual observed in my garden in North London would buzz human intruders and actually settled on my bald head and on several occasions on my spectacles and on the lens of a hand-held camera. *Volucella* species thus hovering will drop onto passing females of their species as has been observed with other Syrphidae. Territory is a word much used in ornithology and little understood elsewhere in the animal kingdom and its investigation throws open a very wide field suitable for investigations by amateurs.

Other general aspects of behaviour are little known, for instance how does a fly spend a normal day? There have been few attempts to find out. Flies, then, are as varied in their behaviour as in other aspects of their biology and structure. Probably we know most about predaceous and courtship behaviour and in some families these two aspects are linked. These aspects are now considered more fully, but clearly the whole subject is ripe for field investigation by the careful amateur.

Predaceous Behaviour

Some flies are predaceous on other insects and invertebrates. Oldroyd (1964; see Chapter 2) suggests that the predaceous habit in adult flies belies a dietary deficiency in the larval stages but there are families in which both stages are predaceous. Empididae and Dolichopodidae are predaceous as adults and larvae. Asilidae are predaceous as adults and have possible predaceous or parasitic larvae and Scathophagidae have varied habits, some being predators, other phytophagous. In the Muscidae two subfamilies, the Coenosiinae and Limnophorinae, are all predators in adult and larval stages but the habit is absent in the other subfamilies. In Anthomyiidae adults of the genus *Paraprosalpia* are predaceous. Among the Acalypterate families in Britain, Micropezidae and some Ephydridae are predaceous as adults and in the Nematocera many Ceratopogonidae are rather specialised predators on many other insects (see Chapter 5).

Poulton (1913) provided an early summary of the type of prey taken by Diptera and discusses predaceous behaviour. Since then most Dipterists have at some time or another provided prey lists for various families and the writings of Hobby and Parmenter are worthy of specific attention. An outstanding study by Melin (1923) on the prey and predaceous behaviour of the Asilidae is a classic and provides a model for such studies. Most predaceous Diptera are opportunist feeders and take what is most readily available, often other Diptera. Some predaceous flies appear to be more specialist feeders either because they take prey of a particular kind or they exploit a particular ecological niche. Asilidae are fairly general predators, but members of the genus *Dioctria* take a higher proportion of Hymenoptera, especially Ichneumonidae, than other Asilidae. In the Empididae species of *Hilara* fly low over water and feed on insects trapped in the surface film and *Microphorus* species feed on the insects trapped in spiders' webs. In the Dolichopodidae *Medetera* and *Neurigona* frequent vertical surfaces, such as tree trunks, and consequently feed on other insects occurring there.

The predaceous habit is naturally reflected in the morphological adaptations that have evolved to meet it. The most obvious adaptation to be expected is in the mouthparts (figs. 1-3). The commonest weapon is the hypopharynx which carries the salivary duct and this can be pushed into the body of the prey like a hypodermic needle and the juices sucked out. The proboscis, too, can be well developed and heavily sclerotized where well protected insects such as beetles and some Hymenoptera constitute the prey. In Asilidae (Fig. 1) the mouthparts mostly point forwards and on the face there are well developed tufts of hair and bristles which probably protect the fly when it impales its prey. In Empididae (Figs. 2-3)

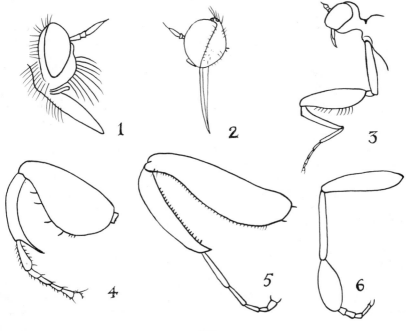

the proboscis is mostly pointed downwards so there is no need for the elaborate facial armature which is so obvious a feature of the asilid head.

Flight is obviously an important factor in chasing or darting after prey and coupled with this is efficiency of vision and development of the wings. In some Asilidae and Empididae (Hybotinae) there are areas of enlarged eye facets in both sexes which aid in prey capture (see also under courtship).

Structural modifications also occur in the legs of predators and such legs are then termed *raptorial* (Figs. 3-6.). Usually the front legs are modified in this way as in *Ochthera mantis* (Ephydridae) (Fig. 4) or in *Hemerodromia* (Empididae) (Fig. 3). In the empid genus *Hilara* the basitarsus may be greatly swollen to accommodate glands from which 'silk' is used to bind up the prey (Fig. 6). In other flies such as *Platypalpus* (Empididae) the middle legs are raptorial (Fig. 5).

Because of their diminutive size and the better known vertebrate blood-sucking habits of *Culicoides*, the Ceratopogonidae are often overlooked when considering the predaceous habit. However most genera of Ceratopogoninae are predaceous in the truest sense of the word and many take whole prey smaller than themselves and have modifications enabling them to do so. Others such as *Forcipomyia* are often much smaller than their prey and feed on the blood of much larger insects such as Neuroptera and mayflies and may be considered ectoparasites. The division is a fine one and is discussed by Downes (1970).

Families in which the larvae only are predaceous are more numerous and are indicated in the section on larvae (chapter 2) but many more careful studies are needed here.

There is still a lot to be learned about the predaceous behaviour of flies, methods of hunting and killing, and the type of prey taken, especially among the smaller empids (e.g. Tachydromiinae), Dolichopodidae and Micropezidae. Comparative studies of prey taken by the same species in different localities and in different environmental conditions would also be valuable.

Courtship Behaviour

Perhaps the most easily detected form of courtship behaviour is that involving mating swarms or aggregations. This habit is common to many families and more frequently involves males than females. There is a relationship between the swarming habit and the type of male eye. Males which swarm often have a larger eye area than the female (e.g. Bibionidae, Simuliidae, many Brachycera, Platypezidae, Pipunculidae, Phoridae, Syrphidae and Calyptratae), the eyes usually touch above (holoptic) and may have clearly demarcated areas of enlarged eye-facets above for use in approaching the female from below. In contrast groups with a distinct courtship or epigamic display usually have males with the eyes separated above (dichoptic). Swarming is thus rare among the Acalyptratae except for Lonchaeidae, Milichiidae and some Heleomyzidae. The huge aggregations of Sepsidae that sometimes occur on vegetation are probably not primarily for courtship.

Swarming often takes place above a 'marker' which may be a tree top, bush, tip of a branch, an animal or even a post or stump, or over water and the swarm can consist of any number from one (e.g. Syrphidae, Muscidae where territorial

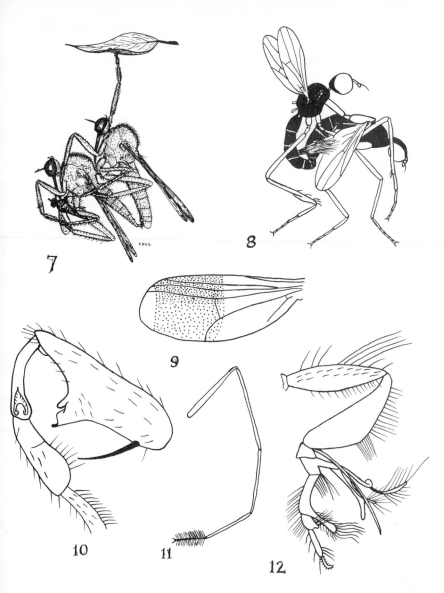

7

8

9

10   11

12

behaviour is involved) to several thousands. Very dense columnar swarms of midges have been mistaken for smoke when situated over roof-tops or towers. The flies usually face into the wind and may be in constant up and down movement (e.g. Trichoceridae) or in a more or less stationary 'hover' (e.g. Simuliidae). The response to the 'marker' appears to be largely visual. Another morphological adaptation to the swarming habit is in the male antenna which is plumose in the families Culicidae, Chaoboridae, Ceratopogonidae and Chironomidae. This type of antenna is an auditory organ which is sensitive to the tone made by the female in

245

flight. The swarms usually consist of males; individual females when ready to mate will fly into the swarms from nearby resting sites. Detailed discussion of the complicated mechanism of swarming is given in Downes (1969), and Oldroyd (1964) is very useful.

In Empididae there is a merging of predaceous and courtship behaviour in that the prey is frequently an essential part of the mating ritual. There appears also to be an evolutionary sequence in the complexity of this behaviour throughout the family as follows: 1) prey devoured by both sexes independently of pairing, e.g. *Platypalpus*, *Hybos*, *Empis trigramma*, *E. punctata*; 2) the prey provided by the male is devoured or sucked by the female during copulation, e.g. many *Empis* (such as *livida* see fig. 7), *Rhamphomyia*; 3) the prey or object provided by the male is not devoured by the female, but becomes an ornament or plaything providing some indispensable stimulus (the behaviourist's 'releaser'), e.g. *Hilara* where inanimate objects may be enclosed in a silken web or indeed the web may be empty. The transference of the prey is usually preceded by an aerial dance in which males alone participate *(Empis opaca)* or females only *(E. livida)* or both sexes *(Hilara* spp.). Even where no prey is used as in *E. trigramma* there is an elaborate male dance. Occasionally Empididae take their own species as prey for the purposes of courtship, but some Ceratopogonidae (e.g. *Probezzia)* show an even more extreme form of courtship cannibalism, as the female, on entering a mating swarm captures the male as prey at the same time as he catches her as a mate and during mating feeds on him through a puncture made in his head (see Downes 1970).

Although closely related to the Empididae, the Dolichopodidae show more specific courtship behaviour of the display type. An easily observed species is *Poecilobothrus nobilitatus*, often to be seen on the muddy edges of ponds or water filled ruts. The male wings (fig. 9) have a subapical dark patch and an apical white patch and he stimulates the female with these by wing wagging displays on each side of her. Dolichopodid males are rich in such sexual adornments for the visual stimulation of the female. In *Argyra* the bodies of the males are clothed in whitish dust which appears silvery in the sunshine and the males perform wild dances before the females and often dash off into the distance as a silvery speck to return just as rapidly a few seconds later. A similar silvery body with accompanying behaviour is exhibited by certain Therevidae such as *Thereva annulata* in which the males perform a frantic dance in groups of up to eight or ten, some four to six feet high, over hot sand in bright sunshine.

Often in Dolichopodidae the legs are modified such as in *Neurigona quadrifasciata* where the male front tarsi (fig. 11) terminate in plumes which are waved over the female's eyes alternately from behind. A further and somewhat novel behavioural speciality of some *Neurigona* is a preference for both hunting and courting on tree trunks within a diameter of between five and eight inches. Surely the most fantastic leg modification in the Dolichopodidae (or any fly?) is that of *Campsicnemus magius* (fig. 12) and when Loew described it Gerstaecker accused him of making a new species from a fly whose legs were deformed by fungoid growth! As yet the function of this leg is unknown but is probably involved in courtship.

In the Syrphidae it is probable that sound may play a part in courtship as well as the more obvious use as a defence mechanism or in territorial behaviour (e.g.

when handled the whining of a syrphid changes to a higher pitch). Most syrphids emit a hum when hovering and this has been observed to be of use in courtship in *Merodon* and possibly in *Eristalis* (Richards 1927). Asilidae and Bombyliidae may also use sound in courtship.

Among the Acalyptratae the behaviour of Drosophilidae has received some attention. The famous fly of many classic genetic studies, *Drosophila melanogaster*, has a complex courtship behaviour. The male expresses his initial sexual excitement by extending one wing at right angles to his body and rapidly vibrates it for a few seconds. This wing vibration is repeated with alternate wings at intervals throughout the courtship until mating is accomplished. Between these wing vibrations there is a slow partial spreading and closing of the wings performed as a 'scissor movement'. During this display the male always faces some part or other of the female. Usually he walks around her in a semi-circle, facing her as he moves. Next he licks the female's ovipositor and bends his abdomen to bring his genitalia under his thorax towards those of the female. If accepted as a mate he then mounts her on her back between her wings and holds on to her wings, thorax or abdomen with his legs.

Two types of courtship behaviour occur in the Sepsidae. In such genera as *Themira* and *Meroplius*, the male has a scent organ (osmeterium) on the hind tibia and the abdomen frequently has tufts of long hairs on the fourth sternite. These hairs not only help disperse the scent but are used to stimulate the female during courtship and mating (fig. 8). The scent is used to attract females and also functions in interspecific recognition. When Sepsidae form vast aggregations (see above) the smell of this scent is very obvious. In *Sepsis* there are no abdominal hair tufts, the hind tibial scent gland is rudimentary and display behaviour involving wing wagging and abdomen waving, usually on cow-pats, is used by the males to stimulate their mates. In both groups the fore legs of the male may be modified for grasping the female (fig. 10). In many Sepsidae and in the otitid *Seioptera vibrans* the wings have a black subapical spot and both species are wing-waggers and these markings are undoubtedly of importance in courtship by the male, although present in both sexes. The Sepsidae is not the only family to use scent in courtship; some females of the ceratopogonid tribe Palpomyiini have eversible glands in the abdomen which are probably used in courtship.

We do not know much about the courtship of calypterate Diptera, but in the Muscidae, *Lispe* with its spoon-shaped palpi may repay observation.

Many families of which habits here are unknown, are known to have elaborate courtship displays abroad. This is a rich field of research in which the amateur can contribute much if he is prepared for patient careful observation. In such work it is vital to make notes and sketches in a field notebook while actually observing or to dictate observations to a companion. Photography, especially high-speed cinematography should reveal many of the finer points of behaviour as yet undetected.

Oviposition

The structure of the ovipositor is closely adapted to specialised function in certain families, usually associated with specialised behaviour. Many groups of flies have a generalised telescopic tube formed by the terminal segments of the abdomen and this is normally sufficient for ovipositing in such media as wet mud, decaying plant material, dung and carrion. In phytophagous species there is often a need to insert eggs into living plant material, this generally entailing an adaptation of the ovipositor. In Tephritidae, Pallopteridae and Lonchaeidae there is a horizontal sheath-knife like blade (some *Pallopiera* and many lonchaeids oviposit into bark). Scathophagid larvae variously breed in plants or are free living in the soil, dung or other media; the structure of the ovipositor is normally specialised in the phytophagous species. Asilidae show a fascinating range of structural and behavioural adaptations to oviposition (Melin); some species oviposit in sand and these have short spiny cerci which act like shovels when eggs are laid in sand whilst other species oviposit in grass flower heads, an activity which requres a long telescopic ovipositor.

Tipulidae, though treated as primitive flies, have a specialised pointed ovipositor though few observations have been made on the act of oviposition, possibly because most species lay eggs at night. Certain species such as *Tipula vittata* and some *Nephrotoma* certainly just hold their abdomen vertically pointed down (this is where long legs are useful) and superficially stab their eggs into the ground. However, Hemmingsen has described how *Tipula juncea* burrows its abdomen right into the soil so that the thorax is flush with the ground. A few species, such as *Tipula vernalis*, have the ovipositor reduced to tiny blunt flaps and presumably in these cases eggs are scattered at random whilst in flight. Some parasitic Diptera have a piercing ovipositor; in Pipunculidae the ovipositor is bent under the abdomen and can act as a clamp to hold the bug it is laying an egg into. Other parasitic flies have very different structures as in Conopidae and Tachinidae.

These comments introduce a fascinating subject which offers plenty of scope since so few life histories are known and observations of oviposition and the structural and behavioural aspects involved are so sparse. The study of ovipositors sometimes gives a clue to life history, but there are many puzzling ovipositors of unknown function, e.g. the long blunt ovipositor of the platypezid *Opetia*.

Legends to figures

Fig. 1. Head of *Asilus crabroniformis* L. (Asilidae)
Fig. 2. Head of *Empis caudatula* Lw. (Empididae)
Fig. 3. Head and front leg of Hemerodromiinae (Empididae)
Fig. 4. Front leg of *Ochthera mantis* Deg. (Ephydridae)
Fig. 5. Middle leg of *Platypalpus* (Empididae)
Fig. 6. Front leg of male *Hilara* (Empididae)

Adaptations to courtship behaviour

Fig. 7. A pair of *Empis livida* L. *in copula* with prey.
Fig. 8. A pair of *Themira leachi* (Mg.) *in copula* (Sepsidae) (after Sulc)
Fig. 9. Wing of male *Poecilobothrus nobilitatus* L. (Dolichopodidae)
Fig. 10. Front leg of male *Themira leachi* (Sepsidae)
Fig. 11. Front leg of male *Neurigona quadrifasciata* F. (Dolichopodidae)
Fig. 12. Front leg of male *Campsicnemus magius* Lw. (after Parent) (Dolichopodidae)

Further Reading

Downes, J. A., 1969. The swarming and mating flight of Diptera. *A. Rev. Ent.* **14:** 271-298.

Downes, J. A., 1970 The ecology of blood-sucking Diptera: an evolutionary perspective (pp. 232-258) in Fallis, A. M. *Ecology and Physiology of Parasites.* A symposium. University of Toronto Press.

Hamm, A. H., 1908-1933. [Papers on behaviour of Empididae] *Entomologist's mon. Mag.* **44:** 181-184; **45:** 132-134, 157-162; **64:** 113-117.

Hobby B. M. & Smith, K. G. V., 1961-1962. [Papers on behaviour of Empididae] *Entomologist's mon. Mag.* **97:** 2-10; 204-208.

Melin, D., 1923. Contributions to the knowledge of the biology, metamorphosis and distribution of the Swedish Asilids in relation to the whole family of Asilids. *Zool. Bidr. Upps.* **8:** 1-317.

Parmenter, L., 1954. The courtship of Diptera. *Proc. S. Lond. ent. nat. Hist. Soc.* **1952-3:** 104-109.

Poulton, E. B., 1913. Empidae and their prey in relation to courtship. *Entomologist's mon Mag.* **49:** 177-180.

Richards, O. W., 1927. Sexual selection and allied problems in the insects. *Biol. Rev.* **2:** 298-364.

Chapter 8

The Fly in Time
THE FOSSIL RECORD OF THE ORDER DIPTERA
by Edmund A. Jarzembowski

General Considerations

The order has its roots amongst the four-winged mecopterous insects of the late Palaeozoic (Permian). The Permotanyderidae from the Upper Permian of Australia (250 million years Before Present) are now considered to be the earliest Diptera and this family was apparently four-winged. The order is next recognised with certainty in the late Triassic (Rhaetic: 210 m.y. B.P.) and apart from several enigmatic forms, these insects belong in the suborder Nematocera which is well represented in the succeeding Lower Jurassic. The early Nematocera include Tipulomorpha, Bibionomorpha, chironomoid Culicomorpha and Psychodomorpha-like forms; although now extinct, some of these were comparatively advanced.

The Brachycera (Orthorrhapha) had evolved by the late Lower Jurassic (Toarcian: 180 m.y. B.P.) e.g. *Protobrachyceron liasinum* from Germany, referred to the Tabanoidea. The Diptera were thus well established by the Jurassic, and further work on insect-bearing strata of latest Permian and early Mesozoic age may well provide important evidence regarding their evolution.

Culicomorpha (Ceratopogonidae) are present in the late Jurassic of England (140 m.y. B.P.) and the late Jurassic/early Cretaceous of Turkestan has yielded Orthorrhapha including Nemestrinidae (Tabanoidea) and possible Asiloidea. Psychodomorpha (Psychodidae: Phlebotominae), Culicomorpha (Chironomidae: Podonominae), Bibionomorpha (Cecidomyiidae and mycetophiloids) occur in Lebanese amber of Lower Cretaceous age (120 m.y. B.P.) as well as rare Aschiza-like flies. Orthorrhapha (Empidoidea) are represented by Empididae in the same deposit and Dolichopodidae are found in late Cretaceous amber from Canada (75 m.y. B.P). The latter resin also contains orthocladiine Chironomidae amongst the Culicomorpha, Anisopodidae, Scatopsidae, Bibionidae and extant mycetophiloid families in the Bibionomorpha and Stratiomyidae in the Tabanoidea. Aschizous Cyclorrhapha are represented by Phoroidea (Sciadoceridae, Platypezidae) and possible Syrphoidea; Schizophora are represented by a single chloropid. Muscoidea (Calliphoridae) are also known from Canada from deposits of similar age. Thus by the close of the Mesozoic, aschizous Cyclorrhapha were established and both acalypterates and calypterates appear in the fossil record just before the end. A number of familiar nematocerous families were present, notable exceptions being Tipulidae, Culicidae, Psychodidae (Psychodinae) and these are known in an advanced state from certain Lower Tertiary deposits (40-50 m.y. B.P.). Common orthorrhaphous families not recorded until the Lower Tertiary include Tabanidae (Tabanoidea) and Bombyliidae (Asiloidea).

By the mid Tertiary (30 m.y. B.P.) pupiparous Cyclorrhapha (Hippoboscidae) had appeared and the Diptera were modern in many respects, though the Schizophora appear to be few. In the main, significant evolution in the Caenozoic was confined to the higher Cyclorrhapha. In other groups, a considerable number of genera were either modern or closely related by mid-Tertiary times. The distribution of certain taxa was notably different from the present day: thus the tsetse flies *(Glossina)* occurred in North America in the Oligocene. Climatic changes culminating in the Pleistocene glaciation (2 m.y. B.P. – ? present) influenced dipterous distribution especially in the Holarctic Region.

British Record

The earliest British dipteron is a poorly-known nematoceran from the Lower Jurassic (Lower Lias) possibly belonging to the Protorhyphidae, an extinct family of Bibionomorpha. The Tipulomorpha are represented by an architipulid, *Liassotipula anglicana,* higher up in the Lower Jurassic (Upper Lias) of Gloucestershire. During late Jurassic and early Cretaceous times much of southern England formed a subsiding coastal plain where the Purbeck and Wealden Beds were deposited over some 30 m.y. Diptera were obtained from the lower part of the succession in the last century and recent work by the author indicates that the order also occurs in the uppermost part of the sequence. Tipulomorpha, Culicomorpha, Bibionomorpha and Tabanoidea are represented by forms allied to modern families.

The interbasaltic Ardtun Leaf Beds on the Isle of Mull have yielded a bibionid and a cylindrotomine tipulid. The age of these strata is slightly problematical but they are probably of early Tertiary age. Some seventy-five species of fossil Diptera are known from the younger Lower Tertiary of the Hampshire Basin (Bembridge Marls: 35 m.y. B.P.) and comprise Tipulomorpha (Tipulidae), Psychodomorpha (Psychodinae), Culicomorpha (Dixidae, Culicidae, Chironomidae), Bibionomorpha (Blephariceridae, Anisopodidae, Bibionidae, Mycetophilidae s. lat.), Orthorrhapha (Rhagionidae, Tabanidae, Stratiomyidae, Asiloidea, Empididae, Dolichopodidae) acalypterate Schizophora (Otitidae, Sphaeroceridae, Ephydridae, Chloropidae). Study by the author of several insect groups from this deposit indicates that the British fauna contained a number of exotic elements at this time and this is also true of the Diptera.

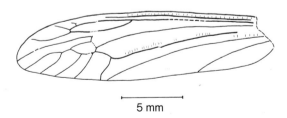

5 mm

Wing of *Ischnotoma vasifera* (Cockerell & Haines), Tipulidae, Bembridge Marls (holotype). The genus is currently confined to South America and Australia and the fossil species comes closest to *Ischnotoma par* (Walker) from New South Wales (Vane-Wright 1967).

Pieces of Tertiary Baltic amber are sometimes found on the east coast of England, especially in Norfolk and Suffolk, and may contain dipterous inclusions. Diptera have been found by me in the overlaying Hampstead Beds, the youngest Palaeogene strata in the Hampshire Basin.

Further Reading

Craig, D.A. 1977. A re-assessment of the systematic position of *Pseudosimulium humidum* (Westwood), an Upper Jurasic fossil dipteran. *Entomologist's Gaz.*, **28**: 175-179.

Jarzembowski, E.A. 1976. Report of Easter Field Meeting: the Lower Tertiaries of the Isle of Wight. *Tertiary Res.* **1**: 11-16.

McAlpine, J.F. 1970. First record of calypterate flies in the Mesozoic Era (Diptera: Calliphoridae). *Can. Ent.* **102**: 342-346.

— & Martin, J.E.H 1969. Canadian amber — a paleontological treasure-chest. *Can. Ent.*, **101**: 819-838

Riek, E.F. 1953. Fossil Mecopteroid Insects from the Upper Permian of New South Wales. *Rec. Aust. Mus.* **23**: 55-8, pls 5-6.

Rohdendorf, B.B. 1962. Order Diptera. *In* B.B. Rohdendorf (ed.), *Basics of Palaeontology, Arthropoda, Tracheata and Chelicerata* : 307-344, Moscow (in Russian).

Tillyard, R.J. 1933. *The Panorpoid Complex in the British Rhaetic and Lias.* 79 pp., 1.pl. London.

Zeuner, F.E. 1941. The Eocene Insects of the Ardtun Beds, Isle of Mull, Scotland. *Ann. Mag. nat. Hist.* (11) **7**: 82-100, pl. 1

THE ICE AGE AND POST-GLACIAL PERIOD

by Alan E. Stubbs

Though a relatively new subject, studies of insect remains in geological and archaeological deposits have already produced some very important results. Beetles have been found to preserve particularly well in some peats and certain other deposits of the Pleistocene Period (the last Ice Age, dating back to well over 1 million years Before Present) and also those of the Holocene Period (post-glacial times; the last 10,000 years). It has been shown how cold and warm climate faunas occupied Britain according to climate fluctuations, the invasions and retreats of these faunas reacting with remarkable rapidity. At times Britain had species characteristic of southern Europe or Siberia or in one case a beetle only now known from Tibet. In archaeological deposits one may find the early occurrences of synanthropic species and of those of habitats now largely destroyed by man (e.g. we have lost various dead wood species) and even in the Holocene, climatic fluctuations affected the insect fauna. One of the major surprises is that there is no evidence of beetle evolution over the last 1 million plus years, even genitalia characters having remained constant, so that identification relates directly to present day species. For the most part it would seem that the ecology of the species has also remained fairly constant; thus it is possible to interpret the past environment of Britain on the basis of the assemblages of species.

The interesting point is that Diptera also occur in these deposits. Wings have been found in peat but of greater value is the occurrence of head capsules of Nematocera and larvae and puparia of Brachycera and Cyclorrhapha. For instance various chironomid genera have been recorded from the Hoxnian interglacial (250,000 years B.P.). Also the bibionid *Dilophus* is known from the Upton

Warren Interstadial Complex (30,000 years B.P.) as well as chironomids and tipulids. Archaeological digs have produced records of *Musca domestica* and *Stomoxys calcitrans* in Roman age deposits, of interest since neither of these synanthropic species is likely to be truly native. Further work is of course required on present day larvae and puparia before reliable identification of these past faunas is possible at a specific level. However, there is clearly considerable potential in this field of entomology and the day may come when the changes in the Diptera fauna of Britain can be discussed on a similar basis to those of the Coleoptera. The literature is steadily increasing in this subject area. The methods given in the first reference below would also have application to the analysis of present day insect remains in bird and animal pellets and droppings. Recent changes in the British dipterous fauna are dealt with by Smith (1974).

Further Reading

Buckland, P. C., 1976. The use of insect remains in the interpretation of archaeological environments. *Geoarchaeology, Earth Science and the Past.* Duckworth Press, London. Section 4;p. 369-96.

Shotton, F.W. & Osborne, P. J., 1965. The fauna of the Hoxnian Interglacial deposits of Nechells, Birmingham. *Phil. Trans. R. Soc.* B, **248:** 353-378, pl. 30.

Smith, K. G. V., 1974. Changes in the British Dipterous Fauna. In. Hawksworth, D. L. *The Changing Flora and Fauna of Britain.* pp. 371-391. Systematics Association Special Vol. No. 6, London.

TIME AND THE LIVING FLY
by Alan E. Stubbs

Length of Life

An adult fly may live the matter of several hours or several weeks depending on the species, and of course the hazards which the individual meets. In viewing the existence of the adult, one must assume its sole function is to reproduce and ensure that further generations continue the species. Thus an adult only has to live long enough to achieve that end – to mate, and, if it is a female, to lay as many eggs as possible in the best places.

Whilst little field information is available it must be assumed that many species complete the essential functions of being an adult within the matter of hours of emergence. This is the case in some tipulids where the males may mate with the female as soon as it is out of the pupa and most of the eggs may be laid the same day (e.g. *Tipula paludosa*). In this and perhaps most cases it is general for the males to emerge a few days before the females so that plenty of males are at hand when the females appear. The average length of life may be less than a day, though some individuals last longer. There is thus an advantage in synchronising the emergence so that there is maximum chance of meeting the opposite sex. It is a fairly well recognised feature with insects that many of the rarities have short synchronised emergence whilst some of the commoner ones have a more extended emergence period. However, if the fly is a tasty morsel to predators, such as some craneflies, even a common species can obtain advantage by suddenly appearing in such large numbers that the local predators are insufficient to make any impact and the whole episode is over before predators are attracted from elsewhere. Despite the advantage of getting the adult process over with as soon as possible before a predator finds the adult, many flies plan their life style for a longer innings. There simply may not be enough time in one day to do all that is necessary or the weather may change and upset plans. Also the required food for the next generation may not be available. Some tipulids and other diptera are not mature when they emerge. Although such tipulids do not appear to feed, the females take several days for their ovaries to mature before egg laying commences. In the case of some predatory flies and blood suckers such as mosquitoes, the females benefit from a meal to supplement the body resources built up as a larva, leading to the ability to lay more eggs.

Many flies are faced with a major problem if the conditions in their environment are wrong. The choice is to stay put and wait for conditions to improve or to migrate to an area where conditions are right − both of which require ability to survive. Thus there may be huge numbers of fungus gnats but no fungi and it must be assumed that, despite the apparent lack of feeding, the adults keep going until the required fungi appear − this may even involve aestivation (summer hibernation). Others such as hoverflies, may have to search out aphid colonies, a very energy demanding process when aphids are scarce and perhaps for this reason they are such ardent attendants at flowers. They must survive long enough to find aphids, or to wait for aphids to appear or migrate locally or even internationally.

The winter poses another unconscious decision. At what stage in the life cycle is it safest to overwinter. There is no easy solution and no doubt even single families may demonstrate every alternative. Some adults hibernate, such as *Pollenia*,and others of course opt for carrying through their full life cycle during the end part of the year, such as the winter gnats. It is clear that some adults are living for six months.

The longevity of the other stages − egg, larva and pupa also shows a wide range of variation according to species and life style. If food is abundant and the temperature warm, some of the smaller species manage 2, 3 and even more generations a year (e.g. *Drosophila* cultures). However, at the other extreme the diet may be poor. The British record would seem to be held by the larva of the tree rot hole hoverfly *Callicera rufa* which took 7 years to produce an adult, though it is not clear whether or not several years were spent quiescent in the puparium.

Time of Day

It is easy to assume that the day is a fairly constant period of activity when it is not. A whole sequence of dipterous events occur through a day but the variability of the British climate readily obscures many of the features of a daily rhythm. There is a long way to go before the natural rhythm is understood and the superimposed effects of climate interpreted. Those who rear insects soon recognize that there are certain times of day when newly emerged adults are to be discovered. This biological rhythm is usually obeyed regardless of how puparia are kept, even in the dark where the fly cannot possibly recognise daylight time. The time of emergence in a given species is normally within the range of a few hours and the timing varies according to species.

Other activities show a rhythm, most markedly so if account is taken of the peaks of activity of the species as a whole, rather than for the stray individual. The time of swarming and of mating, the time of feeding, the time of oviposition all tend to have a pattern. Presumably some species do just keep going from day break to sun set but this is probably far from typical. There are days when the morning yields plenty of flies, then numbers just fade away as if everything has gone off for a siesta. Another day, perhaps because the temperature and humidity are just right, everything seems to keep going. A rhythm tends to develop when there are several good sunny days in succession but a sunny day after several dull wet days reveals everything 'making hay while the sun shines'.

There are plenty of observations of different species doing different things at different times of day. This certainly applies to some hoverflies which are normally only seen in accessible ground level situations for a few hours a day yet are believed to be active in the canopy at other times. Often it is only possible to find one sex and the explanation may frequently be that the other sex is in a different place at that time of day doing something completely different.

There is plenty of simple recording that could be done on the daily rhythm of what is caught by sweeping and the sequence of fly species visiting flowers during the day. Who would have thought to look at Plantain *(Plantago)* flowers between 5 and 7 a.m. to realise that this is when *Melanostoma* (Syrphidae) visits this plant. Also many species are active at night yet little is recorded. Night sweeping and light traps are sampling methods. There is reason to believe that many Tipulidae and some Mycetophilidae are active at night, since these come readily to light and this may explain why many craneflies have not been observed ovipositing. There may be flower visitors too. Virtually any family of fly could be involved in this way, especially among Nematocera and Acalypterates.